W B Yeats was born in Dublin, Ireland, in 1865 and spent much of his childhood in County Sligo, a place he loved and often wrote about. Yeats is often said to be a man of contradictions: he was profoundly intelligent and yet committed to spiritualism and the supernatural; he was philosophical and yet emotionally bound to a woman who did not return his devotion; he was aristocratic and detached and yet motivated by and artistically concerned with the most elementary of human impulses.

In 1922 he was elected a senator of the Irish Free Republic and the following year he won the Nobel Prize for Literature. W B Yeats is remembered as an important cultural leader and as one of the greatest poets of the century. He died in 1939.

Representative
Irish Tales

edited by

W B Yeats

HOUSE OF
STRATUS

First published in 1891

Copyright by Michael B Yeats

This edition published in 2002 by House of Stratus, an imprint of House of Stratus Ltd, Thirsk Industrial Park, York Road, Thirsk, North Yorkshire, YO7 3BX, UK.
Also at: House of Stratus Inc., 2 Neptune Road, Poughkeepsie, NY 12601, USA.

www.houseofstratus.com

Typeset, printed and bound by House of Stratus.

A catalogue record for this book is available from the British Library and the Library of Congress.

ISBN 1-84232-632-5

CONTENTS

A LIST OF SOURCES

Yeats does not identify his sources for all of the materials he includes in *Representative Irish Tales* and the references he does give are not always complete or accurate. The list below gives the earliest editions of Yeats' sources. Some of Yeats' editorial changes are also indicated.

Volume I

Maria Edgeworth. *Castle Rackrent*. Dublin: P Wogan, 1800. Yeats includes the complete text, including notes by the novelist's father, Richard Lovell Edgeworth.

John Banim. 'The Stolen Sheep'. This story first appeared in *The Bit O'Writing* (London, 1838), a collection of tales by 'The O'Hara Family', the pseudonym of John and Michael Banim.

Michael Banim. 'The Mayor of Wind-Gap'. This story is comprised of two separate scenes from Michael Banim's novel, *The Mayor of Wind-Gap*. Dublin: Duffy, 1834.

William Carleton. 'Wildgoose Lodge'. *Traits and Stories of the Irish Peasantry*. Dublin: Curry, 1830–1833. Yeats' deletion of the two final paragraphs of background information necessary to understand the story makes his selection much more mysterious than Carleton's original story. Yeats had included the entire text in *Stories from Carleton* (1889).

William Carleton. 'Condy Cullen and the Gauger'. Story is entitled 'Condy Cullen or the Exciseman Defeated' in Yeats' personal copy of an edition of some of Carleton's tales,

Barney Brady's Goose; The Hedge School, The Three Tasks; and other Irish Tales (n.d., n.p.), and 'Condy Cullen; or, The Irish Rake' in Carleton's *Tales and Sketches, Illustrating the Character, Usages, Traditions, Sports, and Pastimes of the Irish Peasantry.* Dublin: Duffy, 1845.

William Carleton. 'The Curse'. An excerpt from a story entitled 'Party Fight and Funeral' in *Traits and Stories*. Neither the foolish gullibility of the peasantry, nor the condescending tone of the narrator, which pervades the rest of the story, is found in Yeats' excerpt.

William Carleton. 'The Battle of the Factions', From *Traits and Stories*.

Volume II

Samuel Lover. 'Barny O'Reirdon, the Navigator'. From Lover's *Legends and Stories of Ireland*, second series. Dublin: W F Wakeman, 1834.

Samuel Lover. 'Paddy the Piper'. From Lover's *Legends and Stories of Ireland*, first series. Dublin: W F Wakeman, 1831. Yeats omits a quotation from *Much Ado About Nothing* at the beginning of the story and credits the story to Lover, even though in a note following the story Lover had admitted obtaining the story from a friend.

'Father Tom and the Pope'. Yeats omits Chapter IV in which Father Tom kisses the Pope's housekeeper. The story had been published anonymously in *Blackwood's Magazine*, 43 (May 1838), pp. 614-17, and was generally attributed to Maginn until Lady Ferguson revealed her husband was the real author in her *Sir Samuel Ferguson in the Ireland of his Day* (1895). In *Representative Irish Tales* Yeats attributed the story to Maginn, but later corrected his error in 'Irish National Literature, IV: A List of the Best Irish Books', Bookman (October 1895).

SOURCES

T Crofton Croker. 'The Confessions of Tom Bourke'. From Croker's *Fairy Legends and Traditions of the South of Ireland*, Vol. I, London: John Murray, 1825. Yeats had also used the story in *Fairy and Folk Tales of the Irish Peasantry* (1888).

Gerald Griffin. 'The Knight of the Sheep'. Yeats incorrectly states that the story is from Griffin's collection *Holland-Tide* (1827); the story is from Griffin's three-volume *Tales of My Neighbourhood*. London: Saunders and Otley, 1835.

Gerald Griffin. 'The Death of the Huntsman'. A scene from a chapter in Griffin's novel *The Collegians*. Dublin: Duffy, 1825.

Charles Lever. 'Trinity College'. An excerpt from Lever's novel *Charles O'Malley, The Irish Dragoon*. Dublin: William Curry, 1841.

Charles Kickham. 'The Pig-Driving Peelers'. An excerpt from Kickham's novel *For the Old Land*. Dublin: Gill, 1886. In his 'Introduction' to *Stories from Carleton* (1889) Yeats praises this scene from the novel.

Rosa Mulholland. 'The Hungry Death'. Previously unpublished story sent to Yeats by Father Matthew Russell, editor of *The Irish Monthly* in which Rosa Mulholland, Lady Gilbert (1841–1921), had published numerous stories and articles. In *The Irish Monthly* (July 1891), p. 372, Father Russell referred to her as 'if not the greatest living novelist, is the best known Irish writer of the present day'.

'The Jackdaw'. According to Yeats, this anonymous tale was from a chap-book entitled *Hibernian Tales*. However, the tale is not in *Hibernian Tales, A Choice Collection of Popular Stories Descriptive of Irish Life from Several Eminent Authors.* Dublin: James M'Cormick, 1844. It is in *The Royal Hibernian Tales: Being a Collection of the Most Entertaining Stories Now Extant*. Dublin: C M Warren, n.d. (c. 1829), pp. 94-97. Yeats also used the tale in *Fairy and Folk Tales of the Irish Peasantry* (1888).

SOURCES

'Darby Doyle's Visit to Quebec'. Yeats presents this as a story told in the first person, although it had originally appeared as a letter from 'Darby Doyle' to the editor of the *Dublin Penny Journal*, 1, No. 24 (8 December 1832).

DEDICATION

1

There was a green branch hung with many a bell
    When her own people ruled in wave-worn Eri,
    And from its murmuring greenness, calm of faery
– A Druid kindness – on all hearers fell.

2

It charmed away the merchant from his guile,
    And turned the farmer's memory from his cattle,
    And hushed in sleep the roaring ranks of battle,
For all who heard it dreamed a little while.

3

Ah, Exiles, wandering over many seas,
    Spinning at all times Eri's good tomorrow,
    Ah, world-wide Nation, always growing Sorrow,
I also bear a bell branch full of ease.

4

I tore it from green boughs winds tossed and hurled,
    Green boughs of tossing always, weary, weary,
    I tore it from the green boughs of old Eri,
The willow of the many-sorrowed world.

5

Ah, Exiles, wandering over many lands,
 My bell branch murmurs: the gay bells bring laughter,
 Leaping to shake a cobweb from the rafter;
The sad bells bow the forehead on the hands.

6

A honied ringing! under the new skies
 They bring you memories of old village faces,
 Cabins gone now, old well-sides, old dear places,
And men who loved the cause that never dies.

W B YEATS

INTRODUCTION

Chance and Destiny have between them woven two-thirds of all history, and of the history of Ireland wellnigh the whole. The literature of a nation, on the other hand, is spun out of its heart. If you would know Ireland – body and soul – you must read its poems and stories. They came into existence to please nobody but the people of Ireland. Government did not make them on the one hand, nor bad seasons on the other. They are Ireland talking to herself. In these two little volumes I give specimens of a small part of this literature – the prose tales of modern Irish life. I have made the selection in such a way as to illustrate as far as possible the kind of witness they bear to Irish character. In this introduction I intend to explain the fashion I read them in, the class limitations I allow for, the personal bias that seems to me to have directed this novelist or that other. These limitations themselves, this bias even, will show themselves to be moods characteristic of the country.

I notice very distinctly in all Irish literature two different accents – the accent of the gentry, and the less polished accent of the peasantry and those near them; a division roughly into the voice of those who lived lightly and gayly, and those who took man and his fortunes with much seriousness and even at times mournfully. The one has found its most typical embodiment in the tales and novels of Croker, Lover, and Lever, and the other in the ruder but deeper work of Carleton, Kickham, and the two Banims.

There is perhaps no other country in the world the style and nature of whose writers have been so completely governed by their birth and social standing. Lever and Lover, and those like them, show constantly the ideals of a class that held its acres once at the sword's point, and a little later were pleased by the tinsel villainy of the Hell Fire Club – a class whose existence has, on the whole, been a pleasant thing enough for the world. It introduced a new wit – a humour whose essence was dare-devilry and good-comradeship, half real, half assumed. For Ireland, on the other hand, it has been almost entirely an evil, and not the least of its sins against her has been the creation in the narrow circle of its dependants of the pattern used later on for that strange being called sometimes 'the stage Irishman'. They had found the serious passions and convictions of the true peasant troublesome, and longed for a servant who would make them laugh, a tenant who would always appear merry in his checkered rags. The result was that there grew up round about the big houses a queer mixture of buffoonery and chicanery tempered by plentiful gleams of better things – hearts, grown crooked, where laughter was no less mercenary than the knavery. The true peasant remained always in disfavour as 'plotter', 'rebel', or man in some way unfaithful to his landlord. The knave type flourished till the decay of the gentry themselves, and is now extant in the boatmen, guides, and mendicant hordes that gather round tourists, while they are careful to trouble at no time any one belonging to the neighbourhood with their century-old jokes. The tourist has read of the Irish peasant in the only novels of Irish life he knows, those written by and for an alien gentry. He has expectations to be fulfilled. The mendicants follow him for fear he might be disappointed. He thinks they are types of Irish poor people. He does not know that they are merely a portion of the velvet of aristocracy now fallen in the dust.

Samuel Lover, confined by the traditions of his class, and having its dependants about him, took pleasure in celebrating the only peasant-life he knew. His stories, with seldom more than the allowable exaggerations of the humorist, describe the buffoon Irishman with the greatest vigour and humour. 'Barry O'Reirdon' is an incomparable chronicle. The error is with those who have taken from his novels their notion of all Irishmen. 'Handy Andy' has been the cause of much misconception, and yet, like all he wrote, is full of truthful pages and poetic feeling. Samuel Lover had a deal more poetry in him than Lever. It gives repose and atmosphere to his stories and crops up charmingly in his songs. 'The Whistling Thief', for instance, is no less pretty than humorous. But at all times it is the kind of poetry that shines round ways of life other than our own. It is the glamour of distance, and is the same feeling that in a previous age crowded the boards of theatres with peasant girls in high-heeled shoes, and shepherds carrying crooks fluttering with ribbons. At the same time it has a real and quite lawful charm.

Crofton Croker, the historian of the fairies and an accomplished master of this kind of poetry, was much more palpably injured than was Lover by his narrow conception of Irish life. He had to deal with materials dug out of the very soul of the populace. You feel the falsity at once. The people take the fairies and spirits much more seriously. Under his hands the great kingdom of the *sidhe* lost its nobility and splendour. 'The gods of the earth' dwindled to dancing mannikins – buffoons of the darkness. The slighter matters of other-world life – the humour, the pathos – fared better. 'The Priest's Supper' and 'Daniel O'Rourke' deserve to be immortal. I was unfortunately prevented by the plan of these volumes – a plan that does not allow me to stray from Irish human nature to Irish fairy nature – from including either, but I have substituted a fine conversation with an Irish 'fairy doctor', or village seer.

Charles Lever, unlike Lover and Croker, wrote mainly for his own class. His books are quite sufficiently truthful, but more than any other Irish writer has he caught the ear of the world and come to stand for the entire nation. The vices and virtues of his characters are like those of the gentry – a gentry such as Ireland has had, with no more sense of responsibility, as a class, than have the *dullahans, thivishes, sowlths, bowas,* and *water sheries* of the spirit-ridden peasantry. His characters, however, are in no way lacking in the qualities of their defects – having at most times a hospitable, genial, good soldier-like disposition.

Croker and Lover and Lever were as humorists go, great fellows. They must always leave some kind of recollection; but, to my mind, there is one thing lacking among them. I miss the deep earth song of the peasant's laughter. Maginn went nearer to attain it than they did. In 'Father Tom and the Pope' he put himself into the shoes of an old peasant hedge school-master, and added to the wild humour of the people one crowning perfection – irresponsibility. In matters where irresponsibleness is a hindrance the Irish gentry have done little. They have never had a poet. Poetry needs a God, a cause, or a country. But witty have they been beyond question. If one excepts 'The Traits and Stories', all the most laughable Irish books have been by them.

The one serious novelist coming from the upper classes in Ireland, and the most finished and famous produced by any class there, is undoubtedly Miss Edgeworth. Her first novel, 'Castle Rackrent', is one of the most inspired chronicles written in English. One finds no undue love for the buffoon, rich or poor, no trace of class feeling, unless, indeed, it be that the old peasant who tells the story is a little decorative, like a peasant figure in the background of an old-fashioned autumn landscape painting. An unreal light of poetry shines round him, a too tender lustre of faithfulness and innocence. The virtues, also, that she gives him are those a poor man may show his superior, not those of poor man dealing with poor man. She has made him supremely poetical, however, because in her love for him there was nothing of the half contemptuous affection that Croker and Lover felt for their personages. On the other hand, he has not the reality of Carleton's men and women. He stands in the charming twilight of illusion and half-knowledge. When writing of people of her own class she saw everything about them as it really was. She constantly satirised their recklessness, their love for all things English, their oppression of and contempt for their own country. The Irish ladies in 'The Absentee' who seek laboriously after an English accent, might have lived today. Her novels give, indeed, systematically the mean and vulgar side of all that gay life celebrated by Lever.

About 1820, twenty years after the publication of 'Castle Rackrent', a new power began in literary Ireland. Carleton commenced writing for the *Christian Examiner*. He had gone to Dublin from his father's farm in Tyrone, turned Protestant, and begun vehemently asserting his new notion of things in controversial tales and sketches. The Dublin *dilettanti*, and there were quite a number in those days, were delighted. Here was a passion, a violence, new to their polite existence. They could not foresee that some day this stormy satire would be turned against themselves, their church, and, above all, this proselytising it now sought to spread. The true peasant was at last speaking, stammeringly, illogically, bitterly, but nonetheless with the deep and mournful accent of the people. Ireland had produced her second great novelist. Beside Miss Edgeworth's well-finished four-square house of the intelligence, Carleton raised his rough clay 'rath' of humour and passion. Miss Edgeworth has outdone writers like Lover and Lever because of her fine judgment, her serene culture, her well-balanced mind. Carleton, on the other hand, with no conscious art at all, and living a half-blind, groping sort of life, drinking and borrowing, has, I believe, outdone not only them but her also by the sheer force of his powerful nature. It was not for nothing that his ancestors had dug the ground. His great body, that could leap twenty-one feet on a level, was full of violent emotions and brooding melancholy.

Carleton soon tired of controversy, and wrote his famous 'Traits and Stories'. Peasant though he was, he could not wholly escape the convention of his time. There was as yet no national cultivated public, and he was forced to write for a class who wished to laugh a great deal, and who did not mind weeping a little, provided he allowed them always to keep their sense of superiority. In the more early tales, peasant life is used mainly as material for the easier kinds of mirth and pathos. He put himself sometimes in the position of his readers and looked at the life of the people from without. The true peasant had been admitted into the drawing-room of the big house and asked to tell a story, but the lights and the strange faces bewildered him, and he could not quite talk as he would by his own fireside. He at first exaggerated, in deference to his audience, the fighting, and the dancing, and the merriment, and made the life of his class seem more exuberant and buoyant than it was. What did these ladies and gentlemen, he thought, with their foreign tastes, care for the tragic life of the fields?

As time went on, his work grew deeper in nature, and in the second series he gave all his heart to 'The Poor Scholar', 'Tubber Derg', and 'Wildgoose Lodge'. The humorist found his conscience, and, without throwing away laughter, became the historian of his class. It was not, however, until a true national public had arisen with Ferguson and Thomas Davis and the 'Young Ireland' people, that Carleton ventured the creation of a great single character and wrote 'Fardorougha the Miser'. In 'Fardorougha' and the two or three novels that followed he was at his finest. Then came decadence – ruinous, complete.

It seems to be a pretty absolute law that the rich like reading about the poor, the poor about the rich. In Ireland, at any rate, they have liked doing so. Each places its *Teer-nan-oge*, where 'you will get happiness for a penny', its land of unknown adventure, in the kind of life that is just near enough to interest, just far enough to leave the imagination at liberty. Either because he had said all he had to say about the peasantry, or because the cultivated public that read 'Fardorougha' and 'The Black Prophet' was gone – the best among them in the convict ship, – or because of a growing wish to please the more numerous and less intelligent of the class he had sprung from, or from a combination of all these reasons, Carleton started a series of novels dealing with the life of the gentry. They are almost worthless, except when he touches incidentally on peasant life, as in the jury-room scene in 'Willy Reilly'. One or two of them have, for all that, turned out very popular with the Irish uneducated classes. People who love tales of beautiful ladies, supremely brave outlaws, and villains wicked beyond belief, have read fifty editions of 'Willy Reilly'. In these novels landlords, agents, and their class are described as falsely as peasants are in the books of Lover and Croker. In 'Valentine McClutchy', the first novel of his decadence, there is no lack of misdirected power. The land-agent Orangeman, the hypocrite-solicitor, and the old blaspheming landlord who dies in the arms of his drunken mistress, are figures of unforgettable horror. They are the peasant's notion of that splendid laughing world of Lever's. The peasant stands at the roadside, cap in hand, his mouth full of 'your honours' and 'my ladies', his whole voice softened by the courtesy of the powerless, but men like Carleton show the thing that is in his heart. He is not appeased because the foot that passes over him is shod with laughter.

John Banim and his brother Michael, who both have the true peasant accent, are much more unequal writers than Carleton. Unlike him, they covered the peasant life they knew with a melodramatic horde of pirates and wealthy libertines whom they did not know. John Banim, who seems to have invented the manner of 'The O'Hara Tales', lived mostly in London, surrounded by English taste, and had just enough culture to admire and learn and imitate the literary fashion of his age. At times he would write pages, terrible and frank, like all the first half of 'The Nolans', and then suddenly seem to remind himself that the public expected certain conventional incidents and sentiments, and what he did his brother Michael copied. Neither had culture enough to tell them to leave the conventionalities alone and follow their own honest natures. For this reason it is mainly the minor characters – personages like 'The Mayor of Windgap' – that show the Banim genius. They seemed to indulge themselves in these fine creations as though they said 'the public will forgive our queer country-bred taste for very truth if we keep it in holes and corners'. Carleton, on the other hand, when he began writing, knew nothing about the public and its tastes. He had little more education than may be picked up at fair greens and chapel greens, and wrote, as a man naturally wants to write, of the things he understood. The Banims' father was a small shopkeeper; Carleton's a peasant, who perforce brought up his son well out of the reach of fashions from oversea. With less education John Banim might have written stories no less complete than those of Carleton, and with more have turned out a great realist – more like those of France and Russia than of England. The first third of 'The Nolans' is as fine as almost any novel anywhere, and here and there melodrama and realism melt into one and make an artistic unity, like 'John Doe', but much that both he and his brother wrote was of little account.

Neither brother had any trace of Carleton's humour, and John Banim had instead an abiding cold and dry-eyed sadness, produced by ill-health perhaps, wholly different from the tear-dashed melancholy of Carleton's 'Black Prophet' – a melancholy as of gray clouds slumbering on the rim of the sea.

In Gerald Griffin, the most finished storyteller among Irish novelists, and later on in Charles Kickham, I think I notice a new accent – not quite clear enough to be wholly distinct; the accent of people who have not the recklessness of the landowning class, nor the violent passions of the peasantry, nor the good frankness of either. The accent of those middle-class people who find Carleton rough and John Banim coarse, who when they write stories cloak all unpleasant matters, and moralise with ease, and have yet a sense of order and comeliness that may sometime give Ireland a new literature. Many things

are at work to help them: the papers, read by the Irish at home
and elsewhere, are in their hands. They are closer to the peasant
than to the gentry, for they take all things Irish with conscience,
with seriousness. Their main hindrances are a limited and
diluted piety, a dread of nature and her abundance, a distrust of
unsophisticated life. But for these, Griffin would never have
turned aside from his art and left it for the monastery; nor
would he have busied himself with anything so filmy and
bloodless as the greater portion of his short stories. As it is, he
has written a few perfect tales. The dozen pages or so I have
selected seem to me charming, and there are many people who,
repelled by the frieze-coated power of Carleton, think his really
very fine 'Collegians' the best Irish novel. Kickham also, with
his idealising haze, pleases some who do not care for the great
Tyrone peasant; not that Kickham was a man naturally given to
idealise and cloak the unpleasant, and sophisticate life. His first
novel 'Sally Kavanagh', is direct enough – but having come out
of jail, he saw everything with the rose-spectacles of the
returned exile. His great knowledge of Irish life kept him
always an historian, though one who cared only to record the
tender and humane elements of the life of the common people,
and of the small farming and shopkeeping class he came from.
When he wrote of the gentry, he fell like Carleton into
caricature. The Orangemen, landlords, and agents of 'Sally
Kavanagh' and 'Knocnagow' are seldom in any way human, nor
are they even artistically true. The loss of accurate copying has
always been more destructive to Irish national writers than to
the better educated novelists of the gentry. Croker had art
enough to give an ideal completeness to his shallowest
inventions. Carleton and Banim and Kickham, when once they
strayed from the life they had knowledge of, had not art enough
to evade the most manifest conventionality and caricature. No
modern Irish writer has ever had anything of the high culture
that makes it possible for an author to do as he will with life, to
place the head of a beast upon a man, or the head of a man

upon a beast, to give to the most grotesque creation the reality
of a spiritual existence.

Meanwhile a true literary consciousness – national to the
centre – seems gradually forming out of all this disguising and
prettifying, this penumbra of half-culture. We are preparing
likely enough for a new Irish literary movement – like that of
'48 – that will show itself at the first lull in this storm of politics.
Carleton scarcely understood the true tendency of anything
he did. His pages served now one cause, now another, according
to some interest or passion of the moment. Things have
changed since then. These new folk, limited though they be, are
conscious. They have ideas. They understand the purpose of
letters in the world. They may yet formulate the Irish culture
of the future. To help them, is much obscure feeling for
literature diffused throughout the country. The clerks, farmers'
sons, and the like, that make up the 'Young Ireland' societies
and kindred associations, show an alertness to honour the words
'poet', 'writer', 'orator', not commonly found among their class.
Many a poor countryside has its peasant verse-maker. I have
seen stories – true histories – by a village shoemaker that only
needed a fine convention to take their place in fiction. The
school of Davis and Carleton and Ferguson has gone. Most
things are changed now – politics are different, life is different.
Irish literature is and will be, however, the same in one thing for
many a long day – in its nationality, its resolve to celebrate in
verse and prose all within the four seas of Ireland. And why
should it do otherwise? A man need not go further than his own
hill-side or his own village to find every kind of passion and
virtue. As Paracelsus wrote: 'If thou tastest a crust of bread, thou
tastest all the stars and all the heavens.'

W B YEATS

MARIA EDGEWORTH

1767–1849

Miss Edgeworth was born in the year 1767 at Hare Hack, Berkshire. Her father, Richard Lovell Edgeworth, was an Oxford student of a powerful mechanical kind of intelligence. He had come to Oxford from his father's estate in Ireland, his mind choke-full of Rousseau and the French deists, and there fallen in love with a Miss Elers, a lady of German extraction, and married her much against his father's will. He was but twenty years old on the birth of his daughter. When Miss Edgeworth was still a small child her mother died, and her father married again in four months. 'I am not a man of prejudices,' he wrote in later life; 'I have had four wives, the second and third were sisters, and I was in love with the second during the lifetime of the first.' In 1775 she was sent to school at Derby, after a visit to Ireland, in which she had amused herself by cutting out the squares in a checked tablecloth and in trampling through the glass in a number of hot-house frames, delighting in the crash she made. In 1780, she was removed to a fashionable London school. Her holidays were usually spent with Mr Day, the eccentric author of 'Sandford and Merton', whose influence, together with that of her father, started the strange love for the didactic, so harmful to her writings. This unfortunate genius, with her natural talent for the unexpected – witness the hot-house frames, – was ground between these

1

two philosophers, who sought to reduce all things to rule and formula.

At the age of sixteen she returned with her father to Edgeworthstown, the name of the family estate in Longford. The state of the country, its general dilapidation, the character of the people, all greatly moved her and developed the fruitful and sympathetic side of her nature visible later on in 'Castle Rackrent'. For some time she acted as her father's agent, who wished to get rid of the middle-man and see things with his own and his daughter's eyes. In this way she learnt to see far down into the causes of Irish discontent. She was all the more at leisure to study the poor people about her, because neither she nor her father sought the company of the drinking and sport-loving squires and squireens of the neighbourhood. In 1795 and 1796, amid premonitory muttering of the great rebellion, Miss Edgeworth's first books appeared: 'A plea for the Education of Women' and an educational manual called 'The Parents Assistant', respectively. She began also her 'Moral Tales', not published until 1801. A number of educational books for children came next – 'Harry and Lucy', 'Frank and Rosamond', 'Early Lessons', and others, some written by herself, others with help from her father. Fairy tales and all such pleasant impossibilities were to be driven from the nursery and a despotism of the strictly true set up in their place. The nursery, however, has gallantly routed the utilitarian horde. The invasion is as dead as the great outburst of Ninety-eight, amid whose noise it set forth.

After the rebellion Mr Edgeworth entered the Irish Parliament and was among those who voted against the union. In 1800, Miss Edgeworth's imagination burst free from her didacticism and 'Castle Rackrent' was written and published. I have spoken of this great novel in the introduction, and need say no more of it here than that its author never perhaps reached again the same tide mark of power and humour. 'Belinda', a tale of fashionable life, and the 'Essay on Irish Bulls', followed. The last was the joint work of father and daughter and was planned out as she tells us, 'to show the English public the eloquence and wit and talents of the lower classes of people in Ireland'. In 1802 Mr Edgeworth travelled with his family through France and the Low Countries. His daughter, now a famous writer, saw many foreign celebrities at Paris. Now too, in her thirty-sixth year, she fell in love with a young Swede, a M. Edelcrantz, private secretary to the king. He returned her love, but as neither would leave their own country, they talked to each other of duty, and parted – was she not bound to Edgeworthstown, he to the Swedish court? On returning to Ireland Miss Edgeworth tried to forget the Swede in preparing for the press her 'Popular Tales', and in writing 'Leonora', a romantic work, intended to please him. Innumerable 'novels with a purpose', archetypes and forerunners of their class, came year after year from her untiring pen. Many were published under the title of 'Tales from Fashionable Life'. One of these, 'The Absentee', has chapters no less moving than those of 'Castle Rackrent'. Macaulay has, indeed, described the scene in which Lord Colambry discovers himself to his tenantry, as the best thing of its kind since Homer wrote the twenty-second book of the Odyssey.

In 1813 Miss Edgeworth visited London with her father, and was the lion of the season. Byron, who met her at this time, wrote in his journal that she was 'a nice little unassuming "Jeanie Deans" looking body,…and if not handsome, certainly not ill-looking'. In 1817 Mr Edgeworth died, in his seventy-fourth year. A fortnight before his death he wrote the preface to 'Ormond', one of his daughter's most celebrated stories, and one in which she reached a level never again attained by her. In the succeeding year, with the exception of occasional visits to London and Paris, she continued to live on at Edgeworthstown. In 1820 she completed and published her memoir of her father, a task that had long filled her thoughts. The first volume had been left ready written by Mr Edgeworth himself, the second was her work. 'Harry', 'Lucy', and 'Orlando', and other stories followed at intervals. She was getting old, and her pen worked more slowly. The last years of her life were saddened by the famine. She worked hard at the distribution of relief. The children of Boston subscribed together and sent a hundred and fifty barrels of flour for her poor. This greatly pleased her; she was pleased also because the men who carried the barrels to the shore refused to be paid, and knitted a comforter for each of them.

On May 22, 1849, she fell suddenly ill – pains in the heart being the symptom, – and died after a few hours.

Madame de Stael said, after reading her 'Tales of Fashionable Life': 'Que Miss Edgeworth etait digne de l'enthousiasme, mais qu'elle s'est perdue dans la triste utilité.' Great genius though she was, she could not persuade herself to trust nature, to set down in tale and novel the emotions and longings and chances that seemed to her pleasant and beautiful. She could not forget the schooling of her father, and of the author of 'Sandford and Merton', and felt bound to see whither every line she wrote tended, to do nothing she could not prove was for the good of man. Here and there, as in 'Castle Rackrent', she has risen above her own intellect, and produced a work of the greatest kind. In the larger number of her writings, one sees how extreme conscientiousness had injured the spontaneity of her nature. She did everything, no less in life than in novel-writing, with the same elaborate scrupulousness. A relation of mine once got a servant from her. The 'character' filled three sheets of paper. She does the same with the people of her novels. She sends them out into the world with a careful and long-considered judgment attached to each one.

CASTLE RACKRENT

By MARIA EDGEWORTH

Monday Morning.

Having, out of friendship for the family, upon whose estate, praised be Heaven! I and mine have lived rent-free time out of mind, voluntarily undertaken to publish the MEMOIRS OF THE RACKRENT FAMILY, I think it my duty to say a few words, in the first place, concerning myself. My real name is Thady Quirk, though in the family I have always been known by no other than 'Honest Thady', afterward, in the time of Sir Murtagh, deceased, I remember to hear them calling me 'Old Thady', and now I've come to 'Poor Thady'; for I wear a long great-coat[1] winter and summer, which is very handy, as I never put my arms into the sleeves; they are as good as new, though come Hollantide next I've had it these seven years; it holds on by a single button round my neck, cloak fashion. To look at me, you would hardly think 'Poor Thady' was the father of Attorney Quirk; he is a high gentleman, and never minds what poor Thady says, and having better than fifteen hundred a year, landed estate, looks down upon honest Thady; but I wash my hands of his doings, and as I have lived so will I die, true and loyal to the family. The family of the Rackrents is, I am proud to say, one of the most ancient in the kingdom. Everybody knows this is not the old family name, which was O'Shaughlin, related to the kings of Ireland – but that was before my time.

My grandfather was a driver to the great Sir Patrick O'Shaughlin, and I heard him, when I was a boy, telling how the Castle Rackrent estate came to Sir Patrick; Sir Tallyhoo Rackrent was cousin-german to him, and had a fine estate of his own, only never a gate upon it, it being his maxim that a car was the best gate. Poor gentleman! he lost a fine hunter and his life, at last, by it, all in one day's hunt. But I ought to bless that day, for the estate came straight into the family, upon one condition, which Sir Patrick O'Shaughlin at the time took sadly to heart, they say, but thought better of it afterwards, seeing how large a stake depended upon it; that he should, by Act of Parliament, take and bear the surname and arms of Rackrent.

Now it was that the world was to see what was *in* Sir Patrick. On coming into the estate he gave the finest entertainment ever was heard of in the country; not a man could stand after supper but Sir Patrick himself, who could sit out the best man in Ireland, let alone the three kingdoms itself. He had his house, from one year's end to another, as full of company as ever it could hold, and fuller; for rather than be left out of the parties at Castle Rackrent, many gentlemen, and those men of the first consequence and landed estates in the country – such as the O'Neills of Ballynagrotty, and the Moneygawls of Mount Juliet's Town, and O'Shannons of New Town Tullyhog – made it their choice, often and often, when there was no room to be had for love nor money, in long winter nights, to sleep in the chicken-house, which Sir Patrick had fitted up for the purpose of accommodating his friends and the public in general, who honoured him with their company unexpectedly at Castle Rackrent; and this went on I can't tell you how long. The whole country rang with his praises! – Long life to him! I'm sure I love to look upon his picture, now opposite to me; though I never saw him, he must have been a portly gentleman – his neck something short, and remarkable for the largest pimple on his nose, which, by his particular desire, is still extant in his picture, said to be a striking likeness, though taken when young. He is said also to be the inventor of raspberry whiskey, which is very likely, as nobody has ever appeared to dispute it with him, and as there still exists a broken punch-bowl at Castle Rackrent, in the garret, with an inscription to that effect – a great curiosity. A few days before his death he was very merry; it being his honour's birthday, he called my grandfather in – God bless him! – to drink the company's health, and filled a bumper himself, but could not carry it to his head, on account of the great shake in his hand; on this he cast his joke, saying: "What would my poor father say to me if he was to pop out of the grave, and see me now? I remember when I was a little boy, the first bumper of claret he gave me after dinner, how he praised me for carrying it so steady to my mouth. Here's my thanks to him – a bumper toast." Then he fell to singing the favourite song he learned from his father – for the last time, poor gentleman – he sung it that night as loud and as hearty as ever, with a chorus:

He that goes to bed, and goes to bed sober,
Falls as the leaves do, falls as the leaves do, and dies in
    October;
But he that goes to bed, and goes to bed mellow,
Lives as he ought to do, lives as he ought to do, and dies
    an honest fellow.

Sir Patrick died that night: just as the company rose to drink his health with three cheers, he fell down in a sort of fit, and was carried off; they sat it out, and were surprised, on inquiry in the morning, to find that it was all over with poor Sir Patrick. Never did any gentleman live and die more beloved in the country by rich and poor. His funeral was such a one as was never known before or since in the county! All the gentlemen in the three counties were at it; far and near, how they flocked! my great-grandfather said, that to see all the women, even in their red cloaks, you would have taken them for the army drawn out. Then such a fine whillaluh! you might have heard it to the farthest end of the county, and happy the man who could get but a sight of the hearse! But who'd have thought it? Just as all was going on right, through his own town they were passing, when the body was seized for debt – a rescue was apprehended from the mob; but the heir, who attended the funeral, was against that, for fear of consequences, seeing that those villians who came to serve acted under the disguise of the law: so, to be sure, the law must take its course, and little gain had the creditors for their pains. First and foremost, they had the curses of the country: and Sir Murtagh Rackrent, the new heir, in the next place, on account of this affront to the body, refused to pay a shilling of the debts, in which he was countenanced by all the best gentlemen of property, and others of his acquaintance; Sir Murtagh alleging in all companies that he had all along meant to pay his father's debts of honour, but the moment the law was taken of him, there was an end of honour to be sure. It was whispered (but none but the enemies of the family believe it) that this was all a sham seizure to get quit of the debts which he had bound himself to pay in honour.

It's a long time ago, there's no saying how it was, but this for certain, the new man did not take at all after the old gentleman; the cellars were never filled after his death, and no open house, or anything as it used to be; the tenants even were sent away without their whiskey. I was ashamed myself, and knew not what to say for the honour of the family; but I made the best of a bad case, and laid it all at my lady's door, for I did not like her anyhow, nor anybody else; she was of the family of the Skinflints, and a widow; it was a strange match for Sir Murtagh; the people in the country thought he demeaned himself greatly, but I said nothing; I knew how it was. Sir Murtagh was a great lawyer, and looked to the great Skinflint estate; there, however, he overshot himself; for, though one of the co-heiresses, he was never the better for her, for she outlived him many's the long day – he could not see that to be sure when he married her. I must say for her, she made him the best of wives, being a very notable, stirring woman, and looking close to every thing. But I always suspected she had Scotch blood in her veins; anything else I could have looked over in her, from a regard to the family. She was a strict observer, for self and servants, of Lent and all fast-days, but not holidays. One of the maids having fainted three times the last day of Lent, to keep soul and body together we put a morsel of roast beef into her mouth, which came from Sir Murtagh's dinner, who never fasted, not he; but somehow or other it unfortunately reached my lady's ears, and the priest of the parish had a complaint made of it the next day, and the poor girl was forced, as soon as she could walk, to do penance for it, before she could get any peace or absolution, in the house or out of it. However, my lady was very charitable in her own way. She had a charity school for poor children, where they were taught to read and write gratis, and where they were kept well to spinning gratis for my lady in return; for she had always heaps of duty yarn from the tenants, and got all her household linen out of the estate from first to last; for after the spinning, the weavers on the estate took it in hand for nothing, because of the looms my lady's interest could get from the Linen Board to distribute gratis. Then there was a bleach-yard near us, and the tenant dare refuse my lady nothing, for fear of a lawsuit Sir Murtagh kept hanging over him about the watercourse. With these ways of managing, 't is surprising how cheap my lady got things done, and how proud she was of it. Her table the same way, kept for next to nothing; duty fowls, and duty turkeys, and duty geese, came as fast as we could eat 'em, for my lady kept a sharp lookout, and knew to a tub of butter everything the tenants had, all round. They knew her way, and what with fear of driving for rent and Sir Murtagh's lawsuits, they were kept in such good order, they never thought of coming near Castle Rackrent without a present of something or other – nothing too much or too little for my lady – eggs, honey, butter, meal, fish, game, grouse, and herrings, fresh or salt, all went for something. As for their young pigs, we had them, and the best bacon and hams they could make up, with all young chickens in spring; but they were a set of poor wretches, and we had nothing but misfortunes with them, always breaking and running away. This, Sir Murtagh and my lady said, was all their former landlord Sir Patrick's fault, who let 'em all get the half-year's rent into arrear: there was something in that to be sure. But Sir Murtagh was as much the contrary way; for let alone making English tenants of them, every soul, he was always driving and driving, and pounding and pounding, and canting and canting, and replevying and replevying, and he made a good living of trespassing cattle; there was always some tenant's pig, or horse, or cow, or calf, or goose, trespassing, which was so great a gain to Sir Murtagh, that he did not like to hear me talk of repairing fences. Then his heriots and duty-work brought him in something, his turf was cut, his potatoes set and dug, his hay brought home, and, in short, all the work about his house done for nothing: for in all our leases there were strict clauses heavy with penalties, which Sir Murtagh knew well how to enforce; so many days' duty work of man and horse, from every tenant, he was to have, and had, every year; and when a man vexed him, why the finest day he could pitch on, when the cratur was getting in his own harvest, or thatching his cabin, Sir Murtagh made it a principle to call upon him and his horse: so he taught 'em all, as he said, to know the law of landlord and tenant. As for law, I believe no man, dead or alive, ever loved it so well as Sir Murtagh. He had once sixteen suits pending at a time, and I never saw him so much himself: roads, lanes, bogs, wells, ponds, eelwires, orchards, trees, tithes, vagrants, gravel-pits, sandpits, dunghills, and nuisances, everything upon the face of the earth furnished him good matter for a suit. He used to boast that he had a lawsuit for every letter in the alphabet. How I used to wonder to see Sir Murtagh in the midst of the papers in his office! Why, he could hardly turn about for them. I made bold to shrug my shoulders once, in his presence, and thanked my stars I was not born a gentleman to so much toil and trouble;

but Sir Murtagh took me up short with his old proverb, 'Learning is better than house or land.' Out of forty-nine suits which he had, he never lost one but seventeen; the rest he gained with costs, double costs, treble costs sometimes; but even that did not pay. He was a very learned man in the law, and had the character of it; but how it was I can't tell, these suits that he carried cost him a power of money: in the end he sold some hundreds a year of the family estate; but he was a very learned man in the law, and I know nothing of the matter, except having a great regard for the family; and I could not help grieving when he sent me to post up notices of the sale of the fee simple of the lands and appurtenances of Timoleague.

'I know, honest Thady,' says he, to comfort me, 'what I'm about better than you do; I'm only selling to get the ready money wanting to carry on my suit with spirit with the Nugents of Carrickashaughlin.'

He was very sanguine about that suit with the Nugents of Carrickashaughlin. He could have gained it, they say, for certain, had it pleased Heaven to have spared him to us, and it would have been at the least a plump two thousand a year in his way; but things were ordered otherwise – for the best to be sure. He dug up a fairy-mount[2] against my advice, and had no luck afterwards. Though a learned man in the law, he was a little too incredulous in other matters. I warned him that I heard the very Banshee[3] that my grandfather heard under Sir Patrick's window a few days before his death. But Sir Murtagh thought nothing of the Banshee, nor of his cough, with a spitting of blood, brought on, I understand, by catching cold in attending the courts, and overstraining his chest with making himself heard in one of his favourite causes. He was a great speaker, with a powerful voice; but his last speech was not in the courts at all. He and my lady, though both of the same way of thinking in some things, and though she was as good a wife and great economist as you could see, and he the best of husbands, as to looking into his affairs, and making money for his family; yet I don't know how it was, they had a great deal of sparring and jarring between them. My lady had her privy purse; and she had her weed ashes, and her sealing money upon the signing of all the leases, with something to buy gloves besides; and, besides, again often took money from the tenants, if offered properly, to speak for them to Sir Murtagh about abatements and renewals. Now the weed ashes and the glove money he allowed her clear perquisites; though once when he saw her in a new gown saved out of the weed ashes, he told her to my face (for he could say a sharp thing) that she should not put on her weeds before her husband's death. But in a dispute about an abatement my lady would have the last word, and Sir Murtagh grew mad; I was within hearing of the door, and now I wish I had made bold to step in. He spoke so loud, the whole kitchen was out on the stairs. All on a sudden he stopped, and my lady too. Something has surely happened, thought I; and so it was, for Sir Murtagh in his passion broke a blood-vessel, and all the law in the land could do nothing in that case. My lady sent for five physicians, but Sir Murtagh died and was buried. She had a fine jointure settled upon her, and took herself away, to the great joy of the tenantry. I never said anything one way or the other, whilst she was part of the family, but got up to see her go at three o'clock in the morning.

'It's a fine morning, honest Thady,' says she; 'good-by to ye.' And into the carriage she stepped, without a word more, good or bad, or even half-a-crown; but I made my bow, and stood to see her safe out of sight for the sake of the family.

Then we were all bustle in the house, which made me keep out of the way, for I walk slow and hate a bustle; but the house was all hurry-skurry, preparing for my new master. Sir Murtagh, I forgot to notice, had no childer[4]; so the Rackrent estate went to his younger brother, a young dashing officer, who came amongst us before I knew for the life of me whereabouts I was, in a gig or some of them things, with another spark along with him, and led horses, and servants, and dogs, and scarce a place to put any Christian of them into; for my late lady had sent all the featherbeds off before her, and blankets and household linen, down to the very knife-cloths, on the cars to Dublin, which were all her own, lawfully paid for out of her own money. So the house was quite bare, and my young master, the moment ever he set foot in it out of his gig, thought all those things must come of themselves, I believe, for he never looked after anything at all, but harum-scarum called for everything as if we were conjurers, or he in a public-house. For my part, I could not bestir myself anyhow; I had been so much used to my late master and mistress, all was upside down with me, and the new servants in the servants' hall were quite out of my way; I had nobody to talk to, and if it had not been for my pipe and tobacco, should, I verily believe, have broke my heart for poor Sir Murtagh.

But one morning my new master caught a glimpse of me as I was looking at his horse's heels, in hopes of a word from him. 'And is that old Thady?' says he, as he got into his gig; I loved him from that day to this, his voice was so like the family; and he threw me a guinea out of his waistcoat pocket, as he drew up the reins with the other hand, his horse rearing too; I thought I never set my eyes on a finer figure of a man, quite another sort from Sir Murtagh, though withal, to *me*, a family likeness. A fine life we should have led, had he stayed amongst us, God bless him! He valued a guinea as little as any man; money to him was no more than dirt, and his gentleman and groom, and all belonging to him, the same; but the sporting season over, he grew tired of the place, and having got down a great architect for the house, and an improver for the grounds, and seen their plans and elevations, he fixed a day for settling with the tenants, but went off in a whirlwind to town, just as some of them came into the yard in the morning. A circular letter came next post from the new agent, with news that the master was sailed for England, and he must remit £500 to Bath for his use before a fortnight was at an end; bad news still for the poor tenants, no change still for the better with them. Sir Kit Rackrent, my young master, left all to the agent; and though he had the spirit of a prince, and lived away to the honour of his country abroad, which I was proud to hear of, what were we the better for that at home? The agent was one of your middlemen[5], who grind the face of the poor, and can never bear a man with a hat upon his head; he ferreted the tenants out of their lives; not a week without a call for money, drafts upon drafts from Sir Kit; but I laid it all to the fault of the agent, for, says I, what can Sir Kit do with so much cash, and he a single man? But still it went. Rents must be all paid up to the day, and afore; no allowance for improving tenants, no consideration for those who had built upon their farms; no sooner was a lease out but the land was advertised to the highest bidder; all the old tenants turned out, when they spent their substance in the hope and trust of a renewal from the landlord. All was now let at the highest penny to a parcel of poor wretches, who meant to run away, and did so after taking two crops out of the ground. Then fining down the year's rent came into fashion – anything for the ready penny; and with all this and presents to the agent and the driver, there was no such thing as standing it. I said nothing, for I had a regard for the family, but I walked about thinking if his honour Sir Kit knew all this, it would go hard with him but he'd see us righted; not that I had anything for my own share to complain of, for the agent was always very civil to me when he came down into the country, and took a great deal of notice of my son Jason. Jason Quirk, though he be my son, I must say was a good scholar from his birth, and a very 'cute lad; I thought to make him a priest, but he did better for himself; seeing how he was as good a clerk as any in the country, the agent gave him his rent accounts to copy, which he did first of all for the pleasure of obliging the gentleman, and would take nothing at all for his trouble, but was always proud to serve the family. By and by a good farm bounding us to the east fell into his honour's hands, and my son put in a proposal for it; why shouldn't he, as well as

14

another? The proposals all went over to the master at the Bath, who knowing no more of the land than the child unborn, only having once been out a-grousing on it before he went to England; and the value of lands, as the agent informed him, falling every year in Ireland, his honour wrote over in all haste a bit of a letter, saying he left it all to the agent, and that he must let it as well as he could – to the best bidder, to be sure – and send him over £200 by return of post; with this the agent gave me a hint, and I spoke a good word for my son, and gave out in the country that nobody need bid against us. So his proposal was just the thing, and he a good tenant, and he got a promise of an abatement in the rent after the first year, for advancing the half-year's rent at signing the lease, which was wanting to complete the agent's £200 by the return of the post, with all which my master wrote back he was well satisfied. About this time we learnt from the agent, as a great secret, how the money went so fast, and the reason of the thick coming of the master's drafts: he was a little too fond of play, and Bath, they say, was no place for a young man of his fortune, where there were so many of his own countrymen, too, hunting him up and down day and night, who had nothing to lose. At last, at Christmas, the agent wrote over to stop the drafts, for he could raise no more money on bond or mortgage, or from the tenants, or anyhow, nor had he any more to lend himself, and desired at the same time to decline the agency for the future, wishing Sir Kit his health and happiness, and the compliments of the season, for I saw the letter before ever it was sealed, when my son copied it. When the answer came there was a new turn in affairs, and the agent was turned out, and my son Jason, who had corresponded privately with his honour occasionally on business, was forthwith desired by his honour to take the accounts into his own hands, and look them over, till further orders. It was a very spirited letter to be sure; Sir Kit sent his service, and the compliments of the season, in return to the agent, and he would fight him with pleasure tomorrow, or any day, for sending him such a letter, if he was born a gentleman, which he was sorry (for both their sakes) to find (too late) he was not. Then, in a private postscript, he condescended to tell us that all would be speedily settled to his satisfaction, and we should turn over a new leaf, for he was going to be married in a fortnight to the grandest heiress in England, and had only immediate occasion at present for £200, as he would not choose to touch his lady's fortune for travelling expenses home to Castle Rackrent, where he intended to be, wind and weather permitting, early in the next month; and desired fires, and the house to be painted, and the new building to go on as fast as possible, for the reception of him and his lady before that time; with several words besides in the letter, which we could not make out, because, God bless him! he wrote in such a flurry. My heart warmed to my new lady when I read this: I was almost afraid it was too good news to be true; but the girls fell to scouring, and it was well they did, for we soon saw his marriage in the paper, to a lady with I don't know how many tens of thousand pounds to her fortune; then I watched the post office for his landing; and the news came to my son of his and the bride being in Dublin, and on their way home to Castle Rackrent. We had bonfires all over the country, expecting him down the next day, and we had his coming of age still to celebrate, which he had not time to do properly before he left the country; therefore, a great ball was expected, and great doings upon his coming, as it were, fresh to take possession of his ancestors' estate. I never shall forget the day he came home; we had waited and waited all day long till eleven o'clock at night, and I was thinking of sending the boy to lock the gates, and giving them up for that night, when there came the carriages thundering up to the great hall door. I got the first sight of the bride; for when the carriage door opened, just as she had her foot on the steps, I held the flame full in her face to light her, at which she shut her eyes, but I had a full view of the rest of her, and greatly shocked I was, for by that light she was little better than a blackamoor, and seemed crippled; but that was only sitting so long in the chariot.

'You're kindly welcome to Castle Rackrent, my lady,' says I (recollecting who she was). 'Did your honour hear of the bonfires?'

His honour spoke never a word, nor so much as handed her up the steps – he looked to me no more like himself than nothing at all; I know I took him for the skeleton of his honour. I was not sure what to say to one or t' other, but seeing she was a stranger in a foreign country, I thought it but right to speak cheerful to her; so I went back again to the bonfires.

'My lady,' say I, as she crossed the hall, 'there would have been fifty times as many; but for fear of the horses, and frightening your ladyship, Jason and I forbid them, please your honour.'

With that she looked at me a little bewildered.

'Will I have a fire lighted in the stateroom tonight?' was the next question I put to her, but never a word she answered; so I concluded she could not speak a word of English, and was from foreign parts. The short and the long of it was, I couldn't tell what to make of her; so I left her to herself, and went straight down to the servants' hall to learn something for certain about her. Sir Kit's own man was tired, but the groom set him a-talking at last, and we had it all out before ever I closed my eyes that night. The bride might well be a great fortune – she was a *Jewish* by all accounts, who are famous for their great riches. I had never seen any of that tribe or nation before, and could only gather that she spoke a strange kind of English of her own, that she could not abide pork or sausages, and went neither to church or mass. Mercy upon his honour's poor soul, thought I; what will become of him and his, and all of us, with his heretic blackamoor at the head of the Castle Rackrent estate? I never slept a wink all night for thinking of it; but before the servants I put my pipe in my mouth, and kept my mind to myself, for I had a great regard for the family; and after this, when strange gentlemen's servants came to the house, and would begin to talk about the bride, I took care to put the best foot foremost, and passed her for a nabob in the kitchen, which accounted for her dark complexion and everything.

The very morning after they came home, however, I saw plain enough how things were between Sir Kit and my lady, though they were walking together arm in arm after breakfast, looking at the new building and the improvements.

'Old Thady,' said my master, just as he used to do, 'how do you do?'

'Very well, I thank your honour's honour,' said I; but I saw he was not well pleased, and my heart was in my mouth as I walked along after him.

'Is the large room damp, Thady?' said his honour.

'Oh, damp, your honour! how should it be but as dry as a bone,' says I, 'after all the fires we have kept in it day and night? It's the barrack room your honour's talking on.'

'And what is a barrack room, pray, my dear?' were the first words I ever heard out of my lady's lips.

'No matter, my dear,' said he, and went on talking to me, ashamed-like I should witness her ignorance. To be sure, to hear her talk one might have taken her for an innocent, for it was, 'What's this, Sir Kit?' and 'What's that, Sir Kit?' all the way we went. To be sure, Sir Kit had enough to do to answer her.

'And what do you call that, Sir Kit?' said she; 'that – that looks like a pile of black bricks, pray, Sir Kit?'

'My turfstack, my dear,' said my master, and bit his lip.

Where have you lived, my lady, all your life, not to know a turfstack when you see it? thought I; but I said nothing. Then, by-and-by, she takes out her glass, and begins spying over the country.

'And what's all that black swamp out yonder, Sir Kit?' says she.

'My bog, my dear,' says he, and went on whistling.

'It's a very ugly prospect, my dear,' says she.

18

'You don't see it, my dear,' says he; 'for we've planted it out; when the trees grow up in summertime – ' says he.

'Where are the trees,' said she, 'my dear?' still looking through her glass.

'You are blind, my dear,' says he: 'what are these under your eyes?'

'These shrubs?' said she.

'Trees,' said he.

'Maybe they are what you call trees in Ireland, my dear,' said she, 'but they are not a yard high, are they?'

'They were planted out but last year, my lady,' says I, to soften matters between them, for I saw she was going the way to make his honour mad with her: 'they are very well grown for their age, and you'll not see the bog of Allyballycarrick-o'shaughlin at-all-at-all through the skreen, when once the leaves come out. But, my lady, you must not quarrel with any part or parcel of Allyballycarricko'shaughlin, for you don't know how many hundred years that same bit of bog has been in the family; we would not part with the bog of Allybally-carricko'shaughlin upon no account at all; it cost the late Sir Murtagh two hundred good pounds to defend his title to it and boundaries against the O'Learys, who cut a road through it.'

Now one would have thought this would have been hint enough for my lady, but she fell to laughing like one out of their right mind, and made me say the name of the bog over, for her to get it by heart, a dozen times; then she must ask me how to spell it, and what was the meaning of it in English – Sir Kit standing by whistling all the while. I verily believed she laid the cornerstone of all her future misfortunes at that very instant; but I said no more, only looked at Sir Kit.

There were no balls, no dinners, no doings; the country was all disappointed – Sir Kit's gentleman said in a whisper to me, it was all my lady's own fault, because she was so obstinate about the cross.

'What cross?' says I, 'is it about her being a heretic?'

'Oh, no such matter,' says he, 'my master does not mind her heresies, but her diamond cross – it's worth I can't tell you how much, and she has thousands of English pounds concealed in diamonds about her, which she as good as promised to give up to my master before he married; but now she won't part with any of them, and she must take the consequences.'

Her honeymoon, at least her Irish honeymoon, was scarcely well over, when his honour one morning said to me, 'Thady, buy me a pig!' and then the sausages were ordered, and here was the first open breaking-out of my lady's troubles. My lady came down herself into the kitchen to speak to the cook about the sausages, and desired never to see them more at her table. Now my master had ordered them, and my lady knew that. The cook took my lady's part, because she never came down into the kitchen and was young and innocent in housekeeping, which raised her pity; besides, said she, at her own table, surely my lady should order and disorder what she pleases. But the cook soon changed her note, for my master made it a principle to have the sausages, and swore at her for a Jew herself, till he drove her fairly out of the kitchen; then, for fear of her place, and because he threatened that my lady should give her no discharge without the sausages, she gave up, and from that day forward always sausages, or bacon, or pig meat in some shape or other, went up to table; upon which my lady shut herself in her own room, and my master said she might stay there, with an oath; and to make sure of her, he turned the key in the door, and kept it ever after in his pocket. We none of us ever saw or heard her speak for seven years after that[6]: he carried her dinner himself. Then his honour had a great deal of company to dine with him, and balls in the house, and was as gay and gallant, and as much himself as before he was married; and at dinner he always drank my Lady Rackrent's good health and so did the company, and he sent out always a servant with his compliments to my Lady Rackrent, and the company was drinking her ladyship's health, and begged to know if there was anything at table he might send her, and the man came back, after the sham errand, with my Lady Rackrent's compliments, and she was very much obliged to Sir Kit – she did not wish for anything, but drank the company's health. The country, to be sure, talked and wondered at my lady's being shut up, but nobody chose to interfere or ask any impertinent questions, for they knew my master was a man very apt to give a short answer himself, and likely to call a man out for it afterwards: he was a famous shot, had killed his man before he came of age, and nobody scarce dared look at him whilst at Bath. Sir Kit's character was so well known in the country that he lived in peace and quietness ever after, and was a great favourite with the ladies, especially when in process of time, in the fifth year of her confinement, my Lady Rackrent fell ill and took entirely to her bed, and he gave out she was now skin and bone, and could not last through the winter, in this he had two physicians' opinions to back him (for now he called in two physicians for her), and tried all his arts to get the diamond cross from her on her deathbed, and to get her to make a will in his favour of her separate possessions, but there she was too tough for him. He used to swear at her behind her back after kneeling to her face, and call her in the presence of his gentleman his stiff-necked Israelite, though before he married her that same gentleman told me he used to call her (how he could bring it out, I don't know) 'my pretty Jessica!' To be sure it must have been hard for her to guess what sort of a husband he reckoned to make her. When she was lying, to all expectation, on her deathbed of a broken heart, I could not but pity her, though she was a Jewish, and considering too it was no fault of hers to be taken with my master, so young as she was at the Bath, and so fine a gentleman as Sir Kit was when he courted her; and considering too, after all they had heard and seen of him as a husband, there were now no less than three ladies in our county talked of for his second wife, all at daggers drawn with each other, as his gentleman swore, at the balls, for Sir Kit for their partner – I could not but think them

21

bewitched, but they all reasoned with themselves that Sir Kit would make a good husband to any Christian but a Jewish, I suppose, and especially as he was now a reformed rake; and it was not known how my lady's fortune was settled in her will, nor how the Castle Rackrent estate was all mortgaged, and bonds out against him, for he was never cured of his gaming tricks; but that was the only fault he had, God bless him!

My lady had a sort of fit, and it was given out that she was dead, by mistake; this brought things to a sad crisis for my poor master. One of the three ladies showed his letters to her brother, and claimed his promises, whilst another did the same. I don't mention names. Sir Kit, in his defence, said he would meet any man who dared to question his conduct; and as to the ladies, they must settle it amongst them who was to be his second, and his third, and his fourth, whilst his first was still alive, to his mortification and theirs. Upon this, as upon all former occasions, he had the voice of the country with him, on account of the great spirit and propriety he acted with. He met and shot the first lady's brother; the next day he called out the second, who had a wooden leg, and their place of meeting by appointment being in a new-ploughed field, the wooden-leg man stuck fast in it. Sir Kit, seeing his situation, with great candour fired his pistol over his head; upon which the seconds interposed, and convinced the parties there had been a slight misunderstanding between them; thereupon they shook hands cordially, and went home to dinner together. This gentleman, to show the world how they stood together, and by the advice of the friends of both parties, to re-establish his sister's injured reputation, went out with Sir Kit as his second, and carried his message next day to the last of his adversaries; I never saw him in such fine spirits as that day he went out – sure enough he was within amesace of getting quit handsomely of all his enemies; but unluckily, after hitting the toothpick out of his adversary's finger and thumb, he received a ball in a vital part, and was brought home, in little better than an hour after the affair, speechless on a hand-barrow to my lady. We got the key out of his pocket the first thing we did, and my son Jason ran to unlock the barrack room, where my lady had been shut up for seven years, to acquaint her with the fatal accident. The surprise bereaved her of her senses at first, nor would she believe but we were putting some new trick upon her, to entrap her out of her jewels, for a great while, till Jason bethought himself of taking her to the window, and showed her the men bringing Sir Kit up the avenue upon the hand-barrow, which had immediately the desired effect; for directly she burst into tears, and pulling her cross from her bosom, she kissed it with as great devotion as ever I witnessed, and lifting up her eyes to heaven uttered some ejaculation which none present heard; but I take the sense of it to be, she returned thanks for this unexpected interposition in her favour when she had least reason to expect it. My master was greatly lamented: there was no life in him when we lifted him off the barrow, so he was laid out immediately, and 'waked' the same night. The country was all in an uproar about him, and not a soul but cried shame upon his murderer, who would have been hanged surely, if he could have been brought to his trial, whilst the gentlemen in the country were up about it; but he very prudently withdrew himself to the Continent before the affair was made public. As for the young lady who was the immediate cause of the fatal accident, however innocently, she could never show her head after at the balls in the county or any place; and by the advice of her friends and physicians she was ordered soon after to Bath, where it was expected, if anywhere on this side of the grave, she would meet with the recovery of her health and lost peace of mind. As a proof of his great popularity, I need only add that there was a song made upon my master's untimely death in the newspapers, which was in everybody's mouth, singing up and down through the country, even down to the mountains, only three days after his unhappy exit. He was also greatly bemoaned at the Curragh, where his cattle were well known; and all who had taken up his bets were particularly inconsolable for his loss to society. His stud sold at the cant at the greatest price ever known in the county; his favourite horses were chiefly disposed of amongst his particular friends, who would give any price for them, for his sake; but no ready money was required by the new heir, who wished not to displease any of the gentlemen of the neighbourhood just upon his coming to settle amongst them; so a long credit was given where requisite, and the cash has never been gathered in from that day to this.

But to return to my lady. She got surprisingly well after my master's decease. No sooner was it known for certain that he was dead, than all the gentlemen within twenty miles of us came in a body, as it were, to set my lady at liberty, and to protest against her confinement, which they now for the first time understood was against her own consent. The ladies too were as attentive as possible, striving who should be foremost with their morning visits; and they that saw the diamonds spoke very handsomely of them, but thought it a pity they were not bestowed, if it had so pleased God, upon a lady who would have become them better. All these civilities wrought little with my lady, for she had taken an unaccountable prejudice against the country, and everything belonging to it, and was so partial to her native land, that after parting with the cook, which she did immediately upon my master's decease, I never knew her easy one instant, night or day, but when she was packing up to leave us. Had she meant to make any stay in Ireland, I stood a great chance of being a great favourite with her; for when she found I understood the weathercock, she was always finding some pretence to be talking to me, and asking me which way the wind blew, and was it likely, did I think, to continue fair for England. But when I saw she had made up her mind to spend the rest of her days upon her own income and jewels in England, I considered her quite as a foreigner, and not at all any longer as part of the family. She gave no veils to the servants at Castle Rackrent at parting, notwithstanding the old proverb of 'as rich as a Jew', which, she being a Jewish, they built upon with reason. But from first to last she brought nothing but misfortunes amongst us; and if it had not been all along with her, his honour, Sir Kit, would have been now alive in all appearance. Her diamond cross was, they say, at the bottom of it all; and it was a shame for her, being his wife, not to show more duty, and to have given it up when he condescended to ask so often for such a bit of a trifle in his distresses, especially when he all along made it no secret he married for money. But we will not bestow another thought upon her. This much I thought it lay upon my conscience to say, in justice to my poor master's memory.

'T is an ill wind that blows nobody no good; the same wind that took the Jew Lady Rackrent over to England brought over the new heir to Castle Rackrent.

Here let me pause for breath in my story, for though I had a great regard for every member of the family, yet without compare Sir Conolly, commonly called, for short, amongst his friends, Sir Condy Rackrent, was ever my great favourite, and indeed, the most universally beloved man I had ever seen or heard of, not excepting his great ancestor Sir Patrick, to whose memory he, amongst other instances of generosity, erected a handsome marble stone in the church of Castle Rackrent, setting forth in large letters his age, birth, parentage, and many other virtues, concluding with the compliment so justly due, that 'Sir Patrick Rackrent lived and died a monument of old Irish hospitality'.

1. The cloak, or mantle, as described by Thady, is of high antiquity. Spenser, in his 'View of the State of Ireland', proves that it is not, as some have imagined, peculiarly derived from the Scythians, but that 'most nations of the world anciently used the mantle; for the Jews used it, as you may read of Elias' mantle, etc.; the Chaldees also used it, as you may read of in Diodorus; the Egyptians likewise used it, as you may read in Herodotus, and may be gathered by the description of Berenice in the Greek Commentary upon Callimachus; the Greeks also used it anciently, as appeared by Venus'

mantle lined with stars, though afterwards they changed the form thereof into their cloaks, called Pallai, as some of the Irish also use: and the ancient Latins and Romans used it, as you may read in Virgil, who was a great antiquary, that Evander, when Aeneas came to him at his feast, did entertain and feast him sitting on the ground, and lying on mantles: insomuch that he useth the very word mantile for a mantle:

'Humi mantilia sternunt':

so that it seemeth that the mantle was a general habit to most nations, and not proper to the Scythians only'.

Spenser knew the convenience of the said mantle, as housing, bedding, and clothing:

'*Iren.* Because the commodity doth not countervail the discommodity: for the inconveniences which thereby do arise are much more many; for it is a fit house for an outlaw, a meet bed for a rebel, and an apt cloak for a thief. First, the outlaw being, for his many crimes and villainies, banished from the towns and houses of honest men, and wandering in waste places, far from danger of law, maketh his mantle his house, and under it covereth himself from the wrath of Heaven, from the offence of the earth, and from the sight of men. When it raineth, it is his pent-house; when it bloweth, it is his tent; when it freezeth, it is his tabernacle. In summer he can wear it loose; in winter he can wrap it close; at all times he can use it; never heavy, never cumbersome. Likewise for a rebel it is as serviceable; for in this war that he maketh (if at least it deserves the name of war), when he still flieth from his foe, and lurketh in the *thick woods* (this should be *black bogs*) and straight passages, waiting for advantages, it is his bed, yea, and almost his household stuff.'

2. These fairy-mounts are called ant-hills in England. They are held in high reverence by the common people in Ireland. A gentleman, who in laying out his lawn had occasion to level one of these hillocks, could not prevail upon any of his labourers to begin the ominous work. He was obliged to take a *loy* from one of their reluctant hands, and began the attack himself. The labourers agreed that the vengeance of the fairies would fall upon the head of the presumptuous mortal who first disturbed them in their retreat.

3. The Banshee is a species of aristocratic fairy, who, in the shape of a little hideous old woman, has been known to appear, and heard to sing in a mournful supernatural voice under the windows of great houses, to warn the family that some of them are soon to die. In the last century every great family in Ireland had a Banshee, who attended regularly; but latterly their visits and songs have been discontinued.

4. Childer: this is the manner in which many of Thady's rank, and others in Ireland, formerly pronounced the word *children*.
5. *Middlemen.* – There was a class of men, termed middlemen, in Ireland, who took large farms on long leases from gentlemen of landed property, and let the land again in small portions to the poor, as under-tenants, at exorbitant rents. The *head landlord*, as he was called, seldom saw his *under-tenants*; but if he could not get the *middleman* to pay his rent punctually, he *went to his land and drove the land for his rent* – that is to say, he sent his steward, or bailiff, or driver, to the land to seize the cattle, hay, corn, flax, oats, or potatoes belonging to the under-tenants, and proceeded to sell these for his rents. It sometimes happened that these unfortunate tenants paid their rent twice over, once to the *middleman*, and once to the *head landlord*.

The characteristics of a middleman were servility to his superiors and tyranny towards his inferiors; the poor detested this race of beings. In speaking to them, however, they always used the most abject language, and the most humble tone and posture – *'Please your honour; and please your honour's honour,'* they knew must be repeated as a charm at the beginning and end of every equivocating, exculpatory, or supplicatory sentence; and they were much more alert in doffing their caps to those new men than to those of what they call *good old families*. A witty carpenter once termed these middlemen *journeymen gentlemen*.

6. This part of the history of the Rackrent family can scarcely be thought credible; but in justice to honest Thady, it is hoped the reader will recollect the history of the celebrated Lady Cathcart's conjugal imprisonment. The editor was acquainted with Colonel M'Guire, Lady Cathcart's husband; he has lately seen and questioned the maid-servant who lived with Colonel M'Guire during the time of Lady Cathcart's imprisonment. Her ladyship was locked up in her own house for many years, during which period her husband was visited by the neighbouring gentry, and it was his regular custom at dinner to send his compliments to Lady Cathcart, informing her that the company had the honour to drink her ladyship's health, and begging to know whether there was anything at table that she would like to eat? The answer was always, 'Lady Cathcart's compliments, and she has every thing she wants.' An instance of honesty in a poor Irishwoman deserves to be recorded. Lady Cathcart had some remarkably fine diamonds, which she had concealed from her husband, and which she was anxious to get out of the house, lest he should discover them. She had neither servant nor friend to whom she could entrust them, but she had observed a poor beggar-woman, who used to come to the house; she spoke to her from the window of the room in which she was confined; the woman promised to do what she desired, and Lady Cathcart threw a parcel containing the jewels to

her. The poor woman carried them to the person to whom they were directed, and several years afterwards, when Lady Cathcart recovered her liberty, she received her diamonds safely.

At Colonel M'Guire's death her ladyship was released. The editor, within this year, saw the gentleman who accompanied her to England after her husband's death. When she first was told of his death she imagined that the news was not true, and that it was told only with an intention of deceiving her. At his death she had scarcely clothes sufficient to cover her; she wore a red wig, looked scared, and her understanding seemed stupefied; she said that she scarcely knew one human creature from another; her imprisonment lasted about twenty years. These circumstances may appear strange to an English reader; but there is no danger in the present times, that any individual should exercise such tyranny as Colonel M'Guire's with impunity, the power being now all in the hands of government, and there being no possibility of obtaining from Parliament an act of indemnity for any cruelties.

CONTINUATION OF THE MEMOIRS OF THE RACKRENT FAMILY

HISTORY OF SIR CONOLLY RACKRENT

Sir Condy Rackrent, by the grace of God heir-at-law to the Castle Rackrent estate, was a remote branch of the family. Born to little or no fortune of his own, he was bred to the bar, at which, having many friends to push him and no mean natural abilities of his own, he doubtless would in process of time, if he could have borne the drudgery of that study, have been rapidly made King's Counsel at the least, but things were disposed of otherwise, and he never went the circuit but twice, and then made no figure for want of a fee and being unable to speak in public. He received his education chiefly in the College of Dublin, but before he came to years of discretion lived in the country, in a small but slated house within view of the end of the avenue. I remember him, barefooted and headed, running through the street of O'Shaughlin's Town, and playing at pitch-and-toss, ball, marbles, and what not, with the boys of the town, amongst whom my son Jason was a great favourite with him. As for me, he was ever my white-headed boy; often 's the time, when I would call in at his father's where I was always made welcome, he would slip down to me in the kitchen, and love to sit on my knee whilst I told him stories of the family and the blood from which he was sprung, and how he might look forward, if the then present man should die without childer, to being at the head of the Castle Rackrent estate. This was then

29

spoke quite and clear, at random to please the child, but it pleased Heaven to accomplish my prophecy afterwards, which gave him a great opinion of my judgment in business. He went to a little grammar school with many others, and my son amongst the rest, who was in his class, and not a little useful to him in his book-learning, which he acknowledged with gratitude ever after. These rudiments of his education thus completed, he got a-horseback, to which exercise he was ever addicted, and used to gallop over the country while yet but a slip of a boy, under the care of Sir Kit's huntsman, who was very fond of him, and often lent him his gun, and took him out a-shooting under his own eye. By these means he became well acquainted and popular amongst the poor in the neighbour-hood early, for there was not a cabin at which he had not stopped some morning or other, along with the huntsman, to drink a glass of burnt whiskey out of an egg-shell, to do him good and warm his heart and drive the cold out of his stomach. The old people always told him he was a great likeness of Sir Patrick, which made him first have an ambition to take after him, as far as his fortune should allow. He left us when of an age to enter the college, and there completed his education and nineteenth year, for as he was not born to an estate, his friends thought it incumbent on them to give him the best education which could be had for love or money, and a great deal of money consequently was spent upon him at College and Temple. He was a very little altered for the worse by what he saw there of the great world, for when he came down into the country to pay us a visit, we thought him just the same man as ever – hand and glove with everyone, and as far from high, though not without his own proper share of family pride, as any man ever you see. Latterly, seeing how Sir Kit and the Jewish lived together, and that there was no-one between him and the Castle Rackrent estate, he neglected to apply to the law as much as was expected of him, and secretly many of the tenants and others advanced him cash upon his note of hand value received, promising bargains of leases and lawful interest, should he ever come into the estate. All this was kept a great secret for fear the present man, hearing of it, should take it into his head to take it ill of poor Condy, and so should cut him off for ever by levying a fine, and suffering a recovery to dock the entail. Sir Murtagh would have been the man for that; but Sir Kit was too much taken up philandering to consider the law in this case, or any other. These practices I have mentioned to account for the state of his affairs – I mean Sir Condy's upon his coming into the Castle Rackrent estate. He could not command a penny of his first year's income, which, and keeping no accounts, and the great sight of company he did, with many other causes too numerous to mention, was the origin of his distresses. My son Jason, who was now established agent, and knew everything, explained matters out of the face to Sir Conolly, and made him sensible of his embarrassed situation. With a great nominal rent-roll, it was almost all paid away in interest; which being for convenience suffered to run on, soon doubled the principal, and Sir Condy was obliged to pass new bonds for the interest, now grown principal, and so on. Whilst this was going on, my son, requiring to be paid for his trouble and many years' service in the family gratis, and Sir Condy not willing to take his affairs into his own hands, or to look them even in the face, he gave my son a bargain of some acres which fell out of lease at a reasonable rent. Jason let the land, as soon as his lease was sealed, to under-tenants, to make the rent, and got two hundred a year profit rent; which was little enough considering his long agency. He bought the land at twelve years' purchase two years afterwards, when Sir Condy was pushed for money on an execution, and was at the same time allowed for his improvements thereon. There was a sort of hunting-lodge upon the estate, convenient to my son Jason's land, which he had his eye upon about this time; and he was a little jealous of Sir Condy, who talked of letting it to a stranger who was just come into the country – Captain Moneygawl was the man. He was son and heir to the Moneygawls of Mount Juliet's Town, who had a great estate in the next county to ours; and my master was loath to disoblige the young gentleman, whose heart was set upon the Lodge; so he wrote him back that the Lodge was at his service, and if he would honour him with his company at Castle Rackrent, they could ride over together some morning and look at it before signing the lease. Accordingly, the captain came over to us, and he and Sir Condy grew the greatest friends ever you see, and were for ever out a-shooting or hunting together, and were very merry in the evenings; and Sir Condy was invited of course to Mount Juliet's Town; and the family intimacy that had been in Sir Patrick's time was now recollected, and nothing would serve Sir Condy but he must be three times a week at the least with his new friends, which grieved me, who knew, by the captain's groom and gentleman, how they talked of him at Mount Juliet's Town, making him quite, as one may say, a laughing-stock and a butt for the whole company; but they were soon cured of that by an accident that surprised 'em not a little, as it did me. There was a bit of a scrawl found upon the waiting-maid of old Mr Moneygawl's youngest daughter, Miss Isabella, that laid open the whole; and her father, they say, was like one out of his right mind, and swore it was the last thing he ever should have thought of, when he invited my master to his house, that his daughter should think of such a match. But their talk signified not a straw, for as Miss Isabella's maid reported, her young mistress was fallen over head and ears in love with Sir Condy from the first time that ever her brother brought him into the house to dinner. The servant who waited that day behind my master's chair was the first who knew it, as he says; though it's hard to believe him, for he did not tell it till a great while afterwards; but, however, it's likely enough, as the thing turned out, that he was not far out of the way, for towards the middle of dinner, as he says, they were talking of stage-plays, having a playhouse, and being great play-actors at Mount Juliet's Town; and Miss Isabella turns short to my master, and says:

'Have you seen the play-bill, Sir Condy?'

'No, I have not,' said he.

'Then more shame for you,' said the captain her brother, 'not to know that my sister is to play Juliet tonight, who plays it better than any woman on or off the stage in all Ireland.'

'I am very happy to hear it,' said Sir Condy; and there the matter dropped for the present.

But Sir Condy all this time, and a great while afterward, was at a terrible non-plus; for he had no liking, not he, to stage-plays, nor to Miss Isabella either – to his mind, as it came out over a bowl of whiskey-punch at home, his little Judy M'Quirk, who was daughter to a sister's son of mine, was worth twenty of Miss Isabella. He had seen her often when he stopped at her father's cabin to drink whiskey out of the egg-shell, out hunting, before he came to the estate, and, as she gave out, was under something like a promise of marriage to her. Anyhow, I could not but pity my poor master, who was so bothered between them, and he an easy-hearted man, that could not disoblige nobody – God bless him! To be sure, it was not his place to behave ungenerous to Miss Isabella, who had disobliged all her relations for his sake, as he remarked; and then she was locked up in her chamber, and forbid to think of him any more, which raised his spirit, because his family was, as he observed, as good as theirs at any rate, and the Rackrents a suitable match for the Moneygawls any day in the year; all which was true enough. But it grieved me to see that, upon the strength of all this, Sir Condy was growing more in the mind to carry off Miss Isabella to Scotland, in spite of her relations, as she desired.

'It's all over with our poor Judy!' said I, with a heavy sigh, making bold to speak to him one night when he was a little cheerful, and standing in the servants' hall all alone with me, as was often his custom.

'Not at all,' said he. 'I never was fonder of Judy than at this present speaking; and to prove it to you,' said he – and he took from my hand a halfpenny change that I had just got along with my tobacco – 'and to prove it to you, Thady,' says he, 'it's a toss-up with me which I should marry this minute, her or Mr Moneygawl of Mount Juliet's Town's daughter – so it is.'

'Oh – boo! boo!'[1] says I, making light of it, to see what he would go on to next; 'your honour's joking, to be sure; there's no compare between our poor Judy and Miss Isabella, who has a great fortune, they say.'

'I'm not a man to mind a fortune, nor never was,' said Sir Condy, proudly, 'whatever her friends may say; and to make short of it,' says he, 'I'm come to a determination upon the spot.' With that he swore such a terrible oath as made me cross myself. 'And by this book,' said he, snatching up my ballad book, mistaking it for my prayer book, which lay in the window; 'and by this book,' says he, 'and by all the books that ever were shut and opened, it's come to a toss-up with me, and I'll stand or fall by the toss; and so Thady, hand me over that pin[2] out of the ink-horn'; and he makes a cross on the smooth side of the halfpenny; 'Judy M'Quirk,' says he, 'her mark.'[3]

God bless him! his hand was a little unsteadied by all the whiskey-punch he had taken, but it was plain to see his heart was for poor Judy. My heart was all as one as in my mouth when I saw the halfpenny up in the air, but I said nothing at all; and when it came down I was glad I had kept myself to myself, for to be sure now it was all over with poor Judy.

'Judy's out of luck,' said I, striving to laugh.

'I'm out a luck,' said he; and I never saw a man look so cast down: he took up the halfpenny off the flag, and walked away quite sober-like by the shock. Now, though as easy a man, you would think, as any in the wide world, there was no such thing as making him unsay one of these sort of vows,[4] which he had learned to reverence when young, as I well remember teaching him to toss up for bogberries on my knee. So I saw the affair was as good as settled between him and Miss Isabella, and I had no more to say but to wish her joy, which I did the week afterwards, upon her return from Scotland with my poor master.

My new lady was young, as might be supposed of a lady that had been carried off by her own consent to Scotland; but I could only see her at first through her veil, which, from bashfulness or fashion, she kept over her face.

'And am I to walk through all this crowd of people, my dearest love?' said she to Sir Condy, meaning us servants and tenants, who had gathered at the back gate.

'My dear,' said Sir Condy, 'there's nothing for it but to walk, or to let me carry you as far as the house, for you see the back road is too narrow for a carriage, and the great piers have tumbled down across the front approach: so there's no driving the right way, by reason of the ruins.'

'Plato, thou reasonest well!' said she, or words to that effect, which I could noways understand; and again, when her foot stumbled against a broken bit of a car-wheel, she cried out, 'Angels and ministers of grace defend us!' Well, thought I, to be sure, if she's no Jewish, like the last, she is mad-woman for certain, which is as bad: it would have been as well for my poor master to have taken up with poor Judy, who is in her right mind anyhow.

She was dressed like a mad-woman, moreover, more than like anyone I ever saw afore or since, and I could not take my eyes off her, but still followed behind her; and her feathers on the top of her hat were broke going in at the low back door, and she pulled out her little bottle out of her pocket to smell when she found herself in the kitchen, and said, 'I shall faint with the heat of this odious, odious place.'

'My dear, it's only three steps across the kitchen, and there's a fine air if your veil was up,' said Sir Condy; and with that threw back her veil, so that I had then a full sight of her face. She had not at all the colour of one going to faint, but a fine complexion of her own, as I then took it to be, though her maid told me after it was all put on; but even, complexion and all taken in, she was no way, in point of good looks, to compare to poor Judy, and withal she had a quality toss with her; but maybe it was my over-partiality to Judy, into whose place I may say she stepped, that made me notice all this.

To do her justice, however, she was, when we came to know her better, very liberal in her housekeeping – nothing at all of the skinflint in her; she left everything to the housekeeper, and her own maid, Mrs Jane, who went with her to Scotland, gave her the best of characters for generosity. She seldom or ever wore a thing twice the same way, Mrs Jane told us, and was always pulling her things to pieces and giving them away, never being used, in her father's house, to think of expense in anything; and she reckoned to be sure to go on the same way at Castle Rackrent; but when I came to inquire, I learned that her father was so mad with her for running off, after his locking her up and forbidding her to think any more of Sir Condy, that he would not give her a farthing; and it was lucky for her she had a few thousands of her own, which had been left to her by a good grandmother, and these were convenient to begin with. My master and my lady set out in great style; they had the finest coach and chariot, and horses and liveries, and cut the greatest dash in the county, returning their wedding visits; and it was immediately reported that her father had undertaken to pay all my master's debts, and of course all his tradesmen gave him a new credit, and everything went on smacksmooth, and I could not but admire my lady's spirit, and was proud to see Castle Rackrent again in all its glory. My lady had a fine taste for building, and furniture, and playhouses, and she turned everything topsy-turvy, and made the barrack room into a theatre, as she called it, and she went on as if she had a mint of money at her elbow; and to be sure I thought she knew best, especially as Sir Condy said nothing to it one way or the other. All he asked, God bless him! was to live in peace and quietness, and have his bottle or his whiskey-punch at night to himself. Now this was little enough, to be sure, for any gentleman; but my lady couldn't abide the smell of the whiskey-punch.

'My dear,' says he, 'you liked it well enough before we were married, and why not now?'

'My dear,' said she, 'I never smelt it, or I assure you I should never have prevailed upon myself to marry you.'

'My dear, I am sorry you did not smell it, but we can't help that now,' returned my master, without putting himself in a passion or going out of his way, but just fair and easy helped himself to another glass, and drank it off to her good health.

All this the butler told me, who was going backwards and forwards unnoticed with the jug, and hot water and sugar, and all he thought wanting. Upon my master's swallowing the last glass of whiskey-punch, my lady burst into tears, calling him an ungrateful, base, barbarous wretch, and went off into a fit of hysterics, as I think Mrs Jane called it; and my poor master was greatly frightened, this being the first thing of the kind he had seen, and he fell straight on his knees before her, and, like a good-hearted cratur as he was, ordered the whiskey-punch out of the room, and bid 'em throw open all the windows, and cursed himself; and then my lady came to herself again, and when she saw him kneeling there, bid him get up, and not forswear himself any more, for that she was sure he did not love her, and never had. This we learned from Mrs Jane, who was the only person left present at all this.

'My dear,' returns my master, thinking to be sure, of Judy, as well he might, 'whoever told you so is an incendiary, and I'll have 'em turned out of the house this minute, if you'll only let me know which of them it was.'

'Told me what?' said my lady, starting upright in her chair.

'Nothing at all, nothing at all,' said my master, seeing he had overshot himself, and that my lady spoke at random; 'but what you said just now, that I did not love you, Bella; who told you that?'

'My own sense,' she said, and she put her handkerchief to her face and leant back upon Mrs Jane, and fell to sobbing as if her heart would break.

'Why now, Bella, this is very strange of you,' said my poor master; 'if nobody has told you nothing, what is it you are taking on for at this rate, and exposing yourself and me for this way?'

'Oh, say no more, say no more; every word you say kills me,' cried my lady; and she ran on like one, as Mrs Jane says, raving, 'Oh, Sir Condy, Sir Condy! I that had hoped to find in you – '

'Why now, faith, this is a little too much; do, Bella, try to recollect yourself, my dear; am not I your husband, and of your own choosing, and is not that enough?'

'Oh, too much! too much!' cried my lady, wringing her hands.

'Why, my dear, come to your right senses, for the love of Heaven. See, is not the whiskey-punch, jug and bowl and all, gone out of the room long ago? What is it, in the wide world, you have to complain of?'

But still my lady sobbed and sobbed, and called herself the most wretched of women; and among other out-of-the-way, provoking things, asked my master was he fit company for her, and he drinking all night? This nettling him, which it was hard to do, he replied that, as to drinking all night, he was then as sober as she was herself, and that it was no matter how much a man drank, provided it did no ways affect or stagger him; that as to being fit company for her, he thought himself of a family to be fit company for any lord or lady in the land; but that he never prevented her from seeing and keeping what company she pleased, and that he had done his best to make Castle Rackrent pleasing to her since her marriage, having always had the house full of visitors, and if her own relations were not amongst them, he said that was their own fault, and their pride's fault, of which he was sorry to find her ladyship had so unbecoming a share. So concluding, he took his candle and walked off to his room, and my lady was in her tantrums for three days after, and would have been so much longer, no doubt, but some of her friends, young ladies and cousins and second cousins, came to Castle Rackrent, by my poor master's express invitation, to see her, and she was in a hurry to get up, as Mrs Jane called it, a play for them, and so got well, and was as finely dressed and as happy to look at as ever; and all the young ladies, who used to be in her room dressing of her, said in Mrs Jane's hearing that my lady was the happiest bride ever they had seen, and that, to be sure, a love-match was the only thing for happiness where the parties could anyway afford it.

As to affording it, God knows it was little they knew of the matter: my lady's few thousands could not last for ever, especially the way she went on with them, and letters from tradesfolk came every post thick and threefold, with bills as long as my arm, of years' and years' standing. My son Jason had 'em all handed over to him, and the pressing letters were all unread by Sir Condy, who hated trouble, and could never be brought to hear talk of business, but still put it off and put it off, saying, 'Settle it anyhow,' or 'Bid 'em call again tomorrow,' or 'Speak to me about it some other time.' Now it was hard to find the right time to speak, for in the mornings he was a-bed, and in the evenings over his bottle, where no gentleman chooses to be disturbed. Things in a twelve-month or so came to such a pass there was no making a shift to go on any longer, though we were all of us well enough used to live from hand to mouth at Castle Rackrent. One day, I remember, when there was a power of company, all sitting after dinner in the dusk, not to say dark, in the drawing-room, my lady having rung five times for candles and none to go up, the housekeeper sent up the footman, who went to my mistress and whispered behind her chair how it was.

'My lady,' says he, 'there are no candles in the house.'

'Bless me,' says she; 'then take a horse and gallop off as fast as you can to Carrick O'Fungus, and get some.'

'And in the meantime tell them to step into the playhouse, and try if there are not some bits left,' added Sir Condy, who happened to be within hearing. The man was sent up again to my lady to let her know there was no horse to go but one that wanted a shoe.

'Go to Sir Condy, then; I know nothing at all about horses,' said my lady; 'why do you plague me with such things?' How it was settled I really forget, but to the best of my remembrance the boy was sent down to my son Jason's to borrow candles for the night. Another time, in the winter, and on a desperate cold day, there was no turf in for the parlour and above stairs, and scarce enough for the cook in the kitchen. The little *gossoon*[5] was sent off to the neighbours to see and beg or borrow some, but none could he bring back with him for love or money, so, as needs must, we were forced to trouble Sir Condy – 'Well, and if there's no turf to be had in the town or country, why, what signifies talking any more about it; can't ye go and cut down a tree?'

'Which tree, please your honour?' I made bold to say.

'Any tree at all that's good to burn,' said Sir Condy; 'send off smart and get one down and the fires lighted before my lady gets up to breakfast, or the house will be too hot to hold us.'

He was always very considerate in all things about my lady, and she wanted for nothing whilst he had it to give. Well, when things were tight with them about this time, my son Jason put in a word again about the Lodge, and made a genteel offer to lay down the purchase-money, to relieve Sir Condy's distresses. Now Sir Condy had it from the best authority that there were two writs come down to the sheriff against his person, and the sheriff, as ill-luck would have it, was no friend of his, and talked how he must do his duty, and how he would do it, if it was against the first man in the country, or even his own brother, let alone one who had voted against him at the last election, as Sir Condy had done. So Sir Condy was fain to take the purchase-money of the Lodge from my son Jason to settle matters; and sure enough it was a good bargain for both parties, for my son bought the fee-simple of a good house for him and his heirs for ever, for little or nothing, and by selling of it for that same my master saved himself from a gaol. Every way it turned out fortunate for Sir Condy, for before the money was all gone there came a general election, and he being so well beloved in the county, and one of the oldest families, no one had a better right to stand candidate for the vacancy; and he was called upon by all his friends, and the whole county, I may say, to declare himself against the old member, who had little thought of a contest. My master did not relish the thoughts of a troublesome canvass and all the ill-will he might bring upon himself by disturbing the peace of the county, besides the expense, which was no trifle; but all his friends called upon one another to subscribe, and they formed themselves into a committee, and wrote all his circular letters for him, and engaged all his agents, and did all the business unknown to him; and he was well pleased that it should be so at last, and my lady herself was very sanguine about the election; and there was open house kept night and day at Castle Rackrent, and I thought I never saw my lady look so well in her life as she did at that time. There were grand dinners, and all the gentlemen drinking success to Sir Condy till they were carried off; and then dances and balls, and the ladies all finishing with a raking pot of tea in the morning. Indeed, it was well the company made it their choice to sit up all nights, for there were not half beds enough for the sights of people that were in it, though there were shake-downs in the drawing-room always made up before sunrise for those that liked it. For my part, when I saw the doings that were going on, and the loads of claret that went down the throats of them that had no right to be asking for it, and the sights of meat that went up to table and never came down, besides what was carried off to one or t'other below stair, I couldn't but pity my poor master, who was to pay for all; but I said nothing, for fear of gaining myself ill-will. The day of election will come sometime or other, says I to myself, and all will be over; and so it did, and a glorious day it was as any I ever had the happiness to see.

'Huzza! huzza! Sir Condy Rackrent for ever!' was the first thing I hears in the morning, and the same and nothing else all day, and not a soul sober only just when polling, enough to give their votes as became 'em, and to stand the browbeating of the lawyers, who came tight enough upon us; and many of our freeholders were knocked off, having never a freehold that they could safely swear to, and Sir Condy was not willing to have any man perjure himself for his sake, as was done on the other side, God knows; but no matter for that. Some of our friends were dumbfounded by the lawyers asking them: 'Had they ever been upon the ground where their freeholds lay?' Now, Sir Condy, being tender of the consciences of them that had not been on the ground, and so could not swear to a freehold when cross-examined by them lawyers, sent out for a couple of cleavefuls[6] of the sods of his farm of Gulteeshinnagh[7]; and as soon as the sods came into town, he set each man upon his sod, and so then, ever after, you know, they could fairly swear they had been upon the ground.[8] We gained the day by this piece of honesty. I thought I should have died in the streets for joy when I seed my poor master chaired, and he bareheaded, and it raining as hard as it could pour; but all the crowds following him up and down, and he bowing and shaking hands with the whole town.

'Is that Sir Condy Rackrent in the chair?' says a stranger man in the crowd.

'The same,' says I. 'Who else could it be? God bless him!'

'And I take it, then, you belong to him?' says he.

'Not at all,' says I; 'but I live under him, and have done so these two hundred years and upwards, me and mine.'

'It's lucky for you, then,' rejoins he, 'that he is where he is; for was he anywhere else but in the chair, this minute he'd be in a worse place; for I was sent down on purpose to put him up,[9] and here's my order for so doing in my pocket.'

It was a writ that villain the wine merchant had marked against my poor master for some hundreds of an old debt, which it was a shame to be talking of at such a time as this.

'Put it in your pocket again, and think no more of it anyways for seven years to come, my honest friend,' says I; 'he's a member of Parliament now, praised be God, and such as you can't touch him; and if you'll take a fool's advice, I'd have you keep out of the way this day, or you'll run a good chance of getting your deserts amongst my master's friends, unless you choose to drink his health like everybody else.'

'I've no objection to that in life,' said he. So we went into one of the public-houses kept open for my master; and we had a great deal of talk about this thing and that. 'And how is it,' says he, 'your master keeps on so well upon his legs? I heard say he was off Holantide twelve-month past.'

'Never was better or heartier in his life,' said I.

'It's not that I'm after speaking of,' said he; 'but there was a great report of his being ruined.'

'No matter,' says I; 'the sheriffs two years running were his particular friends, and the sub-sheriffs were both of them gentlemen, and were properly spoken to; and so the writs lay snug with them, and they, as I understand by my son Jason the custom in them cases is, returned the writs as they came to them to those that sent 'em – much good may it do them! – with a word in Latin, that no such person as Sir Condy Rackrent, Bart., was to be found in those parts.'

'Oh, I understand all those ways better – no offence – than you,' says he, laughing, and at the same time filling his glass to my master's good health, which convinced me he was a warm friend in his heart after all, though appearances were a little suspicious or so at first. 'To be sure,' says he, still cutting his joke, 'when a man's over head and shoulders in debt, he may live the faster for it, and the better if he goes the right way about it, or else how is it so many live on so well, as we see every day after they are ruined?'

'How is it,' says I, being a little merry at the time; 'how is it but just as you see the ducks in the chicken-yard, just after their heads are cut off by the cook, running round and round faster than when alive?'

At which conceit he fell a-laughing, and remarked he had never had the happiness yet to see the chicken-yard at Castle Rackrent.

'It won't be long so, I hope,' says I; 'you'll be kindly welcome there, as everybody is made by my master; there is not a freer-spoken gentleman or a better beloved, high or low, in all Ireland.'

And of what passed after this I'm not sensible, for we drank Sir Condy's good health and the downfall of his enemies till we could stand no longer ourselves. And little did I think at the time, or till long after, how I was harbouring my poor master's greatest of enemies myself. This fellow had the impudence, after coming to see the chicken-yard, to get me to introduce him to my son Jason; little more than the man that never was born did I guess at his meaning by this visit; he gets him a correct list fairly drawn out from my son Jason of all my master's debts, and goes straight round to the creditors and buys them all up, which he did easy enough, seeing the half of them never expected to see their money out of Sir Condy's hands. Then when this base-minded limb of the law, as I afterwards detected him in being, grew to be sole creditor over all, he takes him out a custodiam on all the denominations and sub-denominations, and even carton and half-carton upon the estate; and not content with that, must have an execution against the master's goods and down to the furniture, though little worth, of Castle Rackrent itself. But this is a part of my story I'm not come to yet, and it's bad to be forestalling; ill news flies fast enough all the world over.

To go back to the day of the election, which I never think of but with pleasure and tears of gratitude for those good times, after the election was quite and clean over, there comes shoals

of people from all parts, claiming to have obliged my master
with their votes, and putting him in mind of promises which he
could never remember himself to have made: one was to have
a freehold for each of his four sons; another was to have a
renewal of a lease; another an abatement; one came to be paid
ten guineas for a pair of silver buckles sold my master on the
hustings, which turned out to be no better than copper gilt;
another had a long bill for oats, the half of which never went
into the granary to my certain knowledge, and the other half
was not fit for the cattle to touch; but the bargain was made the
week before the election, and the coach- and saddle-horses
were got into order for the day, besides a vote fairly got by them
oats; so no more reasoning on that head. But then there was no
end to them that were telling Sir Condy he had engaged to
make their sons excisemen, or high constables, or the like; and
as for them that had bills to give in for liquor, and beds, and
straw, and ribands, and horses, and post-chaises for the
gentlemen freeholders that came from all parts and other
counties to vote for my master, and were not, to be sure, to be
at any charges, there was no standing against all these; and,
worse than all, the gentlemen of my master's committee, who
managed all for him, and talked how they'd bring him in
without costing him a penny, and subscribed by hundreds very
genteelly, forgot to pay their subscriptions, and had laid out in
agents' and lawyers' fees and secret-service money to the Lord
knows how much; and my master could never ask one of them
for their subscription you are sensible, nor for the price of a fine
horse he had sold one of them; so it all was left at his door. He
could never, God bless him again! I say, bring himself to ask a
gentleman for money, despising such sort of conversation
himself; but others, who were not gentlemen born, behaved
very uncivil in pressing him at this very time, and all he could
do to content 'em all was to take himself out of the way as fast
as possible to Dublin, where my lady had taken a house fitting
for him as a member of Parliament, to attend his duty in there

all the winter. I was very lonely when the whole family was gone, and all the things they had ordered to go, and forgot, sent after them by the car. There was then a great silence in Castle Rackrent, and I went moping from room to room, hearing the doors clap for want of right locks, and the wind through the broken windows, that the glazier never would come to mend, and the rain coming through the roof and best ceilings all over the house for want of the slater, whose bill was not paid, besides our having no slates or shingles for that part of the old building which was shingled and burnt when the chimney took fire, and had been open to the weather ever since. I took myself to the servants' hall in the evening to smoke my pipe as usual, but missed the bit of talk we used to have there sadly, and ever after was content to stay in the kitchen and boil my little potatoes,[10] and put up my bed there, and every post-day I looked in the newspaper, but no news of my master in the House; he never spoke good or bad, but, as the butler wrote down word to my son Jason, was very ill-used by the Government about a place that was promised him and never given, after his supporting them against his conscience very honourably, and being greatly abused for it, which hurt him greatly, he having the name of a great patriot in the country before. The house and living in Dublin, too, were not to be had for nothing, and my son Jason said: 'Sir Condy must soon be looking out for a new agent, for I've done my part and can do no more. If my lady had the Bank of Ireland to spend, it would go all in one winter, and Sir Condy would never gainsay her, though he does not care the rind of a lemon for her all the while.'

Now I could not bear to hear Jason giving out after this manner against the family, and twenty people standing by in the street. Ever since he had lived at the Lodge of his own, he looked down, howsomever, upon poor old Thady, and was grown quite a great gentleman, and had none of his relations near him; no wonder he was no kinder to poor Sir Condy than to his own kith or kin.[11] In the spring it was the villain that got the list of the debts from him brought down the custodiam, Sir Condy still attending his duty in Parliament; and I could scarcely believe my own old eyes, or the spectacles with which I read it, when I was shown my son Jason's name joined in the custodiam, but he told me it was only for form's sake, and to make things easier than if all the land was under the power of a total stranger. Well, I did not know what to think; it was hard to be talking ill of my own, and I could not but grieve for my poor master's fine estate, all torn by these vultures of the law; so I said nothing, but just looked on to see how it would all end.

It was not till the month of June that he and my lady came down to the country. My master was pleased to take me aside with him to the brewhouse that same evening, to complain to me of my son and other matters, in which he said he was confident I had neither art nor part; he said a great deal more to me, to whom he had been fond to talk ever since he was my white-headed boy before he came to the estate; and all that he said about poor Judy I can never forget, but scorn to repeat. He did not say an unkind word of my lady, but wondered, as well he might, her relations would do nothing for him or her, and they in all this great distress. He did not take anything long to heart, let it be as it would, and had no more malice or thought of the like in him than a child that can't speak; this night it was all out of his head before he went to his bed. He took his jug of whiskey-punch – my lady was grown quite easy about the whiskey-punch by this time, and so I did suppose all was going on right betwixt them, till I learnt the truth through Mrs Jane, who talked over the affairs to the housekeeper, and I within hearing. The night my master came home, thinking of nothing at all but just making merry, he drank his bumper toast 'to the deserts of that old curmudgeon my father-in-law, and all enemies at Mount Juliet's Town'. Now my lady was no longer in the mind she formerly was, and did noways relish hearing her own friends abused in her presence, she said.

'Then why don't they show themselves your friends,' said my master, 'and oblige me with the loan of the money I condescended by your advice, my dear, to ask? It's now three posts since I sent off my letter, desiring in the postscript a speedy answer by the return of the post, and no account at all from them yet.'

'I expect they'll write to *me* next post,' says my lady, and that was all that passed then; but it was easy from this to guess there was a coolness betwixt them, and with good cause.

The next morning, being post-day, I sent off the gossoon early to the post office, to see was there any letter likely to set matters to rights, and he brought back one with the proper postmark upon it, sure enough, and I had no time to examine or make any conjecture more about it, for into the servants' hall pops Mrs Jane with a blue bandbox in her hand, quite entirely mad.

'Dear ma'am, and what's the matter?' says I.

'Matter enough,' says she; 'don't you see my bandbox is wet through, and my best bonnet here spoiled, besides my lady's, and all by the rain coming in through that gallery window that you might have got mended if you'd had any sense, Thady, all the time we were in town in the winter?'

'Sure, I could not get the glazier, ma'am,' says I.

'You might have stopped it up anyhow,' says she.

'So I did, ma'am, to the best of my ability; one of the panes with the old pillow-case, and the other with a piece of the old stage green curtain. Sure I was as careful as possible all the time you were away, and not a drop of rain came in at that window of all the windows in the house, all winter, ma'am, when under my care; and now the family's come home, and it's summer-time, I never thought no more about it, to be sure; but dear, it's a pity to think of your bonnet, ma'am. But here's what will please you, ma'am – a letter from Mount Juliet's Town for my lady.'

With that she snatches it from me without a word more, and runs up the back stairs to my mistress; I follows with a slate to make up the window. This window was in the long passage, or gallery, as my lady gave out orders to have it called, in the gallery leading to my master's bedchamber and hers. And when I went up with the slate, the door having no lock, and the bolt spoilt, was ajar after Mrs Jane, and, as I was busy with the window, I heard all that was saying within.

'Well, what's in your letter, Bella, my dear?' says he. 'You're a long time spelling it over.'

'Won't you shave this morning, Sir Condy?' says she, and put the letter into her pocket.

'I shaved the day before yesterday,' said he, 'my dear, and that's not what I'm thinking of now; but anything to oblige you, and to have peace and quietness, my dear' – and presently I had a glimpse of him at the cracked glass over the chimney-piece, standing up shaving himself to please my lady. But she took no notice, but went on reading her book, and Mrs Jane doing her hair behind.

'What is it you're reading there, my dear? – phoo, I've cut myself with this razor; the man's a cheat that sold it me, but I have not paid him for it yet. What is it you're reading there? Did you hear me asking you, my dear?'

' "The Sorrows of Werter",' replies my lady, as well as I could hear.

'I think more of the sorrows of Sir Condy,' says my master, joking like. 'What news from Mount Juliet's Town?'

'No news,' says she, 'but the old story over again; my friends all reproaching me still for what I can't help now.'

'Is it for marrying me?' said my master, still shaving. 'What signifies, as you say, talking of that, when it can't be help'd now?'

With that she heaved a great sigh that I heard plain enough in the passage.

'And did not you use me basely, Sir Condy,' says she, 'not to tell me you were ruined before I married you?'

'Tell you, my dear!' said he. 'Did you ever ask me one word about it? And had not you friends enough of your own, that were telling you nothing else from morning to night, if you'd have listened to them slanders?'

'No slanders, nor are my friends slanderers; and I can't bear to hear them treated with disrespect as I do,' says my lady, and took out her pocket-handkerchief; 'they are the best of friends, and if I had taken their advice – . But my father was wrong to lock me up, I own. That was the only unkind thing I can charge him with; for if he had not locked me up, I should never have had a serious thought of running away as I did.'

'Well, my dear,' said my master, 'don't cry and make yourself uneasy about it now, when it's all over, and you have the man of your own choice, in spite of 'em all.'

'I was too young, I know, to make a choice at the time you ran away with me, I'm sure,' says my lady, and another sigh, which made my master, half-shaved as he was, turn round upon her in surprise.

'Why, Bella,' says he, 'you can't deny what you know as well as I do, that it was at your own particular desire, and that twice under your own hand and seal expressed, that I should carry you off as I did to Scotland, and marry you there.'

'Well, say no more about it, Sir Condy,' said my lady, pettishlike; 'I was a child then, you know.'

'And as far as I know, you're little better now, my dear Bella, to be talking in this manner to your husband's face; but I won't take it ill of you, for I know it's something in that letter you put into your pocket just now that has set you against me all on a sudden, and imposed upon your understanding.'

'It's not so very easy as you think it, Sir Condy, to impose upon my understanding,' said my lady.

'My dear,' says he, 'I have, and with reason, the best opinion of your understanding of any man now breathing; and you know I have never set my own in competition with it till now, my dear Bella,' says he, taking her hand from her book as kind as could be – 'till now, when I have the great advantage of being quite cool, and you not; so don't believe one word your friends say against your own Sir Condy, and lend me the letter out of your pocket, till I see what it is they can have to say.'

'Take it then,' says she, 'and as you are quite cool, I hope it is a proper time to request you'll allow me to comply with the wishes of all my own friends, and return to live with my father and family, during the remainder of my wretched existence, at Mount Juliet's Town.'

At this my poor master fell back a few paces, like one that had been shot.

'You're not serious, Bella,' says he, 'and could you find it in your heart to leave me this way in the very middle of my distresses, all alone?' But recollecting himself after his first surprise, and a moment's time for reflection, he said, with a great deal of consideration for my lady. 'Well, Bella, my dear, I believe you are right; for what could you do at Castle Rackrent, and an execution against the goods coming down, and the furniture to be canted, and an auction in the house all next week? So you have my full consent to go, since that is your desire; only you must not think of my accompanying you, which I could not in honour do upon the terms I always have been, since our marriage, with your friends. Besides, I have business to transact at home; so in the meantime, if we are to have any breakfast this morning, let us go down and have it for the last time in peace and comfort, Bella.'

Then as I heard my master coming to the passage door, I finished fastening up my slate against the broken pane; and when he came out I wiped down the window-seat with my wig,[12] and bade him a 'good-morrow' as kindly as I could, seeing he was in trouble, though he strove and thought to hide it from me.

'This window is all racked and tattered,' says I, 'and it's what I'm striving to mend.'

'It *is* all racked and tattered, plain enough,' says he, 'and never mind mending it, honest old Thady,' says he; 'it will do well enough for you and I, and that's all the company we shall have left in the house by-and-bye.'

'I'm sorry to see your honour so low this morning,' says I, 'but you'll be better after taking your breakfast.'

'Step down to the servants' hall,' said he, 'and bring me up the pen and ink into the parlour, and get a sheet of paper from Mrs Jane, for I have business that can't brook to be delayed; and come into the parlour with the pen and ink yourself, Thady, for I must have you to witness my signing a paper I have to execute in a hurry.'

Well, while I was getting of the pen and ink-horn, and the sheet of paper, I ransacked my brains to think what could be the papers my poor master could have to execute in such a hurry, he that never thought of such a thing as doing business afore breakfast in the whole course of his life, for any man living; but this was for my lady, as I afterwards found, and the more genteel of him after all her treatment.

I was just witnessing the paper that he had scrawled over, and was shaking the ink out of my pen upon the carpet, when my lady came in to breakfast, and she started as if it had been a ghost; as well she might, when she saw Sir Condy writing at this unseasonable hour.

'That will do very well, Thady,' says he to me, and took the paper I had signed to, without knowing what upon the earth it might be, out of my hands, and walked, folding it up, to my lady.

'You are concerned in this, my Lady Rackrent,' said he, putting it into her hands; 'and I beg you'll keep this memorandum safe, and show it to your friends the first thing you do when you get home; but put it in your pocket now, my dear, and let us eat our breakfast, in God's name.'

'What is all this?' said my lady, opening the paper in great curiosity.

'It's only a bit of a memorandum of what I think becomes me to do whenever I am able,' says my master; 'you know my situation, tied hand and foot at the present time being, but that can't last always, and when I'm dead and gone the land will be to the good, Thady, you know; and take notice it's my intention your lady should have a clear five hundred a year jointure off the estate afore any of my debts are paid.'

'Oh, please your honour,' says I, 'I can't expect to live to see that time, being now upwards of fourscore years of age, and you a young man, and likely to continue so by the help of God.'

I was vexed to see my lady so insensible too, for all she said was: 'This is very genteel of you, Sir Condy. You need not wait any longer, Thady.' So I just picked up the pen and ink that had tumbled on the floor, and heard my master finish with saying: 'You behaved very genteel to me, my dear, when you threw all the little you had in your power along with yourself into my hands; and as I don't deny but what you may have had some things to complain of' – to be sure he was thinking then of Judy, or of the whiskey-punch, one or t'other, or both, – 'and as I don't deny but you may have had something to complain of, my dear, it is but fair you should have something in the form of compensation to look forward to agreeably in the future; besides, it's an act of justice to myself, that none of your friends, my dear, may ever have it to say against me, I married for money, and not for love.'

'That is the last thing I should ever have thought of saying of you, Sir Condy,' said my lady, looking very gracious.

'Then, my dear,' said Sir Condy, 'we shall part as good friends as we met; so all's right.'

I was greatly rejoiced to hear this, and went out of the parlour to report it all to the kitchen. The next morning my lady and Mrs Jane set out for Mount Juliet's Town in the jaunting-car. Many wondered at my lady's choosing to go away, considering all things, upon the jaunting-car, as if it was only a party of pleasure; but they did not know till I told them that the coach was all broke in the journey down, and no other vehicle but the car to be had. Besides, my lady's friends were to send their coach to meet her at the crossroads; so it was all done very proper.

My poor master was in great trouble after my lady left us. The execution came down, and everything at Castle Rackrent was seized by the gripers, and my son Jason, to his shame be it spoken, amongst them. I wondered, for the life of me, how he could harden himself to do it; but then he had been studying the law, and had made himself Attorney Quirk; so he brought down at once a heap of accounts upon my master's head. To cash lent, and to ditto, and to ditto, and to ditto and oats, and bills paid at milliner's and linen-draper's, and many dresses for the fancy balls in Dublin for my lady, and all the bills to the workmen and tradesmen for the scenery of the theatre, and the chandler's and grocer's bills, and tailors, besides butcher's and baker's, and worse than all, the old one of that base wine merchant's, who wanted to arrest my poor master for the amount on the election day, for which amount Sir Condy afterwards passed his note of hand, bearing lawful interest from the date thereof; and the interest and compound interest was now mounted to a terrible deal on many other notes and bonds for money borrowed, and there was, besides, hush-money to the sub-sheriffs, and sheets upon sheets of old and new attorney's bills, with heavy balances, 'as per former account furnished', brought forward with interest thereon; then there was a powerful deal due to the Crown for sixteen years' arrears of quit-rent of the townlands of Carrickshaughlin, with driver's fees, and a compliment to the receiver every year for letting the quit-rent run on to oblige Sir Condy, and Sir Kit afore him. Then there were bills for spirits and ribands at the election time, and the gentlemen of the committee's accounts unsettled, and their subscription never gathered; and there were cows to be paid for, with the smith and farrier's bills to be set against the rent of the demesne, with calf and hay money; then there was all the servants' wages, since I don't know when, coming due to them, and sums advanced for them by my son Jason for clothes, and boots, and whips, and odd moneys for sundries expended by them in journeys to town and elsewhere, and pocket-money for the master continually, and messengers and postage before his being a Parliament man. I can't myself tell you what besides; but this I know, that when the evening came on the which Sir Condy had appointed to settle all with my son Jason, and when he comes into the parlour, and sees the sight of bills and load of papers all gathered on the great dining-table for him, he puts his hands before both his eyes, and cried out, 'Merciful Jasus! what is it I see before me?' Then I sets an armchair at the table for him, and with a deal of difficulty he sits down, and my son Jason hands him over the pen and ink to sign to this man's bill and t'other man's bill, all which he did without making the least objections. Indeed, to give him his due, I never seen a man more fair and honest, and easy in all his dealings, from first to last, as Sir Condy, or more willing to pay every man his own as far as he was able, which is as much as anyone can do.

'Well,' says he, joking-like with Jason, 'I wish we could settle it all with a stroke of my gray goose-quill. What signifies making me wade through all this ocean of papers here; can't you now, who understand drawing out an account, debtor and creditor, just sit down here at the corner of the table and get it done out for me, that I may have a clear view of the balance, which is all I need be talking about, you know?'

'Very true, Sir Condy; nobody understands business better than yourself,' says Jason.

'So I've a right to do, being born and bred to the bar,' says Sir Condy. 'Thady, do step out and see are they bringing in the things for the punch, for we've just done all we have to do for this evening.'

I goes out accordingly, and when I came back Jason was pointing to the balance, which was a terrible sight to my poor master.

'Pooh! pooh! pooh!' says he. 'Here's so many noughts they dazzle my eyes, so they do, and put me in mind of all I suffered laming of my numeration table when I was a boy at the day school along with you, Jason – units, tens, hundreds, tens of hundreds. Is the punch ready, Thady?' says he, seeing me.

'Immediately; the boy has the jug in his hand; it's coming upstairs, please your honour, as fast as possible,' says I, for I saw his honour was tired out of his life; but Jason, very short and cruel, cuts me off with – 'Don't be talking of punch yet awhile: it's no time for punch yet a bit – units, tens, hundreds,' goes he on, counting over the master's shoulder, 'units, tens, hundreds, thousands.'

'A-a-ah! hold your hand,' cries my master. 'Where in this wide world am I to find hundreds, or units itself, let alone thousands.'

'The balance has been running on too long,' says Jason, sticking to him as I could not have done at the time if you'd have given both the Indies and Cork to boot; 'the balance has been running on too long, and I'm distressed myself on your account, Sir Condy, for money, and the thing must be settled now on the spot, and the balance cleared off,' says Jason.

'I'll thank you if you'll only show me how,' says Sir Condy.

'There's but one way,' says Jason, 'and that's ready enough. When there's no cash, what can a gentleman do but go to the land?'

'How can you go to the land, and it under custodiam to yourself already?' says Sir Condy; 'and another custodiam hanging over it? And no one at all can touch it, you know, but the custodees.'

'Sure, can't you sell, though at a loss? Sure you can sell, and I've a purchaser ready for you,' says Jason.

'Have you so?' says Sir Condy. 'That's a great point gained. But there's a thing now beyond all, that perhaps you don't know yet, barring Thady has let you into the secret.'

'Sarrah bit of a secret, or anything at all of the kind, has he learned from me these fifteen weeks come St John's Eve,' says I, 'for we have scarce been upon speaking terms of late. But what is it your honour means of a secret?'

'Why, the secret of the little keepsake I gave my Lady Rackrent the morning she left us, that she might not go back empty-handed to her friends.'

'My Lady Rackrent, I'm sure, has baubles and keepsakes enough, as those bills on the table will show,' says Jason; 'but whatever it is,' says he, taking up his pen, 'we must add it to the balance, for to be sure it can't be paid for.'

'No, nor can't till after my decease,' says Sir Condy; 'that's one good thing.' Then colouring up a good deal, he tells Jason of the memorandum of the five-hundred-a-year jointure he had settled upon my lady; at which Jason was indeed mad, and said a great deal in very high words, that it was using a gentleman who had the management of his affairs, and was, moreover, his principal creditor, extremely ill to do such a thing without consulting him, and against his knowledge and consent. To all which Sir Condy had nothing to reply, but that, upon his conscience, it was in a hurry and without a moment's thought on his part, and he was very sorry for it, but if it was to do over again he would do the same; and he appealed to me, and I was ready to give my evidence, if that would do, to the truth of all he said.

So Jason, with much ado, was brought to agree to a compromise.

'The purchaser that I have ready,' says he, 'will be much displeased, to be sure, at the incumbrance on the land, but I must see and manage him. Here's a deed ready drawn up; we have nothing to do but to put in the consideration money and our names to it.'

'And how much am I going to sell? – the lands of O'Shaughlin's Town, and the lands of Gruneaghoolaghan, and the lands of Crookagnawaturgh,' says he, just reading to himself. 'And – oh, murder, Jason! sure you won't put this in – the castle, stable, and appurtenances of Castle Rackrent?'

'Oh, murder!' says I, clapping my hands; 'this is too bad, Jason.'

'Why so?' said Jason. 'When it's all, and a good deal more to the back of it, lawfully mine, was I to push for it.'

'Look at him,' says I, pointing to Sir Condy, who was just leaning back in his armchair, with his arms falling beside him like one stupefied; 'Is it you, Jason, that can stand in his presence, and recollect all he has been to us, and all we have been to him, and yet use him so at the last?'

'Who will you find to use him better, I ask you?' said Jason; 'if he can get a better purchaser, I'm content; I only offer to purchase, to make things easy, and oblige him; though I don't see what compliment I am under, if you come to that. I have never had, asked, or charged more than sixpence in the pound, receiver's fees, and where would he have got an agent for a penny less?'

'Oh, Jason! Jason! how will you stand to this in the face of the county, and all who know you?' says I; 'and what will people think and say when they see you living here in Castle Rackrent, and the lawful owner turned out of the seat of his ancestors, without a cabin to put his head into, or so much as a potato to eat?'

Jason, whilst I was saying this and a great deal more, made me signs, and winks, and frowns; but I took no heed, for I was grieved and sick at heart for my poor master, and couldn't but speak.

'Here's the punch,' says Jason, for the door opened; 'here's the punch!'

Hearing that, my master starts up in his chair, and recollects himself, and Jason uncorks the whiskey.

'Set down the jug here,' says he, making room for it beside the papers opposite to Sir Condy, but still not stirring the deed that was to make over all.

Well, I was in great hopes he had some touch of mercy about him when I saw him making the punch, and my master took a glass; but Jason put it back as he was going to fill again, saying:

'No, Sir Condy, it sha'n't be said of me I got your signature to this deed when you were half seas over; you know your name and handwriting in that condition would not, if brought before the courts, benefit me a straw; wherefore, let us settle all before we go deeper into the punch-bowl.'

'Settle all as you will,' said Sir Condy, clapping his hands to his ears; 'but let me hear no more. I'm bothered to death this night.'

'You've only to sign,' said Jason, putting the pen to him.

'Take all, and be content,' said my master. So he signed; and the man who brought in the punch witnessed it, for I was not able, but crying like a child; and besides, Jason said, which I was glad of, that I was no fit witness, being so old and doting. It was so bad with me, I could not taste a drop of the punch itself, though my master himself, God bless him! in the midst of his trouble, poured out a glass for me, and brought it up to my lips.

'Not a drop; I thank your honour's honour as much as if I took it, though.' And I just set down the glass as it was, and went out, and when I got to the street door the neighbours' childer, who were playing at marbles there, seeing me in great trouble, left their play, and gathered about me to know what ailed me; and I told them all, for it was a great relief to me to speak to these poor childer, that seemed to have some natural feeling left in them; and when they were made sensible that Sir Condy was going to leave Castle Rackrent for good and all, they set up a whillalu that could be heard to the farthest end of the street; and one – fine boy he was – that my master had given an apple to that morning, cried the loudest; but they all were the same sorry, for Sir Condy was greatly beloved amongst the childer, for letting them go a-nutting in the demesne, without saying a word to them, though my lady objected to them. The people in the town, who were the most of them standing at their doors, hearing the childer cry, would know the reason of it; and when the report was made known, the people one and all gathered in great anger against my son Jason, and terror at the notion of his coming to be landlord over them, and they cried: 'No Jason! no Jason! Sir Condy! Sir Condy! Sir Condy Rackrent for ever!' And the mob grew so great and so loud, I was frightened, and made my way back to the house to warn my son to make his escape or hide himself for fear of the consequences. Jason would not believe me till they came all round the house, and to the windows, with great shouts. Then he grew quite pale, and asked Sir Condy what had he best do?

'I'll tell you what you had best do,' said Sir Condy, who was laughing to see his fright; 'finish your glass first, then let's go to the window and show ourselves, and I'll tell 'em – or you shall, if you please – that I'm going to the Lodge for change of air and for my health, and by my own desire, for the rest of my days.'

'Do so,' said Jason, who never meant it should have been so, but could not refuse him the Lodge at this unseasonable time. Accordingly, Sir Condy threw up the sash and explained matters, and thanked all his friends, and bid them look in at the punchbowl, and observe that Jason and he had been sitting over it very good friends; so the mob was content, and he sent them out some whiskey to drink his health, and that was the last time his honour's health was ever drunk at Castle Rackrent.

The very next day, being too proud, as he said to me, to stay an hour longer in a house that did not belong to him, he sets off to the Lodge, and I along with him not many hours after. And there was great bemoaning through all O'Shauglin's Town, which I stayed to witness, and gave my poor master a full account of when I got to the Lodge. He was very low, and in his bed when I got there, and complained of a great pain about his heart; but I guessed it was only trouble and all the business, let alone vexation, he had gone through of late, and knowing the nature of him from a boy, I took my pipe, and whilst smoking it by the chimney began telling him how he was beloved and regretted in the county, and it did him a deal of good to hear it.

'Your honour has a great many friends yet that you don't know of, rich and poor, in the county,' says I; 'for as I was coming along the road I met two gentlemen in their own carriages, who asked after you, knowing me, and wanted to know where you was and all about you, and even how old I was. Think of that.'

Then he wakened out of his doze and began questioning me who the gentlemen were. And the next morning it came into my head to go, unknown to anybody, with my master's compliments, round to many of the gentlemen's houses where he and my lady used to visit, and people that I knew were his great friends, and would go to Cork to serve him any day in the year, and I made bold to try to borrow a trifle of cash from them. They all treated me very civil for the most part, and asked a great many questions very kind about my lady and Sir Condy and all the family, and were greatly surprised to learn from me Castle Rackrent was sold, and my master at the Lodge for health; and they all pitied him greatly, and he had their good wishes, if that would do; but money was a thing they unfortunately had not any of them at this time to spare. I had my journey for my pains, and I, not used to walking, nor supple as formerly, was greatly tired, but had the satisfaction of telling my master when I got to the Lodge all the civil things said by high and low.

'Thady,' says he, 'all you've been telling me brings a strange thought into my head. I've a notion I shall not be long for this world anyhow, and I've a great fancy to see my own funeral afore I die.' I was greatly shocked, at the first speaking, to hear him speak so light about his funeral, and he to all appearance in good health; but recollecting myself, answered:

'To be sure it would be as fine a sight as one could see,' I dared to say, 'and one I should be proud to witness, and I did not doubt his honour's would be as great a funeral as ever Sir Patrick O'Shaughlin's was, and such a one as that had never been known in the county afore or since.' But I never thought he was in earnest about seeing his own funeral himself till the next day he returns to it again.

'Thady,' says he, 'as far as the wake[13] goes, sure I might without any great trouble have the satisfaction of seeing a bit of my own funeral.'

'Well, since your honour's honour's so bent upon it,' says I, not willing to cross him, and he in trouble, 'we must see what we can do.'

So he fell into a sort of sham disorder, which was easy done, as he kept his bed, and no one to see him; and I got my shister, who was an old woman very handy about the sick, and very skilful, to come up to the Lodge to nurse him; and we gave out, she knowing no better, that he was just at his latter end, and it answered beyond anything; and there was a great throng of people, men, women, and childer, and there being only two rooms at the Lodge, except what was locked up full of Jason's furniture and things, the house was soon as full and fuller than it could hold, and the heat, and smoke, and noise wonderful great; and standing amongst them that were near the bed, but not thinking at all of the dead, I was startled by the sound of my master's voice from under the greatcoats that had been thrown all at top, and I went close up, no one noticing.

'Thady,' says he, 'I've had enough of this; I'm smothering, and can't hear a word of all they're saying of the deceased.'

'God bless you, and lie still and quiet,' says I, 'a bit longer, for my shister's afraid of ghosts, and would die on the spot with fright was she to see you come to life all on a sudden this way without the least preparation.'

So he lays him still, though wellnigh stifled, and I made all haste to tell the secret of the joke, whispering to one and t'other, and there was a great surprise, but not so great as we had laid out it would. 'And aren't we to have the pipes and tobacco, after coming so far tonight?' said some; but they were all well enough pleased when his honour got up to drink with them, and sent for more spirits from a shebeen-house,[14] where they very civilly let him have it upon credit. So the night passed off very merrily, but to my mind Sir Condy was rather upon the sad order in the midst of it all, not finding there had been such a great talk about himself after his death as he had always expected to hear.

The next morning, when the house was cleared of them, and none but my shister and myself left in the kitchen with Sir Condy, one opens the door and walks in, and who should it be but Judy M'Quirk herself! I forgot to notice that she had been married long since, whilst young Captain Moneygawl lived in the Lodge, to the captain's huntsman, who after a whilst 'listed and left her, and was killed in the wars. Poor Judy fell off greatly in her good looks after her being married a year or two; and being smoke-dried in the cabin, and neglecting herself like, it was hard for Sir Condy himself to know her again till she spoke; but when she says, 'It's Judy M'Quirk, please your honour; don't you remember her?'

'Oh, Judy, is it you?' says his honour. 'Yes, sure, I remember you very well; but you're greatly altered, Judy.'

'Sure it's time for me,' says she, 'and I think your honour, since I seen you last – but that's a great while ago – is altered too.'

'And with reason, Judy,' says Sir Condy, fetching a sort of a sigh. 'But how's this, Judy?' he goes on. 'I take it a little amiss of you that you were not at my wake last night.'

'Ah, don't be being jealous of that,' says she; 'I didn't hear a sentence of your honour's wake till it was all over, or it would have gone hard with me but I would been at it, sure; but I was forced to go ten miles up the country three days ago to a wedding of a relation of my own's, and didn't get home till after the wake was over. But,' says she, 'it won't be so, I hope, the next time,[15] please your honour.'

'That we shall see, Judy,' says his honour, 'and maybe sooner than you think for, for I've been very unwell this while past, and don't reckon anyway I'm long for this world.'

At this Judy takes up the corner of her apron, and puts it first to one eye and then to t'other, being to all appearance in great trouble; and my shister put in her word, and bid his honour have a good heart, for she was sure it was only the gout that Sir Patrick used to have flying about him, and he ought to drink a glass or a bottle extraordinary to keep it out of his stomach; and he promised to take her advice, and sent out for more spirits immediately; and Judy made a sign to me, and I went over to the door to her, and she said: 'I wonder to see Sir Condy so low; has he heard the news?'

'What news?' says I.

'Didn't ye hear it, then?' says she; 'my Lady Rackrent that was is kilt and lying for dead, and I don't doubt but it's all over with her by this time.'

'Mercy on us all,' says I; 'how was it?'

'The jaunting-car it was that ran away with her,' says Judy. 'I was coming home that same time from Biddy M'Guggin's marriage, and a great crowd of people, too, upon the road coming from the fair of Crookaghnawaturgh, and I sees a jaunting-car standing in the middle of the road, and with the two wheels off and all tattered. "What's this?" says I. "Didn't ye hear of it?" says they that were looking on; "it's my Lady Rackrent's car, that was running away from her husband, and the horse took fright at a carrion that lay across the road, and so ran away with the jaunting-car, and my Lady Rackrent and her maid screaming, and the horse ran with them against a car that was coming from the fair with the boy asleep on it, and the lady's petticoat hanging out of the jaunting-car caught, and she was dragged I can't tell you how far upon the road, and it all broken up with the stones just going to be pounded, and one of the road-makers, with his sledge-hammer in his hand, stops the horse at the last, but my Lady Rackrent was all kilt[16] and smashed, and they lifted her into a cabin hard by, and the maid was found after where she had been thrown in the gripe of a ditch, her cap and bonnet all full of bog water, and they say my lady can't live anyway. Thady, pray now is it true what I'm told for sartain, that Sir Condy has made over all to your son Jason?'

'All,' says I.

'All entirely?' says she again.

'All entirely,' says I.

'Then,' says she, 'that's a great shame; but don't be telling Jason what I say.'

'And what is it you say?' cries Sir Condy, leaning over betwixt us, which made Judy start greatly. 'I know the time when Judy M'Quirk would never have stayed so long talking at the door and I in the house.'

'Oh!' says Judy, 'for shame, Sir Condy; times are altered since then, and it's my Lady Rackrent you ought to be thinking of.'

'And why should I be thinking of her, that's not thinking of me now?' says Sir Condy.

'No matter for that,' says Judy, very properly; 'it's time you should be thinking of her, if ever you mean to do it at all, for don't you know she's lying for death?'

'My Lady Rackrent!' says Sir Condy, in a surprise; 'why, it's but two days since we parted, as you very well know, Thady, in her full health and spirits, and she, and her maid along with her, going to Mount Juliet's Town on her jaunting-car.'

'She'll never ride no more on her jaunting-car,' said Judy; 'for it has been the death of her sure enough.'

'And is she dead, then?' says his honour.

'As good as dead, I hear,' says Judy; 'but there's Thady here has just learnt the whole truth of the story as I had it, and it's fitter he or anybody else should be telling it you than I, Sir Condy: I must be going home to the childer.'

But he stops her, but rather from civility in him, as I could see very plainly, than anything else, for Judy was, as his honour remarked at her first coming in, greatly changed, and little likely, as far as I could see – though she did not seem to be clear of it herself, – little likely to be my Lady Rackrent now, should there be a second toss-up to be made. But I told him the whole story out of the face, just as Judy had told it to me, and he sent off a messenger with his compliments to Mount Juliet's Town that evening to learn the truth of the report, and Judy bid the boy that was going call in at Tim M'Enerney's shop in O'Shaughlin's Town and buy her a new shawl.

'Do so,' said Sir Condy, 'and tell Tim to take no money from you, for I must pay him for the shawl myself.' At this my shister throws me over a look, and I says nothing, but turned the tobacco in my mouth, whilst Judy began making a many words about it, and saying how she could not be beholden for shawls to any gentleman. I left her there to consult with my shister, did she think there was anything in it, and my shister thought I was blind to be asking her the question, and I thought my shister must see more into it than I did, and recollecting all past times and everything, I changed my mind, and came over to her way of thinking, and we settled it that Judy was very like to be my Lady Rackrent after all, if a vacancy should have happened.

The next day, before his honour was up, somebody comes with a double knock at the door, and I was greatly surprised to see it was my son Jason.

'Jason, is it you?' said I; 'what brings you to the Lodge?' says I. 'Is it my Lady Rackrent? We know that already since yesterday.'

'Maybe so,' says he; 'but I must see Sir Condy about it.'

'You can't see him yet,' says I; 'sure he is not awake.'

'What then,' says he, 'can't he be wakened, and I standing at the door.'

'I'll not be disturbing his honour for you, Jason,' says I; 'many's the hour you've waited in your time, and been proud to do it, till his honour was at leisure to speak to you. His honour,' says I, raising my voice, at which his honour wakens of his own accord, and calls to me from the room to know who it was I was speaking to. Jason made no more ceremony, but follows me into the room.

'How are you, Sir Condy?' says he; 'I'm happy to see you looking so well; I came up to know how you did today, and to see did you want for anything at the Lodge.'

'Nothing at all, Mr Jason, I thank you,' says he; for his honour had his own share of pride, and did not choose, after all that had passed, to be beholden, I suppose, to my son; 'but pray take a chair and be seated, Mr Jason.'

Jason sat him down upon the chest, for chair there was none, and after he had sat there some time, and a silence on all sides,

'What news is there stirring in the country, Mr Jason M'Quirk?' says Sir Condy, very easy, yet high like.

'None that's news to you, Sir Condy, I hear,' says Jason. 'I am sorry to hear of my Lady Rackrent's accident.'

'I'm much obliged to you, and so is her ladyship, I'm sure,' answered Sir Condy, still stiff; and there was another sort of a silence, which seemed to lie the heaviest on my son Jason.

'Sir Condy,' says he at last, seeing Sir Condy disposing himself to go to sleep again, 'Sir Condy, I dare say you recollect mentioning to me the little memorandum you gave to Lady Rackrent about the £500-a-year jointure.'

'Very true,' said Sir Condy; 'it is all in my recollection.'

'But if my Lady Rackrent dies, there's an end of all jointure,' says Jason.

'Of course,' says Sir Condy.

'But it's not a matter of certainty that my Lady Rackrent won't recover,' says Jason.

'Very true, sir,' says my master.

'It's a fair speculation, then, for you to consider what the chance of the jointure of those lands, when out of custodiam, will be to you.'

'Just five hundred a year, I take it, without any speculation at all,' said Sir Condy.

'That's supposing the life dropt, and the custodiam off, you know; begging your pardon, Sir Condy, who understands business, that is a wrong calculation.'

'Very likely so,' said Sir Condy; 'but, Mr Jason, if you have anything to say to me this morning about it, I'd be obliged to you to say it, for I had an indifferent night's rest last night, and wouldn't be sorry to sleep a little this morning.'

'I have only three words to say, and those more of consequence to you, Sir Condy, than me. You are a little cool, I observe; but I hope you will not be offended at what I have brought here in my pocket,' and he pulls out two long rolls, and showers down golden guineas upon the bed.

'What's this?' said Sir Condy; 'it's long since' – but his pride stops him.

'All these are your lawful property this minute, Sir Condy, if you please,' said Jason.

'Not for nothing, I'm sure,' said Sir Condy, and laughs a little. 'Nothing for nothing, or I'm under a mistake with you, Jason.'

'Oh, Sir Condy, we'll not be indulging ourselves in any unpleasant retrospects,' says Jason; 'it's my present intention to behave, as I'm sure you will, like a gentleman in this affair. Here's two hundred guineas, and a third I mean to add if you should think proper to make over to me all your right and title to those lands that you know of.'

'I'll consider of it,' said my master; and a great deal more, that I was tired listening to, was said by Jason, and all that, and the sight of the ready cash upon the bed, worked with his honour; and the short and the long of it was, Sir Condy gathered up the golden guineas, and tied them up in a handkerchief, and signed some paper Jason brought with him as usual, and there was an end of the business: Jason took himself away, and my master turned himself round and fell asleep again.

I soon found what had put Jason in such a hurry to conclude this business. The little gossoon we had sent off the day before with my master's compliments to Mount Juliet's Town, and to know how my lady did after her accident was stopped early this morning, coming back with his answer through O'Shaughlin's Town, at Castle Rackrent, by my son Jason, and questioned of all he knew of my lady from the servant at Mount Juliet's Town; and the gossoon told him my Lady Rackrent was not expected to live overnight; so Jason thought it high time to be moving to the Lodge, to make his bargain with my master about the jointure afore it should be too late, and afore the little gossoon should reach us with the news. My master was greatly vexed – that is, I may say, as much as ever I seen him – when he found how he had been taken in; but it was some comfort to have the ready cash for immediate consumption in the house, anyway.

And when Judy came up that evening, and brought the childer to see his honour, he unties the handkerchief, and – God bless him! whether it was little or much he had, 't was all the same with him – he gives 'em all round guineas apiece.

'Hold up your head,' says my shister to Judy, as Sir Condy was busy filling out a glass of punch for her eldest boy – 'Hold up your head, Judy; for who knows but we may live to see you yet at the head of the Castle Rackrent estate?'

'Maybe so,' says she, 'but not the way you are thinking of.'

I did not rightly understand which way Judy was looking when she made this speech till a while after.

'Why, Thady, you were telling me yesterday that Sir Condy had sold all entirely to Jason, and where then does all them guineas in the handkerchief come from?'

'They are the purchase-money of my lady's jointure,' says I.

Judy looks a little puzzled at this. 'A penny for your thoughts, Judy,' says my shister; 'hark, sure Sir Condy is drinking her health.'

He was at the table in the room,[17] drinking with the exciseman and the gauger, who came up to see his honour, and we were standing over the fire in the kitchen.

'I don't much care is he drinking my health or not,' says Judy; 'and it is not Sir Condy I'm thinking of, with all your jokes, whatever he is of me.'

'Sure you wouldn't refuse to be my Lady Rackrent, Judy, if you had the offer?' says I.

'But if I could do better!' says she.

'How better?' says I and my shister both at once.

'How better?' says she. 'Why, what signifies it to be my Lady Rackrent and no castle? Sure what good is the car, and no horse to draw it?'

'And where will ye get the horse, Judy?' says I.

'Never mind that,' says she; 'maybe it is your own son Jason might find that.'

'Jason!' says I; 'don't be trusting to him, Judy. Sir Condy, as I have good reason to know, spoke well of you when Jason spoke very indifferently of you, Judy.'

'No matter,' says Judy; 'it's often men speak the contrary just to what they think of us.'

'And you the same way of them, no doubt,' answered I. 'Nay, don't be denying it, Judy, for I think the better of ye for it, and shouldn't be proud to call ye the daughter of a shister's son of mine, if I was to hear ye talk ungrateful, and any way disrespectful of his honour.'

'What disrespect,' says she, 'to say I'd rather, if it was my luck, be the wife of another man?'

'You'll have no luck, mind my words, Judy,' says I; and all I remembered about my poor master's goodness in tossing up for her afore he married at all came across me, and I had a choking in my throat that hindered me to say more.

'Better luck, anyhow, Thady,' says she, 'than to be like some folk, following the fortunes of them that have none left.'

'Oh! King of Glory!' says I, 'hear the pride and ungratitude of her, and he giving his last guineas but a minute ago to her childer, and she with the fine shawl on her he made her a present of but yesterday!'

'Oh, troth, Judy, you're wrong now,' says my shister, looking at the shawl.

'And was not he wrong yesterday, then,' says she, 'to be telling me I was greatly altered, to affront me?'

'But, Judy,' says I, 'what is it brings you here then at all in the mind you are in; is it to make Jason think the better of you?'

'I'll tell you no more of my secrets, Thady,' says she, 'nor would have told you this much, had I taken you for such an unnatural fader as I find you are, not to wish your own son preferred to another.'

'Oh, troth, you are wrong now, Thady,' says my shister.

Well, I was never so put to it in my life; between these womens, and my son, and my master, and all I felt and thought just now, I could not, upon my conscience, tell which was the wrong from the right. So I said not a word more, but was only glad his honour had not the luck to hear all Judy had been saying of him, for I reckoned it would have gone nigh to break his heart; not that I was of opinion he cared for her as much as she and my shister fancied, but the ungratitude of the whole from Judy might not plase him; and he could never stand the notion of not being well spoken of or beloved-like behind his back. Fortunately for all parties concerned, he was so much elevated at this time, there was no danger of his understanding anything, even if it had reached his ears. There was a great horn at the Lodge, ever since my master and Captain Moneygawl was in together, that used to belong originally to the celebrated Sir Patrick, his ancestor; and his honour was fond often of telling the story that he learned from me when a child, how Sir Patrick drank the full of this horn without stopping, and this was what no other man afore or since could without drawing breath. Now Sir Condy challenged the gauger, who seemed to think little of the horn, to swallow the contents, and had it filled to the brim with punch; and the gauger said it was what he could not do for nothing, but he'd hold Sir Condy a hundred guineas he'd do it.

'Done,' says my master; 'I'll lay you a hundred golden guineas to a tester[18] you don't.'

'Done,' says the gauger; and done and done's enough between two gentlemen. The gauger was cast, and my master won the bet, and thought he'd won a hundred guineas, but by the wording it was adjudged to be only a tester that was his due by the exciseman. It was all one to him; he was as well pleased, and I was glad to see him in such spirits again.

The gauger – bad luck to him! – was the man that next proposed to my master to try himself, could he take at a draught the contents of the great horn.

'Sir Patrick's horn!' said his honour; 'hand it to me: I'll hold you your own bet over again I'll swallow it.'

'Done,' says the gauger; 'I'll lay ye anything at all you do no such thing.'

'A hundred guineas to sixpence I do,' says he; 'bring me the handkerchief.' I was loth, knowing he meant the handkerchief with the gold in it, to bring it out in such company, and his honour not very able to reckon it. 'Bring me the handkerchief, then, Thady,' says he, and stamps with his foot; so with that I pulls it out of my greatcoat pocket, where I had put it for safety. Oh how it grieved me to see the guineas counting up the table, and they the last my master had! Says Sir Condy to me: 'Your hand is steadier than mine tonight, old Thady, and that's a wonder; fill you the horn for me.' And so, wishing his honour success, I did; but I filled it, little thinking of what would befall him. He swallows it down, and drops like one shot. We lifts him up, and he was speechless, and quite black in the face. We put him to bed, and in a short time he wakened, raving with a fever on his brain. He was shocking either to see or hear.

'Judy! Judy! have you no touch of feeling? Won't you stay to help us nurse him?' says I to her, and she putting on her shawl to go out of the house.

'I'm frightened to see him,' says she, 'and wouldn't nor couldn't stay in it: and what use? He can't last till the morning.' With that she ran off. There was none but my shister and myself left near him of all the many friends he had.

The fever came and went, and came and went, and lasted five days, and the sixth he was sensible for a few minutes, and said to me, knowing me very well, 'I'm in a burning pain all withinside of me, Thady.' I could not speak, but my shister asked him would he have this thing or t'other to do him good? 'No,' says he, 'nothing will do me good no more,' and he gave a terrible screech with the torture he was in; then again a minute's ease – 'brought to this by drink,' says he. 'Where are all the friends? – where's Judy? Gone, hey? Ay, Sir Condy has been a fool all his days,' said he; and there was the last word he spoke, and died. He had but a very poor funeral after all.

If you want to know any more, I'm not very well able to tell you; but my Lady Rackrent did not die, as was expected of her, but was only disfigured in the face ever after by the fall and bruises she got; and she and Jason, immediately after my poor master's death, set about going to law about that jointure; the memorandum not being on stamped paper, so me say it is worth nothing, others again it may do; others say Jason won't have the lands at any rate; many wishes it so. For my part, I'm tired wishing for anything in this world, after all I've seen in it; but I'll say nothing – it would be folly to be getting myself ill-will in my old age. Jason did not marry, or think of marrying, Judy, as I prophesied, and I am not sorry for it: who is? As for all I have here set down from memory and hearsay of the. family there's nothing but truth in it from beginning to end. That you may depend upon, for where's the use of telling lies about the things which everybody knows as well as I do?

The Editor could have readily made the catastrophe of Sir Condy's history more dramatic and more pathetic, if he thought it allowable to varnish the plain round tale of faithful Thady. He lays it before the English reader as a specimen of manners and character which are perhaps unknown in England. Indeed, the domestic habits of no nation in Europe were less known to the English than those of their sister country till within these few years.

Mr Young's picture of Ireland, in his tour through that country, was the first faithful portrait of its inhabitants. All the features in the foregoing sketch were taken from the life, and they are characteristic of that mixture of quickness, simplicity, cunning, carelessness, dissipation, disinterestedness, shrewdness, and blunder, which, in different forms and with various success, has been brought upon the stage or delineated in novels.

It is a problem of difficult solution to determine whether a union will hasten or retard the amelioration of this country. The few gentlemen of education who now reside in this country will resort to England. They are few, but they are in nothing inferior to men of the same rank in Great Britain. The best that can happen will be the introduction of British manufacturers in their places.

Did the Warwickshire militia, who were chiefly artisans, teach the Irish to drink beer? or did they learn from the Irish to drink whiskey?

1. *Boo! Boo!* – an exclamation equivalent to pshaw or nonsense.
2. *Pin*, read *pen*. It formerly was vulgarly pronounced *pin* in Ireland.
3. *Her mark.* – It was the custom in Ireland for those who could not write to make a cross to stand for their signature, as was formerly the practice of our English monarchs. The Editor inserts the form of such a 'signature' which may hereafter be valuable to a judicious antiquary:

Her

Judy x M'Quirk,

Mark

In bonds or notes signed in this manner a witness is requisite, as the name is frequently written by him or her.

4. *Vows*. – It has been maliciously and unjustly hinted that the lower classes of the people of Ireland pay but little regard to oaths; yet it is certain that some oaths or vows have great power over their minds. Sometimes they swear they will be revenged on some of their neighbours; this is an oath that they are never known to break. But, what is infinitely more extraordinary and unaccountable, they sometimes make and keep a vow against whiskey; these vows are usually limited to a short time. A woman who has a drunken husband is most fortunate if she can prevail upon him to go to the priest, and make a vow against whiskey for a year, or a month, or a week, or a day.

5. *Gossoon*: a little boy – from the French word *garçon*. In most Irish families there used to be a barefooted gossoon, who was slave to the cook and the butler, and who, in fact, without wages, did all the hard work of the house. Gossoons were always employed as messengers. The Editor has known a gossoon to go on foot, without shoes or stockings, fifty-one English miles between sunrise and sunset.

6. A cleave is a large basket. – ED.

7. At St Patrick's meeting, London, March, 1806, the Duke of Sussex said he had the honour of bearing an Irish title, and, with the permission of the company, he should tell them an anecdote of what he had experienced on his travels. When he was at Home he went to visit an Irish seminary, and when they heard who it was, and that he had an Irish title, some of them asked him: 'Please your Royal Highness, since you are an Irish peer, will you tell us if you ever trod upon Irish ground?' When he told them he had not, 'Oh, then,' said one of the Order, 'you shall soon do so.' They then spread some earth which had been brought from Ireland on a marble slab, and made him stand upon it.

8. This was actually done at an election in Ireland.

9. *To put him up*: to put him in gaol.

10. *My little potatoes*. – Thady does not mean by this expression that his potatoes were less than other people's, or less than the usual size. *Little* is here used only as an Italian diminutive, expressive of fondness.

11. *Kith* and *kin*: family or relations. *Kin* from *kind*; *kith* from we know not what.

12. Wigs were formerly used instead of brooms in Ireland for sweeping or dusting tables, stairs, etc. The Editor doubted the fact till he saw a labourer of the old school sweep down a flight of stairs with his wig; he afterwards put it on his head again with the utmost composure, and said, 'Oh, please your honour, it's never a bit the worse.'

It must be acknowledged that these men are not in any danger of catching cold by taking off their wigs occasionally, because they usually have fine crops of hair growing under their wigs. The wigs are often yellow, and the hair which appears from beneath them black; the wigs are usually too small, and are raised up by the hair beneath or by the ears of the wearers.

13. A 'wake' in England is a meeting avowedly for merriment; in Ireland it is a nocturnal meeting avowedly for the purpose of watching and bewailing the dead, but in reality for gossiping and debauchery.

14. Shebeen-house, a hedge alehouse. Shebeen properly means weak, small beer, taplash.

15. At the coronation of one of our monarchs the King complained of the confusion which happened in the procession. The great officer who presided told his Majesty that 'it should not be so next time'.

16. 'Kilt and smashed'. Our author is not here guilty of an anti-climax. The mere English reader, from a similarity of sound between the words 'kilt' and 'killed', might be induced to suppose that their meanings are similar, yet they are not by any means in Ireland synonymous terms. Thus you may hear a man exclaim: 'I'm kilt and murdered!' but he frequently means only that he has received a black eye or a slight contusion. 'I'm kilt all over' means that he is in a worse state than being simply 'kilt'. Thus, 'I'm kilt with the cold' is nothing to 'I'm kilt all over with the rheumatism'.

17. 'The room': the principal room in the house.

18. 'Tester', sixpence; from the French word *tête*, a head – a piece of silver stamped with a head, which in old French was called *un testion*, and which was about the value of an old English sixpence. 'Tester' is used in Shakespeare.

JOHN AND MICHAEL BANIM

Michael, 1796–1874
John, 1798–1842

In the last century there lived in Kilkenny a seller of fishing-tackle and fowling-pieces, named Banim. To him was born in August, 1796, a son, Michael, and in April, 1798, amid the noise of the great rebellion, a second son, John. These two became close friends, and it is in all ways rightful that the same biographical account should serve for both; besides, there is little or no record of Michael except in so far as he comes into the life of his more famous brother.

John Banim got all his schooling in Kilkenny. We first hear of him at a dame's school, kept by a teacher who was 'good-humoured, quiet, and fat', unlearned and simple; and next at the English academy of one Charles George Beauchanon, who was learned and far from simple, judging by the account of him under the name of Charles George Buchmahon in 'Father Connell'. When ten years old he was moved to a school, famous in its day, taught by a Rev. Mr Magraw, and next to one belonging to a Terence Doyle. But looking back on these times, in later life, it seemed to him that his best education was picked up when reading romances under a hayrick. He busied himself with writing, too, both in prose and in verse. He had turned writer when too small to reach the table comfortably from any chair, and so had been compelled to write on a sheet of paper spread out on the floor. Once every year, a few days before his

77

birthday, it was his custom to solemnly go through the year's work and condemn it to a birthday burning.

Several of these fires must have flickered up the chimney before he entered, in his thirteenth year, that Kilkenny college described in 'The Fetches'. He there developed a faculty for drawing that decided him to become an artist. Accordingly, when about eighteen, one finds him in Dublin, a student at the art schools of the Royal Dublin Society, and lodging with a certain Oliver Wheeler, who gave him the anti-type for the lodging-house keeper in 'The Nolans'. He was not long in Dublin before the need to turn his art into money drove him down to Kilkenny again and started him as drawing-master.

At one of the schools where he taught was a pretty girl of seventeen, named Anne D— , the natural daughter of a local squire. She and the young drawing-master fell in love, and thereby began one of the mournfulest love episodes extant. Before long John Banim put on his best clothes and set out to ask her of her father. He found him a violent and bitter old man, who received him with abuse. They parted, quarrelling fiercely; Banim answering in kind the old man's insults. After this Banim found the school doors closed against him. He managed, however, to sit near his sweetheart in chapel, disguised in the hooded cloak of a peasant woman and to thrust into her hands as the people trooped out letters and verses vowing eternal affection. The old squire at last sent a woman, a female relation of the girl, to pretend sympathy and so find out if she still cared for Banim. Quite deceived, she told all, and was at once taken to a place twenty-five miles off, where she would be well out of the way of the young drawing-master and his hooded cloak. The carriage passed by the Banims' shop and John saw it, and running out placed himself before the horses. They were pulled up to prevent his being run over. His eyes met the eyes of Anne D— for a moment, and then the carriage passed on. He never saw her again. He went in among the fishing-lines and threw himself down in some corner. A messenger came in and laid a package in his hands. It was a miniature of his sweetheart he had painted and given to her. It was returned without any letter or message. Thinking her faithless, he wrote an upbraiding letter. It was the only letter of his she was allowed to see. He wrote many more, and in wholly different mood, but all were intercepted. Months passed; then one day he heard that Anne D— was dead, and was told that she had fretted herself out of the world. The body lay in a house belonging to her mother's family. He started away riding, but when no more than a mile on his road, dismounted and sent the horse home with a boy he had met with. He could not bear the sitting still on horseback. He walked the rest of the twenty-five miles, but never knew what route he took. It was evening when he went into the farmhouse and stood beside the body. One can imagine the scene: the half-awed whispering of men and women; the young girl there in the midst; the traditional wallflowers about her, and the flickering light of three candles. At first no one noticed the new-comer. At last a half-sister of the dead girl saw him and cried out that he was the murderer of her sister and bid them drive him away. He went out, and going into an outhouse, lay down on a heap of wet straw. He lay there till morning, when the noise of people arriving told him it was time for the funeral. He followed the procession to the graveyard, and when all had gone, lay down upon the grave. He could never remember where he slept that night. Somewhere under the stars, on some ditch side! The next day his brother found him wandering about some ten miles from home, ill and feeble, not having eaten for three days. He led him homeward, neither speaking a word. For a year he merely lived, no more. The night on the wet straw, the fatigue, the despair, the starvation, weakened his constitution permanently, and left there the seeds of the illness that ultimately killed him.

The year 1818 found him somewhat better. He was again able to write and draw, though it was now becoming clear to him that writing, not drawing, was the business of his life. He returned to Dublin and there wrote and published his first book, 'The Celts' Paradise', a poem on the beautiful old Irish legend of *Teernan Oge*, the Gaelic Island of the Blest; a subject that has moved a number of writers, Gaelic and English-speaking, to make their best verses, but wholly unsuitable for Banim's realistic faculty. He next moved over to London and offered a tragedy, he had had for some while on the stocks, to Macready, who accepted it and produced it with great success at Covent Garden Theatre on the 28th of May, 1821. Banim was now twenty-four, and felt he had his foot well fixed on the first rung of the ladder. He returned to Ireland and talked over with Michael a scheme for celebrating the national life in a series of novels that were 'to insinuate through fiction', as Michael has said, 'the causes of Irish discontent, and to insinuate also that if crime were consequent on discontent, it was no great wonder; a conclusion to be arrived at by the reader, not by insisting on it on the part of the author, but by sympathy with the criminals'. Michael had never written anything but shop accounts, and it was with much difficulty that John persuaded him to contribute to the venture. His persuasions were successful, however. Michael was to become Barnes O'Hara and John, Abel O'Hara, and the series was to be called 'The Tales of the O'Hara Family'.

When John returned to London he brought with him a wife aged eighteen. Her father, a Mr Ruth, furnished the least objectionable characteristics of 'Aby Nolan' in 'The Nolans'. For sometime London used the pair badly. Mrs Banim fell ill, and what with doctors' bills and the rest, they saw much of poverty. 'By the life of Pharaoh, Sir,' John wrote to his brother, 'if I do not ply and tear the brain as wool-combers tear wool, the fire should go out, and the spit cease to turn.' Presently he fell ill himself with a renewal of the wracking pains that followed his visit to the wake and funeral of Anne D— . At last he got somewhat out of his monetary troubles by the publication of some old essays, – 'The Revelations of the Dead Alive', satires on contemporary life by a man who is supposed to have the power of going out of his body in sleep – of projecting his *scin laca*, *astral body*, *doppelganger*, or what you will.

Meanwhile, the first volume of O'Hara Tales had been gradually forming itself: John writing steadily at it amid all his troubles; Michael thinking out his contributions while he sold catgut and trout flies, and setting them on paper when the shutters were put up for the night. In 1825 came out in one volume 'Crohors of the Bellhook', by Barnes, and 'John Doe', and 'The Fetches', by Abel O'Hara. The book was a great success, and poverty left John's door for a little. In the next four years were published: 'The Boyne Water', an historical romance still much read in Ireland; 'The Nolans', the most powerful, and 'The Denounced', the feeblest, of the O'Hara Tales, by John Banim; and 'The Croppy', by Michael. It is not easy, however, to fix where the work of one begins and that of the other ends. It was their custom to write chapters in each other's tales; Michael paying visits to London for the purpose, and John going over to Ireland from time to time, to talk things over with Michael while he was studying the localities of his stories. By the time 'The Denounced' was published the health of John Banim was hopelessly wrecked. The feebleness of the book was merely an index of bodily decay. Overwork and constant illness had worn him out. He looked forty, his hair was gray, his face wrinkled, and his step tottering.

He was ordered to France for his health, and while there a play of his, founded on 'The Fetches', was acted in London and condemned by *The Times* newspaper: 'The perpetuation of such absurd phantasies as fetches and fairies – witches and wizards – is not merely ridiculous, but it is mischievous'; – a remarkable criticism. In 1832 he wrote to his brother: 'My legs are quite gone and I suffer in the extreme, yet I try to work for all that.' He was but thirty-four, and yet it was getting clear enough that his working days were over. The younger Sterling – Carlyle's Sterling – had been a friend of his in London, and now the elder wrote to *The Times* and opened a subscription for him. A public meeting likewise was held in Dublin, at which Sheil spoke and the Lord Mayor presided, and a considerable sum was collected. In 1835 he returned to Kilkenny almost dying, and received an enthusiastic public reception. He lingered on a few years. He made his home in a cottage on Wind-Gap Hill and was called the Mayor of Wind-Gap, after a personage in one of his brother's stories. Too feeble to write, he spent his time gardening. One day he overheard a traveller on the stage coach as it passed by say, 'He will never see the bushes an inch higher,' and heard the driver reply, 'He is booked for the whole journey.' In 1837 he received a small pension from the civil list. In 1842 he died. His brother had started 'Father Connell', and he could not keep his hands off. The work killed him.

Michael Banim survived his brother many years, but wrote nothing of value after his death. He was postmaster of his native town and once mayor. He died in 1874, aged seventy-eight.

'John Doe' and 'The Nolans' are, I imagine, the best of John Banim's stories, and 'Father Connell' the best of Michael's. Whether it be justifiable to divide the work of one from the work of the other in this way I do not know. They worked constantly, as I have said, upon each other's stories, and were so alike in faculty that it is impossible to fix with confidence the march lands of either. The genius of John Banim was certainly the more vehement and passionate. He had likewise a faculty for verse absent in his brother. His 'Sogarth Aroon' is one of the most beautiful and popular of all Irish poems. The greater number of his verses were, however, of no value.

THE STOLEN SHEEP

An Irish Sketch

By JOHN AND MICHAEL BANIM

The faults of the lower orders of the Irish are sufficiently well known; perhaps their virtues have not been proportionately observed or recorded for observation. At all events, it is but justice to them, and it cannot conflict with any established policy, or do any one harm to exhibit them in a favourable light to their British fellow-subjects, as often as strict truth will permit. In this view the following story is written – the following facts, indeed; for we have a newspaper report before us, which shall be very slightly departed from while we make our copy of it.

The Irish plague, called typhus fever, raged in its terrors. In almost every third cabin there was a corpse daily. In everyone, without an exception, there was what had made the corpse – hunger. It need not be added that there was poverty too. The poor could not bury their dead. From mixed motives of self-protection, terror, and benevolence, those in easier circumstances exerted themselves to administer relief, in different ways. Money was subscribed (then came England's munificent donation – God prosper her for it!) – wholesome food, or food as wholesome as a bad season permitted, was provided; and men of respectability, bracing their minds to avert the danger that threatened themselves by boldly facing it, entered the infected house, where death reigned almost alone, and took measures to cleanse and purify the close-cribbed air, and the rough bare walls. Before proceeding to our story, let us be permitted to mention some general marks of Irish virtue, which, under those circumstances, we personally noticed. In poverty, in abject misery, and at a short and fearful notice, the poor man died like a Christian. He gave vent to none of the poor man's complaints or invectives against the rich man who had neglected him, or who he might have supposed had done so till it was too late. Except for a glance – and, doubtless, a little inward pang while he glanced – at the starving and perhaps infected wife, or child, or old parent as helpless as the child – he blessed God and died. The appearance of a comforter at his wretched bedside, even when he knew comfort to be useless, made his heart grateful and his spasmed lips eloquent in thanks. In cases of indescribable misery – some members of his family lying lifeless before his eyes, or else some dying – stretched upon damp and unclean straw on an earthen floor, without cordial for his lips, or potatoes to point out to a crying infant – often we have heard him whisper to himself (and to another who heard him): 'The Lord giveth, and the Lord taketh away, blessed be the name of the Lord.' Such men need not always make bad neighbours.

In the early progress of the fever, before the more affluent roused themselves to avert its career, let us cross the threshold of an individual peasant. His young wife lies dead; his second child is dying at her side; he has just sunk into the corner himself, under the first stun of disease, long resisted. The only persons of his family who have escaped contagion, and are likely to escape it, are his old father, who sits weeping feebly upon the hob, and his first-born, a boy of three or four years, who, standing between the old man's knees, cries also for food.

We visit the young peasant's abode some time after. He has not sunk under 'the sickness'. He is fast regaining his strength, even without proper nourishment; he can creep out-of-doors, and sit in the sun. But in the expression of his sallow and emaciated face there is no joy for his escape from the grave, as he sits there alone silent and brooding. His father and his surviving child are still hungry – more hungry, indeed, and more helpless than ever; for the neighbours who had relieved the family with a potato and a mug of sour milk are now stricken down themselves, and want assistance to a much greater extent than they can give it.

'I wish Mr Evans was in the place,' cogitated Michaul Carroll, 'a body could spake forn'ent him, and not spake for nothin', for all that he's an Englishman; and I don't like the thoughts o' goin' up to the house to the steward's face; it wouldn't turn kind to a body. Maybe he'd soon come home to us, the masther himself.'

Another fortnight elapsed. Michaul's hope proved vain. Mr Evans was still in London; though a regular resident on a small Irish estate, since it had come into his possession, business unfortunately – and he would have said so himself – now kept him an unusually long time absent. Thus disappointed, Michaul overcame his repugnance to appear before the 'hard' steward. He only asked for work, however. There was none to be had. He turned his slow and still feeble feet into the adjacent town. It was market-day, and he took up his place among a crowd of other claimants for agricultural employment, shouldering a spade, as did each of his companions. Many farmers came to the well known 'stannin', and hired men at his right and at his left, but no one addressed Michaul. Once or twice, indeed, touched perhaps by his sidelong looks of beseeching misery, a farmer stopt a moment before him, and glanced over his figure; but his worn and almost shaking limbs giving little promise of present vigor in the working field, worldly prudence soon conquered the humane feeling which started up towards him in the man's heart, and, with a choking in his throat, poor Michaul saw the arbiter of his fate pass on.

He walked homeward without having broken his fast that day. 'Bud, *musha*, what's the harm o' that,' he said to himself, 'only here's the ould father, an' *her* pet boy, the weenock, without a pyatee either. Well, *asthore*, if they can't have the pyatees, they must have better food, that's all; aye – ' he muttered, clenching his hands at his side, and imprecating fearfully in Irish – 'an' so they must.'

He left his house again, and walked a good way to beg a few potatoes. He did not come back quite empty-handed. His father and his child had a meal. He ate but a few himself, and when he was about to lie down in his corner for the night, he said to the old man, across the room, 'Don't be a-crying to-night father, you and the child there; but sleep well, and ye 'll have the good break'ast afore ye in the mornin'.' 'The good break'ast, *ma bouchal?*[1] a then, an' where 'll id come from?' 'A body promised it to me, father.' '*Avich*! Michaul, an' sure its fun you 're makin' of us, now, at any rate; but the good-night, a chorra,[2] an' my blessin' on your head, Michaul; an' if we keep trust in the good God, an' ax his blessin', too, mornin' an' evenin', gettin' up an lyin' down, He'll be a friend to us at last; that was always an' ever my word to you, poor boy, since you was at the years o' your weenock, now fast asleep at my side; and it's my word to you now, *ma bouchal*, an' you won't forget id; an there's one sayin' the same to you, out o' heaven, this night – herself, an' her little angel in glory by the hand, Michaul, a *vourneen*.'

Having thus spoken in the fervent and rather exaggerated, though every-day, words of pious allusion of the Irish poor man, old Carroll soon dropped asleep, with his arms round his little grandson, both overcome by an unusually abundant meal. In the middle of the night he was awakened by a stealthy noise. Without moving, he cast his eyes round the cabin. A small window, through which the moon broke brilliantly, was open. He called to his son, but received no answer. He called again and again; all remained silent. He arose, and crept to the corner where Michaul had lain down. It was empty. He looked out through the window into the moonlight. The figure of a man appeared at a distance, just about to enter a pasture-field belonging to Mr Evans.

The old man leaned his back against the wall of the cabin, trembling with sudden and terrible misgivings. With him, the language of virtue, which we have heard him utter, was not cant. In early prosperity, in subsequent misfortunes, and in his late and present excess of wretchedness, he had never swerved in practice from the spirit of his own exhortations to honesty before men, and love for and dependence upon God, which, as he has truly said, he had constantly addressed to his son since his earliest childhood, and hitherto that son had indeed walked by his precepts, further assisted by a regular observance of the duties of his religion. Was he now about to turn into another path? to bring shame on his father in his old age? to put a stain on their family and their name? 'the name that a rogue or a bowld woman never bore,' continued old Carroll, indulging in some of the pride and egotism for which an Irish peasant is, under his circumstances, remarkable. And then came the thought of the personal peril incurred by Michaul; and his agitation, incurred by the feebleness of age, nearly overpowered him.

He was sitting on the floor, shivering like one in an ague fit, when he heard steps outside the house. He listened, and they ceased; but the familiar noise of an old barn-door creaking on its crazy hinges came on his car. It was now day-dawn. He dressed himself, stole out cautiously, peeped into the barn through a chink of the door, and all he had feared met full confirmation. There, indeed, sat Michaul, busily and earnestly engaged, with a frowning brow and a haggard face, in quartering the animal he had stolen from Mr Evans' field.

The sight sickened the father; the blood on his son's hands and all. He was barely able to keep himself from falling. A fear, if not a dislike, of the unhappy culprit also came upon him. His unconscious impulse was to re-enter their cabin unperceived, without speaking a word; he succeeded in doing so; and then he fastened the door again, and undressed, and resumed his place beside his innocent grandson.

About an hour afterwards, Michaul came in cautiously through the still open window, and also undressed and reclined on his straw, after glancing towards his father's bed, who pretended to be asleep. At the usual time for arising, old Carroll saw him suddenly jump up and prepare to go abroad. He spoke to him, leaning on his elbow:

'And what *hollg*[3] is on you, *ma bouchal?*' 'Going for the good break'ast I promised you, father dear.' 'An' who's the good Christhin'll give id to us, Michaul?' 'Oh, you'll know that soon, father; now, a good-bye' – he hurried to the door. 'A good-bye, then, Michaul; bud tell me, what 's that on your hand?' 'No – nothin',' stammered Michaul, changing colour, as he hastily examined the hand himself; 'nothin' is on it; what could there be?' (nor was there, for he had very carefully removed all evidence of guilt from his person, and the father's question was asked upon grounds distinct from anything he then saw). 'Well, *avich*, an' sure I didn't say anything was on it wrong, or any thing to make you look so quare, an' spake so sthrange to your father, this mornin'; only I'll ax you, Michaul, over agin, who has took such a sudd'n likin' to us, to send us the good break'ast? an' answer me sthraight, Michaul, what is id to be that you call it so *good?*' 'The good mate, father' – he was again passing the threshold. 'Stop!' cried his father, 'stop, an' turn foment me. Mate? – the good mate? What ud bring mate into our poor house, Michaul? Tell me, I bid you again an' again, who is to give id to you?' 'Why, as I said afore, father, a body that – ' 'A body that thieved id, Michaul Carroll!' added the old man, as his son hesitated, walking close up to the culprit; 'a body that thieved id, an' no other body. Don't think to blind me, Michaul. I am ould, to be sure, but sense enough is left in me to look round among the neighbours, in my own mind, an' know that none of 'em that has the will has the power to send us the mate for our break'ast in an honest way. An' I don't say outright that you had the same thought wid me when you consented to take it from a thief; I don't mean to say that you'd go to turn a thief's recaiver at this hour o' your life, an' afther growin' up from a boy to a man without bringin' a spot o' shame on yourself, or on your *weenock*, or on one of us. No, I won't say that. Your heart was scalded, Michaul, an' your mind was darkened, for a start; an' the thought o' gettin' comfort for the ould father, an' for the little son, made you consent in a hurry, without lookin' well afore you, or widout lookin' up to your good God.' 'Father, father, let me alone! don't spake them words to me,' interrupted Michaul, sitting on a stool, and spreading his large and hard hands over his face. 'Well, thin, an' I won't, *avich*; I won't; nothing to trouble you, sure; I didn't mean it – only this, *a vourneen*, don't bring a mouthful o' the bad, unlucky victuals into this cabin; the pyatees, the wild berries o' the bush, the wild roots o' the arth, will be sweeter to us, Michaul; the hunger itself will be sweeter; an' when we give God thanks afther our poor meal, or afther no meal at all, our hearts will be lighter and our hopes for tomorrow sthronger, *avich, ma chree*, than if we faisted on the fat o' the land, but couldn't ax a blessing on our faist.' 'Well, thin, I won't either, father – I won't; an' sure you have your way now. I'll only go out a little while from you to beg, or else as you say, to root down in the ground, with my nails, like a baste brute, for our break'ast.' 'My *vourneen* you are, Michaul, an' my blessin' on your head; yes, to be sure, *avich*, beg, an' I'll beg wid you; sorrow a shame is in that – no, but a good deed, Michaul, when it's done to keep us honest. So come, we'll go among the Christhins together; only, before we go, Michaul, my own dear son, tell me – tell one thing.' 'What, father?' Michaul began to suspect. 'Never be afraid to tell me, Michaul Carroll, *ma bouchal*, I won't – I can't be angry wid you now. You are sorry, an' your Father in heaven forgives you, and so do I. But you know, *avich*, there would be danger in quittin' the place widout hidin' every scrap of

89

anything that could tell on us.' 'Tell on us! what can tell on us?' demanded Michaul; 'what's in the place to tell on us?' 'Nothin' in the cabin, I know, Michaul; but – ' 'But what, father?' 'Have you left nothin' in the way out there?' whispered the old man, pointing towards the barn. 'Out there? Where? What? What do you mean at all, now, father? Sure you know it's your own self has kept me from as much as laying a hand on it.' 'Ay, today mornin'; bud you laid a hand on it last night, *avich*, an' so – ' '*Curp an duoul*!' imprecated Michaul, 'this is too bad at any rate, no, I didn't – last night – let me alone, I bid you, father.' 'Come back again, Michaul,' commanded old Carroll, as the son once more hurried to the door, and his words were instantly obeyed. Michaul, after a glance abroad, and a start, which the old man did not notice, paced to the middle of the floor, hanging his head, an saying in a low voice: 'Hushth, now, father – it's time.' 'No, Michaul, I will not hushth, an' it's not time; come out with me to the barn.' 'Hushth!' repeated Michaul, whispering sharply; he had glanced sideways to the square patch of strong morning sunlight on the ground of the cabin, defined there by the shape of the open door, and saw it intruded upon by the shadow of a man's bust leaning forward in an earnest posture. 'Is it in your mind to go back into your sin, Michaul, an' tell me you were not in the barn at daybreak the mornin'?' asked his father, still unconscious of a reason for silence. 'Arrah, hushth, old man!' Michaul made a hasty sign towards the door, but was disregarded. 'I saw you in id,' pursued old Carroll, sternly, 'ay, and at your work in id too.' 'What's that you're sayin', ould Peery Carroll?' demanded a well-known voice. 'Enough to hang his son!' whispered Michaul to his father, as Mr Evans' land steward, followed by his herdsman and two policemen, entered the cabin. In a few minutes afterwards the policemen had in charge the dismembered carcass of the sheep, dug up out of the floor of the barn, and were escorting Michaul, handcuffed, to the county gaol, in the vicinity of the next town. They could find no trace of the animal's skin, though they sought attentively for it; this seemed to disappoint them and the steward a good deal.

From the moment that they entered the cabin, till their departure, old Carroll did not speak a word. Without knowing it, as it seemed, he sat down on his straw bed, and remained staring stupidly around him, or at one or another of his visitors. When Michaul was about to leave his wretched abode, he paced quickly towards his father, and holding out his ironed hands, and turning his cheek for a kiss, said smiling miserably: 'God be wid you, father, dear.' Still the old man was silent, and the prisoner and all his attendants passed out on the road. But it was then the agony of old Carroll assumed a distinctness. Uttering a fearful cry, he snatched up his still sleeping grandson, ran with the boy in his arms till he overtook Michaul; and, kneeling down before him in the dust, said: 'I ax pardon o' you, *avich*; won't you tell me I have id afore you go? an' here, I've brought little Peery for you to kiss; you forgot *him, a vourneen.*' 'No, father, I didn't,' answered Michaul, as he stooped to kiss the child; 'an' get up, father, get up; my hands are not my own, or I wouldn't let you do that afore your son. Get up, there's nothin' for you to throuble yourself about; that is, I mean, I have nothin' to forgive you; no, but everything to be thankful for, an' to love you for; you were always an' ever the good father to me; an' – ' The many strong and bitter feelings, which till now he had almost perfectly kept in, found full vent, and poor Michaul could not go on. The parting from his father, however, so different from what it had promised to be, comforted him. The old man held him in his arms, and wept on his neck. They were separated with difficulty.

Peery Carroll, sitting on the roadside after he lost sight of the prisoner, and holding his screaming grandson on his knees, thought the cup of his trials was full. By his imprudence he had fixed the proof of guilt on his own child; that reflection was enough for him, and he could indulge in it only generally. But he was yet to conceive distinctly in what dilemma he had involved himself, as well as Michaul. The policemen came back to compel his appearance before the magistrate; then, when the little child had been disposed of in a neighbouring cabin, he understood, to his consternation and horror, that he was to be the chief witness against the sheep stealer. Mr Evans' steward knew well the meaning of the words he had overheard him say in the cabin, and that if compelled to swear all he was aware of, no doubt would exist of the criminality of Michaul, in the eyes of a jury. ' 'Tis a sthrange thing to ax a father to do,' muttered Peery, more than once, as he proceeded to the magistrate's, 'it's a very sthrange thing.'

The magistrate proved to be a humane man. Notwithstanding the zeal of the steward and the policemen, he committed Michaul for trial, without continuing to press the hesitating and bewildered old Peery into any detailed evidence; his nature seemed to rise against the task, and he said to the steward: 'I have enough of facts for making out a committal; if you think the father will be necessary on the trial, subpoena him.'

The steward objected that Peery would abscond, and demanded to have him bound over to prosecute, on two sureties, solvent and respectable. The magistrate assented; Peery could name no bail; and consequently he also was marched to prison, though prohibited from holding the least intercourse with Michaul.

The assizes soon came on. Michaul was arraigned; and, during his plea of 'not guilty', his father appeared, unseen by him, in the gaoler's custody, at the back of the dock, or rather in an inner dock. The trial excited a keen and painful interest in the court, the bar, the jury box, and the crowds of spectators. It was universally known that a son had stolen a sheep, partly to feed a starving father; and that out of the mouth of that father it was now sought to condemn him. 'What will the old man do?' was the general question which ran through the assembly; and while few of the lower orders could contemplate the possibility of his swearing to the truth, many of their betters scarcely hesitated to make out for him a case of natural necessity to swear falsely.

The trial began. The first witness, the herdsman, proved the loss of the sheep, and the finding the dismembered carcass in the old barn. The policemen and the steward followed to the same effect, and the latter added the allusions which he had heard the father make to the son, upon the morning of the arrest of the latter. The steward went down from the table. There was a pause, and complete silence, which the attorney for the prosecution broke by saying to the crier, deliberately: 'Call Peery Carroll.' 'Here, sir,' immediately answered Peery, as the gaoler led him, by a side door, out of the back dock to the table. The prisoner started round; but the new witness against him had passed for an instant into the crowd.

The next instant, old Peery was seen ascending the table, assisted by the gaoler and by many other commiserating hands, near him. Every glance fixed upon his face. The barristers looked wistfully up from their seats round the table; the judge put a glass to his eye, and seemed to study his features attentively. Among the audience there ran a low but expressive murmur of pity and interest.

Though much emaciated by confinement, anguish, and suspense, Perry's cheeks had a flush, and his weak blue eyes glittered. The half-gaping expression of his parched and haggard lips was miserable to see. And yet he did not tremble much, nor appear so confounded as upon the day of his visit to the magistrate.

The moment he stood upright on the table, he turned himself fully to the judge, without a glance towards the dock. 'Sit down, sit down, poor man,' said the judge. 'Thanks to you, my lord, I will,' answered Peery, 'only, first, I'd ax you to let me kneel, for a little start'; and he accordingly did kneel, and after bowing his head, and forming the sign of the cross on his forehead, he looked up, and said: 'My Judge in heaven above, 'tis you I pray to keep me to my duty, afore my earthly judge, this day – amen'; and then, repeating the sign of the cross, he seated himself.

The examination of the witness commenced, and humanely proceeded as follows – (the counsel for the prosecution taking no notice of the superfluity of Peery's answers) – 'Do you know Michaul, or Michael, Carroll, the prisoner at the bar?' 'Afore that night, sir, I believed I knew him well; every thought of his mind; every bit of the heart in his body; afore that night, no living creature could throw a word at Michaul Carroll, or say he ever forgot his father's renown, or his love of his good God; an' sure the people are afther telling you, by this time, how it come about that night; an' you, my lord – an' ye, gintlemen – an' all good Christians that hear me; here I am to help to hang him – my own boy, and my only one – but for all that, gintlemen, ye ought to think of it; 'twas for the *weenock* and the ould father that he done it; indeed, an' deed, we hadn't a pyatee in the place, an' the sickness was among us, a start afore; it took the wife from him, an' another babby; an' id had' himself down, a week or so beforehand; an' all that day he was looking for work, but couldn't get' a hand's turn to do; an' that's the way it was; not a mouthful for me an' little Peery; an' more betoken, he grew sorry for id, in the mornin', an' promised me not to touch a scrap of what was in the barn – ay, long afore the steward and the peelers came on us – but was willin' to go among the neighbours an' beg our break'ast, along wid myself, from door to door, sooner than touch it.' 'It is my painful duty,' resumed the barrister, when Peery would at length cease, 'to ask you for closer information. You saw Michael Carroll in the barn, that night?' '*Musha* – the Lord pity him and me – I did, sir.' 'Doing what?' 'The sheep between his hands,' answered Peery, dropping his head, and speaking almost inaudibly. 'I must still give you pain, I fear; stand up, take the crier's rod, and if you see Michael Carroll in court, lay it on his head.' '*Och, musha, musha*, sir, don't ax me to do that!' pleaded Peery, rising, wringing his hands, and for the first time weeping, 'Och, don't, my lord, don't, and may your own judgment be favourable the last day.' 'I am sorry to command you to do it, witness, but you must take the rod,' answered the judge, bending his head close to his notes, to hide his own tears, and, at the same time, many a veteran barrister rested his forehead on the edge of the table. In the body of the court were heard sobs. 'Michaul, *avich*! Michaul, *a chorra ma chree*!' exclaimed Peery, when at length he took the rod, and faced round to his son, 'is id your father they make to do it, *ma bouchal*?' 'My father does what is right,' answered Michaul, in Irish. The judge immediately asked to have his words translated; and, when he learned their import, regarded the prisoner with satisfaction. 'We rest here, my lord,' said the counsel, with the air of a man freed from a painful task.

The judge instantly turned to the jury box.

'Gentlemen of the jury. That the prisoner at the bar stole the sheep in question, there can be no shade of moral doubt. But you have a very peculiar case to consider. A son steals a sheep that his own famishing father and his own famishing son may have food. His aged parent is compelled to give evidence against him here for the act. The old man virtuously tells the truth, and the whole truth, before you and me. He sacrifices his natural feelings – and we have seen that they are lively – to his honesty, and to his religious sense of the sacred obligations of an oath. Gentlemen, I will pause to observe that the old man's conduct is strikingly exemplary, and even noble. It teaches all of us a lesson. Gentlemen, it is not within the province of a judge to censure the rigour of the proceedings which have sent him before us. But I venture to anticipate your pleasure that, notwithstanding all the evidence given, you will be enabled to acquit that old man's son, the prisoner at the bar. I have said there cannot be the shade of a moral doubt that he has stolen the sheep, and I repeat the words. But, gentlemen, there is a legal doubt, to the full benefit of which he is entitled. The sheep has not been identified. The herdsman could not venture to identify it (and it would have been strange if he could) from the dismembered limbs found in the barn. To his mark on its skin, indeed, he might have positively spoken; but no skin has been discovered. Therefore, according to the evidence, and you have sworn to decide by that alone, the prisoner is entitled to your acquittal. Possibly now that the prosecutor sees the case in its full bearing, he may be pleased with this result.'

While the jury, in evident satisfaction, prepared to return their verdict, Mr Evans, who had but a moment before returned home, entered the court, and becoming aware of the concluding words of the judge, expressed his sorrow aloud, that the prosecution had ever been undertaken; that circumstances had kept him uninformed of it, though it had gone on in his name; and he begged leave to assure his lordship that it would be his future effort to keep Michaul Carroll in his former path of honesty, by finding him honest and ample employment, and, as far as in him lay, to reward the virtue of the old father.

While Peery Carroll was laughing and crying in a breath, in the arms of his delivered son, a subscription, commenced by the bar, was mounting into a considerable sum for his advantage.

1. My boy.
2. Term of endearment.
3. 'What are you about'!

THE MAYOR OF WIND-GAP

An Extract

By MICHAEL BANIM

It was the eve of the twenty-fourth of June, about fifty-five years ago. All Irish readers pretty well know that it has been the practice, time immemorial, of the humbler classes, upon this night, to kindle bonfires throughout the country. We have read many learned discussions touching the origin of this custom; notwithstanding which, and contrary to the nature of the theme, or at least of its origin, we have been as much in the dark as ever, whether the lighting of bonfires on St John's Eve be a remnant of pagan rites, by which our ancestors sacrificed to the palpable deity of the earth, the dispenser of light and heat, or whether it be a custom of more recent origin, we honestly admit we cannot say. Nor shall we pause to submit any grave surmises on the matter. The people themselves, who are the actual incendiaries, can give no rational account of the meaning of what they do.

The unexplained practice is, while we write, lamentably fallen into decay, like many similar and even more intelligible ones.[1] But the bonfires of the twenty-third of June, 1779, in and around our city, blazed grandly and numerously. To whatever point of the suburbs, or of the distant country, the citizen turned his glance – along the high-road, or at the corner of cross-roads, or in the bottoms of the remote valleys, or upon

97

the bosoms of still more distant hills, – columns of flame arose. Even in the streets of his town the houses seemed red-hot, from the flaming upon them of vast fires, composed of furze, cows' horns, bones, tar-barrels, sugar-barrels, trunks or branches of trees, and all other combustibles that could not be called staple consumption for the thrifty domestic hearths of the place.

Within and without, and far beyond our city, all was rejoicing glare. Yet, to the honour of Wind-gap be it recorded, the bonfire upon its height was brilliant beyond comparison: honour, indeed, its inhabitants expected and received from the circumstance; a reflected glory proportioned to the magnificence of their conflagration. Many battles had been fought between the 'boys of Wind-gap' (the elderly men were termed boys, along with the rest), and the other boys of other outlets, in sallies for necessary materials. In all such encounters, the former had been victors, dragging up with shouts of victory, to the topmost point of their high ground, abundance of everything required for a bonfire of gigantic dimensions.

The long-wished for evening fell, the pile was heaped, the brand was applied to it: as its flame shot up, 'even into the skies,' young and old, man and woman, maid and widow, boy and girl and child sent after it a cloud-cleaving shout of exultation.

At this crisis of the mystical festivity, a fellow uncouthly swathed from his neck to his heels in twisted straw ropes, wearing a ridiculous mask, and wielding a stick with a puffed bladder tied to its extremity, flapped and banged his way through the motley crowd with as much agility as his cumbrous clothing would permit. Indeed he resembled a great, half-tamed dancing bear. He was followed by another man of proportions as muscular as his own, fantastically dressed in female attire, also wearing a grotesquely terrific mask, and armed in the same manner as his supposed protector. This absurd pair dashed through the shouting throng, dealing indiscriminately their blows on every head, which blows, like the words of a babbling tongue, were more noisy than mischievous. The people, however, half of their own accord, ran here and there, pursued by their two grotesque sergeants-at-arms, until these active police of Wind-gap had ranged them to their satisfaction. After a little time order was restored, and the proceedings of the night went forward with official regularity.

At one side, where a line of temporary benches covered with green sods had been erected for the occasion, sat the more aged portion of the men of Wind-gap. Squatted on the ground below them, were ranged, dressed in their high-cauled caps and holiday garments, the as elderly females of the principality. Half a dozen sycamore chairs, placed near the benches, were occupied by as many gray-headed, sage-looking, and very old men. Opposite to those gathered the promiscuous group of every inferior age or degree (for age *meant* degree) of the dwellers of the place.

The foolish fellow armoured in straw, and the swaggering unfeminine, would-be female, his companion, strode up and down, pummelling all who did not assume attitudes and faces of the required gravity; at the same time that their own grotesque tricks abundantly caused the loud merriment they affected to discountenance. The glare of the bonfire shot in between the seated elders and the confronting throngs, so that the faces of all glowed like heated metal, while their backs remained in black shadow.

The mumming fool in straw approached the old men seated on the chairs, flourished his stick with its appendage, struck the latter against the ground, and attempted a few unwieldy movements. An aged man arose and came forward: 'Neighbours all, both the ould and the young o' ye, listen to the words from my mouth. The fire is blazing for the midsummer; the eve of St John's Day is come round to us again, praise be given above for the blessin' of another year. We are behouldin' to choose a Mayor of Wind-gap for the year that's afore us. Fifteen midsummer nights are come and gone since the same man first had the Mayorship of rule and sway over us. To this hour he has kept the pace an' the Christian good-will inside our dours, and outside our thrasholds; quashing down scrimmages and ructions, makin' a settlement of all our quarrels, an' keepin' us out of the law of the town below there, that might bring the *Meeroch*[2] on us, if we had anything to do with it. Honest neighbours that hearken to me, my word goes for it; that a more honester or a more worshipfuller Mayor nor Maurteen Maher couldn't hould the sway on Wind-gap.'

Like other reporters of popular oratory we might have broken up this speech with many parenthetical cheers: the spokesman and his subject are as much favourites of ours as any other public speaker ever has been in the eyes of our brethren. We think, however, that we show more real art by keeping our whole volley of hurrahs for the close of the oration; and by declaring with strict truth, that the air was rent, after our friend sat down, with shouts of every calibre. The next instant Maurteen Maher, by public acclamation, was re-elected Mayor of Wind-gap.

Maurteen had been seated on one of the sycamore chairs before spoken of; he now stood up. The oldest man of the assembly, one almost bent double with age, came to his side, and placed a long osier wand, peeled white, in his Worship's right hand.

'Will you make promises before the neighbours to be the honest fair judge among us and to dale out the thrue justice on Wind-gap hill?' queried his ancient installer.

'I'll do my duty like a thrue, honest man,' responded Maurteen Maher.

'Neighbours, do ye promise to be loyal and dutiful to your Mayor?' demanded the same aged person of the assembled crowd.

'Loyal and dutiful!' shouted all.

'The chair, the chair!' was now the cry.

A large, two-armed, wicker chair was brought forward. To its sides were nailed loops of leather; through these strong poles were put. With perfect gravity of manner, Maurteen Maher took his seat, clutching in his right hand his long wand of office, and in the other a huge nosegay. His subjects seized the poles, mounted them on their shoulders, and, preceded by a piper and a fiddler, the Mayor of Wind-gap was thrice borne round the bonfire, to which, during his progress, many fagots of furze, innumerable cows' horns, half the trunk of a goodly tree, and the entire skeleton of a horse, were added, for the purpose of conferring a kind of glory upon his inauguration, as well as of exciting the new and excelling shouts which attested it.

The Mayor's chair was then placed on a turfy eminence raised above the grassy bench before described. A foaming brown pitcher of home-brewed ale was handed to him. He quaffed it, wishing the *sha-dhurth*[3] to all around him. And then the vessel was passed on, of course after having been replenished, while each prayed a long reign for their newly and curiously elected civic magistrate.

Maurteen Maher arose. Amidst all this half-farcical, half-serious scene, profound silence ensued.

'It is in the knowledge of all o' ye, neighbours,' he said, 'that scence the first time ye made me Mayor of Wind-gap, 'tis my rule to choose my council, that, wid their help, I may give good advice to ye, on hard points. The same council that I called the first year o' my Mayorship I'll call this present year. Shawn Leeach and Gregory Roche, take your places.'

Shawn Leeach, the very old man who, as it may be said, had sworn in the Mayor, and Gregory Roche, one not much younger, very demurely took their stations, the one at his right hand, the other at his left.

'Shawn Leeach and Gregory Roche,' continued Maurteen, 'ye are the Mayor's council for the year to come; no man is to gainsay our judgments, upon the peril of being put out of good fellowship with his neighbours. Come before my face, Meehawl O'Moore.'

The hitherto merely foolish fellow, in the case of straw, waddled towards his Worship's chair.

'Meehawl O'Moore, I put you in the post of the Mayor's bailiff. I give you the power to desthrain and to make desthress, under the ordher of the Mayor's Coort of Wind-gap. Are ye all content, and do ye know your own minds, this St John's Eve – that Meehawl O'Moore should have this place over ye, by ordher o' the Coort?'

It was curious that the boisterously inclined crowd wore really serious faces, while they answered to this question in the affirmative.

'Well, then,' rejoined Maurteen, 'my hearty neighbours, let the dance go on, and the *shannachus* [4] be tould, and let the good sheebeen be dhrunk, till the fire burns down and the Colloch's hour comes. Meehawl O'Moore keep the ring reg'lar. Keep the gossoons on their good behav'er to the colleens. Keep the *sheebeen* rangin' its rounds in rason. Let no one pass the gap windout payin' the towl. [5] If there's any unruly doin's or pickin' of quarrels, or any undacent conduct, bring the offendher before me. And so, neighbours, *Sha-dhurth* to ye agin; and hearty and prosperous may we all be, man, woman, and child, ould and young, until St John's Eve comes round to us the next year.'

The Mayor took another willing draught. New cheers were given at the close of his harangue; more fagots and other combustibles were thrown on the fire. The piper and the fiddler, preceded and followed by the 'boys and girls,' adjourned to an adjacent level spot, under the clamorous direction of Meehawl O'Moore; and the dance quickly commenced with all the life and vigour for which Irish 'boys and girls' are so justly celebrated.

Maurteen Maher possessed his osier armchair in quiet dignity; his council placed their lesser chairs at his right and at his left; the other old men, and all the old women, kept their former stations. The *weenocks* sat in a ring round the blaze, and began plays suitable to their age. Over the whole Maurteen kept his eye of authority, ordaining order, encouraging amusement, talking *shannachus*; occasionally tasting his *sheebeen*; commanding that the same beverage should moisten the piper's chanter, rosin the fiddler's bow, give to the dancers' feet spirit for their pastime, and – (superfluous injunction!) oil the well-practised tongues of the old women seated near his chair.

A rather violent stir here took place, among the dancers at a little distance; and six or eight stout young fellows, heralded by the man of straw, and his herculean helpmate, dragged towards the Mayor's chair two individuals wearing large mantles and broad-brimmed hats. As the parties confronted the judgment-seat, hat and cloak were torn from the person of the foremost culprit. Almost in the middle of the gossip, which had occupied itself about him, 'the sthrange man o' the Inch' stood fully in view. His *nom de guerre* was shouted by more than one voice; immediately those who had held him loosed their grasp; and he stood in the blaze of the fire, laughing loudly at the ludicrous confusion caused by his presence.

Among the old women there ensued a hideous discord of screams. They tumbled over each other in their hasty, though not successful, attempt to avoid the neighbourhood of one whom they themselves had magnified into a very formidable being.

After the retreat of the old women, his mocking laughter suddenly gave way to a bold, imperious manner.

'Come, make way here, fellows,' he said. 'I have a strong inclination to punish a score or two of you, for your rough handling, now that you have dared to rob me of my cloak and hat. Make way, I say, or I will score some ugly marks on your foolish faces'; and he tapped the short crooked sword at his side.

All the old men around Maurteen, and all the young people who had followed from the dancing ground, were receding to make way accordingly, when Maurteen Maher clutched his osier wand, and, sitting very upright in his chair, cried out in a sonorous voice: 'Stop! stop awhile, genteel, and give an account of yourself.'

The strange man of the Inch turned suddenly round, and glared at the questioner.

'Yes,' resumed Maurteen, 'I'd have a word or two wid ye, afore ye lave our place.'

The summoned person was evidently much surprised and offended at this interruption. He walked rapidly over to his worship, fixed a stern look upon him, was silent for an instant, and at last burst forth in a question:

'Who the devil are *you* that stop *me*?'

Maurteen Maher did not wince before the strange man of the Inch. He held his head loftily, and his tone was bold, without being arrogant, as he answered:

'*I* am the Mayor of Wind-gap, far above the Mayor of the town below us, as you may learn by looking on the hight of this place, and how low the town lies at our feet.'

'Take your foolish mummery to some other market, you old, ridiculous fool,' cried the strange man of the Inch, again vehemently turning to go away.

'There's no mummery about me,' said Maurteen. 'I govern the people here by their own freewill and consent. And I govern them for their good.'

'You're an old gray-headed idiot, I take it. You look d – d impertinently at me, and I've half a mind to change your tone,' continued the 'sthrange man.'

' 'Tisn't by fighting with the sword I should be able to rule over my neighbours. But for all that, I'm not afeeard o' ye, as wicked as they say ye are, and as fierce as your one eye burns upon me. So you need not lay your hand upon your crooked hanger: the odds o' the battle 'ud be agin' ye. But I don't want anything but peace and quiet. Listen to me. I'm tould ye said evil words into the ear of a young girl at the dance, and put your arms round her when she didn't want them. For that offence on Wind-gap, you are brought before me, the Mayor. It is time for you to give over foolish and sinful notions and behaviour. The snow of age has not fallen on your locks as thick as it has upon mine; but still I'd have you be thinkin' o' your grave. 'Tis a shkandle to us on Wind-gap to see a middle-aged man runnin' the race o' the wicked. I say to you, repent o' your sins, and larn to be a Christhin.'

This magnificent address, though full of never-to-be-forgotten morality, to the ears of Maurteen's neighbours, seemed to strike the 'sthrange man' as something eminently ridiculous. He burst into a renewal of his former fit of laughter, and hurried, now unobstructed, from the presence of his lecturer.

(Throughout the novel the 'sthrange man' and the Mayor of Wind-gap are confronted as the good and evil powers of the tale. In the first we have Banim at his most melodramatic; in the second, keeping close to life, and describing a personage who had really lived at Wind-gap a little before his day, he has given us one of the most beautiful characters in fiction.)

1. In Kilkenny, Banim means. To this day the custom is universal in the west of Ireland. – ED.
2. Ill luck.
3. Good health.
4. Agreeable gossip.
5. Toll – toll for the bonfire.

WILLIAM CARLETON

1798–1869

William Carleton was born on Shrove Tuesday, in the year 1798, when the pike was trying to answer the pitch-cap. He was the youngest of fourteen children. His father, a farmer of the town land of Prillisk, in the parish of Clogher, County Tyrone, was famous among the neighbours for his great knowledge of all old Gaelic charms, ranns, poems, prophecies, miracle-tales, and tales of ghost and fairy. His mother had the sweetest voice within the range of many baronies. When she sang at a wedding or lifted the keen at a wake, the neighbours would crowd in to hear her, as to some famous *prima donna*. Often, too, when she keened, the other keeners would stand round silent to listen. It was her especial care to know all old Gaelic songs, and many a once noted tune has died with her.

A fit father and mother for a great peasant writer – for one who would be called 'the prose Burns of Ireland.'

As the young Carleton grew up his mind filled itself brimful of his father's stories and his mother's songs. He has recorded how, many times, when his mother sat by her spinning-wheel, singing 'The Trougha,' or 'Shule Agra,' or some other mournful air, he would go over to her and whisper: 'Mother, don't sing that song; it makes me sorrowful.' Fifty years later he could still hum tunes and sing verses dead on all other lips.

His education, such as it was, was beaten into him by hedge schoolmasters. Like other peasants of his time he learnt to read out of the chap-books – 'Freney the Robber,' 'Rogues and Rapparees'; or else, maybe, from the undesirable pages of 'Laugh and Be Fat.' He sat under three schoolmasters in succession – Pat Fryne, called Mat Kavanagh in 'Traits and Stories'; O'Beirne of Findramore; and another, whose name Carleton has not recorded, there being naught but evil to say of him. They were a queer race, bred by government in its endeavour to put down Catholic education. The thing being forbidden, the peasantry had sent their children to learn reading, and writing, and a little Latin even, under the 'hips and haws' of the hedges. The sons of ploughmen were hard at work construing Virgil and Horace, so great a joy is there in illegality.

When Carleton was about fourteen he set out as 'a poor scholar,' meaning to travel into Munster in search of more perfect education. 'The poor scholar' was then common enough in Ireland. Many still living remember him and his little bottle of ink. When a boy had shown great attention to his books he would be singled out to be a priest, and a subscription raised to start him on his way to Maynooth. Every peasant's house, as he trudged upon his road, would open its door to him, such honour had learning and piety among the poor. Carleton, however, was plainly intended for nothing of the kind. He did not get farther than Granard, where he dreamed that he was chased by a mad bull, and taking it for an evil omen, went home.

He felt very happy when he came to his own village again, the uncomfortable priestly ambition well done with. He spent his time now in attending all dances, wakes, and weddings, and grew noted as the best dancer and leaper in his district; nor had he many rivals with a spear and shillelah. When he was about nineteen a second pious fit sent him off on a pilgrimage to St Patrick's Purgatory, in Lough Derg. This 'Purgatory,' celebrated by Calderon, is an island where the saint once killed a great serpent, and turned him into stone, and left his rocky semblance visible forever. Upon his return, his opinions, he states, changed considerably, and began slowly drifting into Protestantism.

One day he came on a translation of 'Gil Blas,' and was set all agog to see the world and try its chances. Accordingly, he again left his native village, this time not to return. For a while he lingered teaching in Louth, and then starting away again, reached Dublin with the proverbial half-crown in his pocket. After a hard struggle with poverty, in which he turned or tried to turn his hand to many things, he met with Caesar Otway, a well-known anti-papal controversialist, who set him down to write an account of Lough Derg. It was soon written, and published, and well praised. As it now stands, many controversial passages taken out by Carleton's later judgment, it is a tale of the most vivid kind, though its picturesque troops of praying peasants and avowed *votheens* are somewhat injured in simplicity, and also doubtless in truth to nature, by the zeal of the convert.

From this on there is little to record but the publication of his works. The authorities for facts concerning him are few indeed. He married, and eked out his income by teaching his hedge-school Latin. When about thirty he published the 'Traits and Stories of the Irish Peasantry,' and became famous in a fashion. Then came 'Irish Life and Character,' and 'Fardorougha the Miser,' the miser himself being the largest in conception and most finished in execution of all his characters. 'The Emigrants of Ahadara,' 'Valantine McClutchy,' and 'The Black Prophet,' with its sombre and passionate dialogue, followed rapidly.

By this time the 'Young Ireland' movement was in full swing, and 'the National Library,' founded by Davis, selling in thousands. Carleton, who had more and more with each succeeding story returned to the beliefs and feelings of his fathers, felt bound to do his part. He wrote a series of short stories in such a style as to be read by the peasantry: 'Paddy Go Easy,' a temperance tale, said by Father Mathew to be the best in existence; 'Redmond Count O'Hanlon,' the life of a famous outlaw; and 'Roddy the Rover,' on a favourite theme of his – the secret societies. Rody is an *agent provocateur*, a creature bred in all ages by government in Ireland.

On the death of John Banim, in 1842, an attempt was made to have his pension transferred to Carleton, but some official having discovered that this writer of a temperance tale, read through the whole country like a chap-book, himself drank a deal more than was wholesome, the pension was refused. It might have saved Carleton from years of stumbling decadence brought on by years of hack work. Government has never much minded a drunken magistrate or so, but grows very particular when a man of genius is in question.

Carleton in the latter years of his life wrote little to any good purpose. Poor, feeble stories came from his desk in rapid succession. One or two succeeded, so capricious is public taste; a semi-historical romance of this period being now in its twentieth edition, a success not granted to 'Fardorougha' or 'The Black Prophet,' both great novels and both out of print. The greater number of the books of his decadence failed, however, and he lived in much poverty almost to his death in 1869. A short time before it he was given the pension refused many years earlier.

WILDGOOSE LODGE

An Extract

By WILLIAM CARLETON

I had read the anonymous summons, but, from its general import, I believed it to be one of those special meetings convened for some purpose affecting the usual objects and proceedings of the body; at least, the terms in which it was conveyed to me had nothing extraordinary or mysterious in them beyond the simple fact that it was not to be a general but a select meeting: this mark of confidence flattered me, and I determined to attend punctually. I was, it is true, desired to keep the circumstance entirely to myself; but there was nothing startling in this, for I had often received summonses of a similar nature. I therefore resolved to attend, according to the letter of my instructions, 'on the next night, at the solemn hour of midnight, to deliberate and act upon such matters as should then and there be submitted to my consideration.' The morning after I received this message I arose and resumed my usual occupations; but from whatever cause it may have proceeded, I felt a sense of approaching evil hang heavily upon me; the beats of my pulse were languid, and an undefinable feeling of anxiety pervaded my whole spirit; even my face was pale, and my eye so heavy that my father and brothers concluded me to be ill – an opinion which I thought at the time to be correct, for I felt exactly that kind of depression which precedes a severe fever. I could not understand what I experienced, nor can I yet, except by supposing that there is in human nature some mysterious faculty by which, in coming calamities, the dread of some fearful evil is anticipated, and that it is possible to catch a dark presentiment of the sensations which they subsequently produce. For my part, I can neither analyse nor define it; but on that day I knew it by painful experience, and so have a thousand others in similar circumstances.

It was about the middle of winter. The day was gloomy and tempestuous almost beyond any other I remember; dark clouds rolled over the hills about me, and a close, sleet-like rain fell in slanting drifts that chased each other rapidly towards the earth on the course of the blast. The outlying cattle sought the closest and calmest corners of the fields for shelter; the trees and young groves were tossed about, for the wind was so unusually high that it swept in hollow gusts through them with that hoarse murmur which deepens so powerfully on the mind the sense of dreariness and desolation.

As the shades of night fell, the storm, if possible, increased. The moon was half gone, and only a few stars were visible by glimpses, as a rush of wind left a temporary opening in the sky. I had determined, if the storm should not abate, to incur any penalty rather than attend the meeting; but the appointed hour was distant, and I resolved to be decided by the future state of the night.

Ten o'clock came, but still there was no change; eleven passed, and on opening the door to observe if there were any likelihood of its clearing up, a blast of wind, mingled with rain, nearly blew me off my feet. At length it was approaching to the hour of midnight; and on examining the third time, I found it had calmed a little, and no longer rained.

I instantly got my oak stick, muffled myself in my great-coat, strapped my hat about my ears, and, as the place of meeting was only a quarter of a mile distant, I presently set out.

The appearance of the heavens was lowering and angry, particularly in that point where the light of the moon fell against the clouds, from a seeming chasm in them, through which alone she was visible. The edges of this chasm were faintly bronzed, but the dense body of the masses that hung piled on each side of her was black and impenetrable to sight. In no other point of the heavens was there any part of the sky visible; a deep veil of clouds overhung the horizon, yet was the light sufficient to give occasional glimpses of the rapid shifting which took place in this dark canopy, and of the tempestuous agitation with which the midnight storm swept to and fro beneath it.

At length I arrived at a long slated house, situated in a solitary part of the neighbourhood; a little below it ran a small stream, which was now swollen above its banks, and rushing with mimic roar over the flat meadows beside it. The appearance of the bare slated building in such a night was particularly sombre, and to those, like me, who knew the purpose to which it was usually devoted, it was, or ought to have been, peculiarly so. There it stood, silent and gloomy, without any appearance of human life or enjoyment about or within it. As I approached, the moon once more had broken out of the clouds, and shone dimly upon the wet, glittering slates and windows with a death-like lustre, that gradually faded away as I left the point of observation and entered the folding-door. It was the parish chapel.

The scene which presented itself here was in keeping not only with the external appearance of the house, but with the darkness, the storm, and the hour, which was now a little after midnight. About eighty persons were sitting in dead silence upon the circular steps of the altar. They did not seem to move; and as I entered and advanced the echo of my footsteps rang through the building with a lonely distinctness, which added to the solemnity and mystery of the circumstances about me. The windows were secured with shutters on the inside, and on the altar a candle was lighted, which burned dimly amid the surrounding darkness, and lengthened the shadow of the altar itself, and those of six or seven persons who stood on its upper steps, until they mingled in the obscurity which shrouded the lower end of the chapel. The faces of the men who sat on the altar steps were not distinctly visible, yet their prominent and more characteristic features were in sufficient relief, and I observed that some of the most malignant and reckless spirits in the parish were assembled. In the eyes of those who stood at the altar, and whom I knew to be invested with authority over the others, I could perceive gleams of some latent and ferocious purpose, kindled, as I soon observed, into a fiercer expression of vengeance by the additional excitement of ardent spirits, with which they had stimulated themselves to a point of determination that mocked at the apprehension of all future responsibility, either in this world or the next.

The welcome which I received on joining them was far different from the boisterous good-humour that used to mark our greetings on other occasions: just a nod of the head from this or that person, on the part of those *who sat*, with a *ghud dhemur tha thu*?[1] in a suppressed voice, even below a common whisper; but from the standing group, who were evidently the projectors of the enterprise, I received a conclusive grasp of the hand, accompanied by a fierce and desperate look, that seemed to search my eye and countenance, to try if I were a person not likely to shrink from whatever they had resolved to execute. It is surprising to think of the powerful expression which a moment of intense interest or great danger is capable of giving to the eye, the features, and the slightest actions, especially in those whose station in society does not require them to constrain nature, by the force of social courtesies, into habits that conceal their natural emotions. None of the standing group spoke; but as each of them wrung my hand in silence, his eye was fixed on mine with an expression of drunken confidence and secrecy, and an insolent determination not to be

114

gainsayed without peril. If looks could be translated with certainty, they seemed to say: 'We are bound upon a project of vengeance, and if you do not join us, remember that we *can* revenge.' Along with this grasp they did not forget to remind me of the common bond by which we were united, for each man gave me the secret grip of Ribbonism in a manner that made the joints of my fingers ache for some minutes afterwards.

There was one present, however – the highest in authority – whose actions and demeanour were calm and unexcited. He seemed to labour under no unusual influence whatever, but evinced a serenity so placid and philosophical that I attributed the silence of the sitting group, and the restraint which curbed in the outbreaking passion of those who *stood*, entirely to his presence. He was a schoolmaster, who taught his daily school in that chapel, and acted also, on Sunday, in the capacity of clerk to the priest – an excellent and amiable old man, who knew little of his illegal connections and atrocious conduct.

When the ceremonies of brotherly recognition and friendship were past, the captain (by which title I shall designate the last mentioned person) stooped, and raising a jar of whiskey on the corner of the altar, held a wine-glass to its neck, which he filled, and, with a calm nod, handed it to me to drink. I shrunk back, with an instinctive horror at the profaneness of such an act, in the house, and on the altar, of God, and peremptorily refused to taste the proffered draught. He smiled mildly at what he considered my superstition, and added quietly, and in a low voice: 'You'll be wantin' it, I'm thinkin', afther the wettin' you got.'

'Wet or dry,' said I –

'Stop, man!' he replied, in the same tone; 'spake low. But why wouldn't you take the whiskey? Sure, there's as holy people to the fore as you; didn't they all take it? An' I wish we may never do worse nor dhrink a harmless glass o' whiskey to keep the cowld out, any way.'

'Well,' said I, 'I'll jist trust to God and the consequences for the cowld, Paddy, *ma bouchal*; but a blessed dhrop of it won't be crossin' my lips, *avich*; so no more *ghosther* about it – dhrink it yourself, if you like. Maybe you want it as much as I do; wherein I've the patthern of a good big coat upon me, so thick, your sowl, that if it was rainin' bullocks a dhrop wouldn't get under the nap of it.'

He gave me a calm but keen glance, as I spoke.

'Well, Jim,' said he, 'it's a good comrade you've got for the weather that's in it; but in the meantime, to set you a dacent patthern, I'll just take this myself' – saying which, with the jar still upon its side, and the forefinger of his left hand in its neck, he swallowed the spirits. 'It's the first I dhrank tonight,' he added, 'nor would I dhrink it now, only to show you that I've heart an' spirit to do the thing that we're all bound an' sworn to, when the proper time comes'; after which he laid down the glass, and turned up the jar, with much coolness, upon the altar.

During our conversation those who had been summoned to this mysterious meeting were pouring in fast; and as each person approached the altar he received from one to two or three glasses of whiskey, according as he chose to limit himself; but, to do them justice, there were not a few of those present who, in spite of their own desire, and the captain's express invitation, refused to taste it in the house of God's worship. Such, however, as were scrupulous he afterwards recommended to take it on the outside of the chapel door, which they did, as, by that means, the sacrilege of the act was supposed to be evaded.

About one o'clock they were all assembled except six; at least, so the captain asserted, on looking at a written paper.

'Now, boys,' said he, in the same low voice, 'we are all present except the thraitors whose names I am goin' to read to you; not that we are to count thim thraitors, till we know whether or not it was in their power to come. Anyhow, the night's terrible – but, boys, you're to know that neither fire nor wather is to prevint yees, when duly summoned to attind a meeting – particularly whin the summons is widout a name, as you have been told that there is always something of consequence to be done *thin*.'

He then read out the names of those who were absent, in order that the real cause of their absence might be ascertained, declaring that they would be dealt with accordingly. After this, with his usual caution, he shut and bolted the door, and having put the key in his pocket, ascended the steps of the altar, and for sometime traversed the little platform, from which the priest usually addresses the congregation.

Until this night I had never contemplated the man's countenance with any particular interest; but as he walked the platform I had an opportunity of observing him more closely. He was slight in person, apparently not thirty; and, on a first view, appeared to have nothing remarkable in his dress or features. I, however, was not the only person whose eyes were fixed upon him at that moment; in fact, everyone present observed him with equal interest, for hitherto he had kept the object of the meeting perfectly secret, and of course we all felt anxious to know it. It was while he traversed the platform that I scrutinized his features with a hope, if possible, to gain from them some evidence of what was passing within him. I could, however, mark but little, and that little was at first rather from the intelligence which seemed to subsist between him and those whom I have already mentioned as *standing* against the altar than from any indication of his own. Their gleaming eyes were fixed upon him with an intensity of savage and demon-like hope which blazed out in flashes of malignant triumph, as, upon turning, he threw a cool but rapid glance at them, to intimate the progress he was making in the subject to which he devoted the undivided energies of his mind. But in the course of his meditation I could observe, on one or two occasions, a dark shade come over his countenance, that contracted his brow into a deep furrow, and it was then for the first time, that

I saw the Satanic expression of which his face, by a very slight motion of its muscles, was capable. His hands, during this silence, closed and opened convulsively; his eyes shot out two or three baleful glances, first to his confederates, and afterwards vacantly into the deep gloom of the lower part of the chapel; his teeth ground against each other like those of a man whose revenge burns to reach a distant enemy, and finally, after having wound himself up to a certain determination, his features relapsed into their original calm and undistorted expression.

At this moment a loud laugh, having something supernatural in it, rang out wildly from the darkness of the chapel: he stopped, and putting his open hand over his brows, peered down into the gloom, and said calmly, in Irish: '*Bee dhu husth; ha nihl anam inh* – hold your tongue, it is not yet the time.'

Every eye was now directed to the same spot, but, in consequence of its distance from the dim light on the altar, none could perceive the person from whom the laugh proceeded. It was, by this time, near two o'clock in the morning.

He now stood for a few moments on the platform, and his chest heaved with a depth of anxiety equal to the difficulty of the design he wished to accomplish.

'Brothers,' said he – 'for we are all brothers – sworn upon all that's blessed an' holy to obey whatever them that's over us, *manin' among ourselves*,[2] wishes us to do – are you now ready, in the name of God, upon whose althar I stand, to fulfil yer oaths?'

The words were scarcely uttered, when those who had *stood* beside the altar during the night sprang from their places, and descending its steps rapidly, turned round, and raising their arms, exclaimed, 'By all that's sacred an' holy, we're willin'.'

In the meantime, those who *sat* upon the steps of the altar instantly rose, and following the example of those who had just spoken, exclaimed after them, 'To be sure – by all that's sacred an' holy, we're willin'.'

'Now, boys,' said the captain, 'ar' n't yees big fools for your pains? an' one of yees doesn't know what I mane.'

'You're our captain,' said one of those who had stood at the altar, 'an' has yer ordhers from higher quarthers; of coorse, whatever ye command upon us we're bound to obey you in.'

'Well,' said he, smiling, 'I only wanted to thry yees; an' by the oath yees tuck, there's not a captain in the county has as good a right to be proud of his min as I have. Well, yees won't rue it, maybe, when the right time comes; and for that same rason every one of yees must have a glass from the jar; thim that won't dhrink it *in* the chapel can dhrink it *widout*; an' here goes to open the door for them.'

He then distributed another glass to every man who would accept it, and brought the jar afterwards to the chapel door, to satisfy the scruples of those who would not drink within. When this was performed, and all duly excited, he proceeded: 'Now, brothers, you are solemnly sworn to obay me, and I'm sure there's no thraithur here that ud parjure himself for a thrifle; but *I'm* sworn to obay them that's above me, manin' still among ourselves; an' to show you that I don't scruple to do it, here goes!'

He then turned round, and taking the Missal between his hands, placed it upon the altar. Hitherto every word was uttered in a low, precautionary tone; but on grasping the book he again turned round, and looking upon his confederates with the same Satanic expression which marked his countenance before, exclaimed, in a voice of deep determination:

'By this sacred an' holy book of God, I will perform the action which we have met this night to accomplish, be that what it may; an' this I swear upon God's book an' God's althar!'

On concluding he struck the book violently with his open hand.

At this moment the candle which burned before him went suddenly out, and the chapel was wrapped in pitchy darkness; the sound as if of rushing wings fell upon our ears, and fifty voices dwelt upon the last words of his oath with wild and supernatural tones, that seemed to echo and to mock what he had sworn. There was a pause, and an exclamation of horror from all present: but the captain was too cool and steady to be disconcerted. He immediately groped about until he got the candle, and proceeding calmly to a remote corner of the chapel, took up a half-burned turf which lay there, and after some trouble, succeeded in lighting it again. He then explained what had taken place; which indeed was easily done, as the candle happened to be extinguished by a pigeon which sat directly above it. The chapel, I should have observed, was at this time, like many country chapels, unfinished inside, and the pigeons of a neighbouring dove-cote had built nests among the rafters of the unceiled roof; which circumstance also explained the rushing of the wings, for the birds had been affrighted by the sudden loudness of the noise. The mocking voices were nothing but the echoes, rendered naturally more awful by the scene, the mysterious object of the meeting, and the solemn hour of the night.

When the candle was again lighted, and these startling circumstances accounted for, the persons whose vengeance had been deepening more and more during the night rushed to the altar in a body, where each, in a voice trembling with passionate eagerness, repeated the oath, and as every word was pronounced, the same echoes heightened the wildness of the horrible ceremony by their long and unearthly tones. The countenances of these human tigers were livid with suppressed rage; their knit brows, compressed lips, and kindled eyes fell under the dim light of the taper with an expression calculated to sicken any heart not absolutely diabolical.

As soon as this dreadful rite was completed we were again startled by several loud bursts of laughter, which proceeded from the lower darkness of the chapel, and the captain, on hearing them, turned to the place, and reflecting for a moment, said in Irish: '*Guisho nish, avohelhee* – come hither now, boys.'

A rush immediately took place from the corner in which they had secreted themselves all the night; and seven men appeared, whom we instantly recognised as brothers and cousins of certain persons who had been convicted, sometime before, for breaking into the house of an honest poor man in the neighbourhood, from whom, after having treated him with barbarous violence, they took away such firearms as he kept for his own protection.

It was evidently not the captain's intention to have produced these persons until the oath should have been generally taken, but the exulting mirth with which they enjoyed the success of his scheme betrayed them, and put him to the necessity of bringing them forward somewhat before the concerted moment.

The scene which now took place was beyond all power of description: peals of wild, fiend-like yells rang through the chapel, as the party which *stood* on the altar, and that which had crouched in the darkness, met; wringing of hands, leaping in triumph, striking of sticks and firearms against the ground and the altar itself, dancing and cracking of fingers, marked the triumph of some hellish determination. Even the captain for a time was unable to restrain their fury; but at length he mounted the platform before the altar once more, and, with a stamp of his foot, recalled their attention to himself and the matter in hand.

'Boys,' said he, 'enough of this, and too much; an' well for us it is that the chapel is in a lonely place, or our foolish noise might do us no good. Let thim that swore so manfully jist now stand a one side, till the rest kiss the book, one by one.'

The proceedings, however, had by this time taken too fearful a shape for even the captain to compel them to a blindfold oath; the first man he called flatly refused to answer until he should hear the nature of the service that was required. This was echoed by the remainder, who, taking courage from the firmness of this person, declared generally that until they first knew the business they were to execute none of them would take the oath. The captain's lip quivered slightly, and his brow again became knit with the same hellish expression, which I have remarked gave him so much the appearance of an embodied fiend; but this speedily passed away, and was succeeded by a malignant sneer, in which lurked, if there ever did in a sneer, 'a laughing devil,' calmly, determinedly atrocious.

'It wasn't worth yer whiles to refuse the oath,' said he, mildly, 'for the truth is, I had next to nothing for yees to do. Not a hand, maybe, would have to *rise*, only jist to look on, an' if any resistance would be made to show yourselves; yer numbers would soon make them see that resistance would be no use whatever in the present case. At all evints, the oath of *secrecy must* be taken, or woe be to him that will refuse *that*; he won't know the day, nor the hour, nor the minute, when he'll be made a spatchcock ov.'

He then turned round, and placing his right hand on the Missal, swore, 'in the presence of God, and before his holy altar, that whatever might take place that night he would keep secret from man or mortal, except the priest, and that neither bribery, nor imprisonment, nor death would wring it from his heart.'

Having done this, he again struck the book violently, as if to confirm the energy with which he swore, and then calmly descending the steps, stood with a serene countenance, like a man conscious of having performed a good action. As this oath did not pledge those who refused to take the other to the perpetration of any specific crime, it was readily taken by all present. Preparations were then made to execute what was intended; the half-burned turf was placed in a little pot; another glass of whiskey was distributed; and the door being locked by the captain, who kept the key as parish clerk and master, the crowd departed silently from the chapel.

The moment those who lay in the darkness during the night made their appearance at the altar, we knew at once the persons we were to visit; for, as I said before, they were related to the miscreants whom one of those persons had convicted, in consequence of their midnight attack upon himself and his family. The captain's object in keeping them unseen was that those present, not being aware of the duty about to be imposed on them, might have less hesitation about swearing to its fulfilment. Our conjectures were correct, for on leaving the chapel we directed our steps to the house in which this devoted man resided.

The night was still stormy, but without rain; it was rather dark, too, though not so as to prevent us from seeing the clouds careering swiftly through the air. The dense curtain which had overhung and obscured the horizon was now broken, and large sections of the sky were clear, and thinly studded with stars that looked dim and watery, as did indeed the whole firmament; for in some places black clouds were still visible, threatening a continuance of tempestuous weather. The road appeared washed and gravelly; every dike was full of yellow water; and every little rivulet and larger stream dashed its hoarse music in our ears; every blast, too, was cold, fierce, and wintry, sometimes driving us back to a standstill, and again, when a turn in the road would bring it in our backs, whirling us along for a few steps with involuntary rapidity. At length the fated dwelling became visible, and a short consultation was held in a sheltered place between the captain and the two parties who seemed so eager for its destruction. The firearms were now loaded, and their bayonets and short pikes, the latter shod and pointed with iron, were also got ready. The live coal which was brought in the small pot had become extinguished; but to remedy this two or three persons from a remote part of the country entered a cabin on the wayside, and under pretence of lighting their own and their comrades' pipes, procured a coal of fire, for so they called a lighted turf. From the time we left the chapel until this moment a profound silence had been maintained, a circumstance which, when I considered the number of persons present, and the mysterious and dreaded object of their journey, had a most appalling effect upon my spirits.

At length we arrived within fifty perches of the house, walking in a compact body, and with as little noise as possible; but it seemed as if the very elements had conspired to frustrate our design, for on advancing within the shade of the farm-hedge, two or three persons found themselves up to the middle in water, and on stooping to ascertain more accurately the state of the place, we could see nothing but one immense sheet of it – spread like a lake over the meadows which surrounded the spot we wished to reach.

Fatal night! The very recollection of it, when associated with the fearful tempests of the elements, grows, if that were possible, yet more wild and revolting. Had we been engaged in any innocent or benevolent enterprise, there was something in our situation just then that had a touch of interest in it to a mind imbued with a relish for the savage beauties of nature. There we stood, about a hundred and thirty in number, our dark forms bent forward, peering into the dusky expanse of water, with its dim gleams of reflected light, broken by the weltering of the mimic waves into ten thousand fragments, whilst the few stars that overhung it in the firmament appeared to shoot through it in broken lines, and to be multiplied fifty-fold in the gloomy mirror on which we gazed.

Over us was a stormy sky, and around us a darkness through which we could only distinguish, in outline, the nearest objects, whilst the wind swept strongly and dismally upon us. When it was discovered that the common pathway to the house was inundated, we were about to abandon our object and return home. The captain, however, stooped down low for a moment, and, almost closing his eyes, looked along the surface of the waters, and then raising himself very calmly, said, in his usual quiet tone: 'Yees needn't go back, boys, I've found a way; jist follow me.'

He immediately took a more circuitous direction, by which we reached a causeway that had been raised for the purpose of giving a free passage to and from the house during such inundations as the present. Along this we had advanced more than half-way, when we discovered a breach in it, which, as afterwards appeared, had that night been made by the strength of the flood. This, by means of our sticks and pikes, we found to be about three feet deep and eight yards broad. Again we were at a loss how to proceed, when the fertile brain of the captain devised a method of crossing it.

'Boys,' said he, 'of coorse you've all played at leap-frog; very well, strip and go in, a dozen of you; lean one upon the back of another from this to the opposite bank, where one must stand facing the outside man, both their shoulders agin one another, that the outside man may be supported. Then *we* can creep over you, an' a dacent bridge you'll be, any way.'

This was the work of only a few minutes, and in less than ten we were all safely over.

Merciful heaven! how I sicken at the recollection of what is to follow! On reaching the dry bank, we proceeded instantly, and in profound silence, to the house; the captain divided us into companies, and then assigned to each division its proper station. The two parties who had been so vindictive all the night he kept about himself; for of those who were present they only were in his confidence, and knew his nefarious purpose; their number was about fifteen. Having made these dispositions, he, at the head of about five of them, approached the house on the windy side, for the fiend possessed a coolness which enabled him to seize upon every possible advantage. That he had combustibles about him was evident, for in less than fifteen minutes nearly one half of the house was enveloped in flames. On seeing this, the others rushed over to the spot where he and his gang were standing, and remonstrated earnestly, but in vain; the flames now burst forth with renewed violence, and as they flung their strong light upon the faces of the foremost group, I think hell itself could hardly present anything more Satanic than their countenances, now worked up into a paroxysm of infernal triumph at their own revenge. The captain's look had lost all its calmness; every feature started into distinct malignity; the curve in his brow was deep, and ran up to the root of the hair, dividing his face into two segments, that did not seem to have been designed for each other. His lips were half open, and the corners of his mouth a little brought back on each side, like those of a man expressing intense hatred and triumph over an enemy who is in the death struggle under his grasp. His eyes blazed from beneath his knit eyebrows with a fire that seemed to be lighted up in the infernal pit itself. It is unnecessary and only painful to describe the rest of his gang; demons might have been proud of such horrible visages as they exhibited: for they worked under all the power of hatred, revenge, and joy; and these passions blended into one terrible scowl, enough almost to blast any human eye that would venture to look upon it.

When the others attempted to intercede for the lives of the inmates, there were at least fifteen guns and pistols levelled at them.

'Another word,' said the captain, 'an' you're a corpse where you stand, or the first man who will dare to spake for them; no, no, it wasn't to spare them we came here. "No mercy" is the password for the night, an' by the sacred oath I swore beyant in the chapel, any one among yees that will attempt to show it will find none at my hand. Surround the house, boys, I tell ye, I hear them stirring. "No quarther – no mercy," is the ordher of the night.'

Such was his command over these misguided creatures, that in an instant there was a ring round the house to prevent the escape of the unhappy inmates, should the raging element give them time to attempt it; for none present durst withdraw themselves from the scene, not only from an apprehension of the captain's present vengeance, or that of his gang, but because they knew that, even had they then escaped, an early and certain death awaited them from a quarter against which they had no means of defence. The hour now was about half-past two o'clock. Scarcely had the last words escaped from the captain's lips when one of the windows of the house was broken, and a human head, having the hair in a blaze, was descried, apparently a woman's, if one might judge by the profusion of burning tresses, and the softness of the tones, notwithstanding that it called, or rather shrieked aloud, for help and mercy. The only reply to this was the whoop from the captain and his gang of 'No mercy – no mercy!' and that instant the former and one of the latter rushed to the spot, and ere the action could be perceived the head was transfixed with a bayonet and a pike, both having entered it together. The word mercy was divided in her mouth; a short silence ensued; the head hung down on the window, but was instantly tossed back into the flames!

This action occasioned a cry of horror from all present except the gang and their leader, which startled and enraged the latter so much that he ran towards one of them, and had his bayonet, now reeking with the blood of its innocent victim, raised to plunge it in his body, when, dropping the point, he said, in a piercing whisper, that hissed in the ears of all: 'It's no use *now*, you know; if one's to hang, all will hang; so our safest way, you persave, is to leave none of them to tell the story. Ye *may* go now, if you wish; but it won't save a hair of your heads. You cowardly set! I knew if I had tould yees the sport, that none of yees, except my *own* boys, would come, so I jist played a thrick upon you; but remimber what you are sworn to, and stand to the oath ye tuck.'

Unhappily, notwithstanding the wetness of the preceding weather, the materials of the house were extremely combustible; the whole dwelling was now one body of glowing flame, yet the shouts and shrieks within rose awfully above its crackling and the voice of the storm, for the wind once more blew in gusts and with great violence. The doors and windows were all torn open, and such of those within as had escaped the flames rushed towards them, for the purpose of further escape, and of claiming mercy at the hands of their destroyers; but whenever they appeared the unearthly cry of 'NO MERCY' rung upon their ears for a moment, and for a moment only, for they were flung back at the points of the weapons which the demons had brought with them to make the work of vengeance more certain.

As yet there were many persons in the house whose cry for life was as strong as despair, and who clung to it with all the awakened powers of reason and instinct. The ear of man could hear nothing so strongly calculated to stifle the demon of cruelty and revenge within him as the long and wailing shrieks which rose beyond the elements in tones that were carried off rapidly upon the blast, until they died away in the darkness that lay behind the surrounding hills. Had not the house been in a solitary situation, and the hour the dead of night, any person sleeping within a moderate distance must have heard them, for such a cry of sorrow rising into a yell of despair was almost sufficient to have awakened the dead. It was lost, however, upon the hearts and ears that heard it: to them, though in justice be it said, to only comparatively a few of them, it was as delightful as the tones of soft and entrancing music.

The claims of the surviving sufferers were now modified; they supplicated merely to suffer death *by the weapons of their enemies*; they were willing to bear that, provided they should be allowed to escape from the flames; but no – the horrors of the conflagration were calmly and malignantly gloried in by their merciless assassins, who deliberately flung them back into all their tortures. In the course of a few minutes a man appeared upon the side-wall of the house nearly naked; his figure, as he stood against the sky in horrible relief, was so finished a picture of woe-begone agony and supplication that it is yet as distinct in my memory as if I were again present at the scene. Every muscle, now in motion by the powerful agitation of his sufferings, stood out upon his limbs and neck, giving him an appearance of desperate strength, to which by this time he must have been wrought up; the perspiration poured from his frame, and the veins and arteries of his neck were inflated to a surprising thickness. Every moment he looked down into the flames which were rising to where he stood; and as he looked the indescribable horror which flitted over his features might have worked upon the devil himself to relent. His words were few.

'My child,' said he, 'is still safe; she is an infant, a young crathur that never harmed you nor any one – she is still safe. Your mothers, your wives, have young innocent childhre like it. Oh, spare her; think for a moment that it's one of your own: spare it, as you hope to meet a just God, or if you don't, in mercy shoot me first – put an end to me before I see her burned!'

The captain approached him coolly and deliberately. 'You'll prosecute no one now, you bloody informer,' said he: 'you'll convict no more boys for takin' an ould gun an' pistol from you, or for givin' you a neighbourly knock or two into the bargain.'

Just then, from a window opposite him, proceeded the shrieks of a woman, who appeared at it with the infant in her arms. She herself was almost scorched to death; but, with the presence of mind and humanity of her sex, she was about to put the little babe out of the window. The captain noticed this, and, with characteristic atrocity, thrust, with a sharp bayonet, the little innocent, along with the person who endeavoured to rescue it, into the red flames, where they both perished. This was the work of an instant. Again he approached the man. 'Your child is a coal now,' said he, with deliberate mockery; 'I pitched it in myself, on the point of this' – showing the weapon – 'an' now is your turn' – saying which he clambered up, by the assistance of his gang, who stood with a front of pikes and bayonets bristling to receive the wretched man, should he

129

attempt, in his despair, to throw himself from the wall. The captain got up, and placing the point of his bayonet against his shoulder, flung him into the fiery element that raged behind him. He uttered one wild and terrific cry as he fell back, and no more. After this nothing was heard but the crackling of the fire and the rushing of the blast: all that had possessed life within were consumed, amounting either to eleven or fifteen persons.

When this was accomplished, those who took an active part in the murder stood for some time about the conflagration; and as it threw its red light upon their fierce faces and rough persons, soiled as they now were with smoke and black streaks of ashes, the scene seemed to be changed to hell, the murderers to spirits of the damned, rejoicing over the arrival and the torture of some guilty soul. The faces of those who kept aloof from the slaughter were blanched to the whiteness of death: some of them fainted, and others were in such agitation that they were compelled to lean on their comrades. They became actually powerless with horror; yet to such a scene were they brought by the pernicious influence of Ribbonism.

It was only when the last victim went down that the conflagration shot up into the air with the most unbounded fury. The house was large, deeply thatched, and well furnished; and the broad red pyramid rose up with fearful magnificence towards the sky. Abstractedly it had sublimity, but now it was associated with nothing in my mind but blood and terror. It was not, however, without a purpose that the captain and his gang stood to contemplate its effect. 'Boys,' said he, 'we had better be sartin that all's safe; who knows but there might be some of the sarpents crouchin' under a hape o' rubbish, to come out an' gibbet us to-morrow or next day; we had betther wait awhile, anyhow, if it was only to see the blaze.'

Just then the flames rose majestically to a surprising height. Our eyes followed their direction; and we perceived, for the first time, that the dark clouds above, together with the intermediate air, appeared to reflect back, or rather to have caught, the red hue of the fire. The hills and country about us appeared with an alarming distinctness; but the most picturesque part of it was the effect or reflection of the blaze on the floods that spread over the surrounding plains. These, in fact, appeared to be one broad mass of liquid copper, for the motion of the breaking waters caught from the blaze of the high waving column, as reflected in them, a glaring light, which eddied, and rose, and fluctuated as if the flood itself had been a lake of molten fire.

Fire, however, destroys rapidly. In a short time the flames sank – became weak and flickering – by-and-by they shot out only in fits – the crackling of the timbers died away – the surrounding darkness deepened – and, ere long, the faint light was overpowered by the thick volumes of smoke that rose from the ruins of the house and its murdered inhabitants.

'Now, boys,' said the captain, 'all is safe – we may go. Remember, every man of you, what you've sworn this night on the book an' altar of God – not on a heretic Bible. If you perjure yourselves you may hang us; but let me tell you, for your comfort, that if you do, there is them livin' that will take care the lase of your own lives will be but short.'

After this we dispersed every man to his own home.

Reader, not many months elapsed ere I saw the bodies of this captain, whose name was Patrick Devann, and all those who were actively concerned in the perpetration of this deed of horror, withering in the wind, where they hung gibbeted near the scene of their nefarious villainy; and while I inwardly thanked heaven for my own narrow and almost undeserved escape, I thought in my heart how seldom, even in this world, justice fails to overtake the murderer, and to enforce the righteous judgment of God – that 'whoso sheddeth man's blood, by man shall his blood be shed.'

1. How are you?
2. In opposition to the constituted authorities.

131

CONDY CULLEN AND THE GAUGER

By WILLIAM CARLETON

Young Condy Cullen was descended from a long line of private distillers, and, of course, exhibited in his own person all the practical wit, sagacity, cunning, and fertility of invention, which the natural genius of the family, sharpened by long experience, had created from generation to generation, as a standing capital to be handed down from father to son. There was scarcely a trick, evasion, plot, scheme, or manoeuvre that had ever been resorted to by his ancestors, that Condy had not at his finger ends; and though but a lad of sixteen at the time we present him to the reader, yet be it observed that he had his mind, even at that age, admirably trained, by four or five years of keen, vigorous practice, in all the resources necessary to meet the subtle vigilance and stealthy circumvention of that prowling animal – a gauger. In fact, Condy's talents did not merely consist of an acquaintance with the hereditary tricks of his family. These, of themselves, would prove but a miserable defence against the ever varying ingenuity with which the progressive skill of the still-hunter masks his approaches and conducts his designs. On the contrary, every new plan of the gauger must be met and defeated by a counterplan equally novel, but with this difference in the character of both, that whereas the exciseman's devices are the result of mature deliberation, Paddy's, from the very nature of the circumstances, must be necessarily extemporaneous and rapid. The hostility between the parties, being, as it is, carried on through such varied stratagem on both sides, and characterized by such adroit and able duplicity, by so many quick and unexpected turns of incident – it would be utter fatuity in either to rely upon obsolete tricks and stale manoeuvres. Their relative position and occupation do not, therefore, merely exhibit a contest between Law and that mountain nymph, Liberty, or between the Excise Board and the Smuggler – it presents a more interesting point for observation, namely, the struggle between mind and mind, between wit and wit, between roguery and knavery.

It might be very amusing to detail, from time to time, a few of those keen encounters of practical cunning which take place between the poteen distiller and his lynx-eyed foe, the gauger. They are curious, as throwing light upon the national character of our people, and as evidence of the surprising readiness of wit, fertility of invention, and irresistible humour which they mix up with almost every actual concern of life, no matter how difficult or critical it may be. Nay, it mostly happens that the character of the peasant in all its fulness rises in proportion to what he is called upon to encounter; and that the laugh at, or the hoax upon, the gauger keeps pace with the difficulty that is overcome. But now to our short story.

Two men, in the garb of gentlemen, were riding along a remote by-road, one morning in the month of October, about the year 1827 or '28, I am not certain which. The air was remarkably clear, keen, and bracing; a hoar frost for the few preceding nights had set in, and then lay upon the fields about them, melting gradually, however, as the sun got strength, with the exception of the sides of such hills and valleys as his beams could not reach, until evening chilled their influence too much to absorb the feathery whiteness which covered them. Our equestrians had nearly reached a turn in the way, which, we should observe in this place, skirted the brow of a small declivity that lay on the right. In point of fact, it was a moderately inclined plane or slope rather than a declivity; but be this as it may, the flat at its foot was studded over with furze bushes, which grew so close and level that a person might almost imagine it possible to walk upon their surface. On coming within about two hundred and fifty yards of this angle, the horsemen noticed a lad not more than sixteen jogging on towards them with a keg upon his back. The eye of one of them was immediately lit with that vivacious sparkling of habitual sagacity which marks the practised gauger among ten thousand. For a single moment he drew up his horse – an action which, however slight in itself, intimated more plainly than he could have wished the obvious interest which had just been excited in him. Short as was the pause, it betrayed him, for no sooner had the lad noticed it, than he crossed the ditch and disappeared round the angle we have mentioned, and upon the side of the declivity. To gallop to the spot, dismount, cross the ditch also, and pursue him, was only the work of a few minutes.

'We have him,' said the gauger, 'we have him – one thing is clear, that he cannot escape us.'

'Speak for yourself, Stinton,' replied his companion; 'as for me, not being an officer of his majesty's excise, I decline taking any part in the pursuit; it is a fair battle, so fight it out between you – I am with you now only through curiosity.' He had scarcely concluded, when they heard a voice singing the following lines, in a spirit of that hearty hilarity which betokens a cheerful contempt of care, and an utter absence of all apprehension:

> 'Oh! Jemmy, she sez, you are my true lover,
> You are all the riches that I do adore;
> I solemnly swear now, I'll ne'er have anoder,
> My heart it is fixed to never love more.'

The music then changed to a joyous whistle, and immediately they were confronted by a lad, dressed in an old red coat, patched with gray frieze, who, on seeing them, exhibited in his features a most ingenuous air of natural surprise. He immediately ceased to whistle, and with every mark of respect, putting his hand to his hat, said in a voice, the tones of which spoke of kindness and deference:

'God save ye, gintlemen.'

'I say, my lad,' said the gauger, 'where is that customer with the keg on his back? – he crossed over there this moment.'

'When? – where, sir?' said the lad, with a stare of surprise.

'Where? – when? – why, this minute, and in this place.'

'And was it a whiskey keg, sir?'

'Sir, I am not here to be examined by you,' replied Stinton; 'confound me, if the conniving young rascal is not sticking me into a cross-examination already. I say, red coat, where is the boy with the keg?'

'As for a boy, I did see a boy, sir; but the never a keg he had – hadn't he a gray frieze coat, sir?'

'He had.'

'And wasn't it a dauny bit short about the skirts, plase your honor?'

'Again he's at me. Sirrah, unless you tell me where he is in half a second, I shall lay my whip to your shoulders!'

'The sorra keg I seen, then, sir; the last keg I seen was – '

'Did you see a boy without a keg, answering to the description I gave you?'

'You gave no description of it, sir; but even if you did, when I didn't see it, how can I tell your honor anything about it?'

'Where is the fellow, you villain,' exclaimed the gauger, in a fury – 'where is he gone to? You admit you saw him; as for the keg, it cannot be far from us; but where is he?'

''Dad, I saw a boy, with a short frieze coat upon him, crassing the road there below, and runnin' down the other side of that ditch.'

This was too palpable a lie to stand the test even of a glance at the ditch in question, which was nothing more than a slight mound that ran down along a lea field, on which there was not even the appearance of a shrub.

The gauger looked at his companion, then turning to the boy – 'Come, come, my lad,' said he, 'you know that lie is rather cool. Don't you feel in your soul that a rat could not have gone in that direction without our seeing it?'

'Bedad, an' I saw him,' returned the lad; 'wid a gray coat upon him, that was a little too short in the tail; it's better than half an hour agone.'

'The boy I speak of you must have met,' said Stinton; 'it's not five minutes – no, not more than three – since he came inside the field.'

'That my feet may grow to the ground, then, if I seen a boy, in or about this place, widin that time barrin' myself.'

The gauger eyed him closely for a short space, and pulling out half-a-crown, said: 'Harkee, my lad, a word with you in private.'

The fact is, that during the latter part of this dialogue the worthy exciseman observed the cautious distance at which the boy kept himself from the grasp of him and his companion. A suspicion consequently began to dawn upon him that, in defiance of appearances, the lad himself might be the actual smuggler. On reconsidering the matter, this suspicion almost amounted to certainty; the time was too short to permit even the most ingenious cheat to render himself and his keg invisible in a manner so utterly unaccountable. On the other hand, when he reflected on the open, artless character of the boy's song; the capricious change to a light-hearted whistle; the surprise so naturally, and the respect so deferentially expressed, joined to the dissimilarity of dress, he was confounded again, and scarcely knew on which side to determine. Even the lad's reluctance to approach him might proceed from fear of the whip. He felt resolved, however, to ascertain this point, and, with the view of getting the lad into his hands, he showed him half-a-crown, and addressed him as already stated.

The lad, on seeing the money, appeared to be instantly caught by it, and approached him, as if it had been a bait he could not resist – a circumstance which again staggered the gauger. In a moment, however, he seized him.

'Come, now,' said he, unbuttoning his coat, 'you will oblige me by stripping.'

'And why so?' said the lad, with a face which might have furnished a painter or sculptor with a perfect notion of curiosity, perplexity, and wonder.

'Why so?' replied Stinton; 'we shall see – we shall soon see.'

'Surely you don't think I've hid the keg about me?' said the other, his features now relaxing into an appearance of such utter simplicity as would have made any other man but a gauger give up the examination as hopeless, and exonerate the boy from any participation whatsoever in the transaction.

'No, no,' replied the gauger; 'by no means, you young rascal. See here, Cartwright,' he continued, addressing his companion – 'the keg, my precious,' again turning to the lad. 'Oh! no, no, it would be cruel to suspect you of anything but the purest simplicity.'

'Look here, Cartwright' – having stripped the boy of his coat and turned it inside out, 'there's a coat – there's thrift – there's economy for you. Come, sir, tuck on, tuck on instantly; here, I shall assist you – up with your arms, straighten your neck; it will be both straightened and stretched yet, my cherub. What think you now, Cartwright? Did you ever see a metamorphosis in your life so quick, complete, and unexpected?'

His companion was certainly astonished in no small degree, on seeing the red coat, when turned, become a comfortable gray frieze; one precisely such as he who bore the keg had on. Nay, after surveying his person and dress a second time, he instantly recognized him as the same.

The only interest, we should observe, which this gentleman had in the transaction, arose from the mere gratification which a keen observer of character, gifted with a strong relish for humour, might be supposed to feel. The gauger, in sifting the matter, and scenting the trail of the keg, was now in his glory, and certainly when met by so able an opponent as our friend Condy (for it was, indeed, himself) furnished a very rich treat to his friend.

'Now,' he continued, addressing the boy again, 'lose not a moment in letting us know where you've hid the keg.'

'The sorra bit of it I hid – it fell aff o' me, an' I lost it; sure I'm lookin' afther it myself, so I am'; and he moved over while speaking, as if pretending to search for it in a thin hedge, which could by no means conceal it.

'Cartwright,' said the gauger, 'did you ever see anything so perfect as this, so ripe a rascal? – you don't understand him now. Here, you simpleton: harkee, sirrah, there must be no playing the lapwing with me; back here to the same point. We may lay it down as a sure thing that whatever direction he takes from this spot is the wrong one; so back here, you, sir, till we survey the premises about us for your traces.'

The boy walked sheepishly back, and appeared to look about him for the keg, with a kind of earnest stupidity which was altogether inimitable.

'I say, my boy,' asked Stinton, ironically, 'don't you look rather foolish now? Can you tell your right hand from your left?'

'I can,' replied Condy, holding up his left, 'there's my right hand.'

'And what do you call the other?' said Cartwright.

'My left, bedad, anyhow, an' that's true enough.'

Both gentlemen laughed heartily.

'But it's carrying the thing a little *too far*,' said the gauger; 'in the meantime let us hear how you prove it.'

'Aisy enough, sir,' replied Condy, 'bekase I am left-handed; this,' holding up the left, 'is the right hand to me, whatever you may say to the conthrary.'

Condy's countenance expanded, after he had spoken, into a grin so broad and full of grotesque sarcasm, that Stinton and his companion both found their faces, in spite of them, get rather blank under its influences.

'What the deuce!' exclaimed the gauger, 'are we to be here all day? Come, sir, bring us at once to the keg.'

He was here interrupted by a laugh from Cartwright, so vociferous, long, and hearty, that he looked at him with amazement. 'Hey, dey,' he exclaimed, 'what's the matter, what's the matter; what new joke is this?'

For some minutes, however, he could not get a word from the other, whose laughter appeared as if never to end; he walked to and fro in absolute convulsions, bending his body and clapping his hands together with a vehemence quite unintelligible.

'What is it, man?' said the other; 'confound you, what is it?'

'Oh!' replied Cartwright, 'I am sick; perfectly feeble.'

'You have it to yourself, at all events,' observed Stinton.

'And shall keep it to myself,' said Cartwright; 'for, if your sagacity is overreached, you must be contented to sit down under defeat. I won't interfere.'

Now, in this contest between the gauger and Condy, even so slight a thing as one glance of an eye by the latter might have given a proper cue to an opponent so sharp as Stinton. Condy, during the whole dialogue, consequently preserved the most vague and undefinable visage imaginable, except in the matter of his distinction between right and left; and Stinton, who watched his eye with the shrewdest vigilance, could make nothing of it. Not so was it between him and Cartwright; for during the closing paroxysms of his mirth Stinton caught his eye fixed upon a certain mark, barely visible, upon the hoar-frost, which mark extended down to the furze bushes that grew at the foot of the slope where they then stood.

As a stanch old hound lays his nose to the trail of a hare or fox, so did the gauger pursue the trace of the keg down the little hill; for the fact was, that Condy, having no other resource, trundled it off towards the furze, into which it settled perfectly to his satisfaction; and, with all the quickness of youth and practice, instantly turned his coat, which had been made purposely for such rencounters. This accomplished, he had barely time to advance a few yards round the angle of the hedge, and changing his whole manner, as well as his appearance, acquitted himself as the reader has already seen. That he could have carried the keg down to the cover, then conceal it, and return to the spot where they met him, was utterly beyond the reach of human exertion, so that in point of fact they never could have suspected that the whiskey lay in such a place.

The triumph of the gauger was now complete, and a complacent sense of his own sagacity sat visibly on his features. Condy's face, on the other hand, became considerably lengthened, and appeared quite as rueful and mortified as the other's was joyous and confident.

'Who's sharpest now, my knowing one?' said he. 'Whom is the laugh against, as matters stand between us?'

'The sorra give you good of it,' said Condy, sulkily.

'What is your name?' inquired Stinton.

'Barney Keerigan's my name,' replied the other, indignantly; 'and I'm not ashamed of it, nor afeard to tell it to you or any man.'

'What, of the Keerigans of Killoghan?'

'Ay, jist, of the Keerigans of Killoghan.'

'I know the family,' said Stinton; 'they are decent *in their way*; – but, come, my lad, don't lose your temper, and answer me another question. Where were you bringing this whiskey?'

'To a betther man than ever stud in your shoes,' replied Condy, in a tone of absolute defiance – 'to a gintleman, anyway,' with a peculiar emphasis on the word gintleman.

'But what's his name?'

'Mr Stinton's his name – Gauger Stinton.'

The shrewd exciseman stood and fixed his keen eye on Condy for upwards of a minute, with a glance of such piercing scrutiny as scarcely any consciousness of imposture could withstand.

Condy, on the other hand, stood and eyed him with an open, unshrinking, yet angry glance; never winced, but appeared, by the detection of his keg, to have altogether forgotten the line of cunning policy he had previously adopted, in a mortification which had predominated over duplicity and art.

He is now speaking truth, thought the gauger; he has lost his temper, and is completely off his guard.

'Well, my lad,' he continued, 'that is very good so far; but who sent the keg to Stinton?'

'Do you think,' said Condy, with a look of strong contempt at the gauger, for deeming him so utterly silly as to tell him, 'do you think you can make me turn informer? There's none of that blood in me, thank goodness.'

'Do you know Stinton?'

'How could I know the man I never seen?' replied Condy, still out of temper; 'but one thing I don't know, gintlemen, and that is, whether you have any right to take my whiskey or not.'

'As to that, my good lad, make your mind easy; I'm Stinton.'

'You, sir!' said Condy, with well-feigned surprise.

'Yes,' replied the other, 'I'm the very man you were bringing the keg to. And now I'll tell you what you must do for me; proceed to my house with as little delay as possible; ask to see my daughter – ask to see Miss Stinton; take this key and desire her to have the keg put into the cellar; she'll know the key, and let it also be as a token that she is to give you your breakfast; say I desire that keg to be placed to the right of the five-gallon one I seized on Thursday last, that stands on a little stillion under my blunderbuss.'

'Of coorse,' said Condy, who appeared to have misgivings on the matter, 'I suppose I must; but somehow – '

'Why, sirrah, what do you grumble now for?'

Condy still eyed him with suspicion. 'And, sir,' said he, after having once more mounted the keg, 'am I to get nothing for such a weary trudge as I had wid it but my breakfast?'

'Here,' said Stinton, throwing him half-a-crown, 'take that along with it, and now be off – or stop, Cartwright, will you dine with me today, and let us broach the keg? I'll guarantee its excellence, for this is not the first I have got from the same quarter, that's *entre nous*.'

'With all my heart,' replied Cartwright, 'upon the terms you say, that of the broach.'

'Then, my lad,' said Stinton, 'say to my daughter that a friend, perhaps a friend or two, will dine with me to-day – that is enough.'

They then mounted their horses, and were proceeding as before, when Cartwright addressed the gauger as follows: 'Do you not put this lad, Stinton, in a capacity to overreach you yet?'

'No,' replied the other; 'the young rascal spoke the truth after the discovery of the keg; for he lost his temper, and was no longer cool.'

'For my part, hang me if I'd trust him.'

'I should scruple to do so myself,' replied the gauger, 'but, as I said, these Keerigans – notorious illicit fellows, by the way – send me a keg or two every year, and almost about this very time. Besides, I read him to the heart and he never winced. Yes, decidedly, the whiskey was for me; of that I have no doubt whatsoever.'

'I most positively would not trust him.'

'Not that perhaps I ought,' said Stinton, 'on second thought, to place such confidence in a lad who acted so adroitly in the beginning. Let us call him back and re-examine him at all events.'

Now Condy had, during this conversation, been discussing the very same point with himself.

'Bad cess forever attend you, Stinton, agra,' he exclaimed, 'for there's surely something *over you* – a lucky shot from behind a hedge, or a break-neck fall down a cliff, or something of that kind. If the ould boy hadn't his croubs hard and fast in you, you wouldn't let me walk away wid the whiskey, anyhow. Bedad, it's well I thought o' the Keerigans; for sure enough I did hear Barney say that he was to send a keg in to him this week, some day, – and he didn't think I knew him aither. Faix it's many a long day since I knew the sharp *puss* of him, wid an eye like a hawk. But what if they folly me and do up all? Anyway, I'll prevint them from having suspicion on me, before I go a toe farther, the ugly rips.'

He instantly wheeled about a moment or two before Stinton and Cartwright had done the same, for the purpose of sifting him still more thoroughly – so that they found him meeting them.

'Gintlemen,' said he, 'how do I know that aither of you is Mr Stinton, or that the house you directed me to is his? I know that if the whiskey doesn't go to him I may lave the counthry.'

'You are either a deeper rogue or a more stupid fool than I took you to be,' observed Stinton; 'but what security can you give us that you will leave the keg safely at its destination?'

'If I thought you were Mr Stinton I'd be very glad to lave you the whiskey where it is, and even do widout my breakfast. Gintlemen, tell me truth, bekase I'd only be murdhered out of the face.'

'Why, you idiot,' said the gauger, losing his temper and suspicion both together, 'can't you go to the town and inquire where Mr Stinton lives?'

'Bedad, thin, thrue enough, I never thought of that at all at all; but I beg your pardon, gintlemen, an' I hope you won't be angry wid me, in regard that it's kilt and quartered I'd be if I let myself be made a fool of by anybody.'

'Do what I desire you,' said the exciseman; 'inquire for Mr Stinton's house, and you may be sure the whiskey will reach him.'

'Thank you, sir. Bedad, I might have thought of that myself.'

This last clause, which was spoken in a soliloquy, would have deceived a saint himself.

'Now,' said Stinton, after they had recommenced their journey, 'are you satisfied?'

'I am at length,' said Cartwright; 'if his intentions had been dishonest, instead of returning to make himself certain against being deceived, he would have made the best of his way from us – a rogue never wantonly puts himself in the way of danger or detection.'

That evening, about five o'clock, Stinton, Cartwright, and two others arrived at the house of the worthy gauger, to partake of his good cheer. A cold frosty evening gave a peculiar zest to the comfort of a warm room, a blazing fire, and a good dinner. No sooner were the viands discussed, the cloth removed, and the glasses ready, than the generous host desired his daughter to assist the servant in broaching the redoubtable keg.

'That keg, my dear,' he proceeded, 'which the country lad, who brought the key of the cellar, left here today.'

'A keg!' repeated the daughter, with surprise.

'Yes, Maggy, my love, a keg; I said so, I think.'

'But, papa, there came no keg today!'

The gauger and Cartwright both groaned in unison.

'No keg!' said the gauger.

'No keg!' echoed Cartwright.

'No keg! indeed,' re-echoed Miss Stinton; – 'but there came a country boy with the key of the cellar, as a token that he was to get the five-gallon – '

'Oh!' groaned the gauger, 'I'm knocked up, outwitted, – oh!'

'Bought and sold,' added Cartwright.

'Go on,' said the gauger, 'I must hear it out.'

'As a token,' proceeded Miss Stinton, 'that he was to get the five-gallon keg on the little stillion, under the blunderbuss, for Captain Dalton.'

'And he got it?'

'Yes, sir, he got it; for I took the key as a sufficient token.'

'But, Maggy – hell and fury, hear me, child, surely he brought a keg here and left it; and of course it's in the cellar?'

'No, indeed, papa, he brought no keg here; but he did bring the five-gallon one that *was* in the cellar away with him.'

'Stinton,' said Cartwright, 'send round the bottle.'

'The rascal,' ejaculated the gauger, 'we shall drink his health.' And on relating the circumstances, the company drank the sheepish lad's health, that bought and sold the gauger.

THE CURSE [1]

By WILLIAM CARLETON

When he had been *keened* in the street, there being no hearse, the coffin was placed upon two handspikes which were fixed across, but parallel to each other, under it. These were borne by four men, one at the end of each, with the point of it touching his body a little below his stomach; in other parts of Ireland the coffin is borne on the shoulders, but this is more convenient and less distressing.

When we got out upon the road the funeral was of great extent – for Kelly had been highly respected. On arriving at the *merin* which bounded the land he had owned, the coffin was laid down, and a loud and wailing *keena* took place over it. It was again raised, and the funeral proceeded in a direction which I was surprised to see it take, and it was not until an acquaintance of my brother's had explained the matter that I understood the cause of it. In Ireland, when a murder is perpetrated, it is usual, as the funeral proceeds to the graveyard, to bring the corpse to the house of him who committed the crime, and lay it down at his door, while the relations of the deceased kneel down, and, with an appalling solemnity, utter the deepest imprecations, and invoke the justice of Heaven on the head of the murderer. This, however, is usually omitted if the residence of the criminal be completely out of the line of the funeral, but if it be possible, by any circuit, to approach it, this dark ceremony is never omitted. In cases where the crime is doubtful, or unjustly imputed, those who are thus visited come out, and laying their right hand upon the coffin, protest their innocence of the blood of the deceased, calling God to witness the truth of their asseverations; but in cases where the crime is clearly proved against the murderer, the door is either closed, the ceremony repelled by violence, or the house abandoned by the inmates until the funeral passes.

The death of Kelly, however, could not be actually, or, at least, directly, considered a murder, for it was probable that Grimes did not inflict the stroke with an intention of taking away his life, and besides, Kelly survived it four months. Grimes' house was not more than fifteen perches from the road; and when the corpse was opposite the little bridle-way that led up to it, they laid it down for a moment, and the relations of Kelly surrounded it, offering up a short prayer, with uncovered heads. It was then borne towards the house, whilst the *keening* commenced in a loud wailing cry, accompanied with clapping of hands, and every other symptom of external sorrow. But, independent of their compliance with this ceremony as an old usage, there is little doubt that the appearance of anything connected with the man who certainly occasioned Kelly's death awoke a keener and more intense sorrow for his loss. The wailing was thus continued until the coffin was laid opposite Grimes' door; nor did it cease then, but, on the contrary, was renewed with louder and more bitter lamentations.

As the multitude stood compassionating the affliction of the widow and orphans, it was the most impressive and solemn spectacle that could be witnessed. The very house seemed to have a condemned look; and, as a single wintry breeze waved a tuft of long grass that grew on a seat of turf at the side of the door, it brought the vanity of human enmity before my mind with melancholy force. When the *keening* ceased, Kelly's wife, with her children, knelt, their faces towards the house of their enemy, and invoked, in the strong language of excited passion, the justice of Heaven upon the head of the man who had left her a widow, and her children fatherless. I was anxious to know if Grimes would appear to disclaim the intention of murder; but I understood that he was at market – for it happened to be market day.

'Come out!' said the widow – 'come out and look at the sight that's here before you! Come and view *your own work*! Lay but your hand upon the coffin, and the blood of him that you murdhered will spout, before God and these Christhen people, in your guilty face! But, oh! may the Almighty God bring *this home to you*![2] – May you never lave this life, John Grimes, till worse nor has overtaken me and mine falls upon you and yours! May our curse light upon you this day; – the curse, I say, of the widow and the orphans, and that your bloody hand has made us, may it blast you! May you and all belonging to you wither off the 'arth! Night and day, sleeping and waking, – like snow off the ditch may you melt, until your name and your place will be disremimbered, except to be cursed by them that will hear of you and your hand of murdher! Amin, we pray God this day! – and the widow and orphan's prayer will not fall to the ground while your guilty head is above. Childher, did you all say it?'

At this moment a deep, terrific murmur, or rather ejaculation, corroborative of assent to this dreadful imprecation, pervaded the crowd in a fearful manner; their countenances darkened, their eyes gleamed, and their scowling visages stiffened into an expression of determined vengeance.

When these awful words were uttered, Grimes' wife and daughters approached the window in tears, sobbing, at the same time, loudly and bitterly.

'You're wrong,' said the wife – 'you're wrong, Widow Kelly, in saying that my husband *murdhered* him! he did not murdher him; for, when you and yours were far from him, I heard John Grimes declare, before the God who's to judge him, that he had no thought or intention of taking his life; he struck him in anger, and the blow did him an injury that was not intended. Don't curse him, Honor Kelly,' said she – 'don't curse him so fearfully; but, above all, don't curse me and my innocent childher, for *we* never harmed you, nor wished you ill! *But it was this party work did it*! Oh! my God!' she exclaimed, wringing her hands, in utter bitterness of spirit, 'when will it be ended between friends and neighbours, that ought to live in love and kindness together, instead of fighting in this bloodthirsty manner!'

She then wept more violently, as did her daughters.

'May God give me mercy in the last day, Mrs Kelly, as I pity from my heart and soul you and your orphans,' she continued; 'but don't curse us, for the love of God – for you know we should forgive our enemies, as we ourselves, that are the enemies of God, hope to be forgiven.'

'May God forgive me, then, if I have wronged you or your husband,' said the widow, softened by their distress; 'but you know that, whether he intended his life or not, the stroke he gave him has left my childher without a father, and myself dissolate. Oh, heavens above me!' she exclaimed, in a scream of distraction and despair, 'is it possible – is it thrue – that my manly husband, the best father that ever breathed the breath of life, my own Denis, is lying dead – murdhered before my eyes! Put your hands on my head, some of you – put your hands on my head, or it will go to pieces. Where are you, Denis, where are you, the strong of hand, and the tender of heart? Come to me, darling, I want you in my distress. I want comfort, Denis; and I'll take it from none but yourself, for kind was your word to me in all my afflictions!'

All present were affected; and, indeed, it was difficult to say whether Kelly's wife or Grimes' was more to be pitied at the moment. The affliction of the latter and of her daughters was really pitiable: their sobs were loud, and the tears streamed down their cheeks like rain. When the widow's exclamations had ceased, or rather were lost in the loud cry of sorrow which was uttered by the *keeners* and friends of the deceased, they, too, standing somewhat apart from the rest, joined in it bitterly;

and the solitary wail of Mrs Grimes, differing in character from that of those who had been trained to modulate the most profound grief into strains of a melancholy nature, was particularly wild and impressive. At all events, her Christian demeanor, joined to the sincerity of her grief, appeased the enmity of many; so true is it that a soft answer turneth away wrath. I could perceive, however, that the resentment of Kelly's male relations did not at all appear to be in any degree moderated.

1. From 'Party Fight and Funeral'.
2. Does not this usage illustrate the proverb of the guilt being brought home to a man when there is no doubt of his criminality?

THE BATTLE OF THE FACTIONS

By WILLIAM CARLETON
(*Composed into Narrative by a Hedge Schoolmaster*)

'My grandfather, Connor O'Callaghan, though a tall, erect man, with white flowing hair, like snow, that falls profusely about his broad shoulders, is now in his eighty-third year; an amazing age, considhering his former habits. His countenance is still marked with honesty and traces of hard fighting, and his cheeks ruddy and cudgel-worn; his eyes, though not as black as they used to be, have lost very little of that nate fire which characterizes the eyes of the O'Callaghans, and for which I myself have been – but my modesty won't allow me to allude to that: let it be sufficient for the present to say that there never was remembered so handsome a man in his native parish, and that I am as like him as one Corkred phatie is to another; indeed, it has been often said that it would be hard to meet an O'Callaghan without a black eye in his head. He has lost his fore-teeth, however, a point in which, unfortunately, I, though his grandson, have a strong resemblance to him. The truth is, they were knocked out of him in rows, before he had reached his thirty-fifth year – a circumstance which the kind reader will be pleased to receive in extenuation for the same defect in myself. That, however, is but a trifle, which never gave either of us much trouble.

'It pleased Providence to bring us through many hair-breadth escapes with our craniums uncracked; and when we

151

consider that he, on taking a retrogradation of his past life, can indulge in the plasing recollection of having broken two skulls in his fighting days, and myself one, I think we have both rason to be thankful. He was a powerful *bulliah batthagh* in his day, and never met a man able to fight him, except big Mucklemurray, who stood before him the greater part of an hour and a half, in the fair of Knockimdowney, on the day that the first great fight took place – twenty years afther the hard frost – between the O'Callaghans and the O'Hallaghans. The two men fought single hands – for both factions were willing to let them try the engagement out, that they might see what side could boast of having the best man. They began where you enter the north side of Knockimdowney, and fought successfully up to the other end, then back again to the spot where they commenced, and afterwards up to the middle of the town, right opposite to the marketplace, where my grandfather, by the same a-token, lost a grinder; but he soon took satisfaction for that, by giving Mucklemurray a tip above the eye with the end of an oak stick, dacently loaded with lead, which made the poor man feel very quare entirely, for the few days that he survived it.

'Faith, if an Irishman happened to be born in Scotland, he would find it mighty inconvanient – afther losing two or three grinders in a row – to manage the hard oaten bread that they use there; for which rason, God be good to his sowl that first invented the phaties, anyhow, because a man can masticate them without a tooth at all at all. I'll engage, if larned books were consulted, it would be found out that he was an Irishman. I wonder that neither Pastorini nor Columbkill mentions anything about him in their prophecies consarning the church; for my own part, I'm strongly inclined to believe that it must have been Saint Patrick himself; and I think that his driving all kinds of venomous reptiles out of the kingdom is, according to the Socrastic method of argument, an undeniable proof of it. The subject, to a dead certainty, is not touched upon in the

Brehone Code, nor by any of the three Psalters, which is extremely odd, seeing that the earth never produced a root equal to it in the multiplying force of prolification. It is, indeed, the root of prosperity to a fighting people; and many a time my grandfather boasts, to this day, that the first bit of *bread* he ever *ett* was a *phatie*.

'In mentioning my grandfather's fight with Mucklemurray, I happened to name them blackguards, the O'Hallaghans; hard fortune to the same set, for they have no more discretion in their quarrels than so many Egyptian mummies, African buffoons, or any other uncivilized animals. It was one of them, he that's married to my own fourth cousin, Biddy O'Callaghan, that knocked two of my grinders out, for which piece of civility I have just had the satisfaction of breaking a splinter or two in his carcase, being always honestly disposed to pay my debts.

'With respect to the O'Hallaghans, they and our family have been next neighbours since before the flood – and that's as good as two hundred years; for I believe it's one hundred and ninety-eight, anyhow, since my great grandfather's grand-uncle's ould mare was swept out of the "Island," in the dead of the night, about half an hour after the whole country had been *ris* out of their beds by the thunder and lightning. Many a field of oats, and many a life, both of beast and Christian, was lost in it, especially of those that lived on the *holmes* about the edge of the river; and it was true for them that said it came before something; for the *next year* was one of the hottest *summers* ever remembered in Ireland.

'These O'Hallaghans couldn't be at peace with a saint. Before they and our faction began to quarrel, it's said that the O'Connells, or Connells, and they had been at it – and a blackguard set the same O'Connells were, at all times – in fair and market, dance, wake, and berrin, setting the country on fire. Whenever they met, it was heads cracked and bones broken; till by degrees the O'Connells fell away, one after another, from fighting, accidents, and hanging; so that at last there was hardly the name of one of them in the neighbourhood. The O'Hallaghans, after this, had the country under themselves – were the cocks of the walk entirely – who but they? A man darn't look crooked at them, or he was certain of getting his head in his fist. And when they'd get drunk in a fair, it was nothing but "Whoo! for the O'Hallaghans!" and leaping yards high off the pavement, brandishing their cudgels over their heads, striking their heels against their hams, tossing up their hats; and when all would fail, they'd strip off their coats, and trail them up and down the street, shouting. "Who dare touch the coat of an O'Hallaghan? Where's the blackguard Connells now?" – and so on, till flesh and blood couldn't stand it.

'In the course of time, the whole country was turned against them; for no crowd could get together in which they didn't kick up a row, nor a bit of stray fighting couldn't be, but they'd pick it up first – and if a man would venture to give them a contrairy answer, he was sure to get the crame of a good welting for his pains. The very landlord was timorous of them; for when they'd get behind in their *rint*, hard fortune to the bailiff, or proctor, or steward, he could find, that would have anything to say to them. And the more wise they; for, maybe, a month would hardly pass till all belonging to them in the world would be in a heap of ashes: and who could say who did it? for they were as cunning as foxes.

'If one of them wanted a wife, it was nothing but find out the purtiest and richest farmer's daughter in the neighbourhood, and next march into her father's house, at the dead hour of night, tie and gag every mortal in it, and off with her to some friend's place in another part of the country. Then what could be done? If the girl's parents didn't like to give in, their daughter's name was sure to be ruined; at all events, no other man would think of marrying her, and the only plan was to make the worst of a bad bargain; and God he knows, it was making a bad bargain for a girl to have any matrimonial concatenation with the same O'Hallaghans; for they always had the bad drop in them, from first to last, from big to little – the blackguards! But wait, it's not over with them yet.

'The bone of contintion that got between them and our faction was this circumstance: their lands and ours were divided by a river that ran down from the high mountains of Sliew Boglish, and after a coorse of eight or ten miles, disembogued itself – first into George Duffy's mill-dam, and afterwards into that superb stream, the Blackwater, that might be well and appropriately appellated the Irish Niger. This river, which, though small at first, occasionally inflated itself to such a gigantic altitude that it swept away cows, corn, and cottages, or whatever else happened to be in the way – was the march-ditch, or *merin* between our farms. Perhaps it is worthwhile remarking, as a solution for natural philosophers, that these inundations were much more frequent in winter than in summer – though, when they did occur in summer, they were truly terrific.

'God be with the days, when I and half a dozen gorsoons used to go out, of a warm Sunday in summer – the bed of the river nothing but a line of white meandering stones, so hot that you could hardly stand upon them, with a small obscure thread of water creeping invisibly among them, hiding itself, as it were, from the scorching sun – except here and there that you might find a small crystal pool where the streams had accumulated. Our plan was to bring a pocketful of roche lime with us, and put it into the pool, when all the fish used to rise on the instant to the surface, gasping with open mouth for fresh air, and we had only to lift them out of the water; a nate plan, which, perhaps, might be adopted successfully on a more extensive scale by the Irish fisheries. Indeed, I almost regret that I did not remain in that station of life, for I was much happier than ever I was since I began to study and practise larning. But this is vagating from the subject.

'Well, then, I have said that them O'Hallaghans lived beside us, and that this stream divided our lands. About half a quarter

– *i.e.*, to accommodate myself to the vulgar phraseology – or, to speak more scientifically, one eighth of a mile from our house, was as purty a hazel glen as you'd wish to see, near half a mile long – its developments and proportions were truly classical. In the bottom of this glen was a small green island, about twelve yards, diametrically, of Irish admeasurement, that is to say, be the same more or less – at all events, it lay in the way of the river, which, however, ran towards the O'Hallaghan side, and consequently, the island was our property.

'Now, you'll observe, that this river had been, for ages, the *merin* between the two farms, for they both belonged to separate landlords, and so long as it kept the O'Hallaghan side of the little peninsula in question, there could be no dispute about it, for all was clear. One wet winter, however, it seemed to change its mind upon the subject; for it wrought and wore away a passage for itself on our side of the island, and by that means took part, as it were, with the O'Hallaghans, leaving the territory which had been our property for centuries, in their possession. This was a vexations change to us, and, indeed, eventually produced very feudal consequences. No sooner had the stream changed sides, than the O'Hallaghans claimed the island as theirs, according to their tenement; and we, having had it for such length of time in our possession, could not break ourselves of the habitude of occupying it. They incarcerated our cattle, and we incarcerated theirs. They summoned us to their landlord, who was a magistrate; and we summoned them to ours, who was another. The verdicts were north and south. Their landlord gave it in favour of them, and ours in favour of us. The one said he had law on his side; the other, that he had proscription and possession, length of time and usage.

'The two Squires then fought a challenge upon the head of it, and what was more singular, upon the disputed spot itself; the one standing on their side – the other on ours; for it was just *twelve paces* every way. Their friend was a small, light man, with legs like drumsticks; the other was a large, able-bodied gentleman, with a red face and a hooked nose. They exchanged two shots, one only of which – the second – took effect. It pastured upon their landlord's spindle leg, on which he held it out, exclaiming, that while he lived he would never fight another challenge with his antagonist, "because," said he, looking at his own spindle shank, "the man who could hit *that* could hit *anything.*"

'We then were advised by an attorney to go to law with them; and they were advised by another attorney to go to law with us; accordingly, we did so, and in the course of eight or nine years it might have been decided; but just as the legal term approximated in which the decision was to be announced, the river divided itself with mathematical exactitude on each side of the island. This altered the state and law of the question *in toto*; but, in the meantime, both we and the O'Hallaghans were nearly fractured by the expenses. Now during the lawsuit we usually houghed and mutilated each other's cattle, according as they trespassed the premises. This brought on the usual concomitants of various battles, fought and won by both sides, and occasioned the lawsuit to be dropped; for we found it a mighty inconvanient matter to fight it out both ways – by the same a-token that I think it a great proof of stultity to go to law at all at all, as long as a person is able to take it into his own management. For the only incongruity in the matter is this: that, in the one case, a set of lawyers have the law in *their* hands, and, in the other, that you have it in *your own* – that's the only difference, and 'tis easy knowing where the advantage lies.

'We, however, paid the most of the expenses, and would have *ped* them all with the greatest integrity, were it not that our attorney, when about to issue an execution against our property, happened somehow to be shot, one evening, as he returned home from a dinner which was given by him that was attorney for the O'Hallaghans. Many a boast the O'Hallaghans made, before the quarrelling between us and them commenced, that they'd sweep the streets with the *fighting*

157

O'Callaghans, which was an epithet that was occasionally applied to our family. We differed, however, materially from them; for we were honourable, never starting out in dozens on a single man or two, and beating him into insignificance. A couple or maybe, when irritated, three were the most we ever set at a single enemy; and, if we left him lying in a state of imperception, it was the most we ever did, except in a regular confliction, when a man is justified in saving his own skull by breaking one of an opposite faction. For the truth of the business is, that he who breaks the skull of him who endeavours to break his own, is safest; and, surely, when a man is driven to such an alternative, the choice is unhesitating.

'O'Hallaghans' attorney, however, had better luck; they were, it is true, rather in the retrograde with him touching the law charges, and, of coorse, it was only candid in him to look for his own. One morning he found that two of his horses had been executed by some *incendiary* unknown, in the course of the night; and on going to look at them he found a taste of a notice posted on the inside of the stable door, giving him intelligence that if he did not find a *horpus corpus* whereby to transfer his body out of the country, he would experience a fate parallel to that of his brother lawyer or the horses. And, undoubtedly, if honest people never perpetrated worse than banishing such varmin, along with proctors, and drivers of all kinds, out of a civilised country, they would not be so very culpable or atrocious.

'After this, the lawyer went to reside in Dublin; and the only bodily injury he received was the death of a land-agent and a bailiff, who lost their lives faithfully in driving for rent. They died, however, successfully; the bailiff having been provided for nearly a year before the agent was sent to give an account of his stewardship – as the authorized version has it.

'The occasion on which the first rencounter between us and the O'Hallaghans took place, was a peaceable one. Several of our respective friends undertook to produce a friendly and oblivious potation between us – it was at a berrin belonging to a corpse who was related to us both; and, certainly in the beginning, we were all as thick as whigged milk. But there is no use now in dwelling too long upon that circumstance: let it be sufficient to assert that the accommodation was effectuated by fists and cudgels, on both sides – the first man that struck a blow being one of the friends that wished to bring about the tranquillity. From that out, the play commenced, and God he knows when it may end; for no dacent faction could give in to another faction, without losing their character, and being kicked, and cuffed, and kilt, every week in the year.

'It is the *great battle*, however, which I am after going to describe; that in which we and the O'Hallaghans had contrived one way or other, to have the parish divided – one half for them, and the other for us; and, upon my credibility, it is no exaggeration to declare that the whole parish, though ten miles by six, assembled itself in the town of Knockimdowney upon this interesting occasion. In thruth, Ireland ought to be a land of mathemathitians; for I'm sure her population is well trained, at all events, in the two sciences of *multiplication* and *division*. Before I adventure, however, upon the narration, I must wax pathetic a little, and then proceed with the main body of the story.

'Poor Rose O'Hallaghan! – or, as she was designated – *Rose Galh*, or *Fair Rose*, and sometimes simply Rose Hallaghan, because the detention of the big O would produce an afflatus in the pronunciation that would be mighty inconvanient to such as did not understand oratory – besides that, the Irish are rather fond of sending the liquids in a guttheral direction – Poor Rose! that faction *fight* was a black *day* to her, the sweet innocent! when it was well known that there wasn't a man, woman, or child, on either side, that wouldn't lay their hands under her feet. However, in order to *insense* the reader better into her character, I will commence a small sub-narration, which will afterwards emerge into the parent stream of the story.

'The chapel of Knockimdowney is a slated house, without any ornament, except a set of wooden cuts, painted red and blue, that are placed *seriatim* around the square of the building in the internal side. Fourteen of these suspend at equal distances on the walls, each set in a painted frame; these constitute a certain species of country devotion. It is usual on Sundays for such of the congregations as are most inclined to piety, to genuflect at the first of these pictures, and commence a certain number of prayers to it; after the repetition of which, they travel on their knees along the bare earth to the second, where they repate another prayer peculiar to *that*, and so on, till they finish the grand *tower* of the interior. Such, however, as are not especially dictated to this kind of locomotive prayer, collect together in various knots, through the chapel, and amuse themselves by auditing or narrating anecdotes, discussing policy or detraction; and in case it be summer, and a day of a fine texture, they scatter themselves into little crowds on the chapel-green, or lie at their length upon the grass in listless groups, giving way to chat and laughter.

'In this mode, laired on the sunny side of the ditches and hedges, or collected in rings round that respectable character, the Academician of the village, or some other well-known *shannahas*, or story-teller, they amuse themselves till the priest's arrival. Perhaps, too, some walking geographer of a pilgrim may happen to be present; and if there be, he is sure to draw a crowd about him, in spite of all the efforts of the learned Academician to the reverse. It is no unusual thing to see such a vagrant, in all the vanity of conscious sanctimony, standing in the middle of the attentive peasants, like the knave and fellows of a cartwheel – if I may be permitted the loan of an apt similitude – repeating some piece of unfathomable and labyrinthine devotion, or perhaps warbling, from stenthorian lungs, some *melodia sacra*, in an untranslatable tongue; or, it may be, exhibiting the mysterious power of an amber bade, fastened as a decade to his *paudareens*, lifting a chaff or light bit of straw by the force of its attraction. This is an exploit which causes many an eye to turn from the bades to his own bearded face, with a hope, as it were, of being able to catch a glimpse of the lurking sanctimony by which the knave hoaxes them in the miraculous.

'The amusements of the females are also nearly such as I have drafted out. Nosegays of the darlings might be seen sated on green banks, or sauntering about with a sly intention of coming in contact with their sweethearts, or, like bachelor's buttons in smiling rows, criticising the young men as they pass. Others of them might be seen screened behind a hedge, with their backs to the spectators, taking the papers off their curls before a small bit of looking-glass placed against the ditch; or perhaps putting on their shoes and stockings – which phrase can be used only by authority of the figure, *heusteron proteron* – inasmuch as if they put on the shoes first, you persave, it would be a scientific job to get on the stockings after; but it's an idiomatical expression, and therefore justifiable. However, it's a general custom in the country, which I dare to say has not yet spread into large cities, for the young women to walk barefooted to the chapel, or within a short distance of it, that they may exhibit their bleached thread stockings and well-greased slippers to the best advantage, not pertermitting a well-turned ankle, and neat leg, which, I may fearlessly assert, my fair countrywomen can show against any other nation living or dead.

'One sunny Sabbath the congregation of Knockimdowney were thus assimilated, amusing themselves in the manner I have just outlined: a series of country girls sat on a little green mount, called the Rabbit Bank, from the circumstance of its having been formerly an open burrow, though of late years it has been closed. It was near twelve o'clock, the hour at which Father Luke O'Shaughran was generally seen topping the rise of the hill at Larry Mulligan's public-house, jogging on his bay hack at something between a walk and a trot – that is to say, his horse moved his fore and hind legs on the off side at one motion, and the fore and hind legs of the near side in another, going at a kind of dog's trot, like the pace of an idiot with sore feet in a shower – a pace, indeed, to which the animal had been set for the last sixteen years, but beyond which, no force, or entreaty, or science, or power, either divine or human, of his reverence, could drive him. As yet, however, he had not become apparent; and the girls already mentioned were discussing the pretensions which several of their acquaintances had to dress or beauty.

'"Peggy," said Katty Carroll to her companion, Peggy Donohue, "were you out last Sunday?"

'"No, in troth, Katty, I was disappointed in getting my shoes from Paddy Malone, though I left him the measure of my foot three weeks agone, and gave him a thousand warnings to make them *duck-nebs*; but instead of that," said she, holding out a very purty foot, "he has made them as sharp in the toe as a pick-axe, and a full mile too short for me; but why do ye ax was I *out*, Katty?"

'"Oh, nothing," responded Katty, "only that you missed a sight, anyway."

'"What was it, Katty, a-hagur?" asked her companion with mighty great curiosity.

'"Why, nothing less, indeed, nor Rose Cuillenan, decked out in a white muslin gown, and a black sprush bonnet, tied under her chin wid a silk ribbon, no less; but what killed us, out and out, was – you wouldn't guess?"

'"Arrah, how could I guess, woman alive? A silk handkerchy, maybe; for I wouldn't doubt the same Rose, but she would be setting herself up for the likes of sich a thing."

'"It's herself that had, as red as scarlet, about her neck; but that's not it."

' "Arrah, Katty, tell it to us at wanst; out with it, a-hagur; sure there's no treason in it, anyhow."

' "Why, thin, nothing less nor a crass-bar red and white pocket-handkerchy, to wipe her pretty complexion wid!"

'To this Peggy replied by a loud laugh, in which it was difficult to say whether there was more of sathir than astonishment.

' "A pocket-handkerchy!" she exclaimed; "musha, are we alive afther that, at all at all! Why, that bates Molly M'Cullagh, and her red mantle entirely; I'm sure, but it's well come up for the likes of her, a poor, imperint crathur, that's sprung from nothing, to give herself sich airs."

' "Molly M'Cullagh, indeed," said Katty; "why, they oughtn't to be mintioned in the one day, woman; Molly's come of a dacent ould stock, and kind mother for her to keep herself in genteel ordher at all times; she seen nothing else, and can afford it, not all as one as the other *flipe*, that would go to the world's end for a bit of dress."

' "Sure she thinks she's a beauty too, if you plase," said Peggy, tossing her head with an air of disdain; "but tell us, Katty, how did the muslin sit upon her at all, the upsetting crathur?"

' "Why, for all the world like a shift on a May-powl, or a stocking on a body's nose; only nothing killed us outright but the pocket-handkerchy!"

' "But," said the other, "what could we expect from a proud piece like her, that brings a Manwill[1] to mass every Sunday, purtending she can read in it, and Jem Finigan saw the wrong side of the book *toards* her, the Sunday of the *Purcession*!"

'At this hit they both formed another risible junction, quite as sarcastic as the former, in the midst of which the innocent object of their censure, dressed in all her obnoxious finery, came up and joined them. She was scarcely sated – I blush to the very point of my pen during the manuscript – when the confabulation assumed a character directly antipodial to that which marked the precedent dialogue.

' "My gracious, Rose, but that's a purty thing you have got in your gown! where did you buy it?"

' "Och, thin, not a one of myself likes it over much. I'm sorry I didn't buy a gingham; I could have got a beautiful patthern, all out, for two shillings less; but they don't wash so well as this. I bought it in Paddy Gartland's, Peggy."

' "Troth, it's nothing else but a great beauty; I didn't see anything on you this long time becomes you so well, and I've remarked that you always look best in white."

' "Who made it, Rose," inquired Katty, "for it sits illegant?"

' "Indeed," replied Rose, "for the differ of the price, I thought it better to bring it to Peggy Boyle, and be sartin of not having it spoiled. Nelly Keenan made the last, and although there was a full breadth more in it nor this, bad cess to the one of her but spoiled it on me; it was ever so much too short in the body, and too tight in the sleeves, and then I had no step at all at all."

' "The sprush bonnet is exactly the fit for the gown," observed Katty; "the black and the white's jist the cut – how many yards had you, Rose?"

' "Jist ten and a half; but the half-yard was for the tucks."

' "Ay, faix! and brave full tucks she left in it; ten would do me, Rose?"

' "Ten! no nor ten and a half; you're a size bigger nor me at the laste, Peggy; but you'd be asy fitted, you're so *well* made."

' "Rose, *darling*," said Peggy, "that's a great beauty, and shows off your complexion all to pieces: you have no notion how well you look in it and the sprush."

'In a few minutes after this, her namesake, Rose Galh O'Hallaghan, came towards the chapel, in society with her father, mother, and her two sisters. The eldest, Mary, was about twenty-one; Rose, who was the second, about nineteen, or scarcely that; and Nancy, the junior of the three, about twice seven.

' "There's the O'Hallaghans," says Rose.

' "Ay," replied Katty; "you may talk of beauty, now; did you ever lay your two eyes on the likes of Rose for downright – musha if myself knows what to call it – but, anyhow, she's the lovely crathur to look at."

'Kind reader, without a single disrespectful insinuation against any portion of the fair sex, you may judge what Rose O'Hallaghan must have been, when even these three were necessitated to praise her in her absence.

' "I'll warrant," observed Katty, "we'll soon be after seeing John O'Callaghan" (he was my own cousin) "sthrolling afther them, at his ase."

' "Why," asked Rose, "what makes you say that?"

' "Bekase," replied the other, "I have a rason for it."

' "Sure, John O'Callaghan wouldn't be thinking of her," observed Rose, "and their families would see other shot; their factions would never have a crass marriage, anyhow."

' "Well," said Peggy, "it's the thousand pities that the same two couldn't go together: for, fair and handsome as Rose is, you'll not deny but John comes up to her: but faix, sure enough it's they that's the proud people on both sides, and dangerous to make or meddle with, not saying that ever there was the likes of the same two for dacency and peaceableness among either of the factions."

' "Didn't I tell yees?" cried Katty; "look at him now, staling afther her, and it'll be the same thing going home agin; and if Rose is not much belied, it's not a bit displeasing to her, they say."

' "Between ourselves," observed Peggy, "it would be no wondher the darling young crathur would fall in love with him, for you might thravel the counthry afore you'd meet with his fellow for face and figure."

' "There's Father Ned," remarked Katty; "we had betther get into the chapel before the *scroodgen* comes an, or your bonnet and gown, Rose, won't be the betther for it."

'They now proceeded to the chapel, and those who had been amusing themselves after the same mode, followed their exemplar. In a short time the hedges and ditches adjoining the chapel were quite in solitude, with the exception of a few persons from the extreme parts of the parish, who might be seen running with all possible velocity "to overtake mass," as the phrase on that point expresses itself.

'The chapel of Knockimdowney was situated at the foot of a range of lofty mountains; a by-road went past the very door, which had under subjection a beautiful extent of cultivated country, diversificated by hill and dale, or rather by hill and hollow; for as far as my own geographical knowledge went, I have uniformly found them inseparable. It was also ornamented with the waving verdure of rich corn-fields and meadows, not pretermitting phatie-fields in full blossom – a part of rural landscape which, to my utter astonishment, has escaped the pen of poet and the brush of painter; although I will risque my reputation as a man of pure and categorical taste, if a finer ingredient in the composition of a landscape could be found than a field of Cork-red phaties, or Moroky *blacks* in full bloom, allowing a man to judge by the pleasure they confer upon the eye, and therefore to the heart. About a mile up from the chapel, towards the south, a mountain-stream – not the one already intimated – over which there was no bridge, crossed the road. But in lieu of a bridge, there was a long double plank laid over it, from bank to bank; and as the river was broad, and not sufficiently incarcerated within its channel, the neighbours were necessitated to throw these planks across the narrowest part they could find in the contiguity of the road. This part was consequently the deepest, and, in floods, the most dangerous; for the banks were elevated as far as they went, and quite tortuositous.

'Shortly after the priest had entered the chapel, it was observed that the hemisphere became, of a sudden, unusually obscured, though the preceding part of the day had not only been uncloudously bright, but hot in a most especial manner. The obscurity, however, increased rapidly, accompanied by that gloomy stillness which always takes precedence of a storm, and fills the mind with vague and interminable terror. But this ominous silence was not long unfractured; for soon after the first appearance of the gloom, a flash of lightning quivered through the chapel, followed by an extravagantly loud clap of thunder, which shook the very glass in the windows, and filled the congregation to the brim with terror. Their dismay, however, would have been infinitely greater, only for the presence of his reverence, and the confidence which might be traced to the solemn occasion on which they were assimilated.

'From this moment the storm became progressive in dreadful magnitude, and the thunder, in concomitance with the most vivid flashes of lightning, pealed through the sky with an awful grandeur and magnificence that were exalted, and even rendered more sublime, by the still solemnity of religious worship. Every heart now prayed fervently – every spirit shrunk into a deep sense of its own guilt and helplessness – and every conscience was terror-stricken, as the voice of an angry God thundered out of his temple of storms through the heavens; for truly, as the authorized version has it, "darkness was under his feet, and his pavilion round about was dark waters, and thick clouds of the skies, because he was wroth."

'The rain now condescended in even down torrents, and thunder succeeded thunder in deep and terrific peals, whilst the roar of the gigantic echoes that deepened and reverberated among the glens and hollows – "laughing in their mountain mirth" – hard fortune to me, but they made the flesh creep on my bones!

'This lasted for an hour, when the thunder slackened; but the rain still continued. As soon as mass was over, and the storm had elapsed, except an odd peal which might be heard rolling at a distance behind the hills, the people began gradually to recover their spirits, and enter into confabulation; but to venture out was still impracticable. For about another hour it rained incessantly, after which it ceased; the hemisphere became lighter, and the sun shone out once more upon the countenance of nature with his former brightness. The congregation then decanted itself out of the chapel – the spirits of the people dancing with that remarkable buoyancy or juvenility which is felt after a thunderstorm, when the air is calm, soople, and balmy, and all nature garmented with glittering verdure and light. The crowd next began to commingle on their way home, and to make the usual observations upon the extraordinary storm which had just passed, and the probable effect it would produce on the fruit and agriculture of the neighbourhood.

'When the three young women, whom we have already introduced to our respectable readers, had evacuated the chapel, they determined to substantiate a certitude, as far as their observation could reach, as to the truth of what Katty Carroll had hinted at, in reference to John O'Callaghan's attachment to Rose Galh O'Hallaghan, and her taciturn approval of it. For this purpose they kept their eye upon John, who certainly seemed in no especial hurry home, but lingered upon the chapel green in a very careless method. Rose Galh, however, soon made her appearance, and, after going up the chapel-road a short space, John slyly walked at some distance behind, without seeming to pay her any particular notice, whilst a person up to the secret might observe Rose's bright eye sometimes peeping back, to see if he was after her. In this manner they proceeded until they came to the river, which, to their great alarm, was almost fluctuating over its highest banks.

'A crowd was now assembled, consulting as to the safest method of crossing the planks, under which the red boiling current ran, with less violence, it is true, but much deeper than in any other part of the stream. The final decision was that the very young and the old, and such as were feeble, should proceed by a circuit of some miles to a bridge that crossed it, and that the young men should place themselves on their knees along the planks, their hands locked in each other, thus forming a support on one side, upon which such as had courage to venture across might lean, in case of accident or megrim. Indeed, anybody that had able nerves might have crossed the planks without this precaution, had they been dry; but, in consequence of the rain, and the frequent attrition of feet, they were quite slippery; and, besides, the flood rolled terrifically two or three yards below them, which might be apt to beget a megrim that would not be felt if there was no flood.

'When this expedient had been hit upon, several young men volunteered themselves to put it in practice; and in a short time a considerable number of both sexuals crossed over, without the occurrence of any unpleasant accident. Paddy O'Hallaghan and his family had been stationed for some time on the bank, watching the success of the plan; and as it appeared not to be attended with any particular danger, they also determined to make the attempt. About a perch below the planks stood John O'Callaghan, watching the progress of those who were crossing them, but taking no part in what was going forward. The river under the planks, and for some perches above and below them, might be about ten feet deep; but to those who could swim it was less perilous, should any accident befall them, than those parts where the current was more rapid, but shallower. The water here boiled, and bubbled, and whirled about; but it was slow, and its yellow surface unbroken by rocks or fords.

'The first of the O'Hallaghans that ventured over it was the youngest, who, being captured by the hand, was encouraged by many cheerful expressions from the young men who were clinging to the planks. She got safe over, however; and when she came to the end, one who was stationed on the bank gave her a joyous pull, that translated her several yards upon *terra firma*.

' "Well, Nancy," he observed, *"you're* safe, anyhow; and if I don't dance at your wedding for this, I'll never say you're dacent."

'To this Nancy gave a jocular promise, and he resumed his station, that he might be ready to render similar assistance to her next sister. Rose Galh then went to the edge of the plank several times, but her courage as often refused to be forthcoming. During her hesitation, John O'Callaghan stooped down, and privately untied his shoes, then unbuttoned his waistcoat, and very gently, being unwilling to excite notice, slipped the knot of his cravat. At long last, by the encouragement of those who were on the plank, Rose attempted the passage, and had advanced as far as the middle of it, when a fit of dizziness and alarm seized her with such violence that she lost all consciousness – a circumstance of which those who handed her along were ignorant. The consequence, as might be expected, was dreadful; for as one of the young men was receiving her hand, that he might pass her to the next, she lost her momentum, and was instantaneously precipitated into the boiling current.

'The wild and fearful cry of horror that succeeded this cannot be laid on paper. The eldest sister fell into strong convulsions, and several of the other females fainted on the spot. The mother did not faint; but, like Lot's wife, she seemed to have been translated into stone: her hands became clenched convulsively, her teeth locked, her nostrils dilated, and her eyes shot halfway out of her head. There she stood, looking upon her daughter struggling in the flood, with a fixed gaze of wild and impotent frenzy, that, for fearfulness, beat the thunderstorm all to nothing. The father rushed to the edge of the river, oblivious of his incapability to swim, determined to save her or lose his own life, which latter would have been a *dead* certainty had he ventured; but he was prevented by the crowd, who pointed out to him the madness of such a project.

' "For God's sake, Paddy, don't attempt it," they exclaimed, "except you wish to lose your own life, widout being able to save hers; no man could swim in that flood, and it upwards of ten feet deep."

'Their arguments, however, were lost upon him; for, in fact, he was insensible to every thing but his child's preservation. He therefore only answered their remonstrances by attempting to make another plunge into the river.

' "Let me alone, will yees," said he – "let me alone! I'll either save my child, Rose, or die along with her! How could I live after her? Merciful God, any of them but *her*! Oh! Rose, darling," he exclaimed, "the favourite of my heart – will no one save you?" All this passed in less than a minute.

'Just as these words were uttered a plunge was heard a few yards above the bridge, and a man appeared in the flood, making his way with rapid strokes to the drowning girl. Another cry now arose from the spectators. "It's John O'Callaghan," they shouted – "It's John O'Callaghan, and they'll be both lost." "No," exclaimed others; "if it's in the power of man to save her, he will!" "Oh, blessed Father, she's lost!" now burst from all present; for, after having struggled and been kept floating for sometime by her garments, she at length sunk, apparently exhausted and senseless, and the thief of a flood flowed over her, as if she had been under its surface.

'When O'Callaghan saw that she went down he raised himself up in the water, and cast his eye towards that part of the bank opposite which she disappeared, evidently, as it proved, that he might have a mark to guide him in fixing on the proper spot where to plunge after her. When he came to the place he raised himself again in the stream, and, calculating that she must by this time have been borne some distance from the spot where she sank, he gave a stroke or two down the river and disappeared after her. This was followed by another cry of horror and despair; for, somehow, the idea of desolation which marks, at all times, a deep, over-swollen torrent, heightened by the bleak mountain scenery around them, and the dark, angry voracity of the river where they had sunk, might have impressed the spectators with utter hopelessness as to the fate

171

of those now engulfed in its vortex. This, however, I leave to those who are deeper read in philosophy than I am.

'An awful silence succeeded the last exclamation, broken only by the hoarse rushing of the waters, whose wild, continuous roar, booming hollowly and dismally in the ear, might be heard at a great distance over all the country. But a new sensation soon invaded the multitude; for, after the lapse of about a minute, John O'Callaghan emerged from the flood, bearing, in his sinister hand, the body of his own Rose Galh – for it's he that loved her tenderly. A peal of joy congratulated them from a thousand voices; hundreds of directions were given to him how to act to the best advantage. Two young men in especial, who were both dying about the lovely creature that he held were quite anxious to give advice.

' "Bring her to the other side, John, ma bouchal; it's the safest," said Larry Carty.

' "Will you let him alone, Carty?" said Simon Tracy, who was the other. "You'll only put him in a perplexity."

'But Carty should order in spite of everything. He kept bawling out, however, so loud that John raised his eye to see what he meant, and was near losing hold of Rose. This was too much for Tracy, who ups with his fist and downs him – so they both at it; for no one there could take themselves off those that were in danger, to interfere between them. But, at all events, no earthly thing can happen among Irishmen without a fight.

'The father, during this, stood breathless, his hands clasped, and his eyes turned to heaven, praying in anguish for the delivery of his darling. The mother's look was still wild and fixed, her eyes glazed, and her muscles hard and stiff; evidently she was insensible to all that was going forward; while large drops of paralytic agony hung upon her cold brow. Neither of the sisters had yet recovered, nor could those who supported them turn their eyes from the more imminent danger, to pay them any particular attention. Many, also, of the other females, whose feelings were too much wound up when the accident occurred; now fainted, when they saw she was likely to be rescued; but most of them were weeping with delight and gratitude.

'When John brought her to the surface, he paused a moment to recover breath and collectedness; he then caught her by the left arm, near the shoulder, and cut, in a slanting direction, down the stream, to a watering-place, where a slope had been formed in the bank. But he was already too far down to be able to work across the stream to this point – for it was here much stronger and more rapid than under the planks. Instead, therefore, of reaching the slope, he found himself, in spite of every effort to the contrary, about a perch below it; and except he could gain this point, against the strong rush of the flood, there was very little hope of being able to save either her or himself – for he was now much exhausted.

'Hitherto, therefore, all was still doubtful, whilst strength was fast failing him. In this trying and almost helpless situation, with an admirable presence of mind, he adopted the only expedient which could possibly enable him to reach the bank. On finding himself receding down, instead of advancing up, the current, he approached the bank, which was here very deep and perpendicular; he then sank his fingers into the firm blue clay with which it was stratified, and by this means advanced, bit by bit, up the stream, having no other force by which to propel himself against it. After this mode did he breast the current with all his strength – which must have been prodigious, or he never could have borne it out – until he reached the slope, and got from the influence of the tide into dead water. On arriving here, his hand was caught by one of the young men present, who stood up to the neck, waiting his approach. A second man stood behind him, holding his other hand, a link being thus formed, that reached out to the firm bank; and a good pull now brought them both to the edge of the liquid. On finding bottom, John took his Colleen Galh in his own arms, carried her out, and pressing his lips to hers, laid her in the bosom of her father; then after taking another kiss of the young drowned flower, he burst into tears, and fell powerless beside her. The truth is, the spirit that kept him firm was now exhausted; both his legs and arms having become nerveless by the exertion.

'Hitherto her father took no notice of John, for how could he? seeing that he was entirely wrapped up in his daughter; and the question was, though rescued from the flood, if life was in her. The sisters were by this time recovered, and weeping over her along with the father – and, indeed, with all present; but the mother could not be made to comprehend what they were all about, at all at all. The country people used every means with which they were intimate to recover Rose; she was brought instantly to a farmer's house beside the spot, put into a warm bed, covered over with hot salt, wrapped in half-scorched blankets, and made subject to every other mode of treatment that could possibly revoke the functions of life. John had now got a dacent draught of whiskey, which revived him. He stood over her, when he could be admitted, watching for the symptomatics of her revival; all, however, was vain. He now determined to try another course: by-and-by he stooped, put his mouth to her mouth, and, drawing in his breath, respired with all his force from the bottom of his very heart into hers; this he did several times rapidly – faith, a tender and agreeable operation, anyhow. But mark the consequence: in less than a minute her white bosom heaved – her breath returned – her pulse began to play, she opened her eyes, and felt his tears of love raining warmly on her pale cheek!

'For years before this, no two of these opposite factions had spoken; nor up to this minute had John and they, even upon this occasion, exchanged a monosyllable. The father now looked at him – the tears stood afresh in his eyes; he came forward – stretched out his hand – it was received; and the next moment he fell into John's arms, and cried like an infant.

'When Rose recovered, she seemed as if striving to recordate what had happened; and after two or three minutes, inquired from her sister, in a weak but sweet voice, "Who saved me?"

' " 'Twas John O'Callaghan, Rose darling," replied the sister, in tears, "that ventured his own life into the boiling flood, to save yours – and did save it, jewel."

'Rose's eye glanced at John; – and I only wish, as I am a bachelor not further than my forty-seventh, that I may ever have the happiness to get such a glance from two blue eyes as she gave him that moment; a faint smile played about her mouth, and a slight blush lit up her fair cheek, like the evening sunbeams on the virgin snow, as the poets have said, for the five hundredth time, to my own personal knowledge. She then extended her hand, which John, you may be sure, was no way backward in receiving, and the tears of love and gratitude ran silently down her cheeks.

'It is not necessary to detail the circumstances of this day further; let it be sufficient to say that a reconciliation took place between those two branches of the O'Hallaghan and O'Callaghan families, in consequence of John's heroism and Rose's soft persuasion, and that there was also every perspective of the two factions being penultimately amalgamated. For nearly a century they had been pell-mell at it, whenever and wherever they could meet. Their forefathers, who had been engaged in the law-suit about the island which I have mentioned, were dead and petrified in their graves; and the little peninsula in the glen was gradationally worn away by the river, till nothing remained but a desert, upon a small scale, of sand and gravel. Even the ruddy, able-bodied squire, with the longitudinal nose projecting out of his face like a broken arch, and the small, fiery magistrate, both of whom had fought the duel, for the purpose of setting forth a good example and bringing the dispute to a *peaceable* conclusion, were also dead. The very memory of the original contention had been lost (except that it was preserved along with the cranium of my grandfather), or became so indistinct that the parties fastened themselves on some more modern provocation, which they kept in view until another fresh motive would start up, and so on. I know not, however, whether it was fair to expect them to give up at once the agreeable recreation of fighting. It's not easy to abolish old customs, particularly diversions; and every one knows that this is the national amusement of the finest peasantry on the face of the earth.

'There were, it is true, many among both factions who saw the matter in this reasonable light, and who wished rather, if it were to cease, that it should die away by degrees, from the battle of the whole parish, equally divided between the factions, to the subordinate row between certain members of them – from that to the faint broil of certain families, and so on, to the single-handed play between individuals. At all events, one half of them were for peace, and two thirds of them equally divided between peace and war.

'For three months after the accident which befell Rose Galh O'Hallaghan, both factions had been tolerably quiet: that is to say, they had no general engagement. Some slight skirmishes certainly did take place on market nights, when the drop was in, and the spirits up; but in those neither John nor Rose's immediate families took any part. The fact was that John and Rose were on the evening of matrimony; the match had been made, the day appointed, and every other necessary stipulation ratified. Now, John was as fine a young man as you would meet in a day's travelling; and as for Rose, her name went far and near for beauty; and with justice, for the sun never shone on a fairer, meeker, or modester virgin than Rose Galh O'Hallaghan.

'It might be, indeed, that there were those on both sides who thought that, if the marriage was obstructed, their own sons and daughters would have a better chance. Rose had many admirers; they might have envied John his happiness: many fathers, on the other side, might have wished their sons to succeed with Rose. Whether I am sinister in this conjecture is more than I can say. I grant, indeed, that a great portion of it is speculation on my part. The wedding day, however, was arranged; but, unfortunately, the fair day of Knockimdowney occurred, in the rotation of natural time, precisely one week before it. I know not from what motive it proceeded, but the factions on both sides were never known to make a more light-hearted preparation for battle. Cudgels of all sorts and sizes (and some of them, to my own knowledge, great beauties) were provided.

'I believe, I may as well take this opportunity of saying, that real Irish cudgels must be root-growing, either oak, blackthorn, or crab-tree – although crab-tree, by the way, is apt to fly. They should not be too long – three feet and a few inches is an accommodating length. They must be naturally top-heavy, and have around the end that is to make acquaintance with the cranium, three or four natural lumps, calculated to divide the flesh in the natest manner, and to leave, if possible, the smallest taste in life of pit in the skull. But if a good root-growing *kippeen* be light at the fighting end, or possess not the proper number of knobs, a hole a few inches deep is to be bored in the end, which must be filled with melted lead. This gives it a widow-and-orphan-making quality, a child-bereaving touch, altogether very desirable. If, however, the top splits in the boring, which, in awkward hands, is not uncommon, the defect may be remediated by putting on an iron ferrule, and driving two or three strong nails into it, simply to preserve it from flying off; not that an Irishman is ever at a loss for weapons when in a fight; for so long as a scythe, flail, spade, pitchfork, or stone is at hand, he feels quite contented with the lot of war. No man, as they say of great statesmen, is more fertile in expedients during a row; which, by the way, I take to be a good quality, at all events.

'I remember the fair day of Knockimdowney well: it has kept me from griddle-bread and tough nutriment ever since. Hard fortune to Jack Roe O'Hallaghan! No man had better teeth than I had, till I met with him that day. He fought stoutly on his own side; but he was *ped* then for the same basting that fell to me, though not by my hands: if to get his jaw dacently divided into three halves could be called a fair liquidation of an old debt – it was equal to twenty shilling in the pound, anyhow.

'There had not been a larger fair in the town of Knockimdowney for years. The day was dark and sunless, but sultry. On looking through the crowd, I could see no man without a cudgel; yet, what was strange, there was no certainty of any sport. Several desultory scrimmages had locality; but they were altogether sequestered from the great factions of the O's. Except that it was pleasant, and stirred one's blood to look at them, or occasioned the cudgels to be grasped more firmly, there was no personal interest felt by any of us in them; they therefore began and ended, here and there, through the fair, like mere flashes in the pan, dying in their own smoke.

'The blood of every prolific nation is naturally hot; but when that hot blood is inflamed by ardent spirits, it is not to be supposed that men should be cool; and, God he knows, there is not on the level surface of this habitable globe a nation that has been so thoroughly inflamed by *ardent spirits* as Ireland.

'Up till four o'clock that day, the factions were quiet. Several relations on both sides had been invited to drink by John and Rose's families, for the purpose of establishing a good feeling between them. But this was, after all, hardly to be expected, for they hated one another with an ardency much too good-humoured and buoyant; and, between ourselves, to bring Paddy over a bottle is a very equivocal mode of giving him an anti-cudgelling disposition. After the hour of four, several of the factions were getting very friendly, which I knew at the time to be a bad sign. Many of them nodded to each other, which I knew to be a worse one; and some of them shook hands with the greatest cordiality, which I no sooner saw than I slipped the knot of my cravat, and held myself in preparation for the sport.

'I have often had occasion to remark – and few men, let me tell you, had finer opportunities of doing so – the differential symptomatics between a Party Fight, that is, a battle between Orangemen and Ribbonmen, and one between two Roman Catholic Factions. There is something infinitely more anxious, silent, and deadly in the compressed vengeance, and the hope of slaughter, which characterize a *party fight*, than is to be seen in a battle between *factions*. The truth is, the enmity is not so deep and well-grounded in the latter as in the former. The feeling is not political nor religious between the factions; whereas, in the other it is both, which is a mighty great advantage; for when this is adjuncted to an intense personal hatred, and a sense of wrong, probably arising from a too intimate recollection of the leaded blackthorn, or the awkward death of some relative by the musket or the bayonet, it is apt to produce very purty fighting, and much respectable retribution.

'In a party fight, a prophetic sense of danger hangs, as it were, over the crowd – the very air is loaded with apprehension; and the vengeance-burst is preceded by a close, thick darkness, almost sulphury, that is more terrifical than the conflict itself, though clearly less dangerous and fatal. The scowl of the opposing parties, the blanched cheeks, the knit brows, and the grinding teeth, not pretermitting the deadly gleams that shoot from their kindled eyes, are ornaments which a plain battle between factions cannot boast, but which, notwithstanding, are very suitable to the fierce and gloomy silence of that premeditated vengeance, which burns with such intensity on the heart, and scorches up the vitals into such a thirst for blood, Not but they come by different means to the same conclusion; because it is the feeling, and not altogether the manner of operation, that is different.

'Now a faction fight doesn't resemble this, at all at all. Paddy's at home here; all song, dance, good-humour, and affection. His cheek is flushed with delight, which, indeed, may derive assistance from the consciousness of having no bayonets or loaded carabines to contend with; but, anyhow, he's at home

– his eye is lit with real glee – he tosses his hat in the air, in the height of mirth – and leaps, like a mountebank, two yards from the ground. Then with what a gracious dexterity he brandishes his cudgel! – what a joyous spirit is heard in his shout at the face of a friend from another faction! His very "whoo!" is contagious, and would make a man, that had settled on running away, return and join the sport with an appetite truly Irish. He is, in fact, while under the influence of this heavenly *afflatus*, in love with everyone – man, woman, and child. If he meet his sweetheart, he will give her a kiss and a hug, and that with double kindness, because he is on his way to thrash her father or brother. It is the *acumen* of his enjoyment; and woe be to him who will adventure to go between him and his amusements. To be sure, skulls and bones are broken, and lives lost; but they are lost in pleasant fighting – they are the consequences of the sport, the beauty of which consists in breaking as many heads and necks as you can; and certainly when a man enters into the spirit of any exercise, there is nothing like elevating himself to the point of excellence. Then a man ought never to be disheartened. If you lose this game, or get your head good-humourly beaten to pieces, why, you may win another, or your friends may mollify two or three skulls as a set-off to yours – but that is nothing.

'When the evening became more advanced, maybe, considering the poor look up there was for anything like dacent sport – maybe, in the early part of the day, wasn't it the delightful sight to see the boys on each side of the two great factions beginning to get frolicksome. Maybe the songs and the shouting, when they began, hadn't melody and music in them, anyhow! People may talk about harmony; but what harmony is equal to that in which five or six hundred men sing and shout, and leap and caper at each other, as a prelude to neighbourly fighting, where they beat time upon the drums of each other's ears and heads with oak drumsticks? That's an Irishman's music; and hard fortune to the *garran* that wouldn't have friendship and kindness in him to join and play a stave along with them! "Whoo! your sowl! Hurroo! Success to our side! Hi for the O'Callaghans! Where's the blackguard to –" I beg pardon, dacent reader – I forgot myself for a moment, or rather I got new life in me, for I am nothing at all at all for the last five months – a kind of nonentity, I may say, ever since that vagabond Burgess occasioned me to pay a visit to my distant relations, till my friends get that last matter of the collar-bone settled.

'The impulse which *faction* fighting gives trade and business in Ireland is truly surprising; whereas *party* fighting depreciates both. As soon as it is perceived that a *party* fight is to be expected, all buying and selling are suspended for the day, and those who are not *up*,[2] and even many who are, take themselves and their property home as quickly as may be convenient. But in a *faction* fight, as soon as there is any perspective of a row, depend upon it, there is quick work at all kinds of negotiation; and truly there is nothing like brevity and decision in buying and selling; for which reason faction fighting, at all events, if only for the sake of national prosperity, should be encouraged and kept up.

'Towards five o'clock, if a man was placed on an exalted station, so that he could look at the crowd, and *wasn't able to fight*, he could have seen much that a man might envy him for. Here a hat went up, or maybe a dozen of them; then followed a general huzza. On the other side, two dozen *caubeens* sought the sky, like so many scaldy crows attempting their own element for the first time, only they were not so black. Then another shout, which was answered by that of their friends on the opposite side; so that you would hardly know which side huzzaed loudest, the blending of both was so truly symphonious. Now there was a shout for the face of an O'Callaghan; this was prosecuted on the very heels by another for the face of an O'Hallaghan. Immediately a man of the O'Hallaghan side doffed his tattered frieze, and catching it by the very extremity of the sleeve, drew it, with a tact known only by an initiation of half a dozen street days, up the pavement after him. On the instant, a blade from the O'Callaghan side *peeled* with equal alacrity, and stretching his *home-made* at full length after him, proceeded triumphantly up the street to meet the other.

'Thundher-an-ages, what's this for, at all at all! I wish I hadn't begun to manuscript an account of it, anyhow; 'tis like a hungry man dreaming of a good dinner at a feast, and afterwards awaking and finding his front ribs and back-bone on the point of union. Reader, is that a blackthorn you carry – tut, where is my imagination bound for? – to meet the other, I say.

' "Where's the rascally O'*Callaghan* that will place his toe or his shilley on this frieze?" "Is there no blackguard O'*Hallaghan* jist to look *crucked* at the coat of an O'Callaghan, or say black's the white of his eye?"

' "Throth and there is, Ned, avourneen, that same on the sod here."

' "Is that Barney?"

' "The same, Ned, ma bouchal – and how is your mother's son, Ned?"

' "In good health at the present time, thank God and you; how is yourself, Barney?"

' "Can't complain as time goes; only take this, anyhow, to mend your health, ma bouchal" – (whack).

' "Success, Barney, and here's at your sarvice, avick, not making little of what I got – anyway" – (crack).

'About five o'clock on a May evening, in the fair of Knockimdowney, was the ice thus broken, with all possible civility, by Ned and Barney. The next moment a general rush took place towards the scene of action, and ere you could bless yourself, Barney and Ned were both down, weltering in their own and each other's blood. I scarcely know, indeed, though with a mighty respectable quota of experimentality myself, how to describe what followed. For the first twenty minutes the general harmony of this fine row might be set to music, according to a scale something like this: – Whick whack – crick crack – which whack – crick crack – &c., &c., &c. "Here yer sowl – (crack) – there yer sowl – (whack). Whoo for the O'Hallaghans!" – (crack, crack, crack). "Hurroo for the O'Callaghans! – (whack, whack, whack). The O'Callaghans for ever!" – (whack). "The O'Hallaghans for ever!" – (crack). "Murther; murther! – (crick, crack) – foul! foul! – (whick, whack). Blood and turf! – (whack, whick) – thundher-an'-ouns!" – (crack, crick). "Hurroo! my darlings! handle your kippeens – (crack, crack) – the O'Hallaghans are going!" – (whack, whack).

'You are to suppose them here to have been at it for about half an hour.

'Whack, crack – "Oh – oh – oh! have mercy upon me, boys – (crack – a shriek of murther! murther! – crack, crack, whack) – my life – my life – (crack, crack – whack, whack) – oh! for the sake of the living Father! – for the sake of my wife and childher, Ned Hallaghan, spare my life."

' "So we will, but take this, anyhow" – (whack, crack, whack, crack).

' "Oh! for the love of God, don't kill –" (whack, crack, whack). "Oh!" – (crack, crack, whack – *dies*).

' "Huzza! huzza! huzza!" from the O'Hallaghans. "Bravo, boys! there's one of them done for. Whoo! my darlings – hurroo! the O'Hallaghans for ever!"

'The scene now changes to the O'Callaghan side.

' "Jack – oh, Jack, avourneen – hell to their sowls for murdherers – Paddy's killed – his skull's smashed – Revinge, boys, Paddy O'Callaghan's killed! On with you, O'Callaghans – on with you – on with you, Paddy O'Callaghan's murdhered – take to the stones – that's it keep it up – down with him! Success! – he's the bloody villain that didn't show him marcy – that's it. Thundher-an'-ouns, is it laying him that way you are afther – let me at him!"

' "Here's a stone, Tom!"

' "No, no, this stick has the lead in it – it'll do him, never fear!"

' "Let him alone, Barney, he got enough."

' "By the powdhers, it's myself that won't; didn't he kill Paddy? – (crack, crack). Take that, you murdhering thief!" – (whack, crack).

' "Oh! – (whack, crack) – my head – I'm killed – I'm" – (crack – *kicks the bucket*).

' "Now, your sowl, that does you, anyway – (crack, whack) – horroo! – huzza! – huzza! Man for man, boys – an O'Hallaghan's done for – whoo! for our side – tol-deroll, lol-deroll, tow, row, row – huzza! – huzza! – tol-deroll – lol-deroll, tow, row, row – huzza for the O'Callaghans!"

'From this moment the battle became delightful; it was now pelt and welt on both sides, but many of the kippeens were broken – many of the boys had their fighting arms disabled by a dislocation or bit of fracture, and those weren't equal to more than doing a little upon such as were down.

'In the midst of the din, such a dialogue as this might be heard: ' "Larry, you're after being done for, for this day" – (whack, crack).

' "Only an eye gone – is that Mickey?" – (whick, whack, crick, crack).

' "That's it, my darlings! – you may say that, Larry – 'tis my mother's son that's in it – (crack, crack, a general huzza. Mickey and Larry) huzza! huzza! huzza for the O'Hallaghans! – What have you got, Larry?" – (crack, crack).

' "Only the bone of my arm, God be praised for it, very purtily snapt across!" – (whack, whack).

' "Is that all? Well, some people have luck!" – (crack, crack, crack).

' "Why, I've no reason to complain, thank God – (whack, crack) – purty play that, any way – Paddy O'Callaghan's settled – did you hear it? – (whack, whack, another shout) – That's it, boys – handle the shillelys! – Success, O'Hallaghans – down with the bloody O'Callaghans!"

' "I did hear it; so is Jem O'Hallaghan – (crack, whack, whack, crack) – you're not able to get up, I see – tare-an'-ounty, isn't it a pleasure to hear that play? – What ails you?"

' "Oh, Larry, I'm in great pain, and getting very weak, entirely" – (*faints*).

' "Faix, and he's settled too, I'm thinking."

' "Oh, murdher, my arm!" (One of the O'Callaghans attacks him – crack, crack).

' "Take that, you bagabone!" – (whack, whack).

' "Murdher, murdher, is it striking a *down* man you're after? – foul, foul, and my arm broke!" – (Crack, crack).

' "Take that, with what you got before, and it'll ase you, maybe."

'(A party of the O'Hallaghans attack the man who is beating him.)

' "Murdher, murdher!" – (crack, whack, whack, crack, crack, whack).

' "Lay on him, your sowls to pirdition – lay on him, hot and heavy – give it to him! He sthruck me, and me down wid my broken arm!"

' "Foul, ye thieves of the world! – (from the O'Callaghan) – foul! – five against one – give me fairplay! – (crack, crack, crack) – Oh! – (whack) – Oh, oh, oh!" – (falls senseless, covered with blood).

' "Ha, hell's cure to you, you bloody thief; you didn't spare me, with my arm broke! – (another general shout). – Bad end to it, isn't it a poor case entirely, that I can't even throw up my caubeen, let alone join in the diversion."

'Both parties now rallied, and ranged themselves along the street, exhibiting a firm, compact phalanx, wedged close against each other, almost foot to foot. The mass was thick and dense, and the tug of conflict stiff, wild, and savage. Much natural skill and dexterity were displayed in their mutual efforts to preserve their respective ranks unbroken, and as the sallies and charges were made on both sides, the temporary rush, the indentation of the multitudinous body, and the rebound into its original position gave an undulating appearance to the compact mass – reeking, groaning, dragging, and huzzaing – as it was, that resembled the serpentine motion of a rushing waterspout in the cloud.

'The women now began to take part with their brothers and sweethearts. Those who had no bachelors among the opposite factions fought along with their brothers; others did not scruple even to assist in giving their enamoured swains the father of a good beating. Many, however, were more faithful to love than to natural affection, and these sallied out, like heroines, under the banners of their sweethearts, fighting with amazing prowess against their friends and relations; nor was it all extraordinary to see two sisters engaged on opposite sides – perhaps tearing each other, as, with dishevelled hair, they screamed with a fury that was truly exemplary. Indeed, it is no untruth to assert that the women do much valuable execution. Their manner of fighting is this – as soon as the fair one decides upon taking a part in the row, she instantly takes off her apron or her stocking, stoops down, and lifting the first four-pounder she can get, puts it in the corner of her apron, or the foot of her stocking, if it has a foot, and marching into the scene of action, lays about her right and left. Upon my credibility, they are extremely useful and handy, and can give mighty nate knockdowns – inasmuch as no guard that a man is acquainted with can ward off their blows. Nay, what is more, it often happens, when a son-in-law is in a faction against his father-in-law and his wife's people generally, that if he and his wife's brother meet, the wife will clink him with the *pet* in her apron, downing her own husband with great skill, for it is not always that marriage extinguishes the hatred of factions: and very often 'tis the brother that is humiliated.

'Up to the death of these two men, John O'Callaghan and Rose's father, together with a large party of their friends on both sides, were drinking in a public-house, determined to take no portion in the fight, at all at all. Poor Rose, when she heard the shouting and terrible strokes, got as pale as death, and sat close to John, whose hand she captured in hers, beseeching him, and looking up in his face with the most imploring sincerity as she spoke, not to go out among them; the tears falling all the time from her fine eyes, the mellow flashes of which, when John's pleasantry in soothing her would seduce a smile, went into his very heart. But when, on looking out of the window where they sat, two of the opposing factions heard that a man on each side was killed; and when, on ascertaining the names of the individuals, and of those who murdhered them, it turned out that one of the murdered men was brother to a person in the room, and his murderer uncle to one of those in the window, it was not in the power of man or woman to keep them asunder, particularly as they were all rather advanced in liquor. In an instant the friends of the murdered man made a rush to the window, before any pacifiers had time to get between them, and catching the nephew of him who had committed the murder, hurled him headforemost upon the stone pavement, where his skull was dashed to pieces, and his brains scattered about the flags.

'A general attack instantly took place in the room between the two factions; but the apartment was too low and crowded to permit of proper fighting, so they rushed out to the street, shouting and yelling, as they do when the battle comes to the real point of doing business. As soon as it was seen that the heads of the O'Callaghans and O'Hallaghans were at work as well as the rest, the fight was recommenced with retrebled spirit; but when the mutilated body of the man who had been flung from the window was observed lying in a pool of his own proper brains and blood, such a cry arose among his friends, as would *cake*[3] the vital fluid in the veins of any one not a party in the quarrel. Now was the work – the moment of interest – men and women groaning, staggering, and lying insensible;

others shouting, leaping, and huzzaing; some singing, and not a few able-bodied spalpeens blurting, like overgrown children, on seeing their own blood; many raging and roaring about like bulls; – all this formed such a group as a faction fight, and nothing else, could represent.

'The battle now blazed out afresh; all kinds of instruments were now pressed into the service. Some got flails, some spades, some shovels, and one man got his hands upon a scythe, with which, unquestionably, he would have taken more lives than one; but, very fortunately, as he sallied out to join the crowd, he was politely visited in the back of the head by a brick-bat, which had a mighty convincing way with it of giving him a peaceable disposition, for he instantly lay down, and did not seem at all anxious as to the result of the battle. The O'Hallaghans were now compelled to give way, owing principally to the introvention of John O'Callaghan, who, although he was as good as sworn to take no part in the contest, was compelled to fight merely to protect himself. But, blood-and-turf! when he *did* begin, he was dreadful. As soon as his party saw him engaged, they took fresh courage, and in a short time made the O'Hallaghans retreat up the churchyard. I never saw anything equal to John; he absolutely sent them down in dozens: and when a man would give him any inconvenience with the stick, he would *down* him with the fist, for right and left were all alike to him. Poor Rose's brother and he met, both roused like two lions; but when John saw who it was, he held back his hand.

' "No, Tom," says he, "I'll not strike you, for Rose's sake. I'm not fighting through ill-will to you or your family; so take another direction, for I can't strike you."

'The blood, however, was unfortunately up in Tom.

' "We'll decide it now," said he; "I'm as good a man as you, O'Callaghan; and let me whisper this in your ear – you'll never warm the one bed with Rose, while God's in heaven – it's past that now – there can be nothing but blood between us!"

'At this juncture two of the O'Callaghans ran with their shillelaghs up, to beat down Tom on the spot.

' "Stop, boys!" said John, "you mustn't touch him; he had no hand in the quarrel. Go boys, if you respect me; lave him to myself."

'The boys withdrew to another part of the fight; and the next instant Tom struck the very man that interfered to save him across the temple, and cut him severely. John put his hand up, and staggered.

' "I'm sorry for this," he observed; "but it's now self-defence with me," and, at the same moment, with one blow, he left Tom O'Hallaghan stretched insensible on the street.

'On the O'Hallaghans being driven to the churchyard, they were at a mighty great inconvenience for weapons. Most of them had lost their sticks, it being a usage in fights of this kind to twist the cudgels from the grasp of the beaten men, to prevent them from rallying. They soon, however, furnished themselves with the best they could find, videlicet, the skull, leg, thigh, and arm bones, which they found lying about the graveyard. This was a new species of weapon, for which the majority of the O'Callaghans were scarcely prepared. Out they sallied in a body – some with these, others with stones, and, making fierce assault upon their enemies, absolutely *druv* them back – not so much by the damage they were doing, as by the alarm and terror which these unexpected species of missiles excited.

'At this moment, notwithstanding the fatality that had taken place, nothing could be more truly comical and facetious than the appearance of the field of battle. Skulls were flying in every direction – so thick, indeed, that it might with truth be asseverated that many who were petrified in the dust had their skulls broken in this great battle between the factions. – God help poor Ireland! when its inhabitants are so pugnacious that even the grave is no security against getting their crowns cracked, and their bones fractured! Well, anyhow, skulls and bones flew in every direction; stones and brick-bats were also put in motion; spades, shovels, loaded whips, pot-sticks, churn-staffs, flails, and all kinds of available weapons were in hot employment.

'But, perhaps, there was nothing more truly felicitous or original in its way than the mode of warfare adopted by little Neal Malone, who was tailor for the O'Callaghan side; for every tradesman is obliged to fight on behalf of his own faction. Big Frank Farrell the miller, being on the O'Hallaghan side, had been sent for, and came up from his mill behind the town, quite fresh. He was never what could be called a *good man*,[4] though it was said that he could lift ten hundredweight. He puffed forward with a great cudgel, determined to commit slaughter out of the face, and the first man he met was the *weeshy* fraction of a tailor, as nimble as a hare. He immediately attacked him, and would probably have taken his measure for life, had not the tailor's activity protected him. Farrell was in a rage; and Neal, taking advantage of his blind fury, slipt round him, and, with a short run sprang upon the miller's back, and planted a foot upon the threshold of each coat-pocket, holding by the mealy collar of his waistcoat. In this position he belaboured the miller's face and eyes with his little hard fist to such purpose that he had him in the course of a few minutes nearly as blind as a mill-horse. The miller roared for assistance, but the pell-mell was going on too warmly for his cries to be available. In fact, he resembled an elephant with a monkey on his back.

' "How do you like that, Farrell?" Neal would say – giving him a cuff; "and that, and that – but that is best of all. Take it again, gudgeon – (two cuffs more) – here's grist for you – (half a dozen additional) hard fortune to you! – (crack, crack). What! going to lie down! by all that's terrible, if you do, I'll *annigulate*[5] you. Here's a *dhuragh*[6] (another half dozen) – long measure, you savage – the baker's dozen, you baste; there's five-an'-twenty to the score, Sampson, and one or two in" – (crack, whack).

' "Oh! murther sheery!" shouted the miller – "murther-an-age, I'm kilt – foul play! foul play!"

' "You lie, big Nebuchodonosor, it's not – this is all fair play, you big baste – *fair* play, Sampson: by the same a-token, here's to jog your memory that it's the *Fair* day of Knockimdowney; *Irish Fair* play, you whale – but I'll whale you" – (crack, crack, whack).

' "Oh – oh!" shouted the miller.

' "Oh – oh! is it? Oh, if I had my scissors here, till I'd clip your ears off, wouldn't I be the happy man, anyhow, you swab, you" – (whack, whack, crack).

' "Murther – murther – murther!" – shouted the miller – "is there no help?"

' "Help, is it? you may say that – (crack, crack); there's a trifle – a small taste in the *milling* style, you know; and here goes to dislodge a *grinder*. Did ye ever hear of the tailor on horseback, Sampson? eh? – (whack, whack): did you ever expect to see a tailor o' horseback of yourself, you baste – (crack). I tell you, if you offer to lie down, I'll *annigulate* you out o' the face."

'Never, indeed, was a miller, before or since, so well dusted; and I daresay Neal would have rode him long enough, but for an O'Hallaghan, who had gone into one of the houses to procure a weapon. This man was nearly as original in his choice of one as the tailor in the position which he selected for beating the miller. On entering the kitchen, he found that he had been anticipated; there was neither tongs, poker, or churn-staff; nor, in fact, anything wherewith he could assault his enemies: all had been carried off by others, There was, however, a goose in the action of being roasted on a spit at the fire. This was enough: honest O'Hallaghan saw nothing but the spit, which he accordingly seized, goose and all, making the best of his way, so armed, to the scene of battle. He just came out as the miller was once more roaring for assistance, and, to a dead certainty, would have spitted the tailor like a cock-sparrow against the miller's carcass, had not his activity once more saved him.

Unluckily, the unfortunate miller got the thrust behind, which was intended for Neal, and roared like a bull. He was beginning to shout "Foul play," when, on turning round, he perceived that the thrust was not intended for him, but for the tailor.

' "Give me that spit," said he; "by all the mills that ever were turned, I'll spit the tailor this blessed minute beside the goose, and we'll roast them both together."

'The other refused to part with the spit; but the miller, seizing the goose, flung it with all his force after the tailor, who stooped, however, and avoided the blow.

' "No man has a better right to the goose than the tailor," said Neal, as he took it up, and disappearing, neither he nor the goose could be seen for the remainder of the day.

'The battle was now somewhat abated. Skulls, and bones, and bricks, and stones were, however, still flying; so that it might be truly said the bones of contention were numerous. The streets presented a woeful spectacle: men were lying with their bones broken – others, though not so seriously injured, lappered in their blood – some were crawling up, but were instantly knocked down by their enemies – some were leaning against the walls, or groping their way silently along them, endeavouring to escape observation, lest they might be smashed down and altogether murdered. Wives were sitting with the bloody heads of their husbands in their laps, tearing their hair, weeping, and cursing, in all the gall of wrath, those who left them in such a state. Daughters performed the same offices to their fathers, and sisters to their brothers; not pretermitting those who did not neglect their broken-pated bachelors, to whom they paid equal attention. Yet was the scene not without abundance of mirth. Many a hat was thrown up by the O'Callaghan side, who certainly gained the day. Many a song was raised by those who tottered about with trickling sconces, half drunk with whiskey, and half stupid with beating. Many a "whoo," and "hurroo," and "huzza," was sent forth by the triumphanters; but truth to tell, they were miserably feeble and faint, compared to what they had been in the beginning of the amusements – sufficiently evincing that, although they might boast of the name of victory, they had got a bellyful of beating – still there was hard fighting.

'I mentioned, some time ago, that a man had adopted a scythe. I wish from my heart there had been no such bloody instrument there that day; but truth must be told. John O'Callaghan was now engaged against a set of the other O's, who had rallied for the third time and attacked him and his party. Another brother of Rose Galh's was in this engagement, and him did John O'Callaghan not only knock down, but cut desperately across the temple. A man, stripped, and covered with blood and dust, at that moment made his appearance, his hand bearing the blade of the aforesaid scythe. His approach was at once furious and rapid – and, I may as well add, fatal; for, before John O'Callaghan had time to be forewarned of his danger, he was cut down, the artery of his neck laid open, and he died without a groan. It was truly dreadful, even to the oldest fighter present, to see the strong rush of red blood that curvated about his neck, until it gurgled – gurgled – gurgled, and lappered, and bubbled out – ending in small red spouts, blackening and blackening, as they became fainter and more faint. At this criticality every eye was turned from the corpse to the murderer; but he had been instantly struck down, and a female, with a large stone in her apron, stood over him, her arms stretched out, her face horribly distorted with agony, and her eyes turned backwards, as it were, into her head. In a few seconds she fell into strong convulsions, and was immediately taken away. Alas! alas! it was Rose Galh; and when we looked at the man she had struck down, he was found to be her brother! flesh of her flesh, and blood of her blood! On examining him more closely, we discovered that his under-jaw hung loose, that his limbs were supple; we tried to make him speak, but in vain – he, too, was a corpse.

'The fact was that, in consequence of his being stripped, and covered by so much blood and dust, she knew him not; and impelled by her feelings to avenge herself on the murderer of her lover, to whom she doubly owed her life, she struck him a deadly blow, without knowing him to be her brother. The shock produced by seeing her lover murdered – and the horror of finding that she herself, in avenging him, had taken her brother's life, was too much for a heart so tender as hers. On recovering from her convulsions, her senses were found to be gone forever! Poor girl! she is still living; but from that moment to this she has never opened her lips to mortal. She is, indeed, a fair ruin, but silent, melancholy, and beautiful as the moon in the summer heaven. Poor Rose Galh! you, and many a mother, and father, and wife, and orphan, have had reason to maledict the *bloody Battles of the Factions!*

'With regard to my grandfather, he says that he didn't see purtier fighting within his own memory; nor since the fight between himself and Big Mucklemurray took place in the same town. But, to do him justice, he condemns the scythe and every other weapon except the cudgels; because, he says, that if they continue to be resorted to, nate fighting will be altogether forgotten in the country.'

1. Manual – a Catholic prayer-book.
2. Initiated into Whiteboyism.
3. Harden.
4. A brave man.
5. Annihilate. Many of the jaw-breakers–and this was certainly such in a double sense–used by the hedge schoolmasters are scattered among the people, by whom they are so twisted that it would be extremely difficult to recognize them.
6. Dhuragh–an additional portion of any thing thrown in from a spirit of generosity, after the measure agreed on is given. When the miller, for instance, receives his toll, the country people usually throw in several handfuls of meal as a *dhuragh.*

SAMUEL LOVER

1797–1868

Samuel Lover was born in Dublin on the 24th of February, 1797. His father was a well-known stock-broker. As young Lover grew up, tales of those innumerable outrages of soldiers and yeomen that had so much to do with bringing on the great rebellion, were dinned into his ears by nurses and servants. Nothing else, perhaps, had so much to do with waking that sympathy with peasant life so visible in his stories. At thirteen he entered his father's office, but spent much of his time, to his father's disgust, in music, painting, verse-writing, and theatricals. At first the angry stockbroker tried obstruction – the paint-box or music-book would get lost mysteriously. Young Lover began more and more to neglect his office-work. When he was eighteen, things came to a climax. He had constructed a marionette show, and his father, unable any longer to bear with such 'frivolities,' broke it into pieces with his walking-stick. Its owner, angry in his turn, left the house never to return.

For two years he lived in lodgings, studying art and making his living in some way that has never become known, but live he did, and not without some comfort, finding money enough to buy a guitar and leisure enough to practise it. At the end of the two years he emerged as a rising miniature painter. The Marquis Wellesley, the Duke of Leinster, and Lord Cloncurry sat to him, and Dublin society made him its latest lion. His handsome and mobile face, his numberless stories and good songs, opened all doors. He soon became known to the general public through the song of 'Rory O'More,' written at the suggestion of Lady Morgan. Many more followed and repeated its success. Some, such as 'Molly Carew' and 'Widow Macree,' are still well known. In 1827 Lover married a Miss Birret, and, in 1834, took advantage of some renewed celebrity gained for him by a miniature of Paganini to move over to London. His two well-known novels, 'Rory O'More' and 'Handy Andy,' were written and published soon after his arrival. Their immense success induced him henceforth to make literature his main reliance. He wrote a number of dramas now forgotten, an adaptation of 'Rory O'More' being the most successful. Indeed, 'Rory O'More,' as story, song, and stage play, was the triumph of his life. In 1846 he went on a lecturing tour in America, reading selections from his own works. His last picture, 'The Kerry Post on Valentine's Day,' was exhibited in Dublin in 1862. He died on July the 6th, 1868.

BARNY O'REIRDON, THE NAVIGATOR

By SAMUEL LOVER

I

Outward Bound

A very striking characteristic of an Irishman is his unwillingness to be outdone. Some have asserted that this arises from vanity, but I have ever been unwilling to attribute an unamiable motive to my countrymen where a better may be found, and one equally tending to produce a similar result; and I consider a deep-seated spirit of emulation to originate this peculiarity. Phrenologists might resolve it by supposing the organ of the love of approbation to predominate in our Irish craniums, and it may be so; but as I am not in the least a metaphysician, and very little of a phrenologist, I leave those who choose to settle the point in question, quite content with the knowledge of the fact with which I started, viz., the unwillingness of an Irishman to be outdone. This spirit, it is likely, may sometimes lead men into ridiculous positions, but it is equally probable that the desire of surpassing one another has given birth to many of the noblest actions, and some of the most valuable inventions; let us, therefore, not fall out with it.

Now having vindicated the *motive* of my countrymen, I will prove the total absence of national prejudice in so doing, by giving an illustration of the ridiculous consequences attendant upon this Hibernian peculiarity.

Barny O'Reirdon was a fisherman of Kinsale, and a heartier fellow never hauled a net or cast a line into deep water; indeed, Barny, independently of being a merry boy among his companions, a lover of good fun and good whiskey, was rather looked up to, by his brother fishermen, as an intelligent fellow, and few boats brought more fish to market than Barny O'Reirdon's; his opinion on certain points in the craft was considered law, and in short, in his own little community, Barny was what was commonly called a leading man. Now, your leading man is always jealous in an inverse ratio to the sphere of his influence, and the leader of a nation is less incensed at a rival's triumph than the great man of a village. If we pursue this descending scale, what a desperately jealous person the oracle of oyster-dredgers and cockle-women must be! Such was Barny O'Reirdon.

Seated one night in a public-house, the common resort of Barny and other marine curiosities, our hero got entangled in debate with what he called a strange sail – that is to say, a man he had never met before, and whom he was inclined to treat rather magisterially upon nautical subjects; at the same time that the stranger was equally inclined to assume the high hand over him, till at last the new-comer made a regular outbreak by exclaiming: 'Ah, tare-an-ouns, lave off your balderdash, Mr O'Reirdon; by the powdhers o' war it's enough, so it is, to make a dog bate his father, to hear you goin' an as if you wor Curlumberus or Sir Crustyphiz. Wran, whin ivery one knows the divil a farther you ivir wor, nor ketchin' crabs or drudgin' oysters.'

'Who towld you that, my Watherford Wondher?' rejoined Barny: 'what the dickens do you know about sayfarin', farther nor fishin' for sprats in a bowl wid your grandmother?'

'Oh, baithershin,' says the stranger.

'And who made you so bowld with my name?' demanded O'Reirdon.

'No matther for that,' says the stranger; 'but if you'd like for to know, shure it's your cousin, Molly Mullins, knows me well, and maybe I don't know you and yours as well as the mother that bore you, ay, in throth; and shure I know the very thoughts o' you as well as if I was inside o' you, Barny O'Reirdon.'

'By my sowl, thin, you know betther thoughts than your own, Mr Whippersnapper, if that's the name you go by.'

'No, it's not the name I go by; I've as good a name as your own, Mr O'Reirdon, for want o' a betther, and that's O'Sullivan.'

'Throth there's more than there's good o' them,' said Barny.

'Good or bad, I'm a cousin o' your own, twice removed by the mother's side.'

'And is it the Widda O'Sullivan's boy you'd be that left this come Candlemas four years?'

'The same.'

'Throth, thin, you might know betther manners to your eldhers, though I'm glad to see you, anyhow, agin; but a little thravellin' puts us beyant ourselves sometimes,' said Barny, rather contemptuously.

'Throth, I niver bragged out o' myself yit, and it's what I say, that a man that's only a fishin' aff the land all his life has no business to compare in the regard o' thrathericks wid a man that has sailed to Fingal.'

This silenced any further argument on Barny's part. Where Fingal lay was all Greek to him; but, unwilling to admit his ignorance, he covered his retreat with the usual address of his countrymen, and turned the bitterness of debate into the cordial flow of congratulation at seeing his cousin again.

The liquor was freely circulated, and the conversation began to take a different turn, in order to lead from that which had nearly ended in a quarrel between O'Reirdon and his relation.

The state of the crops, county cess, road jobs, etc., became topics, and various strictures as to the utility of the latter were indulged in, while the merits of the neighbouring farmers were canvassed.

'Why, thin,' said one, 'that field o' whate o' Michael Coghlan, is the finest field o' whate mortial eyes was ever set upon – divil the likes iv it myself ever seen far or near.'

'Throth, thin, sure enough,' said another, 'it promises to be a fine crap, anyhow; and myself can't help thinkin' it quare that Mickee Coghlan, that's a plain-spoken, quite (quiet) man, and simple-like, should have finer craps than Pether Kelly o' the big farm beyant, that knows all about the great saycrets o' the airth, and is knowledgeable to a degree, and has all the hard words that iver was coined at his fingers' ends.'

'Faith, he has a power o' *blasthogue* about him, sure enough,' said the former speaker, 'if that could do him any good, but he isn't fit to hould a candle to Michael Coghlan in the regard o' farmin'.'

'Why, blur an agers,' rejoined the upholder of science, 'sure he met the Scotch steward that the lord beyant has, one day, that I hear is a wondherful edicated man, and was brought over here to show us all a patthern; – well, Pether Kelly met him one day, and, by gor, he discoorsed him to that degree that the Scotch chap hadn't a word left in his jaw.'

'Well, and what was he the betther o' having more prate than a Scotchman?' asked the other.

'Why,' answered Kelly's friend, 'I think it stands to rayson that the man that done out the Scotch steward ought to know somethin' more about farmin' than Mickee Coghlan.'

'Augh! don't talk to me about knowing,' said the other rather contemptuously. 'Sure I gev into you that he has the power o' prate, and the gift o' the gab, and all to that. I own to you that he has *the-o-ry* and the *che-mis-thery*, but he hasn't the *craps*. Now, the man that has the craps is the man for my money.'

'You're right, my boy,' said O'Reirdon, with an approving thump of his brawny fist on the table; 'it's a little talk goes far – *doin'* is the thing.'

'Ah, yiz may run down larnin' if yiz like,' said the undis-
mayed stickler for theory versus practice; 'but larnin' is a fine
thing, and sure where would the world be at all only for it; sure
where would the staymers (steamboats) be, only for larnin'?'

'Well,' said O'Reirdon, 'and the divil may care if we never
seen them; I'd rather dipind an wind and canvas any day then
the likes o' them. What are they good for but to turn good
sailors into kitchen-maids, all as one bilin' a big pot o' wather
and oilin' their fire-irons, and throwin' coals an the fire? Augh!
thim staymers is a disgrace to the say; they're for all the world
like owld fogies, smokin' from mornin' till night, and doing no
good.'

'Do you call it doin' no good to go fasther nor ships ivir wint
before?'

'Pooh; sure Solomon, queen o' Sheba, said there was time
enough for all things.'

'Thrue for you,' said O'Sullivan, *fair and aisy goes far in a
day*, is a good owld sayin'.'

'Well, maybe you'll own to the improvemint they're makin'
in the harbour o' Howth, beyant in Dublin, is some good?'

'We'll see whether it'll be an improvemint first,' said the
obdurate O'Reirdon.

'Why, man alive, sure you'll own it's the greatest o' good it
is, takin' up the big rocks out o' the harbour.'

'Well, and where's the wondher of that? – sure we done the
same here.'

'Oh, yis, but it was whin the tide was out and the rocks was
bare; but up in Howth they cut away the big rocks from under
the say intirely.'

'Oh, be aisy; why, how could they do that?'

'Ay, there's the matther, that's what larnin' can do; and
wondherful it is intirely! and the way it is is this, as I hear it, for
I never seen it, but hard it described by the lord to some
gintlemin and ladies one day in his garden, where I was helpin'
the gardener to land some salary (celery). You see the ingineer

goes down undher the wather intirely, and can stay there as long as he plazes.'

'Whoo! and what o' that? Sure I heerd the long sailor say, that come from the Aysthern Ingees, that the Ingineers there can almost live undher wather; and goes down lookin' for dimonds, and has a sledge-hammer in their hand, brakein' the dimonds when they're too big to take them up whole, all as one as men brakein' stones an the road.'

'Well, I don't want to go beyant that; but the way the lord's ingineer goes down is, he has a little bell wid him, and while he has that little bell to ring, hurt nor harm can't come to him.'

'Arrah, be aisy.'

'Divil a lie in it.'

'Maybe it's a blessed bell,' said O'Reirdon, crossing himself.

'No, it is not a blessed bell.'

'Why, thin, now do you think me sitch a born nath'ral as to give in to that? – as if the ringin' iv a bell, barrin' it was a blessed bell, could do the like. I tell you it's impossible.'

'Ah, nothin's unpossible to God.'

'Sure I wasn't denyin' that; but I say the bell is unpossible.'

'Why,' said O'Sullivan, 'you see he's not altogether complate in the demonstheration o' the mashine; it is not by the ringin' o' the bell it is done, but – '

'But what?' broke in O'Reirdon, impatiently. 'Do you mane for to say there is a bell in it at all, at all?'

'Yes, I do,' said O'Sullivan.

'I towld you so,' said the promulgator of the story.

'Ay,' said O'Sullivan, 'but it is not by the ringin' iv the bell it is done.'

'Well, how is it done, then?' said the other, with a half-offended, half-supercilious air.

'It is done,' said O'Sullivan, as he returned the look with interest, 'it is done intirely be jommethry.'

'Oh! I undherstan' it now,' said O'Reirdon, with an inimitable affectation of comprehension in the Oh! – 'but to talk of the ringin' iv a bell doing the like is beyant the beyants untirely, barrin', as I said before, it was a blessed bell, glory be to God!'

'And so you tell me, sir, it is jommethry?' said the twice-discomfited man of science.

'Yes, sir,' said O'Sullivan, with an air of triumph, which rose in proportion as he saw he carried the listeners along with him – 'jommethry.'

'Well, have it your own way. There's them that won't hear rayson sometimes, nor have belief in larnin'; and you may say it's jommethry if you plaze: but I heerd them that knows betther than iver you knew say – '

'Whisht, whisht! and bad cess to you both,' said O'Reirdon; 'what the dickens are yiz goin' to fight about now, and sitch good liquor before yiz? Hillo! there, Mrs Quigley, bring uz another quart, i' you plaze; ay, that's the chat, another quart. Augh! yiz may talk till you're black in the face about your invintions, and your staymers, and bell-ringin', and gash, and railroads; but here's long life and success to the man that invinted the impairil (imperial) quart; that was the rail beautiful invintion,' and he took a long pull at the replenished vessel, which strongly indicated that the increase of its dimensions was a very agreeable *measure* to such as Barny.

After the introduction of this and *other* quarts, it would not be an easy matter to pursue the conversation that followed. Let us, therefore, transfer our story to the succeeding morning, when Barny O'Reirdon strolled forth from his cottage, rather later than usual, with his eyes bearing eye-witness to the carouse of the preceding night. He had not a headache, however; whether it was that Barny was too experienced a campaigner under the banners of Bacchus, or that Mrs Quigley's boast was a just one, namely, 'that of all the drink in her house there was n't a headache in a hogshead of it,' is hard to determine, but I rather incline to the strength of Barny's head.

The above-quoted declaration of Mrs Quigley is the favourite inducement held out by every boon companion in Ireland at the head of his own table: 'Don't be afraid of it, my boys! It's the right sort. There's not a headache in a hogshead of it.'

Barny sauntered about in the sun, at which he often looked up, under the shelter of compressed, bushy brows and long-lashed eyelids, and a shadowing hand across his forehead, to see 'what time o' day' it was; and, from the frequency of this action, it was evident the day was hanging heavily with Barny. He retired at last to a sunny nook in a neighbouring field, and stretching himself at full length, basked in the sun, and began 'to chew the cud of sweet and bitter thought'. He first reflected on his own undoubted weight in his little community, but still he could not get over the annoyance of the preceding night, arising from his being silenced by O'Sullivan, 'a chap,' as he said himself, 'that lift the place four years agon a brat iv a boy, and to think of his comin' back and outdoin' his elders, that saw him runnin' about the place, a gassoon, that one could tache a few months before'; 't was too bad. Barny saw his reputation was in a ticklish position, and began to consider how his disgrace could be retrieved. The very name of Fingal was hateful to him; it was a plague-spot on his peace that festered there incurably. He first thought of leaving Kinsale altogether; but flight implied so much of defeat that he did not long indulge in that notion. No; he would stay, 'in spite of all the O'Sullivans, kith and kin, breed, seed, and generation'. But at the same time he knew he should never hear the end of that hateful place, Fingal; and if Barny had had the power, he would have enacted a penal statute, making it death to name the accursed spot, wherever it was; but not being gifted with such legislative authority, he felt Kinsale was no place for him, if he would not submit to be flouted every hour out of the four-and-twenty, by man, woman, and child, that wished to annoy him. What was to be done? He was in the perplexing situation, to use his own words, 'of the cat in the thripe shop,' he did n't know which way to choose. At last, after turning himself over in the sun several times, a new idea struck him. Could n't he go to Fingal himself? and then he'd be equal to that upstart, O'Sullivan. No sooner was the thought engendered than Barny sprang to his feet a new man; his eye brightened, his step became once more elastic, he walked erect, and felt himself to be all over Barny O'Reirdon once more. 'Richard was himself again.'

But where was Fingal? – there was the rub. That was a profound mystery to Barny, which, until discovered, must hold him in the vile bondage of inferiority. The plain-dealing trader will say, 'Couldn't he ask?' No, no; that would never do for Barny; that would be an open admission of ignorance his soul was above; and, consequently, Barny set his brains to work to devise measures of coming at the hidden knowledge by some circuitous route, that would not betray the end he was working for. To this purpose fifty stratagems were raised and demolished in half as many minutes, in the fertile brain of Barny, as he strode along the shore; and as he was working hard at the fifty-first, it was knocked all to pieces by his jostling against someone whom he never perceived he was approaching, so immersed was he in speculations, and on looking up, who should it prove to be but his friend, 'the long sailor from the Aysthern Injees.' This was quite a godsend to Barny, and much beyond what he could have hoped for. Of all the men under the sun, the long sailor was the man in a million for Barny's net at that minute, and accordingly he made a haul of him, and thought it the greatest catch he ever made in his life.

Barny and the long sailor were in close companionship for the remainder of the day, which was closed, as the preceding one, in a carouse; but on this occasion there was only a duet performance in honour of the jolly god, and the treat was at Barny's expense. What the nature of their conversation during the period was I will not dilate on, but keep it as profound a secret as Barny himself, and content myself with saying that

Barny looked a much happier man the next day. Instead of wearing his hat slouched, and casting his eyes on the ground, he walked about with his usual unconcern, and gave his nod and passing word of *'civilitude'* to every friend he met; he rolled his quid of tobacco about in his jaw with an air of superior enjoyment, and if disturbed in his narcotic amusement by a question, he took his own good time to eject 'the leperous distilment' before he answered the querist, with a happy composure, that bespoke a man quite at ease with himself. It was in this agreeable spirit that Barny bent his course to the house of Peter Kelly, the owner of the 'big farm beyant,' before alluded to, in order to put into practice a plan he had formed for the fulfilment of his determination of rivalling O'Sullivan.

He thought it probable that Peter Kelly, being one of the 'snuggest' men in the neighbourhood, would be a likely person to join him in a 'spec,' as he called it (a favourite abbreviation of his for the word speculation), and, accordingly, when he reached the 'big farmhouse,' he accosted its owner with the usual 'God save you.'

'God save you kindly, Barny,' returned Peter Kelly; 'an' what is it brings you here, Barny,' asked Peter, 'this fine day, instead o' bein' out in the boat?'

'Oh, I'll be in the boat soon enough, and it's far enough too I'll be out in her; an' indeed it's partly that same is bringin' me here to yourself.'

'Why, do you want me to go along wid you, Barny?'

'Throth, an' I don't, Mr Kelly. You are a knowledgeable man on land, but I'm afeard it's a bad bargain you'd be at say.'

'And what wor you talking about me and your boat for?'

'Why, you see, sir, it was in the regard of a little bit o' business, an' if you'd come wid me and take a turn in the praty field, I'll be behouldin' to you, and maybe you'll hear somethin' that won't be displazin' to you.'

'An' welkim, Barny,' said Peter Kelly.

When Barny and Peter were in the 'praty field,' Barny opened the trenches (I don't mean the potato trenches), but, in military parlance, he opened the trenches and laid siege to Peter Kelly, setting forth the extensive profits that had been realized by various 'specs' that had been made by his neighbours in exporting potatoes. 'And sure,' said Barny, 'why shouldn't you do the same, and they here ready to your hand? as much as to say, *why don't you profit by me, Peter Kelly?* And the boat is below there in the harbour, and, I'll say this much, the divil a betther boat is betune this and herself.'

'Indeed, I b'lieve so, Barny,' said Peter; 'for considhering where we stand at this present, there's no boat at all at all betune us'; and Peter laughed with infinite pleasure at his own hit.

'Oh! well, you know what I mane, anyhow, an', as I said before, the boat is a darlint boat, and as for him that commands her – I b'lieve I need say nothin' about that,' and Barny gave a toss of his head and a sweep of his open hand, more than doubling the laudatory nature of his comment on himself.

But, as the Irish saying is, 'to make a long story short,' Barny prevailed on Peter Kelly to make an export; but in the nature of the venture they did not agree. Barny had proposed potatoes; Peter said there were enough of them already where he was going, and rejoined: 'Praties were so good in themselves there never could be too much o' thim anywhere.' But Peter, being a knowledgeable man, and up to all the 'saycrets o' the airth, and undherstanding the the-o-ry and the che-mis-thery,' overruled Barny's proposition, and determined upon a cargo of *scalpeens* (which name they give to pickled mackerel) as a preferable merchandise, quite forgetting that Dublin Bay herrings were a much better and as cheap a commodity, at the command of the Fingalians. But in many similar mistakes the ingenious Mr Kelly has been paralleled by other speculators. But that is neither here nor there, and it was all one to Barny whether his boat was freighted with potatoes or *scalpeens*, so long as he had the honour and glory of becoming a navigator, and being as good as O'Sullivan.

Accordingly, the boat was laden and all got in readiness for putting to sea, and nothing was now wanting but Barny's orders to haul up the gaff and shake out the jib of his hooker.

But this order Barny refrained to give, and for the first time in his life exhibited a disinclination to leave the shore. One of his fellow-boatmen at last said to him: 'Why, thin, Barny O'Reirdon, what the divil is come over you at all at all? What's the maynin' of your loitherin' about here, and the boat ready, and a lovely fine breeze aff o' the land?'

'Oh! never you mind; I b'lieve I know my own business, anyhow; an' it's hard, so it is, if a man can't ordher his own boat to sail when he plazes.'

'Oh! I was only thinkin' it quare – and a pity more betoken, as I said before, to lose the beautiful breeze, and – '

'Well, just keep your thoughts to yourself, i' you plaze, and stay in the boat as I bid you, an' don't be out of her on your apperl, by no manner o' manes, for one minit, for you see I don't know when it may be plazin' to me to go aboord an' set sail.'

'Well, all I can say is, I never seen you afeard to go to say before.'

'Who says I'm afeard?' said O'Reirdon; 'you betther not say that agin, or in throth, I'll give you a leatherin' that won't be for the good o' your health – throth, for three sthraws this minit I'd lave you that your own mother wouldn't know you with the lickin' I'd give you; but I scorn your dirty insinuation; no man ever seen Barny O'Reirdon afeard yet, anyhow. Howld your prate, I tell you, and look up to your betthers. What do you know iv navigation? – maybe you think it's as easy for to sail an a voyage as to go start a fishin"; and Barny turned on his heel and left the shore.

The next day passed without the hooker sailing, and Barny gave a most sufficient reason for the delay, by declaring that he had a warnin' given him in a dhrame (glory be to God), and that it was given him to understand (under heaven) that it wouldn't be looky that day.

Well, the next day was Friday, and Barny, of course, would not sail any more than any other sailor who could help it, on this unpropitious day. On Saturday, however, he came, running in a great hurry down to the shore, and, jumping aboard, he gave orders to make all sail, and taking the helm of the hooker, he turned her head to the sea, and soon the boat was cleaving the blue waters with a velocity seldom witnessed in so small a craft, and scarcely conceivable to those who have not seen the speed of a Kinsale hooker.

'Why, thin, you tuk the notion mighty suddint, Barny,' said the fisherman next in authority to O'Reirdon, as soon as the bustle of getting the boat under way had subsided.

'Well, I hope it's plazin' to you at last,' said Barny; 'throth, one 'ud think you were never at say before, you wor in such a hurry to be off; as newfangled a'most as a child with a play-toy.'

'Well,' said the other of Barny's companions, for there were but two with him in the boat, 'I was thinkin' myself as well as Jimmy, that we lost two fine days for nothin', and we'd be there a'most, maybe, now, if we sail'd three days agon.'

'Don't b'lieve it,' said Barny, emphatically. 'Now, don't you know yourself that there is some days that the fish won't come near the lines at all, and that we might as well be castin' our nets an the dhry land as in the say, for all we'll catch if we start an an unlooky day; and sure I towld you I was waitin' only till I had it given to me to undherstan' that it was looky to sail, and I go bail we'll be there sooner than if we started three days agon; for, if you don't start, with good look before you, faix, maybe it's never at all to the end o' your thrip you'll come.'

'Well, there's no use in talkin' about it now anyhow; but when do you expec' to be there?'

'Why, you see we must wait antil I can tell you how the wind is like to hould on, before I can make up my mind to that.'

'But you're sure now, Barny, that you're up to the coorse you have to run?'

'See now, lay me alone, and don't be crass-questionin' me – tare an ouns, do you think me sitch a bladdherang as for to go to shuperinscribe a thing I wasn't aiquil to?'

'No; I was only goin' to ax you what coorse you wor goin' to steer?'

'You'll find out soon enough when we get there; and so I bid you agin lay me alone – just keep your toe in your pump. Shure I'm here at the helm, and a woight on my mind, and it's fitther for you, Jim, to mind your own business and lay me to mind mine; away wid you, there, and be handy; haul taut that foresheet there; we must run close an the wind; be handy, boys; make everything dhraw.'

These orders were obeyed, and the hooker soon passed to windward of a ship that left the harbour before her, but could not hold on a wind with the same tenacity as the hooker, whose qualities in this particular render it peculiarly suitable for the purposes to which it is applied – namely, pilot- and fishing-boats.

We have said that a ship left the harbour before the hooker had set sail, and it is now fitting to inform the reader that Barny had contrived, in the course of his last meeting with the 'long sailor', to ascertain that this ship, then lying in the harbour, was going to the very place Barny wanted to reach. Barny's plan of action was decided upon in a moment; he had now nothing to do but to watch the sailing of the ship and follow in her course. Here was, at once, a new mode of navigation discovered.

The stars, twinkling in mysterious brightness through the silent gloom of night, were the first encouraging, because *visible*, guides to the adventurous mariners of antiquity. Since then the sailor, encouraged by a bolder science, relies on the *unseen* agency of nature, depending on the fidelity of an atom of iron to the mystic law that claims its homage in the north. This is one refinement of science upon another. But the beautiful simplicity of Barny O'Reirdon's philosophy cannot be too much admired. To follow the ship that is going to the same place. Is not this navigation made easy?

But Barny, like many a great man before him, seemed not to be aware of how much credit he was entitled to for his invention, for he did not divulge to his companions the originality of his proceeding; he wished them to believe he was only proceeding in the commonplace manner, and had no ambition to be distinguished as the happy projector of so simple a practice.

For this purpose he went to windward of the ship, and then fell off again, allowing her to pass him, as he did not wish even those on board the ship to suppose he was following in their wake; for Barny, like all people that are quite full of one scheme, and fancy everybody is watching them, dreaded lest any one should fathom his motives. All that day Barny held on the same course as his leader, keeping at a respectful distance, however, 'for fear 't would look like dodging her', as he said to himself; but as night closed in, so closed in Barny with the ship, and kept a sharp lookout that she should not give him the slip in the dark. The next morning dawned, and found the hooker and ship companions still; and thus matters proceeded for four days, during the entire of which time they had not seen land since their first losing sight of it, although the weather was clear.

'By my sowl,' thought Barny, 'the channel must be mighty wide in these parts, and for the last day or so we've bein' goin' purty free with a flowin' sheet, and I wondher we aren't closin' in wid the shore by this time, or maybe it's farther off than I thought it was.' His companions, too, began to question Barny on the subject, but to their queries he presented an impenetrable front of composure, and said 'it was always the best plan to keep a good bowld offin''. In two days more, however, the weather began to be sensibly warmer, and Barny and his companions remarked that it was 'goin' to be the finest sayson, God bless it, that ever kem out o' the skies for many a long year; and maybe it's the whate wouldn't be beautiful, and a great plenty of it'. It was at the end of a week that the ship which Barny had hitherto kept ahead of him showed symptoms of bearing down upon him, as he thought, and, sure enough, she did; and Barny began to conjecture what the deuce the ship could want with him, and commenced inventing answers to the questions he thought it possible might be put to him in case the ship spoke to him. He was soon put out of suspense by being hailed and ordered to run under her lee, and the captain looking over the quarter, asked Barny where he was going.

'Faith, thin, I'm goin' an my business,' said Barny.

'But where?' said the captain.

'Why, sure, an it's no matther where a poor man like me id be goin',' said Barny.

'Only I'm curious to know what the deuce you've been following my ship for for the last week?'

'Follyin' your ship! Why, thin, blur an agers, do you think it's follyin' yiz I am?'

'It's very like it,' said the captain.

'Why, did two people niver thravel the same road before?'

'I don't say they didn't, but there's a great difference between a ship of seven hundred tons and a hooker.'

'Oh, as for that matther,' said Barny, 'the same highroad sarves a coach-and-four and a low-back car, the thravellin' tinker an' a lord a' horseback.'

'That's very true,' said the captain, 'but the cases are not the same, Paddy, and I can't conceive what the devil brings you here.'

'And who ax'd you to consayve anything about it?' asked Barny, somewhat sturdily.

'D—n me if I can imagine what you're about, my fine fellow,' said the captain, 'and my own notion is that you don't know where the devil you're going yourself.'

'O *baithershin*,' said Barny, with a laugh of derision.

'Why, then, do you object to tell?' said the captain.

'Arrah, sure, captain, an' don't you know that sometimes vessels is bound to sail *saycret ordher!*' said Barny, endeavouring to foil the question by badinage.

There was a universal laugh from the deck of the ship at the idea of a fishing-boat sailing under secret orders – for by this time the whole broadside of the vessel was crowded with grinning mouths and wondering eyes at Barny and his boat.

'Oh, it's a thrifle makes fools laugh,' said Barny.

'Take care, my fine fellow, that you don't be laughing at the wrong side of your mouth before long, for I've a notion that you're cursedly in the wrong box, as cunning a fellow as you think yourself. D—n your stupid head, can't you tell what brings you here?'

'Why, thin, begor, one id think the whole say belonged to you, you're so mighty bold in axin' questions an it. Why, tare an ouns, sure I've as much right here as you, though I haven't as a big a ship nor so fine a coat; but maybe I can take as good sailin' out o' the one, and has as bowld a heart under th' other.'

'Very well,' said the captain; 'I see there's no use in talking to you, so go to the devil your own way.' And away bore the ship, leaving Barny in indignation and his companions in wonder.

'And why wouldn't you tell him?' said they to Barny.

'Why, don't you see,' said Barny, whose object was now to blind them, 'don't you see, how do I know but maybe he might be goin' to the same place himself, and maybe he has a cargo of *scalpeens* as well as us, and wants to get before us there?'

'Thrue for you, Barny,' said they. 'Bedad you're right.' And, their inquiries being satisfied, the day passed, as former ones had done, in pursuing the course of the ship.

In four days more, however, the provisions in the hooker began to fail, and they were obliged to have recourse to the *scalpeens* for sustenance, and Barny then got seriously uneasy at the length of the voyage, and the likely greater length for anything he could see to the contrary; and, urged at last by his own alarms and those of his companions, he was enabled, as the wind was light, to gain on the ship, and when he found himself alongside he demanded a parley with the captain.

The captain, on hearing that the 'hardy hooker', as she got christened, was under his lee, came on deck, and, as soon as he appeared, Barny cried out:

'Why, then, blur an agers, captain dear, do you expec' to be there soon?'

'Where?' said the captain.

'Oh, you know yourself,' said Barny.

'It's well for me I do,' said the captain.

'Thrue for you, indeed, your honour,' said Barny, in his most insinuating tone; 'but whin will you be at the ind o' your voyage, captain, jewel?'

'I daresay in about three months,' said the captain.

'Oh, Holy Mother!' ejaculated Barny; 'three months! arrah, it's jokin' you are, captain dear, and only want to freken me.'

'How should I frighten you?' asked the captain.

'Why, thin, your honour, to tell God's thruth, I heard you were goin' *there*, an' as I wanted to go there too, I thought I couldn't do better nor to folly a knowledgeable gintleman like yourself, and save myself the throuble iv findin' it out.'

'And where do you think I *am* going?' said the captain.

'Why, thin,' said Barny, 'isn't it to Fingal?'

'No,' said the captain, ''t is to *Bengal*.'

'Oh! Gog's blakey!' said Barny, 'what'll I do now at all at all?'

II

Homeward Bound

The captain ordered Barny on deck, as he wished to have some conversation with him on what he, very naturally, considered a most extraordinary adventure. Heaven help the captain! he knew little of Irishmen, or he would not have been so astonished. Barny made his appearance. Puzzling question and more puzzling answer followed in quick succession between the commander and Barny, who, in the midst of his dilemma, stamped about, thumped his head, squeezed his caubeen into all manner of shapes, and vented his despair anathematically: –

'Oh, my heavy hathred to you, you tarnal thief iv a long sailor; it's a purty scrape yiv led me into. Begor, I thought it was *Fingal* he said, and now I hear it is *Bingal*. Oh! the divil sweep you for navigation; why did I meddle or make with you at all! And my curse light on you, Teddy O'Sullivan; why did I iver come acrass you, you onlooky vagabone, to put sitch thoughts in my head! An' so it's *Bingal*, and not *Fingal*, you're goin' to, captain?'

'Yes, indeed, Paddy.'

'An' might I be bowld to ax, captain, is Bingal much farther nor Fingal?'

'A trifle or so, Paddy.'

'Och, thin, millia murther, weirasthru, how'll I iver get there at all?' roared out poor Barny.

'By turning about, and getting back the road you've come, as fast as you can.'

'Is it back? O Queen iv Heaven! an' how will I iver get back?' said the bewildered Barny.

'Then you don't know your course, it appears?'

'Oh, faix, I knew it illigant, as long as your honour was before me.'

'But you don't know your course back?'

'Why, indeed, not to say rightly all out, your honour.'

'Can't you steer?' said the captain.

'The divil a betther hand at the tiller in all Kinsale,' said Barny, with his usual brag.

'Well, so far so good,' said the captain. 'And you know the points of the compass – you have a compass, I suppose?'

'A compass! – by my sowl, an' it's not let alone a compass, but a *pair* a compasses I have, that my brother the carpinthir left me for a keepsake whin he wint abroad; but, indeed, as for the points o' thim I can't say much, for the childhren spylt thim intirely, rootin' holes in the flure.'

'What the plague are you talking about?'

'Wasn't your honour discoorsin' me about the points o' the compasses?'

'Confound your thick head!' said the captain. 'Why, what an ignoramus you must be, not to know what a compass is, and you at sea all your life! Do you even know the cardinal points?'

'The cardinal! – faix, an' it's a great respect I have for them, your honour. Sure, aren't they belongin' to the Pope?'

'Confound you, you blockhead!' roared the captain, in a rage; ''t would take the patience of the Pope and the cardinals, and the cardinal virtues into the bargain, to keep one's temper with you. Do you know the four points of the wind?'

'By my sowl I do, and more.'

'Well, never mind more, but let us stick to four. You're sure you know the four points of the wind?'

'Bydad, it would be a quare thing if a sayfarin' man didn't know somethin' about the wind, anyhow. Why, captain dear, you must take me for a nath'ral intirely to suspect me o' the like o' not knowin' all about the wind. Begor, I know as much o' the wind a'most as a pig.'

'Indeed, I believe so,' laughed out the captain.

'Oh, you may laugh if you plaze; and I see by the same that you don't know about the pig, with all your edication, captain.'

'Well, what about the pig?'

'Why, sir, did you never hear a pig can see the wind?'

'I can't say that I did.'

'Oh, thin, he does; and for that rayson, who has a right to know more about it?'

'You don't for one, I dare say, Paddy; and maybe you have a pig aboard to give you information.'

'Sorra taste, your honour, not as much as a rasher o' bacon; but it's maybe your honour never seen a pig tossin' up his snout, consaited like, and running like mad afore a storm.'

'Well, what if I have?'

'Well, sir, that is when they see the wind a-comin'.'

'Maybe so, Paddy; but all this knowledge in piggery won't find you your way home; and, if you take my advice, you will give up all thoughts of endeavouring to find your way back, and come on board. You and your messmates, I dare say, will be useful hands, with some teaching; but, at all events, I cannot leave you here on the open sea, with every chance of being lost.'

'Why, thin, indeed, and I'm behowlden to your honour; and it's the hoighth o' kindness, so it is, your offer; and it's nothin' else but a gintleman you are, every inch o' you; but I hope it's not so bad wid us yet as to do the likes o' that.'

'I think it's bad enough,' said the captain, 'when you are without a compass, and knowing nothing of your course, and nearly a hundred and eighty leagues from land.'

'An' how many miles would that be, captain?'

'Three times as many.'

'I never larned the rule o' three, captain, and maybe your honour id tell me yourself.'

'That is rather more than five hundred miles.'

'Five hundred miles!' shouted Barny. 'Oh, the Lord look down on us! – how 'ill we iver get back?'

'That's what I say,' said the captain; 'and therefore I recommend you to come aboard with me.'

'And where 'ud the hooker be all the time?' said Barny.

'Let her go adrift,' was the answer.

'Is it the darlint boat? Oh, dedad, I'll never hear o' that at all.'

'Well, then, stay in her and be lost. Decide upon the matter at once; either come on board, or cast off'; and the captain was turning away as he spoke, when Barny called after him: 'Arrah, thin, your honour, don't go just for one minit antil I ax you one word more. If I wint wid you, whin would I be home agin?'

'In about seven months.'

'Oh, thin, that puts the wig an it at wanst. I darn't go at all.'

'Why, seven months are not long passing.'

'Thrue for you, in throth,' said Barny, with a shrug of his shoulders. 'Faix, it's myself knows, to my sorrow, the half year comes round mighty suddint, and the lord's agint comes for the thrifle o' rint; and, faix, I know, by Molly, that nine months is not long in goin' over either,' added Barny, with a grin.

'Then what's your objection as to the time?' asked the captain.

'Arrah, sure, sir, what would the woman that owns me do while I was away; – and maybe it's break her heart the craythur would, thinkin' I was lost intirely; and who'd be at home to take care o' the childher, and airn thim the bit and the sup, whin I'd be away? – and who knows but that it's all dead they'd be afore I got back? Och, home! sure the heart id fairly break in my body, if hurt or harm kem to them through me. So say no more, captain dear; only give me a thrifle o' directions how I'm to make an offer at gettin' home, and it's myself that will pray for you night, noon, and mornin' for that same.'

'Well, Paddy,' said the captain, 'as you are determined to go back, in spite of all I can say, you must attend to me well while I give you as simple instructions as I can. You say you know the four points of the wind – north, south, east, and west.'

'Yis, sir.'

'How do you know them? – for I must see that you are not likely to make a mistake. How do you know the points?'

'Why, you see, sir, the sun, God bless it, rises in the aist, and sets in the west, which stands to rayson; and when you stand bechuxt the aist and the west, the north is forninst you.'

'And when the north is foreninst you, as you say, is the east on your right or your left hand?'

'On the right hand, your honour.'

'Well, I see you know that much, however. Now,' said the captain, 'the moment you leave the ship, you must steer a north-east course, and you will make some land near home in about a week, if the wind holds as it is now, and it is likely to do so; but mind me, if you turn out of your course in the smallest degree, you are a lost man.'

'Many thanks to your honour!'

'And how are you off for provisions?'

'Why, thin, indeed, in the regard o' that same, we are in the hoighth o' distress; for exceptin' the scalpeens, sorra a taste passed our lips for these four days.'

'Oh, you poor devils!' said the commander; in a tone of sincere commiseration. 'I'll order you some provisions on board before you start.'

'Long life to your honour! – and *I'd like to drink the health* of so noble a jintleman.'

'I understand you, Paddy; – you shall have grog too.'

'Musha, the heavens shower blessins an you, I pray the Virgin Mary and the twelve apostles, Matthew, Mark, Luke, and John, not forgettin' St Pathrick.'

'Thank you, Paddy; but keep all your prayers for yourself, for you need them all to help you home again.'

'Oh, never fear, whin the thing is to be done, I'll do it, bedad, wid a heart and a half. And sure, your honour, God is good, an' will mind dissolute craythurs like uz, on the wild oceant as well as ashore.'

While some of the ship's crew were putting the captain's benevolent intentions to Barny and his companions into practice, by transferring some provisions to the hooker, the commander entertained himself by further conversation with Barny, who was the greatest original he had ever met. In the course of their colloquy, Barny drove many hard queries at the captain, respecting the wonders of the nautical profession, and at last put the question to him plump.

'Oh, thin, captain dear, and how is it at all at all, that you make your way over the wide says intirely to them furrin parts?'

'You would not understand, Paddy, if I attempted to explain to you.'

'Sure enough, indeed, your honour, and I ask your pardon, only I was curious to know, and sure no wonder.'

'It requires various branches of knowledge to make a navigator.'

'Branches,' said Barny, 'begor, I think it id take *the whole three o' knowledge* to make it out. And that place are you going to, sir, that *Bingal* (oh, bad luck to it for a *Bing*al, it's the sore *Bing*al to me), is it so far off as you say?'

'Yes, Paddy, half round the world.'

'Is it round in airnest, captain dear? Round about?'

'Ay, indeed.'

'Oh, thin, aren't you afeard that whin you come to the top and that you're obleeged to go down, that you'd go sliddherin' away intirely, and never be able to stop maybe. It's bad enough, so it is, goin' down-hill by land, but it must be the dickens all out by wather.'

'But there is no hill, Paddy; don't you know that water is always level?'

'Bedad, it's very *flat*, anyhow; and by the same token, it's seldom I throuble it; but sure, your honour, if the wather is level, how do you make out that it is *round* you go?'

'That is part of the knowledge I was speaking to you about,' said the captain.

'Musha, bad luck to you, knowledge, but you're a quare thing! And where is it Bingal, bad cess to it, would be at all at all?'

'In the East Indies.'

'Oh, that is where they make the *tay*, isn't it, sir?'

'No; where the tea grows is farther still.'

'Farther! – why, that must be ind of the world intirely. And they don't make it, then, sir, but it grows, you tell me.'

'Yes, Paddy.'

'Is it like hay, your honour?'

'Not exactly, Paddy; what puts hay in your head?'

'Oh, only because I hear them call it Bo*hay*.'

'A most logical deduction, Paddy.'

'And is it a great deal farther, your honour, the *tay* country is?'

'Yes, Paddy, China it is called.'

'That's I suppose, what we call Chaynee, sir?'

'Exactly, Paddy.'

'Bedad, I never could come at it rightly before; why, it was nath'ral to dhrink tay out o' chaynee. I ax your honour's pardon for bein' throublesome, but I hard tell from the long sailor iv the place they call Japan in them furrin parts, and *is* it there, your honour?'

'Quite true, Paddy.'

'And I suppose it's there the blackin' comes from?'

'No, Paddy, you're out there.'

'Oh, well, I thought it stood to rayson, as I heerd of japan blackin', sir, that it would be there it kem from; besides, as the blacks themselves – the naygurs, I mane – is in them parts.'

'The negroes are in Africa, Paddy, much nearer to us.'

'God betune uz and harm; I hope I would not be too near them,' said Barny.

'Why, what's your objection?'

'Arrah, sure, sir, they're hardly mortials at all, but has the mark o' the bastes an thim.'

'How do you make out that, Paddy?'

'Why, sure, sir, and didn't nature make thim wid wool on their heads, plainly makin' it unherstood to Chrishthans that they wur little more nor cattle.'

'I think your head is a wool-gathering now, Paddy,' said the captain, laughing.

'Faix, maybe so, indeed,' answered Barny, good-humouredly; 'but it's seldom I ever went out to look for wool and kem home shorn, anyhow,' said he, with a look of triumph.

'Well, you won't have that to say for the future, Paddy,' said the captain, laughing again.

'My name's not Paddy, your honour,' said Barny, returning the laugh, but seizing the opportunity to turn the joke aside that was going against him; 'my name isn't Paddy, sir, but Barny.'

'Oh, if it was Solomon, you'll be bare enough when you go home this time: you have not gathered much this trip, Barny.'

'Sure, I've been gathering knowledge, anyhow, your honour,' said Barny, with a significant look at the captain, and a complimentary tip of his hand to his caubeen, 'and God bless you for being so good to me.'

'And what's your name besides Barny?' asked the captain.

'O'Reirdon, your honour; – Barny O'Reirdon's my name.'

'Well, Barny O'Reirdon, I won't forget your name nor yourself in a hurry, for you are certainly the most original navigator I ever had the honour of being acquainted with.'

'Well,' said Barny, with a triumphant toss of his head, 'I have done out Terry O'Sullivan, at any rate; the divil a half so far he ever was, and that's a comfort. I have muzzled his clack for the rest iv his life, and he won't be comin' over us wid the pride iv his *Fingal*, while I'm to the fore, that was a'most at *Bingal*.'

'Terry O'Sullivan – who is he, pray?' said the captain.

'Oh, he's a scut iv a chap that's not worth your axin' for – he's not worth your honour's notice – a braggin' poor craythur. Oh, wait till I get home, and the divil a more braggin' they'll hear out of his jaw.'

'Indeed, then, Barny, the sooner you turn your face towards home the better,' said the captain; 'since you will go, there is no need in losing more time.'

'Thrue for you, your honour; and sure it's well for me had the luck to meet wid the likes o' your honour, that explained the ins and outs iv it to me, and laid it all down as plain as prent.'

'Are you sure you remember my directions?' said the captain.

'Throth, an' I'll niver forget them to the day o' my death, and is bound to pray, more betoken, for you and yours.'

'Don't mind praying for me till you get home, Barny; but answer me, how are you to steer when you shall leave me?'

'The *nor'aist coorse*, your honour; that's the coorse agin the world.'

'Remember that! Never alter that course till you see land; let nothing make you turn out of a north-east course.'

'Throth, an' that id be the dirty turn, seein' that it was yourself that ordhered it. Oh, no, I'll depend my life an the *nor-aist coorse*; and God help anyone that comes betune me an' it – I'd run him down if he was my father.'

'Well, good-bye, Barny.'

'Good-bye, and God bless you, your honour, and send you safe.'

'That's a wish you want more for yourself, Barny; never fear for me, but mind yourself well.'

'Oh, sure, I'm as good as at home wanst I know the way, barrin' the wind is conthrary; sure, the *nor-aist coorse*'ll do the business complate. Good-bye, your honour, and long life to you, and more power to your elbow, and a light heart and a heavy purse to you evermore, I pray the Blessed Virgin and all the saints, amin!' and so saying, Barny descended the ship's side, and once more assumed the helm of the 'hardy hooker'.

The two vessels now separated on their opposite courses. What a contrast their relative situations afforded! Proudly the ship bore away under her lofty and spreading canvas, cleaving the billows before her, manned by an able crew, and under the guidance of experienced officers; the finger of science to point the course of her progress, the faithful chart to warn of the hidden rock and the shoal, the log line and the quadrant to measure her march and prove her position. The poor little hooker cleft not the billows, each wave lifted her on its crest like a sea-bird; but three inexperienced fishermen to manage her; no certain means to guide them over the vast ocean they had to traverse, and the holding of the 'fickle wind' the only *chance* of their escape from perishing in the wilderness of waters. By the one, the feeling excited is supremely that of man's power; by the other, of his utter helplessness. To the one the expanse of ocean could scarcely be considered 'trackless', to the other it was a waste indeed.

Yet the cheer that burst from the ship, at parting, was answered as gaily from the hooker as though the odds had not been so fearfully against her; and no blither heart beat on board the ship than that of Barny O'Reirdon.

Happy light-heartedness of my poor countrymen! They have often need of all their buoyant spirits. How kindly have they been fortified by Nature against the assaults of adversity; and if they blindly rush into dangers, they cannot be denied the possession of gallant hearts to fight their way out of them.

But each hurrah became less audible; by degrees the cheers dwindled into faintness, and finally were lost in the eddies of the breeze.

The first feeling of loneliness that poor Barny experienced was when he could no longer hear the exhilarating sound. The plash of the surge, as it broke on the bows of his little boat, was uninterrupted by the kindred sound of human voice; and as it fell upon his ear it smote upon his heart. But he rallied, waved his hat, and the silent signal was answered from the ship.

'Well, Barny,' said Jemmy, 'what was the captain sayin' to you all the time you wor wid him?'

'Lay me alone,' said Barny; 'I'll talk to you when I see her out o' sight, but not a word till thin. I'll look afther him, the rale gintleman that he is, while there's a topsail o' his ship to be seen, and thin I'll send my blessin' after him, and pray for his good fortune wherever he goes, for he's the right sort and nothin' else.' And Barny kept his word, and when his straining eye could no longer trace a line of the ship, the captain certainly had the benefit of 'a poor man's blessing'.

The sense of utter loneliness and desolation had not come upon Barny until now; but he put his trust in the goodness of Providence, and in a fervent mental outpouring of prayer resigned himself to the care of his Creator. With an admirable fortitude, too, he assumed a composure to his companions that was a stranger to his heart; and we all know how the burden of anxiety is increased when we have none with whom to sympathize. And this was not all. He had to affect ease and confidence, for Barny not only had no dependence on the firmness of his companions to go through the undertaking before them, but dreaded to betray to them how he had imposed on them in the affair. Barny was equal to all this. He had a stout heart, and was an admirable actor; yet, for the first hour after the ship was out of sight, he could not quite recover himself, and every now and then, unconsciously, he would look back with a wistful eye to the point where last he saw her. Poor Barny had lost his leader.

The night fell, and Barny stuck to the helm as long as nature could sustain want of rest, and then left it in charge of one of his companions, with particular directions how to steer, and ordered if any change in the wind occurred that they should instantly awake him. He could not sleep long, however; the fever of anxiety was upon him, and the morning had not long dawned when he awoke. He had not well rubbed his eyes and looked about him, when he thought he saw a ship in the distance approaching them. As the haze cleared away, she showed distinctly bearing down towards the hooker. On board the ship the hooker, in such a sea, caused surprise as before, and in about an hour she was so close as to hail and order the hooker to run under her lee.

'The divil a state,' said Barny; 'I'll not quit my *nor-aist coorse* for the king of Ingland, nor Bonyparty into the bargain. Bad cess to you, do you think I've nothin' to do but to plaze you?'

Again he was hailed.

'Oh! bad luck to the toe I'll go to you.'

Another hail.

'Spake loudher, you'd betther,' said Barny, jeeringly, still holding on his course.

A gun was fired ahead of him.

'By my sowl, you spoke loudher that time, sure enough,' said Barny.

'Take care, Barny!' cried Jemmy and Peter together. 'Blur an' agers, man, we'll be kilt if you don't go to them!'

'Well, and we'll be lost if we turn out iv our *nor-aist coorse*, and that's as broad as it's long. Let them hit iz if they like; sure it 'ud be a pleasanther death nor starvin' at say. I tell you again, I'll turn out o' my *nor-aist coorse* for no man.'

A shotted gun was fired. The shot hopped on the water as it passed before the hooker.

'Phew! you missed it, like your mammy's blessin',' said Barny.

'Oh, murther!' said Jemmy, 'didn't you see the ball hop aff the wather forninst you? Oh, murther! what 'ud we ha' done if we wor there at all at all?'

'Why, we'd have taken the ball at the hop,' said Barny, laughing, 'accordin' to the owld sayin'.'

Another shot was ineffectually fired.

'I'm thinkin' that's a Connaughtman that's shootin','[1] said Barny, with a sneer. The allusion was so relished by Jemmy and Peter that it excited a smile in the midst of their fears from the cannonade.

Again the report of the gun was followed by no damage.

'Augh! never heed them!' said Barny, contemptuously. 'It's a barkin' dog that never bites, as the owld sayin' says'; and the hooker was soon out of reach of further annoyance.

226

'Now, what a pity it was, to be sure,' said Barny, 'that I wouldn't go aboord to plaze them. Now, who's right? Ah, lave me alone always, Jemmy. Did you ivir know me wrong yet?'

'Oh, you may hillow now that you're out o' the woods,' said Jemmy; 'but, accordin' to my idays, it was runnin' a grate rishk to be contrary wid them at all, and they shootin' balls afther us.'

'Well, what matther?' said Barny, 'since they wor only blind gunners, *an' I knew it*; besides, as I said afore, I won't turn out o' my *nor-aist coorse* for no man.'

'That's a new turn you tuk lately,' said Peter. 'What's the rayson you're runnin' a noir-aist coorse now, an' we never hear'd iv it afore at all, till afther you quitted the big ship?'

'Why, then, are you sich an ignoramus all out,' said Barny, 'as not for to know that in navigation you must lie an a great many different tacks before you can make the port you steer for?'

'Only I think,' said Jemmy, 'that it's back intirely we're goin' now, and I can't make out the rights o' that at all.'

'Why,' said Barny, who saw the necessity of mystifying his companions a little, 'you see, the captain towld me that I kum a round, an' rekimminded me to go th' other way.'

'Faix, it's the first I ever heard o' goin' a round by say,' said Jemmy.

'Arrah, sure, that's part o' the saycrets o' navigation, and the various branches o' knowledge that is requizit for a navigathor; an' that's what the captain, God bless him, and myself was discoorsin' an aboord; and, like a rale gintleman as he is, "Barny," says he; "Sir," says I; "You're come the round," says he. "I know that," says I, "bekase I like to keep a good bowld offin'," says I, "in conthrary places." "Spoke like a good sayman," says he. "That's my prenciples," says I. "They're the right sort," says he. "But," says he, "(no offince), I think you wor wrong," says he, "to pass the short turn in the ladieshoes,"[2] says he. "I know," says I, "you mane beside the threespike headlan'." "That's the spot," says he, "I see you know it." "As well as I know my father," says I.'

'Why, Barny,' said Jemmy, interrupting him, 'we seen no headlan' at all.'

'Whisht, whisht!' said Barny; 'bad cess to you, don't thwart me. We passed it in the night, and you couldn't see it. Well, as I was saying, "I know it as well as I know my father," says I, "but I gev the preferince to go the round," says I. "You're a good sayman for that same," says he, "an' it would be right at any other time than this present," says he, "but it's onpossible now, teetotally, on account o' the war," says he. "Tare alive," says I, "what war?" "An' didn't you hear o' the war?" says he. "Divil a word," says I. "Why," says he, "the naygurs has made war on the king o' Chaynee," says he, "bekase he refused them any more tay; an' with that, what did they do," says he, "but they put a lumbaago on all the vessels that sails the round, an' that's the rayson," says he, "I carry guns, as you may see; and I'd rekimmind you," says he, "to go back, for you're not able for thim, an' that's jist the way iv it." An' now, wasn't it looky that I kem acrass him at all, or maybe we might be cotch by the naygurs, and ate up alive.'

'Oh, thin, indeed, and that's thrue,' said Jemmy and Peter; 'an' when will we come to the short turn?'

'Oh, niver mind,' said Barny; 'you'll see it when we get there; – but wait till I tell you more about the captain and the big ship. He said, you know, that he carried guns afeard o' the naygurs, an' in throth it's the hoight o' care he takes o' them same guns; – and small blame to him, sure they might be the salvation of him. 'Pon my conscience, they're taken betther care of than any poor man's child. I heer'd him cautionin' the sailors about them, and given them ordhers about their clothes.'

'Their clothes!' said his two companions at once, in surprise; 'is it clothes upon cannons?'

'It's truth I'm tellin' you,' said Barny. 'Bad luck to the lie in it, he was talkin' about their aprons and their breeches.'

'Oh, think o' that!' said Jemmy and Peter, in surprise.

'An' 'twas all iv a piece,' said Barny; 'that an' the rest o' the ship all out. She was as nate as a new pin. Throth, I was a'most ashamed to put my fut an the deck, it was so clane, and she painted every colour in the rainbow; and all sorts o' curiosities about her; and instead iv a tiller to steer her, like this darlin' craythur iv ours, she goes wid a wheel, like a coach all as one; and there's the quarest thing you iver seen, to show the way, as the captain gev me to understan', a little round rowly-powly thing in a bowl, that goes waddlin' about as if it didn't know its own way, much more nor show anybody theirs. Throth, myself thought that if that's the way they're obliged to go, that it's with a great deal of *fear and thrimblin'* they find it out.'

Thus it was that Barny continued most marvellous accounts of the ship and the captain to his companions, and by keeping their attention so engaged prevented their being too inquisitive as to their own immediate concerns, and for two days more Barny and the hooker held on their respective course undeviatingly.

The third day Barny's fears for the continuity of his *nor-aist coorse* were excited, as a large brig hove in sight, and the nearer she approached, the more directly she came athwart Barny's course.

'May the divil sweep you,' said Barny; 'and will nothin' else sarve you than comin' forninst me that away? Brig, ahoy, there!' shouted Barny, giving the tiller to one of his messmates, and standing at the bow of his boat. 'Brig, ahoy, there! – bad luck to you, go 'long out o' my *nor-aist coorse*.' The brig, instead of obeying his mandate, hove to, and lay right ahead of the hooker. 'Oh, look at this!' shouted Barny, and he stamped on the deck with rage – 'look at the blackguards where they're stayin', just a purpose to ruin an unfort'nate man like me. My heavy hathred to you; quit this minit, or I'll run down an yez, and if we go to the bottom, we'll hant you for evermore; – go 'long out o' that, I tell you. The curse o' Crummil an you, you stupid vagabones, that won't go out iv a man's *nor-aist coorse!*'

From cursing Barny went to praying as he came closer. 'For the tendher marcy o' heavin, and lave my way. May the Lord reward you, and get out o' my *nor-aist coorse*! May angels make your bed in heavin, and don't ruinate me this a way.' The brig was immovable, and Barny gave up in despair, having cursed and prayed himself hoarse, and finished with a duet volley of prayers and curses together, apostrophizing the hard case of a man being '*done out of his nor-aist coorse*'.

'Ahoy, there!' shouted a voice from the brig, 'put down your helm, or you'll be aboard of us. I say, let go your gib and foresheet; – what are you about, you lubbers?'

'T was true that the brig lay so fair in Barny's course that he would have been aboard, but that instantly the manoeuvre above alluded to was put in practice on board the hooker, as she swept to destruction towards the heavy hull of the brig, and she luffed up into the wind alongside her. A very pale and somewhat emaciated face appeared at the side, and addressed Barny:

'What brings you here?' was the question.

'Throth, thin, and I think I might betther ax what brings *you* here, right in the way o' my *nor-aist coorse*.'

'Where do you come from?'

'From Kinsale; and you didn't come from a betther place, I go bail.'

'Where are you bound to?'

'To Fingal.'

'Fingal – where's Fingal?'

'Why, thin, ain't you ashamed o' yourself an' not to know where Fingal is?'

'It is not in these seas.'

'Oh, that's all you know about it,' says Barny.

'You're a small craft to be so far at sea. I suppose you have provisions on board?'

'To be sure we have; – throth, if we hadn't, this id be a bad place to go a-beggin'.'

'What have you eatable?'

'The finest o' scalpeens.'

'What are scalpeens?'

'Why you're mighty ignorant, intirely,' said Barny; 'why, scalpeens is pickled mackerel.'

'Then you must give us some, for we have been out of everything eatable these three days; and even pickled fish is better than nothing.'

It chanced that the brig was a West India trader, which unfavourable winds had delayed much beyond the expected period of time on her voyage, and though her water had not failed, everything eatable had been consumed, and the crew reduced almost to helplessness. In such a strait the arrival of Barny O'Reirdon and his scalpeens was a most providential succour to them, and a lucky chance for Barny, for he got in exchange for his pickled fish a handsome return of rum and sugar, much more than equivalent to their value. Barny lamented much, however, that the brig was not bound for Ireland, that he might practise his own peculiar system of navigation; but as staying with the brig could do no good, he got himself put into his *nor-aist coorse* once more, and ploughed away towards home.

The disposal of his cargo was a great godsend to Barny in more ways than one. In the first place, he found the most profitable market he could have had; and, secondly, it enabled him to cover his retreat from the difficulty which still was before him of not getting to Fingal after all his dangers, and consequently being open to discovery and disgrace. All these beneficial results were not thrown away upon one of Barny's readiness to avail himself of every point in his favour; and, accordingly, when they left the brig, Barny said to his companions: 'Why, thin, boys, 'pon my conscience, but I'm as proud as a horse wid a wooden leg this minit, that we met them poor unfort'nate craythurs this blessed day, and was enabled to extind our charity to them. Sure, an' it's lost they'd be only for our comin' acrass them, and we, through the blessin' o' God, enabled to do an act of marcy, that is, feedin' the hungry; – and sure every good work we do here is before uz in heavin, and that's a comfort, anyhow. To be sure, now that the scalpeens is sowld, there's no use in goin' to Fingal, and we may jist as well go home.'

'Faix, I'm sorry myself,' said Jemmy, 'for Terry O'Sullivan said it was an iligant place intirely, an' I wanted to see it.'

'To the divil with Terry O'Sullivan,' said Barny; 'how does he know what's an iligant place? What knowledge has he of iligance? I'll go bail, he never was half as far a navigatin' as we; – he wint the short cut, I go bail, and never daar'd for to vinture the round, as I did.'

'Bedad we wor a great dale longer, anyhow, than he towld me he was.'

'To be sure we wor,' said Barny; 'he wint skulkin' by the short cut, I tell you; and was afeard to keep a bowld offin' like me. But come, boys, let uz take a dhrop o' that bottle o' sper'ts we got out o' the brig. Begor it's well we got some bottles iv it; for I wouldn't much like to meddle wid that darlint little kag iv it antil we get home.' The rum was put on its trial by Barny and his companions, and in their critical judgement was pronounced quite as good as the captain of the ship had bestowed upon them, but that neither of those specimens of spirit was to be compared to whiskey. 'Bedad,' says Barny, 'they may rack their brains a long time before they'll make out a purtier invintion than *poteen*; – that rum may do very well for thim that has the misforthin' not to know better; but the whiskey is a more nath'ral sper't, accordin' to my idays.' In this, as in most other of Barny's opinions, Peter and Jemmy coincided.

Nothing particular occurred for the two succeeding days, during which time Barny most religiously pursued his *nor-aist coorse*; but the third day produced a new and important event. A sail was discovered on the horizon, and in the direction Barny was steering, and a couple of hours made him tolerable certain that the vessel in sight was an American; for though it is needless to say that he was not very conversant in such matters, yet from the frequency of his seeing Americans trading to Ireland, his eye had become sufficiently accustomed to their lofty and tapering spars, and peculiar smartness of rig, to satisfy him that the ship before him was of transatlantic build; nor was he wrong in his conjecture.

Barny now determined on a manoeuvre, classing him amongst the first tacticians at securing a good retreat.

Moreau's highest fame rests upon his celebrated retrograde movement through the Black Forest.

Xenophon's greatest glory is derived from the deliverance of his ten thousand Greeks from impending ruin by his renowned retreat.

Let the ancient and the modern hero 'repose under the shadow of their laurels,' as the French have it, while Barny O'Reirdon's historian, with a pardonable jealousy for the honour of his country, cuts down a goodly bough of the classic tree, beneath which our Hibernian hero may enjoy his '*otium cum dignitate*'.

Barny calculated the American was bound for Ireland; and as she lay *almost* as directly in the way of his *nor-aist coorse* as the West Indian brig, he bore up to and spoke to her.

He was answered by a shrewd Yankee captain.

'Faix, an' it's glad I am to see your honour again,' said Barny.

The Yankee had never been to Ireland, and told Barny so.

'Oh, throth, I couldn't forget a gintleman so easy as that,' said Barny.

'You're pretty considerably mistaken now, I guess,' said the American.

'Divil a taste,' said Barny, with inimitable composure and pertinacity.

'Well, if you know me so tarnation well, tell me what's my name?' The Yankee flattered himself he had nailed Barny now.

'Your name, is it?' said Barny, gaining time by repeating the question, 'why, what a fool you are not to know your own name.'

The oddity of the answer posed the American, and Barny took advantage of the diversion in his favour, and changed the conversation.

'Bedad, I've been waitin' here these four or five days, expectin' some of you would be wantin' me.'

'Some of us! How do you mean?'

'Sure an' aren't you from Amerikay?'

'Yes; – and what then?'

'Well, I say I was waitin' for some ship or other from Amerikay, that ud be wantin' me. It's to Ireland you're goin' I dare say.'

'Yes.'

'Well, I suppose you'll be wantin' a pilot?' said Barny.

'Yes, when we get in shore, but not yet.'

'Oh, I don't want to hurry you,' said Barny.

'What port are you a pilot of?'

'Why, indeed, as for the matther o' that,' said Barny, 'they're all aiqual to me a'most.'

'All?' said the American. 'Why, I calculate you couldn't pilot a ship into all the ports of Ireland.'

'Not all at wanst (once),' said Barny, with a laugh, in which the American could not help joining.

'Well, I say, what ports do you know best?'

'Why, thin, indeed,' said Barny, 'it would be hard for me to tell; but wherever you want to go, I'm the man that'll do the job for you complate. Where's your honour goin'?'

'I won't tell you that; – but do you tell me what ports you know best?'

'Why, there's Watherford, and there's Youghal, an' Fingal.'

'Fingal! Where's that?'

'So you don't know where Fingal is. Oh, I see you're a sthranger, sir; – an' then there's Cork.'

'You know Cove, then?'

'Is it the Cove o' Cork, why?'

'Yes.'

'I was bred an' born there, an' pilots as many ships into Cove as any other two min *out* o' it.'

Barny thus sheltered his falsehood under the idiom of his language.

'But what brought you so far out to sea?' asked the captain.

'We wor lyin' out lookin' for ships that wanted pilots, and there kem an the terriblest gale o' wind off the land, an' blew us to say out intirely, an' that's the way iv it, your honour.'

'I calculate we got a share of the same gale; 't was from the nor'-east.'

'Oh, directly!' said Barny, 'faith, you're right enough, 't was the *nor-aist coorse* we wor an, sure enough; but no matther, now that we've met wid you; – sure we'll have a job home, anyhow.'

'Well, get aboard, then,' said the American.

'I will in a minit, your honour, whin I jist spake a word to my comrades here.'

'Why, sure it's not goin' to turn pilot you are?' said Jemmy, in his simplicity of heart.

'Whisht, you omadhaun!' said Barny, 'or I'll cut the tongue out o' you. Now, mind me, Pether. You don't undherstan' navigashin and the various branches o' knowledge, an' so all you have to do is to folly the ship when I get into her, an' I'll show you the way home.'

Barny then got aboard the American vessel, and begged of the captain that as he had been out at sea so long, and had gone through a 'power o' hardship intirely', that he would be permitted to go below and turn in to take a sleep; 'for, in throth, it's myself and sleep that is sthrayngers for some time,' said Barny, 'an' if your honour'll be plazed, I'll be thankful if you won't let them disturb me antil I'm wanted, for sure till you see the land there's no use for me in life; an', throth, I want a sleep sorely.'

Barny's request was granted, and it will not be wondered at that, after so much fatigue of mind and body, he slept profoundly for four-and-twenty hours. He then was called, for land was in sight, and when he came on deck the captain rallied him upon the potency of his somniferous qualities, and 'calculated' he had never met any one who could sleep 'four-and-twenty hours on a stretch before'.

'Oh, sir,' said Barny, rubbing his eyes, which were still a little hazy, 'whiniver *I* go to sleep *I pay attintion to it.*'

The land was soon neared, and Barny put in charge of the ship, when he ascertained the first landmark he was acquainted with; but as soon as the Head of Kinsale hove in sight, Barny gave a 'whoo', and cut a caper that astonished the Yankees, and was quite inexplicable to them, though I flatter myself it is not to those who do Barny the favour of reading his adventures.

'Oh! there you are, my darlint owld head! – an' where's the head like you? Throth, it's little I thought I'd ever set eyes an your good-looking faytures agin. But, God's good!'

In such half-muttered exclamations did Barny apostrophize each well-known point of his native shore, and when opposite the harbour of Kinsale, he spoke the hooker, that was somewhat astern, and ordered Jemmy and Peter to put in there, and tell Molly immediately that he was come back, and would be with her as soon as he could, after piloting the ship into Cove. 'But, an your apperl, don't tell Pether Kelly o' the big farm; nor, indeed, don't mintion to man nor mortial about the navigashin we done antil I come home myself and make them sensible of it, bekase, Jemmy and Pether, neither o' yiz is aiqual to it, and doesn't undherstan' the branches o' knowledge requizit for discoorsin' o' navigashin.'

The hooker put into Kinsale, and Barny sailed the ship into Cove. It was the first ship he had acted the pilot for, and his old luck attended him; no accident befell his charge, and, what was still more extraordinary, he made the American believe he was absolutely the most skilful pilot on the station. So Barny pocketed his pilot's fee, swore the Yankee was a gentleman, for which the republican did not thank him, wished him good-bye, and then pushed his way home with what Barny swore was the easiest made money he ever had in his life. So Barny got himself paid for *piloting* the ship that *showed him the way home*.

All the fishermen in the world may throw their caps at this feat – none but an Irishman, I fearlessly assert, could have executed so splendid a *coup de finesse*.

And now, sweet readers (the ladies I mean), did you ever think Barny would get home? I would give a hundred of pens to hear all the guesses that have been made as to the probable termination of Barny's adventure. They would furnish good material, I doubt not, for another voyage. But Barny did make other voyages, I can assure you, and perhaps he may appear in his character of navigator once more, if his daring exploits be not held valueless by an ungrateful world, as in the case of his great predecessor, Columbus.

As some *curious* persons (I *don't* mean the ladies) may wish to know what became of some of the characters who have figured in this tale, I beg to inform them that Molly continued a faithful wife and timekeeper, as already alluded to, for many years. That Peter Kelly was so pleased with his share in the profits arising from the trip, in the ample return of rum and sugar, that he freighted a large brig with scalpeens to the West Indies, and went supercargo himself.

All he got in return was the yellow fever.

Barny profited better by his share: he was enabled to open a public-house, which had more custom than any ten within miles of it. Molly managed the bar very efficiently, and Barny 'discoorsed' the customers most seductively; in short, Barny, at all times given to the *marvellous*, became a greater romancer than ever, and, for years, attracted even the gentlemen of the neighbourhood, who loved fun, to his house, for the sake of his magnanimous mendacity.

As for the hitherto triumphant Terry O'Sullivan, from the moment Barny's *Bingal* adventure became known, he was obliged to fly the country, and was never heard of more, while the hero of the hooker became a greater man than before, and never was addressed by any other title afterwards than that of THE COMMODORE.

1. This is an allusion of Barny's to a prevalent saying in Ireland, addressed to a sportsman who returns home unsuccessful, 'So you've killed what the Connaughtman shot at.'
2. Some attempt Barny is making at latitudes.

PADDY THE PIPER

By SAMUEL LOVER

The only introduction I shall attempt to the following *'extravaganza'* is, to request the reader to suppose it to be delivered by a frollicking Irish peasant, in the richest brogue and most dramatic manner.

'I'll tell you, sir, a mighty quare story, and it's as thrue as I'm standin' here, and that's no lie: –

'It was in the time of the Rebellion, whin the long summer days, like many a fine fellow's precious life, was cut short by rayson of the martial law – that wouldn't let a dacent boy be out in the evenin', good or bad; for whin the day's work was over, divil a one of uz dar go to meet a frind over a glass, or a girl at the dance, but must go home, and shut ourselves up, and never budge, nor rise latch, nor dhraw boult, until the morning kem agin.

'Well, to come to my story: – 'T was after nightfall, and we wor sittin' round the fire, and the praties wor boilin', and the noggins of butthermilk was standin' ready for our suppers, whin a knock kem to the door.

' "Whisht!" says my father, "here's the sojers come upon us now," says he; "bad luck to thim, the villains, I'm afeard they seen a glimmer of the fire through the crack in the door," says he.

' "No," says my mother, "for I'm afther hanging' an owld sack and my new petticoat agin it awhile ago."

239

' "Well, whisht, anyhow," says my father, "for there's a knock agin"; and we all held our tongues till another thump kem to the door.

' "Oh, it's a folly to purtind any more," says my father, "they're too cute to be put off that-a-way," says he. "Go Shamus," says he to me, "and see who's in it."

' "How can I see who's in it in the dark?" says I.

' "Well," says he, "light the candle thin, and see who's in it, but don't open the door, for your life, barrin' they brake it in," says he, "exceptin to the sojers, and spake thim fair, if it's thim."

'So with that I wint to the door, and there was another knock.

' "Who's there?" says I.

' "It's me," says he.

' "Who are you?" says I.

' "A frind," says he.

' "*Baithershin*," says I, – "who are you at all?"

' "Arrah, don't you know me?" says he.

' "Divil a taste," says I.

' "Sure I'm Paddy the Piper," says he.

' "Oh, thunder an' turf," says I, "is it you, Paddy, that's in it?"

' "Sorra one else," says he.

' "And what brought you at this hour?" says I.

' "By gar," says he, "I didn't like goin' the roun' by the road," says he, "and so I kem the short cut, and that's what delayed me," says he.

' "Oh, murther!" says I; "Paddy, I wouldn't be in your shoes for the king's ransom," says I; "for you know yourself it's a hangin' matther to be cotched out these times," says I.

' "Sure I know that," says he, "and that's what I kem to you for," says he; "so let me in for owld acquaintance sake," says poor Paddy.

' "Oh, by this and that," says I, "I dar'n't open the door for the wide world; and sure you know it; and throth if the Husshians or the Yeos ketches you," says I, "they'll murther you as sure as your name's Paddy."

' "Many thanks to you," says he, "for your good intintions; but plase the pigs, I hope it's not the likes o' that is in store for me, anyhow."

' "Faith, thin," says I, "you had betther lose no time in hidin' yourself," says I; "for, throth I tell you it's a short thrial and a long rope the Husshians would be afther givin' you – for they've no justice and less marcy, the villians!"

' "Faith, thin, more's the rayson you should let me in, Shamus," says poor Paddy.

' "It's a folly to talk," says I, "I dar'n't open the door."

' "Oh, then, millia murther," says Paddy, "what'll become of me, at all at all?" says he.

' "Go aff into the shed," says I, "behin' the house, where the cow is, and there there's an iligant lock o' straw, that you may go sleep in," says I, "and a fine bed it id be for a lord, let alone a piper."

'So off Paddy set to hide in the shed, and, throth, it went to our hearts to refuse him, and turn him away from the door, more by token when the praties was ready – for sure the bit and the sup is always welkim to the poor thraveller. Well, we all wint to bed, and Paddy hid himself in the cow-house; and now I must tell you how it was with Paddy: –

'You see, afther sleepin' for some time, Paddy wakened up, thinkin' it was mornin'; but it wasn't mornin' at all, but only the light o' the moon that desaved him; but, at all evints, he wanted to be stirrin' airly, bekase he was goin' off to the town hard by, it bein' fair day, to pick up a few ha'pence with his pipes – for the divil a betther piper was in all the counthry round nor Paddy; and everyone gave it up to Paddy that he was iligant on the pipes, and played "Jinny bang'd the Weaver" beyant tellin', and the "Hare in the Corn", that you'd think the very dogs was in it, and the horsemen ridin' like mad.

'Well, as I was sayin', he set off to go to the fair, and he went meandherin' along through the fields; but he didn't go far, antil climbin' up through a hedge, when he was comin' out at t'other side, his head kem plump agin somethin' that made the fire flash out iv his eyes. So with that he looks up – and what do you think it was – Lord be marciful to uz! but a corpse hangin' out of a branch of a three.

' "Oh, the top o' the mornin' to you, sir," says Paddy, "and is that the way with you, my poor fellow? Throth, you tuk a start out o' me," says poor Paddy; and 't was thrue for him, for it would make the heart of a stouter man nor Paddy jump, to see the like, and to think of a Chrishthan crathur being hanged up, all as one as a dog.

'Now, 'twas the rebels that hanged this chap – bekase, you see, the corpse had good clothes an him, and that's the rayson that one might know it was the rebels – by rayson that the Husshians and the Orangemen never hanged anybody wid *good* clothes an him, but only the poor and definceless crathurs, like uz; so, as I said before, Paddy knew well it was the *boys* that done it; "and," says Paddy, eyin' the corpse, "by my sowl, thin, but you have a beautiful pair o' boots an you," says he, "and it's what I'm thinkin' you won't have any great use for thim no more; and sure it's a shame for the likes o' me," says he, "the best piper in the sivin counties, to be trampin' wid a pair of owld brogues not worth three *traneens*, and a corpse with such an iligant pair o' boots, that wants someone to wear thim." So, with that, Paddy lays hould of him by the boots, and began a pullin' at thim; but they were mighty stiff; and whether it was by rayson of their bein' so tight, or the branch of the three a-jiggin' up and down, all as one as a weighdeebuckettee, and not lettin' Paddy cotch any right hould o' thim – he could get no *advantage* o' thim at all – and at last he gev it up, and was goin' away, whin, looking behind him agin, the sight of the fine iligant boots was too much for him, and he turned back, determined to have the boots, anyhow, by fair means or foul; and I'm loath to tell you now how he got thim – for indeed it was a dirty turn, and throth, it was the only dirty turn I ever knew Paddy to be guilty av; and you see it was this a-way; 'pon my sowl, he pulled out a big knife, and, by the same token, it was a knife with a fine buck-handle, and a murtherin' big blade, that an uncle o' mine, that was a gardener at the lord's, made Paddy a prisint av; and, more by token, it was not the first mischief that knife done, for it cut love between thim, that was the best of frinds before; and sure 't was the wondher of everyone, that two knowledgeable men, that ought to know betther, would do the likes, and give and take sharp steel in frindship; but I'm forgettin' – well, he outs with his knife, and what does he do, but he cuts off the legs of the corpse; "and," says he, "I can take off the boots at my convaynience"; and, throth, it was, as I said before, a dirty turn.

'Well, sir, he tuck'd the legs under his arms, and at that minit the moon peeped out from behind a cloud. "Oh! is it there you are?" says he to the moon, for he was an impidint chap; – and thin, seein' that he made a mistake, and that the moonlight deceaved him, and that it wasn't the early dawn, as he conceaved; and bein' freken'd for fear himself might be cotched and thrated like the poor corpse he was afther a malthreating, if *he* was found walking the counthry at that time – begor, he turned about, and walked back agin to the cow-house, and, hidin' the corpse's legs in the sthraw, Paddy wint to sleep agin. But what do ye think? Paddy was not long there until the sojers came in airnest, and, by the powers, they carried off Paddy – and, faith, it was only sarvin' him right for what he done to the poor corpse.

'Well, whin the mornin' kem, my father says to me, "Go, Shamus," says he, "to the shed, and bid poor Paddy come in and take share of the praties, for, I go bail, he's ready for his breakquest by this, anyhow?"

'Well, out I wint to the cow-house, and called out, "Paddy!" and afther callin' three or four times, and gettin' no answer, I wint in, and called agin, and dickens an answer I got still.

"Tatthar-an-agers!" says I, "Paddy, where are you, at all at all?" and so, castin' my eyes about the shed, I seen two feet stickin' out from undher the hape o' straw – "Musha! thin," says I, "bad luck to you, Paddy, but you're fond of a warm corner, and maybe you haven't made yourself as snug as a flea in a blanket? but I'll disturb your dhrames, I'm thinkin'," says I, and with that I laid hould of his heels (as I thought, God help me), and givin' a good pull to waken him, as I intinded, away I wint, head over heels, and my brains was a'most knocked out agin the wall.

'Well, when I recovered myself, there I was, an the broad o' my back, and two things stickin' out o' my hands like a pair o' Husshian's horse-pist'ls – and I thought the sight 'id lave my eyes when I seen they were two mortial legs.

'My jew'l, I threw them down like a hot pratee, and jumpin' up, I roared out millia murther. "Oh, you murtherin' villain," says I, shakin' my fist at the cow. "Oh, you unnath'ral *baste*," says I, "you've ate poor Paddy, you thievin' cannible, you're worse than a neygar," says I; "and, bad luck to you, how dainty you are, that nothin' 'id sarve you for your supper, but the best piper in Ireland. *Weirasthru! weirasthru!* what'll the whole counthry say to such an unnath'ral murther? And you lookin' as innocent there as a lamb, and atin' your hay as quiet as if nothin' happened." With that, I run out – for, throth, I didn't like to be near her – and, goin' into the house, I tould them all about it.

' "Arrah, be aisy," says my father.

' "Bad luck to the lie I tell you," says I.

' "Is it ate Paddy?" says they.

' "Divil a doubt of it," says I.

' "Are you sure, Shamus?" says my mother.

' "I wish I was as sure of a new pair of brogues," says I. "Bad luck to the bit she has left of him but his two legs."

' "And do you tell me she ate the pipes too?" says my father.

' "Begor, I b'lieve so," says I.

' "Oh, the divil fly away wid her," says he; "what a cruel taste she has for music!"

' "Arrah," says my mother, "don't be cursin' the cow, that gives the milk to the childher."

' "Yis, I will," says my father; "why shouldn't I curse sich an unnath'ral baste?"

' "You oughtn't to curse any livin' thing that's undher your roof," says my mother.

' "By my sowl, thin," says my father, "she sha'n't be undher my roof any more; for I'll sind her to the fair this minit," says he, "and sell her for whatever she'll bring. Go aff," says he, "Shamus, the minit you've ate your breakquest, and dhrive her to the fair."

' "Throth, I don't like to dhrive her," says I.

' "Arrah, don't be makin' a gommagh of yourself," says he.

' "Faith, I don't," says I.

' "Well, like or no like," says he, "you must dhrive her."

' "Sure, father," says I, "you could take more care iv her yourself."

' "That's mighty good," says he, "to keep a dog, and bark myself"; and, faith, I rec'llected the sayin' from that hour; – "let me have no more words about it," says he, "but be aff wid you."

'So, aff I wint – and it's no lie I'm tellin', whin I say it was sore agin my will I had anything to do with sich a villian of a baste. But, howsowever, I cut a brave, long wattle, that I might dhrive the man-ater iv a thief, as she was, without bein' near her, at all at all.

'Well, away we wint along the road, and mighty throng it wuz wid the boys and the girls – and, in short, all sorts, rich and poor, high and low, crowdin' to the fair.

' "God save you," says one to me.

' "God save you kindly," says I.

' "That's a fine baste you're dhrivin'," says he.

' "Throth, she is," says I; though it wint agin my heart to say a good word for the likes of her.

' "It's to the fair you're goin', I suppose," says he, "with the baste?" (He was a snug-lookin' farmer, ridin' a purty little grey hack.)

' "Faith, thin, you're right enough," says I; "it is to the fair I'm goin'."

' "What do you expec' for her?" says he.

' "Faith, thin, mysel doesn't know," says I – and that was thrue enough, you see, bekase I was bewildhered like about the baste intirely.

' "That's a quare way to be goin' to market," says he, "and not to know what you expec' for your baste."

' "Och," says I – not likin' to let him suspict there was anything wrong wid her – "och," says I, in a careless sort of way, "sure, no one can tell what a baste'll bring, antil they come to the fair," says I, "and see what price is goin'."

' "Indeed, that's nath'ral enough," says he, "But if you wor bid a fair price before you come to the fair, sure you might as well take it," says he.

' "Oh, I've no objection in life," says I.

' "Well, thin, what'll you ax for her?" says he.

' "Why, thin, I wouldn't like to be onraysonable," says I (for the thruth was, you know, I wanted to get rid of her), "and so I'll take four pounds for her," says I, "and no less."

' "No less!" says he.

' "Why, sure that's chape enough," says I.

' "Throth, it is," says he; "and I'm thinkin' it's too cheap it is," says he; "for if there wasn't somethin' the matter, it's not for that you'd be sellin' the fine milch cow, as she is, to all appearance."

' "Indeed, thin," says I; "upon my conscience, she is a fine milch cow."

' "Maybe," says he, "she's gone off her milk, in regard that she doesn't feed well?"

' "Och, by this and that," says I, "in regard o' feedin' there's not the likes o' her in Ireland; so make your mind aisy – and if you like her for the money, you may have her."

' "Why, indeed, I'm not in a hurry," says he, "and I'll wait to see how they go in the fair."

' "With all my heart," says I, purtendin' to be no ways consarned; – but, in throth, I began to be afeard that the people was seein' somethin' unnath'ral about her, and that we'd never get rid of her, at all at all. At last we kem to the fair, and a great sight o' people was in it – throth, you'd think the whole world was there, let alone the standins o' gingerbread and iligant ribbins, and makins o' beautiful gownds, and pitch-and-toss, and merry-go-rouns, and tins with the best av dhrink in them, and the fiddles playin' up t' incourage the boys and girls; but I never minded thim at all, but detarmint to sell the thievin' rogue av a cow afore I'd mind any divarshin in life; so an I drhriv her into the thick av the fair, whin, all of a suddint, as I kem to the door av a tint, up sthruck the pipes to the tune av 'Tather Jack Welsh', and, my jew'l, in a minit the cow cock'd her ears, and was makin' a dart at the tint.

' "Oh, murther!" says I, to the boys standin' by, "hould her," says I, "hould her – she ate one piper already, the vagabone, and, bad luck to her, she wants another now."

' "Is it a cow for to ate a piper?" says one o' them.

' "Not a word o' lie in it, for I seen his corpse myself, and nothin' left but the two legs," says I; and it's a folly to be sthrivin' to hide it, for I see she'll never lave it aff – as poor Paddy Grogan knows to his cost, Lord be merciful to him."

' "Who's that takin' my name in vain?" says a voice in the crowd; and with that, shovin' the throng a one side, who should I see but Paddy Grogan, to all appearance.

' "Oh, hould him too," says I: "keep him aff me, for it's not himself at all, but his ghost," says I, "for he was kilt last night to my sartin knowledge, every inch av him, all to his legs."

'Well, sir, with that, Paddy – for it *was* Paddy himself, as it kem out afther – fell a-laughin', that you'd think his sides 'ud split; and whin he kem to himself, he ups and he tould uz how it was, as I tould you already; and the likes av the fun they made av me was beyant tellin', for wrongfully misdoubtin' the poor cow, and layin' the blame iv atin' a piper an her. So we all wint into the tint to have it explained, and begor, it took a full gallon o' sper'ts t' explain it; and we dhrank health and long life to Paddy and the cow, and Paddy played that day beyant all tellin', and many a one said the likes was never heerd before nor sence, even from Paddy himself – and av coorse the poor slandhered cow was dhruv home agin, and many a quiet day she had wid us afther that; and whin she died, throth, my father had sitch a regard for the poor thing that he had her skinned, and an iligant pair of breeches made out iv her hide, and it's in the family to this day; and isn't it mighty remarkable it is, what I'm goin' to tell you now, but it's as thrue as I'm here, that from that day out, anyone that has thim breeches an, the minit a pair o' pipes sthrikes up, they can't rest, but goes jiggin' and jiggin' in their sate, and never stops as long as the pipes are playin' – and there,' said he, slapping the garment in question that covered his sinewy limb, with a spank of his brawny hand that might have startled nerves more tender than mine – 'there, them is the very breeches that's an me now, and a fine pair they are this minit.'

The foregoing story I heard related by a gentleman, who said he was not aware to whom the original authorship was attributable.

WILLIAM MAGINN

1794–1842

William Maginn was born in Cork in 1794. He entered Trinity very young, and soon showed signs of the wide learning he was noted for later on. *Blackwood* was started in 1817, and Maginn contributed to an early number a translation into Latin of 'Chevy Chase'. For a time he kept a school at Cork, where he came across and befriended Callanan, the first fine translator of old Irish songs, and himself author of some good and well prized verses. In 1823 he married, gave up his school and settled in London, writing for *Blackwood* and the then newly started *Standard*, to the success of which he greatly contributed by his political articles. He quarrelled with *Blackwood* a little later, and founded in competition *Fraser's Magazine*. In 1838 appeared his 'Homeric Ballads', called by Matthew Arnold 'genuine poems of their sort', but now forgotten. He was all this time constantly in debt through wild living. Dissipation brought him more than once to the debtors' prison, but never did he lose his magnificent serenity. A man who saw him just before his death has thus described him: 'He was quite emaciated and worn away; his hands thin, and very little flesh on his face; his eyes appeared brighter and larger than usual, and his hair wild and disordered. He stretched out his hand and saluted me. He is a ruin, but a glorious ruin nevertheless... He lives a rollicking life, and will write you one of his ablest articles while standing in his shirt or sipping brandy. We talked of

Seneca, Homer, Christ, Plato, and Virgil.' He died in 1842, aged forty-eight. He was the origin of Captain Shandon in 'Pendennis'. He left behind little beside a great mass of ephemeral articles. 'Father Tom', however, deserves to be long remembered. Its chief personage was a once well-known Catholic controversialist, Father Tom Maguire, who shortly before it was written had met in public debate and in the opinion of the multitude routed a Protestant clergyman named Pope.

FATHER TOM AND THE POPE

OR, A NIGHT AT THE VATICAN

[*Maga*. May, 1838]

I

How Father Tom Went to Take Pot-luck at the Vatican

When his Riv'rence was in Room, ov coorse the Pope axed him
to take pot-look wid him. More be token, it was on a Friday;
but, for all that, there was plenty of mate; for the Pope gev
himself an absolution from the fast on account ov the great
company that was in it – at least so I'm tould. Howandiver,
there's no fast on the dhrink, anyhow – glory be to God! – and
so, as they wor sitting, afther dinner, taking their sup together,
says the Pope, says he, 'Thomaus' – for the Pope, you know,
spakes that away, all as one as one ov uz – 'Thomaus *a lanna*,'
says he, 'I'm tould you welt them English heretics out ov the
face.'

'You may say that,' says his Riv'rence to him again. 'Be my
sowl,' says he, 'if I put your Holiness undher the table, you
won't be the first Pope I floored.'

Well, his Holiness laughed like to split; for, you know, Pope
was the great Prodesan that Father Tom put down upon
Purgathory; and ov coorse they knewn all the ins and outs of
the conthravarsy at Room. 'Faix, Thomaus,' says he, smiling
across the table at him mighty agreeable – 'it's no lie what they

251

tell me, that yourself is the pleasant man over the dhrop ov good liquor.'

'Would you like to thry?' says his Riv'rence.

'Sure, and am n't I thrying all I can?' says the Pope. 'Sorra betther bottle ov wine's betuxt this and Salamancha, nor's there fornenst you on the table; it's raal Lachrymalchrystal, every spudh ov it.'

'It's mortial could,' says Father Tom.

'Well, man alive,' says the Pope, 'sure and here's the best ov good claret in the cut decanther.'

'Not maning to make little ov the claret, your Holiness,' says his Riv'rence, 'I would prefir some hot wather and sugar, wid a glass ov spirits through it, if convanient.'

'Hand me over the bottle of brandy,' says the Pope to his head butler, 'and fetch up the mater'ls,' says he.

'Ah, then, your Holiness,' says his Riv'rence, mighty eager, 'maybe you'd have a dhrop ov the native in your cellar? Sure it's all one throuble,' says he, 'and, troth, I dunna how it is, but brandy always plays the puck wid my inthrails.'

''Pon my conscience, then,' says the Pope, "it's very sorry I am, Misther Maguire,' says he, 'that it isn't in my power to plase you; for I'm sure and certain that there's not as much whiskey in Room this blessed minit as 'ud blind the eye ov a midge.'

'Well in troth, your Holiness,' says Father Tom, 'I knewn there was no use in axing; only,' says he, 'I didn't know how else to exqueeze the liberty I tuck,' says he, 'of bringing a small taste,' says he, 'of the real stuff,' says he, hauling out an imperi'l quart bottle out ov his coat-pocket; 'that never seen the face ov a gauger,' says he, setting it down on the table fornenst the Pope: 'and if you'll jist thry the full ov a thimble ov it, and it doesn't rise the cockles ov your Holiness' heart, why then, my name,' says he, 'isn't Torn Maguire!' and wid that he outs wid the cork.

Well, the Pope at first was going to get vexed at Father Tom for fetching dhrink thataway in his pocket, as if there wasn't lashins in the house: so says he, 'Misther Maguire,' says he, 'I'd have you to comprehind the differ betuxt an inwitation to dinner from the successor of Saint Pether, and from a common nagur ov a Prodesan squireen that maybe hasn't liquor enough in his cupboard to wet more nor his own heretical whistle. That may be the way wid them that you wisit in Leithrirn,' says he, 'and in Roscommon; and I'd let you know the differ in the prisint case,' says he, 'only that you're a champion ov the Church and entitled to laniency. So,' says he, 'as the liquor's come, let it stay. And in throth I'm curis myself,' says he, getting mighty soft when he found the delightful smell ov the *putteen*, 'in inwistigating the composition ov distilled liquors; it's a branch of natural philosophy,' says he, taking up the bottle and putting it to his blessed nose. Ah! my dear, the very first snuff he got ov it, he cried out, the dear man, 'Blessed Vargin, but it has the divine smell!' and crossed himself and the bottle half-a-dozen times running.

'Well, sure enough, it's the blessed liquor now,' says his Riv'rence, 'and so there can be no harm anyway in mixing a dandy of punch; and,' says he, stirring up the materi'ls wid his goolden muddler – for everything at the Pope's table, to the very shcrew for drawing the corks, was ov vergin goold – 'if I might make bould,' says he, 'to spake on so deep a subjic afore your Holiness, I think it 'ud considherably whacilitate the inwestigation ov its chemisthry and phwarmaceutics, if you'd jist thry the laste sup in life ov it inwardly.'

'Well, then, suppose I do make the same expiriment,' says the Pope, in a much more condescinding way nor you'd have expected – and wid that he mixes himself a real stiff facer.

'Now, your Holiness,' says Father Tom, 'this bein' the first time you ever dispinsed them chymicals,' says he, 'I'll just make bould to lay down one rule ov orthography,' says he, 'for conwhounding them, *secundum mortem*.'

'What's that?' says the Pope.

'Put in the sperits first,' says his Riv'rence; 'and then put in the sugar; and remember, every dhrop ov wather you put in afther that spoils the punch.'

'Glory be to God!' says the Pope, not minding a word Father Tom was saying. 'Glory be to God!' says he, smacking his lips. 'I never knewn what dhrink was afore,' says he. 'It bates the Lachrymalchrystal out ov the face!' says he – 'it's Necthar itself, it is, so it is!' says he, wiping his epistolical mouth wid the cuff ov his coat.

''Pon my secret honour,' says his Riv'rence, 'I'm raally glad to see your Holiness set so much to your satiswhaction; especially,' says he, 'as, for fear ov accidents, I tuck the liberty of fetching the fellow ov that small vesshel,' says he, 'in my other coatpocket. So devil a fear ov our running dhry till the but-end of the evening, anyhow,' says he.

'Dhraw your stool in to the fire, Misther Maguire,' says the Pope, 'for faix,' says he, 'I'm bent on analizing the metaphwysics ov this phinomenon. Come, man alive, clear off,' says he, 'you're not dhrinking at all.'

'Is it dhrink?' says his Riv'rence; 'by Gorra, your Holiness,' says he, 'I'd dhrink wid you till the cows 'ud be coming home in the morning.'

So wid that they tackled to, to the second fugee a-piece, and fell into larned discourse. But it's time for me now to be off to the lecthir at the Boord. Oh my sorra light upon you, Docther Whateley, wid your pilitical econimy and your hydherastatics! What the *dioul* use has a poor hedge-master like me wid such deep larning as is only fit for the likes ov them two that I left over their second tumbler? Howandiver, wishing I was like them, in regard ov the sup ov dhrink, anyhow, I must brake off my norration for the prisint; but when I see you again, I'll tell you how Father Tom made a hare ov the Pope that evening, both in theology and the cube root.

II

How Father Tom Sacked His Holiness in Theology and Logic

Well, the lecthir's over, and I'm kilt out and out. My bitther curse upon the man that invinted the same Boord! I thought ons't I'd fadomed the say ov throuble; and that was when I got through fractions at ould Mat Kavanagh's school, in Firdramore – God be good to poor Mat's sowl, though he did deny the cause the day he suffered! but it's fluxions itself we're set to bottom now, sink or shwim! May I never die if my head isn't as throughother as anything wid their ordinals and cardinals – and, begob, it's all nothing to the econimy lecthir that I have to go to at two o'clock. Howandiver, I mustn't forget that we left his Riv'rence and his Holiness sitting fornenst one another in the parlour ov the Vatican, jist afther mixing their second tumbler.

When they had got well down into the same, they fell, as I was telling you, into larned discourse. For, you see, the Pope was curious to find out whether Father Tom was the great theologian all out that people said; and says he: 'Misther Maguire,' says he, 'what answer do you make to the heretics when they quote them passidges agin thransubstantiation out ov the Fathers?' says he.

'Why,' says his Riv'rence, 'as there should be no sich passidges I make myself mighty aisy about them; but if you want to know how I dispose ov them,' says he, 'just repate one ov them, and I'll show you how to catapomphericate it in two shakes.'

'Why, then,' says the Pope, 'myself disremimbers the particlar passidges they alledge out ov them ould felleys,' says he, 'though sure enough they're more numerous nor edifying – so we'll jist suppose that a heretic was to find sich a saying as this in Austin, "Every sensible man knows that thransubstantiation is a lie," – or this out of Tertullian or Plutarch, "The bishop ov Room is a common imposther," – now tell me, could you answer him?'

'As easy as kiss,' says his Riv'rence. 'In the first, we're to understand that the exprission, "Every sinsible man," signifies simply, "Every man that judges by his nath'ral sinses"; and we all know that nobody folleying them seven deludhers could ever find out the mysthery that's in it, if somebody didn't come in to his assistance wid an eighth sinse, which is the only sinse to be depended on, being the sinse ov the Church. So that, regarding the first quotation which your Holiness has supposed, it makes clane for us, and tee-totally agin the heretics.'

'That's the explanation sure enough,' says his Holiness; 'and now what div you say to my being a common imposther?'

'Faix, I think,' says his Riv'rence, 'wid all submission to the betther judgment ov the learned father that your Holiness has quoted, he'd have been a thrifle nearer the thruth, if he had said that the bishop ov Room is the grand imposther and top-sawyer in that line over us all.'

'What do you mane?' says the Pope, getting quite red in the face.

'What would I mane?' says his Riv'rence, as composed as a docther ov physic, 'but that your Holiness is at the head ov all them – troth I had a'most forgot I wasn't a bishop myself,' says he (the deludher was going to say, as the head of all *uz*) – 'that has the gift ov laying on hands. For sure,' says he, 'imposthur and *imposithir* is all one, so you're only to undherstand *manuum*, and the job is done. Awouich!' says he, 'if any heretic 'ud go for to cast up sich a passidge as that agin me, I'd soon give him a lesson in the p'lite art ov cutting a stick to welt his own back wid.'

''Pon my apostolical word,' says the Pope, 'you've cleared up them two pints in a most satiswhacthemy manner.'

'You see,' says his Riv'rence – by this time they wor mixing their third tumbler – 'the writings ov them Fathers is to be thrated wid great veneration; and it 'ud be the height ov presumption in anyone to sit down to interpret them widout providing himself wid a genteel assortment ov the best figures ov rhetoric, sich as mettonymy, hyperbol, cattychraysis, prolipsis, mettylipsis, superbaton, pollysyndreton, hustheronprotheron, prosodypeia and the like, in ordher that he may never be at a loss for shuitable sintiments when he comes to their high-flown passidges. For unless we thrate them Fathers liberally to a handsome allowance ov thropes and figures, they'd set up heresy at ons't, so they would.'

'It's thrue for you,' says the Pope; 'the figures ov spache is the pillars ov the Church.'

'Bedad,' says his Riv'rence, 'I dunna what we'd do widout them at all.'

'Which one do you prefir?' says the Pope; 'that is,' says he, 'which figure ov spache do you find most usefullest when you're hard set?'

'Metaphour's very good,' says his Riv'rence, 'and so's mettonymy – and I've known prosodypeia stand to me at a pinch mighty well – but for a constancy, superbaton's the figure for my money. Devil be in me,' says he, 'but I'd prove black white as fast as a horse 'ud throt wid only a good stock ov superbaton.'

'Faix,' says the Pope, wid a sly wink, 'you'd need to have it backed, I judge, wid a small taste of assurance.'

'Well, now, jist for that word,' says his Riv'rence, 'I'll prove it widout aither one or other. Black,' says he, 'is one thing and white is another thing. You don't conthravene that? But everything is aither one thing or another thing; I defy the apostle Paul to get over that dilemma. Well! If any thing be one thing, well and good; but if it be another thing, then it's plain it isn't both things, and so can't be two things – nobody can deny that. But what can't be two things must be one thing – *Ergo*, whether it's one thing or another thing it's all one. But black is one thing and white is another thing, – *Ergo*, black and white is all one. *Quod erat demonsthrandum*.'

'Stop a bit,' says the Pope, 'I can't althegither give in to your second minor – no – your second major,' says he, and he stopped. 'Faix, then,' says he, getting confused, 'I don't rightly remimber where it was exactly that I thought I seen the flaw in your premises. Howsomdiver,' says he, 'I don't deny that it's a good conclusion, and one that 'ud be ov materi'l service to the Church if it was dhrawn wid a little more distinctiveness.'

'I'll make it as plain as the nose on your Holiness' face, by superbaton,' says his Riv'rence. 'My adversary says, black is not another colour, that is, white? Now that's jist a parallel passidge wid the one out ov Tartullian that me and Hayes smashed the heretics on in Clarendon Sthreet, "This is my body – that is, the figure ov my body." That's a superbaton, and we showed that it oughtn't to be read that way at all, but this way, "This figure of my body *is* my body." Jist so wid my adversary's proposition, it mustn't be undherstood the way it reads, by no manner of manes; but it's to be taken this way, – "Black – that is, white, is not another colour," – green, if you like, or orange, by dad, for anything I care, for my case is proved. "Black", that is, "white", lave out the "that", by sinnalayphy, and you have the orthodox conclusion, "Black is white", or by convarsion, "White is black".'

'It's as clear as mud,' says the Pope.

'Begad,' says his Riv'rence, 'I'm in great humour for disputin' tonight. I wisht your Holiness was a heretic jist for two minutes,' says he, 'till you'd see the flaking I'd give you!'

'Well then, for the fun o' the thing, suppose me my namesake, if you like,' says the Pope, laughing, 'though, by Jayminy,' says he, 'he's not one that I take much pride ov.'

'Very good – devil a betther joke ever I had,' says his Riv'rence. 'Come, then, Misther Pope,' says he, 'hould up that purty face ov yours, and answer me this question. Which 'ud be the biggest lie, if I said I seen a turkeycock lying on the broad ov his back, and picking the stars out ov the sky, or if I was to say that I seen a gandher in the same intherestin' posture, raycreating himself wid similar asthronomical experiments? Answer me that, you ould swaddler?' says he.

'How durst you call me a swaddler, sir?' says the Pope, forgetting, the dear man, the part that he was acting.

'Don't think for to bully me!' says his Riv'rence, 'I always daar to spake the truth, and it's well known that you're nothing but a swaddling ould sinner ov a saint,' says he, never letting on to persave that his Holiness had forgot what they were agreed on.

'By all that's good,' says the Pope, 'I often hard ov the imperance ov you Irish afore,' says he, 'but I never expected to be called a saint in my own house either by Irishman or Hottentot. I'll till you what, Misther Maguire,' says he, 'if you can't keep a civil tongue in your head, you had betther be walking off wid yourself; for I beg lave to give you to undherstand, that it won't be for the good ov your health if you call me by sich an outprobrious epithet again,' says he.

'Oh, indeed! then things is come to a purty pass,' says his Riv'rence (the dear funny soul that he ever was!) 'when the likes ov you compares one of the Maguires ov Tempo wid a wild Ingine! Why, man alive, the Maguires was kings ov Fermanagh three thousand years afore your grandfather, that was the first ov your breed that ever wore shoes and stockings' (I'm bound to say, in justice to the poor Prodesan, that this was all spoken by his Riv'rence by way of a figure ov spache), 'was sint his Majesty's arrand to cultivate the friendship of Prince Lee Boo in Botteney Bay! Oh, Bryan dear,' says he, letting on to cry, 'if you were alive to hear a *boddagh Sassenagh* like this casting up his counthry to one ov the name ov Maguire!'

'In the name ov God,' says the Pope, very solemniously, 'what *is* the maning ov all this at all at all?' says he.

'Sure,' says his Riv'rence, whispering to him across the table, 'sure you know we're acting a conthrawarsy, and you tuck the part ov the Prodesan champion. You wouldn't be angry wid me, I'm sure, for sarving out the heretic to the best ov my ability.'

'Oh, begad, I had forgot,' says the Pope, the good-natured ould crethur; 'sure enough you were only taking your part, as a good Milesian Catholic ought, agin the heretic Sassenagh. Well,' says he, 'fire away now, and I'll put up wid as many conthroversial compliments as you plase to pay me.'

'Well, then, answer me my question, you santimonious ould dandy,' says his Riv'rence.

'In troth, then,' says the Pope, 'I dunna which 'ud be the biggest lie; to my mind,' says he, 'the one appears to be about as big a bounce as the other.'

'Why, then, you poor simpleton,' says his Riv'rence, 'don't you persave that, forbye the advantage the gandher 'ud have in the length ov his neck, it 'ud be next to onpossible for the turkeycock lying thataway to see what he was about, by rason ov his djollars and other accouthrements hanging back over his eyes? The one about as big a bounce as the other! Oh, you misfortunate crethur! if you had ever larned your ABC in theology, you'd have known that there's a differ betuxt them two lies so great, that, begad, I wouldn't wondher if it'ud make a balance ov five years in purgathory to the sowl that 'ud be in it. Ay, and if it wasn't that the Church is too liberal entirely, so she is, it'ud cost his heirs and successors betther nor ten pounds to have him out as soon as the other. Get along, man, and take half-a-year at dogmatical theology; go and read your Dens, you poor dunce, you!'

'Raaly,' says the Pope, 'you're making the heretic's shoes too hot to hould me. I wundher how the Prodesans can stand afore you at all.'

'Don't think to delude me,' says has Riv'rence, 'don't think to back out ov your challenge now,' says he, 'but come to the scratch like a man, if you are a man, and answer me my question. What's the rason, now, that Julius Caesar and the Vargin Mary was born upon the one day? – answer me that, if you wouldn't be hissed off the platform.'

Well, my dear, the Pope couldn't answer it, and he had to acknowledge himself sacked. Then he axed his Riv'rence to tell him the rason himself; and Father Tom communicated it to him in Latin. But as that is a very deep question, I never hard what the answer was, except that I'm tould it was so mysterious, it made the Pope's hair stand on end.

But there's two o'clock, and I'll be late for the lecthir.

III

How Father Tom Made a Hare of His Holiness in Latin

Oh, Docther Whateley, Docther Whateley, I'm sure I'll never die another death if I don't die aither of consumption or production! I ever and always thought that asthronomy was the hardest science that was till now – and it's no lie I'm telling you, the same asthronomy is a tough enough morsel to brake a man's fast upon – and geolidgy is middling and hard too – and hydherastatics is no joke; but ov all the books of science that ever was opened and shut, that book upon Pilitical Econimy lifts the pins! Well, well, if they wait till they persuade me that taking a man's mints out ov the counthry, and spinding them in forrain parts isn't doing us out ov the same, they'll wait a long time in troth. But you're waiting, I see, to hear how his Riv'rence and his Holiness got on after finishing the disputation I was telling you of. Well, you see, my dear, when the Pope found he couldn't hould a candle to Father Tom in theology and logic, he thought he'd take the shine out ov him in Latin anyhow, so says he, 'Misther Maguire,' says he, 'I quite agree wid you that it's not lucky for us to be spaking on them deep subjects in sich langidges as the evil spirits is acquainted wid; and,' says he, 'I think it'ud be no harm for us to spake from this out in Latin,' says he, 'for fraid the devil'ud undherstand what we are saying.'

'Not a hair I care,' says Father Tom, 'whether he undherstands what we're saying or not, as long as we keep off that last pint we wor discussing, and one or two others. Listners never heard good ov themselves,' says he; 'and if Belzhebub takes anything amiss that aither you or me says in regard ov himself or his faction, let him stand forrid like a man, and, never fear, I'll give him his answer. Howandiver, if it's for a taste ov classic conwersation you are, just to put us in mind ov ould Cordarius,' says he, 'here's at you'; and wid that he lets fly at his Holiness wid his health in Latin.

'Vesthrae Sanctitatis salutem volo!' says he.

'Vestrae Revirintiae salubritati bibo!' says the Pope to him again (haith, it's no joke, I tell you, to remimber sich a power ov larning). 'Here's to you wid the same,' says the Pope, in the raal Ciceronian. 'Nunc poculum alterhum imple,' says he.

'Cum omni jucunditate in vita,' says his Riv'rence. 'Cum summâ concupiscintiâ et animositate,' says he; as much as to say, 'Wid all the veins ov my heart, I'll do that same'; and so wid that, they mixed their fourth gun a-piece.

'Aqua vitae vesthra sane est liquor admirabilis,' says the Pope. 'Verum est pro te, – it's thrue for you,' says his Riv'rence, forgetting the idyim ov the Latin phwraseology, in a manner.

'Prava est tua Latinitas, domine,' says the Pope, finding fault like wid his etymology.

'Parva culpa mihi,' 'small blame to me, that is,' says his Riv'rence; 'nam multum laboro in partibus interioribus,' says he – the dear man! that never was at a loss for an excuse!

'Quid tibi incommodi?' says the Pope, axing him what ailed him.

'Habesne id quod Anglicè vocamus, a looking-glass,' says his Riv'rence.

'Immo, habeo speculum splendidissimum subther operculum pyxidis hujus starnutatoriae,' says the Pope, pulling out a beautiful goold snuff-box, wid a looking-glass in undher the lid; 'Subther operculum pyxidis hujus starnutatorii – no – starnutatoriae – quam dono accepi ab Archi-duce Austhriaco siptuagisima praetheritâ,' says he; as much as to say that he got the box in a prisint from the Queen ov Spain last Lint, if I rightly remimber.

Well, Father Tom laughed like to burst. At last, says he, 'Pather Sancte,' says he, 'sub errore jaces. "Looking-glass" apud nos habet significationem quamdam peculiarem ex tempore diei dependentem' – there was a sthring ov accusatives for yez! – 'nam mane speculum sonat,' says he, 'post prandium vero mat – mat – mat' – sorra be in me but I disremimber the classic appellivation ov the same article. Howandiver, his Riv'rence went on explaining himself in such a way as no scholar could mistake. 'Vesica mea,' says he, 'ab illo ultimo eversore distenditur, donec similis est rumpere. Verbis apertis,' says he, 'Vesthrae Sanctitatis praesentia salvata, aquam facere valde desidhero.'

'Ho, ho, ho!' says the Pope, grabbing up his box; 'si inquinavisses meam pyxidem, excimnicari debuisses. Hillo, Anthony,' says he to his head butler, 'fetch Misther Maguire a –'

'You spoke first!' says his Riv'rence, jumping off his sate: 'You spoke first in the vernacular. I take Misther Anthony to witness,' says he.

'What else would you have me to do?' says the Pope, quite dogged like to see himself bate thataway at his own waypons. 'Sure,' says he, 'Anthony wouldn't undherstand a B from a bull's foot, if I spoke to him any other way.'

'Well, then,' says his Riv'rence, 'in considheration ov the needcessity,' says he, 'I'll let you off for this time; but mind, now, afther I say *praestho*, the first of us that spakes a word of English is the hare – *praestho!*'

Neither of them spoke for near a minit, considhering wid themselves how they wor to begin sich a great thrial ov shkill.

At last, says the Pope – the blessed man! only think how 'cute it was ov him! – 'Domine Maguire,' says he, 'valde desidhero, certiorem fieri de significatione istius verbi *eversor* quo jam jam usus us' – (well, surely I *am* the boy for the Latin!).

'*Eversor*, id est cyathus,' says his Riv'rence, 'nam apud nos *tumbleri*, seu eversores, dicti sunt ab evertendo ceremoniam inter amicos; non, ut Temperantiae Societatis frigidis fautoribus placet, ab evertendis ipsis potatoribus.' (It's not every masther undher the Boord, I tell you, could carry such a car-load ov the dead langidges.) 'In agro vero Louthiano et Midensi,' says he, 'nomine gaudent quodam secundum linguam Anglicanam significante bombardam sen tormentum; quia ex eis tanquam ex telis jaculatorus liquorem faucibus immittere solent. Etiam inter haereticos illos melanostomos' (that was a touch of Greek). 'Presbyterianos Septentrionales, qui sunt terribiles potatores, Cyathi dicti sunt *faceres*, et dimidium Cyathi *hoef-a-glessus*. Dimidium Cyathi verò apud Metropolitanos Hibernicos dicitur *dandy*.' – 'En verbum Anglicanum!' says the Pope, clapping his hands, – 'leporem te fecisti'; as much as to say that he had made a hare ov himself.

'*Dandoeus, dandoeus*, verbum erat,' says his Riv'rence – oh, the dear man, but it's himself that was handy ever and always at getting out of a hobble – '*dandoeus* verbum erat,' says he, 'quod dicturus eram, cum me intherpillavisti.'

'Ast ego dico,' says the Pope, very sharp, 'quod verbum erat *dandy*.'

'Per tibicinem qui coram Mose modulatus est,' says his Riv'rence, 'id flagellat mundum! *Dandoeus* dixi, et tu dicis *dandy*; ergo tu es lepus, non ego – Ah, ha! Saccavi vesthram Sanctitatem!'

'Mendacium est!' says the Pope, quite forgetting himself, he was so mad at being sacked before the sarvints.

Well, if it hadn't been that his Holiness was in it, Father Tom'ud have given him the contints ov his tumbler betuxt the two eyes, for calling him a liar; and, in troth, it's very well it was in Latin the offince was conweyed, for, if it had been in the vernacular, there's no saying what'ud ha' been the consequence. His Riv'rence was mighty angry anyhow. – 'Tu senex lathro,' says he, 'quomodo audes me mendacem praedicare?'

'Et tu, sacrilege nebulo,' says the Pope, 'quomodo audacitatem habeas, me Dei in terris vicarium, lathronem conwiciari?'

'Interroga circumcirca,' says his Riv'rence.

'Abi ex aedibus meis,' says the Pope.

'Abi tu in malem crucem,' says his Riv'rence.

'Excumnicabo te,' says the Pope.

'Diabolus curat,' says his Riv'rence.

'Anathema sis,' says the Pope.

'Oscula meum pod,' – says his Riv'rence – but, my dear, afore he could finish what he was going to say, the Pope broke out into the vernacular, 'Get out o' my house, you reprobate!' says he in sich a rage that he could contain himself widin the Latin no longer.

'Ha, ha, ha! – ho, ho, ho!' says his Riv'rence, 'Who's the hare now, your Holiness? Oh, by this and by that, I've sacked you clane! Clane and clever I've done it, and no mistake! You see what a bit ov desate will do wid the wisest, your Holiness – sure it was joking I was, on purpose to aggrawate you – all's fair, you know, in love, law, and conthravarsy. In troth if I'd thought you'd have taken it so much to heart, I'd have put my head into the fire afore I'd have said a word to offind you,' says he, for he seen that the Pope was very vexed. 'Sure, God forbid that I'd say anything agin your Holiness, barring it was in fun: for aren't you the father ov the faithful, and the thrue vicar ov God upon earth? And am n't I ready to go down on my two knees this blessed minit and beg your apostolical pardon for every word that I said to your displasement?'

'Are you in arnest that it is in fun you wor?' says the Pope.

'May I never die if I am n't,' says his Riv'rence. 'It was all to provoke your Holiness to commit a brache ov the Latin that I tuck the small liberties I did,' says he.

'I'd have you to take care,' says the Pope, 'how you take sich small liberties again, or maybe you'll provoke me to commit a brache of the pace.'

'Well, and if I did,' says his Riv'rence, 'I know a sartan preparation ov chemicals that's very good for curing a brache either in Latinity or friendship.'

'What's that?' says the Pope, quite mollified, and sitting down again at the table that he had ris from in the first pluff of his indignation. 'What's that?' says he, 'for, 'pon my Epistolical 'davy, I think it'ud n't be easy to bate this miraclous mixthir that we've been thrying to anilize this two hours back,' says he, taking a mighty scientifical swig out ov the bottom ov his tumbler.

'It's good for a beginning,' says his Riv'rence; 'it lays a very nate foundation for more sarious operation; but we're now arrived at a pariod of the evening when it's time to proceed wid our shuperstructhure by compass and square, like free and excipted masons as we both are.'

My time's up for the present; but I'll tell you the rest in the evening at home.

Glory be to God! I've done wid their lecthirs – they may all go and be d—d wid their consumption and production. I'm off to Tullymactaggart before daylight in the morning, where I'll thry whether a sod or two o' turf can't consume a cartload ov heresy, and whether a weekly meeting ov the lodge can't produce a new thayory ov rints. But afore I take my lave ov you, I may as well finish my story about poor Father Tom that I hear is coming up to whale the heretics in Adam and Eve during the Lint.

The Pope – and indeed it ill becomes a good Catholic to say anything agin him – no more would I, only that his Riv'rence was in it – but you see the fact ov it is, that the Pope was as envious as ever he could be, at seeing himself sacked right and left by Father Tom, and bate out o' the face, the way he was, on every science and subjec' that was started. So, not to be outdone altogether, he says to his Riv'rence, 'You're a man that's fond of the brute crayation, I hear, Misther Maguire?'

'I don't deny it,' says his Riv'rence, 'I've dogs that I'm willing to run agin any man's, ay, or to match them agin any other dogs in the world for genteel edication and polite manners,' says he.

'I'll hould you a pound,' says the Pope, 'that I've a quadhruped in my possession that's a wiser baste nor any dog in your kennel.'

'Done,' says his Riv'rence, and they staked the money.

'What can this larned quadhruped o' yours do?' says his Riv'rence.

'It's my mule,' says the Pope, 'and, if you were to offer her goolden oats and clover off the meadows o' Paradise, sorra taste ov aither she'd let pass her teeth till the first mass is over every Sunday or holiday in the year.'

'Well, and what'ud you say if I showed you a baste ov mine,' says his Riv'rence, 'that, instead ov fasting till first mass is over only, fasts out the whole four-and-twenty hours ov every Wednesday and Friday in the week as reg'lar as a Christian?'

'Oh, be asy, Masther Maguire,' says the Pope.

'You don't b'lieve me, don't you?' says his Riv'rence; 'very well, I'll soon show you whether or no,' and he put his knuckles in his mouth, and gev a whistle that made the Pope stop his fingers in his ears. The aycho, my dear, was hardly done playing wid the cobwebs in the comnish, when the door flies open, and in jumps Spring. The Pope happened to be sitting next the door, betuxt him and his Riv'rence, and, may I never die, if he didn't clear him, thriple crown and all, at one spang. 'God's presence be about us!' says the Pope, thinking it was an evil spirit come to fly away wid him for the lie that he had tould in regard ov his mule (for it was nothing more nor a thrick that consisted in grazing the brute's teeth): but seeing it was only one ov the greatest beauties ov a greyhound that he'd ever laid his epistolical eyes on, he soon recovered ov his fright, and began to pat him, while Father Tom ris and went to the sideboord, where he cut a slice ov pork, a slice ov beef, a slice ov mutton, and a slice ov salmon, and put them all on a plate thegither. 'Here, Spring, my man,' says he, setting the plate down afore him on the hearthstone, 'here's your supper for you this blessed Friday night.' Not a word more he said nor what I tell you; and, you may believe it or not, but it's the blessed truth that the dog, afther jist tasting the salmon, and spitting it out again, lifted his nose out o' the plate, and stood wid his jaws wathering, and his tail wagging, looking up in his Riv'rence's face, as much as to say, 'Give me your absolution, till I hide them temptations out o' my sight.'

'There's a dog that knows his duty,' says his Riv'rence; 'there's a baste that knows how to conduct himself either in the parlour or the field. You think him a good dog, looking at him here; but I wisht you seen him on the side ov Slieve-an-Eirin! Be my soul, you'd say the hill was running away from undher him. Oh I wisht you had been wid me,' says he, never letting on to see the dog at all, 'one day, last Lent, that I was coming from mass. Spring was near a quarther ov a mile behind me, for the childher was delaying him wid bread and butther at the chapel door, when a lump ov a hare jumped out ov the plantations ov Grouse Lodge and ran acrass the road; so I gev the whilloo, and knowing that she'd take the rise ov the hill, I made over the ditch, and up through Mullaghcashel as hard as I could pelt, still keeping her in view, but afore I had gone a perch, Spring seen her, and away the two went like the wind, up Drumrewmy, and down Clooneen, and over the river, widout his being able ons't to turn her. Well, I run on till I come to the Diffagher, and through it I went, for the wather was low and I didn't mind being wet shod, and out on the other side, where I got up on a ditch, and seen sich a coorse as I'll be bound to say was never seen afore or since. If Spring turned that hare ons't that day, he turned her fifty times, up and down, back and for'ard throughout and about. At last he run her right into the big quarry-hole in Mullaghbawn, and when I went up to look for her fud, there I found him sthretched on his side, not able to stir a foot, and the hare lying about an inch afore his nose as dead as a door-nail, and divil a mark of a tooth upon her. Eh, Spring, isn't that thrue?' says he. Jist at that minit the clock sthruck twelve, and, before you could say thrap-sticks, Spring had the plateful of mate consaled. 'Now,' says his Riv'rence, 'hand me over my pound, for I've won my bate fairly.'

'You'll excuse me,' says the Pope, pocketing his money, 'for we put the clock half an hour back, out ov compliment to your Riv'rence,' says he, 'and it was Sathurday morning afore he came up at all.'

'Well, it's no matther,' says his Riv'rence, putting back his pound-note in his pocket-book, 'only,' says he, 'it's hardly fair to expect a brute baste to be so well skilled in the science ov chronology.'

In troth his Riv'rence was badly used in the same bate, for he won it clever; and, indeed, I'm afeard the shabby way he was thrated had some effect in putting it into his mind to do what he did. 'Will your Holiness take a blast ov the pipe?' says he, dhrawing out his dhudeen.

'I never smoke,' says the Pope, 'but I haven't the least objection to the smell of the tobaccay.'

'Oh, you had betther take a dhraw,' says his Riv'rence, 'it'll relish the dhrink, that'ud be too luscious intirely, widout something to flavour it.'

'I had thoughts,' said the Pope, wid the laste sign ov a hiccup on him, 'ov getting up a broiled bone for the same purpose.'

'Well,' says his Riv'rence, 'a broiled bone'ud do no manner ov harm at this present time; but a smoke,' says he, ' 'ud flavour both the devil and the dhrink.'

'What sort o' tobaccay is it that's in it?' says the Pope.

'Raal nagur-head,' says his Riv'rence; 'a very mild and salubrios spacies of the philosophic weed.'

'Then, I don't care if I do take a dhraw,' says the Pope. Then Father Tom held the coal himself till his Holiness had the pipe lit; and they sat widout saying anything worth mentioning for about five minutes.

At last the Pope says to his Riv'rence: 'I dunna what gev me this plaguy hiccup,' says he. 'Dhrink about,' says he – 'Begorra,' he says, 'I think I'm getting merrier nor's good for me. Sing us a song, your Riv'rence,' says he.

Father Tom then sung him 'Monatagrenoge' and the 'Bunch o' Rushes', and he was mighty well pleased wid both, keeping time wid his hands, and joining in in the choruses, when his hiccup'ud let him. At last, my dear, he opens the lower buttons ov his waistcoat, and the top one of his waistband, and calls to Masther Anthony to lift up one ov the windys. 'I dunna what's wrong wid me, at all at all,' says he, 'I'm mortial sick.'

'I thrust,' says his Riv'rence, 'the pasthry that you ate at dinner hasn't disagreed wid your Holiness' stomach.'

'Oh, my! oh!' says the Pope, 'what's this at all?' gasping for breath, and as pale as a sheet, wid a could swate bursting out over his forehead, and the palms ov his hands spread out to catch the air. 'Oh, my! oh, my!' says he, 'fetch me a basin! – Don't spake to me. – Oh! – oh! – blood alive! – Oh, my head, my head, hould my head! – oh! – ubh! – I'm poisoned! – ach!'

'It was them plaguy pasthries,' says his Riv'rence. 'Hould his head hard,' says he, 'and clap a wet cloth over his timples. If you could only thry another dhraw o' the pipe, your Holiness, it'ud set you to rights in no time.'

'Carry me to bed,' says the Pope, 'and never let me see that wild Irish priest again. I'm poisoned by his manes – ubplsch! – ach! – ach! – He dined wid Cardinal Wayld yestherday,' says he, 'and he's bribed him to take me off. Send for a confissor,' says he, 'for my latther end's approaching. My head's like to split – so it is! – Oh, my! oh, my! – ubplsch! – ach!'

Well, his Riv'rence never thought it worth his while to make him an answer; but, when he seen how ungratefully he was used, afther all his throuble in making the evening agreeable to the ould man, he called Spring, and put the but-end ov the second bottle into his pocket, and left the house widout once wishing, 'Good-night, an' plaisant dhrames to you'; and, in troth, not one of *them* axed him to lave them a lock ov his hair.

That's the story as I heard it tould; but myself doesn't b'lieve over one half of it. Howandiver, when all's done, it's a shame, so it is, that he's not a bishop this blessed day and hour; for, next to the goiant of St Jarlath's, he's out and out the cleverest fellow ov the whole jing-bang.

T CROFTON CROKER

1798–1854

Croker was born in Cork in the year that produced Carleton and John Banim, the year of the great Rebellion. His father was a major in the army, and of course a Protestant. When quite young he was apprenticed to a Cork merchant, but the historian of fairy-land that was to be, stirred already within the mind of the clerk that was, and kept him busy studying local legends and antiquities. In 1818 Major Croker died, and his son started for London to seek his fortune. His namesake, John Wilson Croker, made notorious by Macaulay, a friend but no relation, got him a post in the Admiralty. In 1821 he returned to Ireland, and planned out his first book, 'Researches in the South of Ireland.' It was published in 1824. His famous 'Fairy Legends' followed in 1825, and was so successful that he wrote immediately a second series. The extract I have taken is from this book, and was considered by his friend and fellow-worker, Thomas Keightley, of 'The Fairy Mythology,' to be the most valuable, from a folk-lore point of view, of all his writings, as it gives the actual words of a 'fairy man,' or village seer.

In 1850 Croker retired from the Admiralty Office on a pension, and lived in London until his death in 1854.

Scott, quoted by Mr Alfred Webb, has described him as 'little as a dwarf, keen-eyed as a hawk, of easy, prepossessing manners, something like Tom Moore.' His work is always humorous and full of 'go,' but marred by a constitutional difficulty in believing that any man, unless drunk, could see an apparition, a mode of looking at things more common among educated people in his day than in ours, and at all times destructive to the simplicity and grace of any tale of ghost or goblin that contains it. Nor could he take the peasants themselves quite seriously. The strain to make all things merry and laughable injured his sense of reality. At the same time he had a strong feeling for beauty and romance, and could tell a story better than most men.

THE CONFESSIONS OF TOM BOURKE

By T CROFTON CROKER

Tom Bourke lives in a low, long farmhouse, resembling in outward appearance a large barn, placed at the bottom of the hill, just where the new road strikes off from the old one, leading from the town of Kilworth to that of Lismore. He is of a class of persons who are a sort of black swans in Ireland: he is a wealthy farmer. Tom's father had, in the good old times, when a hundred pounds were no inconsiderable treasure, either to lend or spend, accommodated his landlord with that sum, at interest; and obtained as a return for his civility a long lease, about half-a-dozen times more valuable than the loan which procured it. The old man died worth several hundred pounds, the greater part of which, with his farm, he bequeathed to his son Tom. But besides all this, Tom received from his father, upon his death-bed, another gift, far more valuable than worldly riches, greatly as he prized and is still known to prize them. He was invested with the privilege, enjoyed by few of the sons of men, of communicating with those mysterious beings called 'the good people.'

Tom Bourke is a little, stout, healthy, active man, about fifty-five years of age. His hair is perfectly white, short and bushy behind, but rising in front erect and thick above his forehead, like a new clothes-brush. His eyes are of that kind which I have often observed with persons of a quick but limited intellect – they are small, gray, and lively. The large and projecting eyebrows under, or rather within, which they twinkle, give them an expression of shrewdness and intelligence, if not of cunning. And this is very much the character of the man. If you want to make a bargain with Tom Bourke you must act as if you were a general besieging a town, and make your advances a long time before you can hope to obtain possession. If you march up boldly, and tell him at once your object, you are for the most part sure to have the gates closed in your teeth. Tom does not wish to part with what you wish to obtain; or another person has been speaking to him for the whole of the last week. Or, it may be, your proposal seems to meet the most favourable reception. 'Very well, sir'; 'That's true, sir'; 'I'm very thankful to your honour,' and other expressions of kindness and confidence greet you in reply to every sentence; and you part from him wondering how he can have obtained the character which he universally bears, of being a man whom no one can make anything of in a bargain. But when you next meet him the illusion is dissolved; you find you are a great deal further from your object than you were when you thought you had almost succeeded; his eye and his tongue express a total forgetfulness of what the mind within never lost sight of for an instant; and you have to begin operations afresh, with the disadvantage of having put your adversary completely upon his guard.

Yet, although Tom Bourke is, whether from supernatural revelings, or (as many will think more probable) from the tell-truth experience, so distrustful of mankind, and so close in his dealings with them, he is no misanthrope. No man loves better the pleasures of the genial board. The love of money, indeed, which is with him (and who will blame him?) a very ruling propensity, and the gratification which it has received from habits of industry, sustained throughout a pretty long and successful life have taught him the value of sobriety, during those seasons, at least, when a man's business requires him to keep possession of his senses. He has, therefore, a general rule, never to get drunk but on Sundays. But in order that it should be a general one to all intents and purposes, he takes a method which, according to better logicians than he is, always proves the rule. He has many exceptions; among these, of course, are the evenings of all the fair and market-days that happen in his neighbourhood; so also all the days in which funerals, marriages, and christenings take place among his friends within many miles of him. As to this last class of exceptions, it may appear at first very singular, that he is much more punctual in his attendance at the funerals than at the baptisms or weddings of his friends. This may be construed as an instance of disinterested affection for departed worth, very uncommon in this selfish world. But I am afraid that the motives which lead Tom Bourke to pay more court to the dead than the living are precisely those which lead to the opposite conduct in the generality of mankind – a hope of future benefit and a fear of future evil. For the good people, who are a race as powerful as they are capricious, have their favourites among those who inhabit this world; often show their affection by easing the objects of it from the load of this burdensome life; and frequently reward or punish the living according to the degree of reverence paid to the obsequies and the memory of the elected dead.

Some may attribute to the same cause the apparently humane and charitable actions which Tom, and indeed the other members of his family, are known frequently to perform. A beggar has seldom left their farmyard with an empty wallet, or without obtaining a night's lodging, if required, with a sufficiency of potatoes and milk to satisfy even an Irish beggar's appetite; in appeasing which, account must usually be taken of the auxiliary jaws of a hungry dog, and of two or three still more hungry children, who line themselves well within, to atone for their nakedness without. If one of the neighbouring poor be seized with a fever, Tom will often supply the sick wretch with some untenanted hut upon one of his two large farms (for he has added one to his patrimony), or will send his labourers to construct a shed at a hedge-side, and supply straw for a bed while the disorder continues. His wife, remarkable for the largeness of her dairy, and the goodness of everything it contains, will furnish milk for whey; and their good offices are frequently extended to the family of the patient, who are, perhaps, reduced to the extremity of wretchedness, by even the temporary suspension of a father's or a husband's labour.

If much of this arises from the hopes and fears to which I above alluded, I believe much of it flows from a mingled sense of compassion and of duty, which is sometimes seen to break from an Irish peasant's heart, even where it happens to be enveloped in a habitual covering of avarice and fraud; and which I once heard speak in terms not to be misunderstood: "When we get a deal, 'tis only fair we should give back a little of it."

It is not easy to prevail on Tom to speak on those good people, with whom he is said to hold frequent and intimate communications. To the faithful, who believe in their power, and their occasional delegation of it to him, he seldom refuses, if properly asked, to exercise his high prerogative when any unfortunate being is *struck* in his neighbourhood. Still he will not be won unsued: he is at first difficult of persuasion, and must be overcome by a little gentle violence. On these occasions he is unusually solemn and mysterious, and if one word of reward be mentioned he at once abandons the unhappy patient, such a proposition being a direct insult to his supernatural superiors. It is true that, as the labourer is worthy of his hire, most persons gifted as he is do not scruple to receive a token of gratitude from the patients or their friends *after* their recovery. It is recorded that a very handsome gratuity was once given to a female practitioner in this occult science, who deserves to be mentioned, not only because she was a neighbour and a rival of Tom's, but from the singularity of a mother deriving her name from her son. Her son's name was Owen, and she was always called *Owen sa vauher* (Owen's mother). This person was, on the occasion to which I have alluded, *persuaded* to give her assistance to a young girl who had lost the use of her right leg; *Owen sa vauher* found the cure a difficult one. A journey of about eighteen miles was essential for the purpose, probably to visit one of the good people who resided at that distance; and this journey could only be performed by *Owen sa vauher* travelling upon the back of a white hen. The visit, however, was accomplished; and at a particular hour, according to the prediction of this extraordinary woman, when the hen and her rider were to reach their journey's end, the patient was seized with an irresistible desire to dance, which she gratified with the most perfect freedom of the diseased leg, much to the joy of her anxious family. The gratuity in this case was, as it surely ought to have been, unusually large, from the difficulty of procuring a hen willing to go so long a journey with such a rider.

To do Tom Bourke justice, he is on these occasions, as I have heard from many competent authorities, perfectly disinterested. Not many months since he recovered a young woman (the sister of a tradesman living near him), who had been struck speechless after returning from a funeral, and had continued so for several days. He steadfastly refused receiving any compensation, saying that even if he had not as much as would buy him his supper, he could take nothing in this case, because the girl had offended at the funeral of one of the good people belonging to his own family, and though he would do her a kindness, he could take none from her.

About the time this last remarkable affair took place, my friend Mr Martin, who is a neighbour of Tom's, had some business to transact with him, which it was exceedingly difficult to bring to a conclusion. At last Mr Martin, having tried all quiet means, had recourse to a legal process, which brought Tom to reason, and the matter was arranged to their mutual satisfaction, and with perfect good-humour between the parties. The accommodation took place after dinner at Mr

Martin's house, and he invited Tom to walk into the parlour and take a glass of punch, made of some excellent *potteen*, which was on the table; he had long wished to draw out his highly endowed neighbour on the subject of his supernatural powers, and as Mrs Martin, who was in the room, was rather a favourite of Tom's, this seemed a good opportunity.

'Well, Tom,' said Mr Martin, 'that was a curious business of Molly Dwyer's, who recovered her speech so suddenly the other day.'

'You may say that, sir,' replied Tom Bourke; 'but I had to travel far for it: no matter for that now. Your health, ma'am,' said he, turning to Mrs Martin.

'Thank you, Tom. But I am told you had some trouble once in that way in your own family,' said Mrs Martin.

'So I had, ma'am; trouble enough: but you were only a child at that time.'

'Come, Tom,' said the hospitable Mr Martin, interrupting him, 'take another tumbler'; and he then added: 'I wish you would tell us something of the manner in which so many of your children died. I am told they dropped off, one after another, by the same disorder, and that your eldest son was cured in a most extraordinary way, when the physicians had given him over.'

' 'Tis true for you, sir,' returned Tom; 'your father, the doctor (God be good to him, I won't belie him in his grave), told me, when my fourth boy was a week sick, that himself and Dr Barry did all that man could do for him; but they could not keep him from going after the rest. No more they could, if the people that took away the rest wished to take him too. But they left him; and sorry to the heart I am I did not know before why they were taking my boys from me; if I did, I would not be left trusting to two of 'em now.'

'And how did you find it out, Tom?' inquired Mr Martin.

'Why, then, I'll tell you, sir,' said Bourke. 'When your father said what I told you, I did not know very well what to do. I walked down the little *bohereen* you know, sir, that goes to the riverside near Dick Heafy's ground; for 'twas a lonesome place, and I wanted to think of myself. I was heavy, sir, and my heart got weak in me, when I thought I was to lose my little boy; and I did not well know how to face his mother with the news, for she doted down upon him. Besides, she never got the better of all she cried at his brother's *berrin*[1] the week before. As I was going down the *bohereen* I met an old *bocough*, that used to come about the place once or twice a year, and used always to sleep in our barn while he stayed in the neighbourhood. So he asked me how I was. "Bad enough, Shamous,"[2] says I. "I'm sorry for your trouble," says he; "but you're a foolish man, Mr Bourke. Your son would be well enough if you would only do what you ought with him." "What more can I do with him, Shamous?" says I; "the doctors give him over." "The doctors know no more what ails him than they do what ails a cow when she stops her milk," says Shamous; "but go to such a one," telling me his name, "and try what he'll say to you." '

'And who was that, Tom?' asked Mr Martin.

'I could not tell you that, sir,' said Bourke, with a mysterious look; 'however, you often saw him, and he does not live far from this. But I had a trial of him before; and if I went to him at first, may be I'd have now some of them that's gone, and so Shamous often told me. Well, sir, I went to this man, and he came with me to the house. By course, I did everything as he bid me. According to his order, I took the little boy out of the dwelling-house immediately, sick as he was, and made a bed for him and myself in the cow-house. Well, sir, I lay down by his side in the bed, between two of the cows, and he fell asleep. He got into a perspiration, saving your presence, as if he was drawn through the river, and breathed hard, with a great *impression* on his chest, and was very bad – very bad entirely through the night. I thought about twelve o'clock he was going at last, and I was just getting up to go call the man I told you of; but there was no occasion. My friends were getting the better of them that wanted to take him away from me. There was nobody in the cow-house but the child and myself. There was only one half-penny candle lighting it, and that was stuck in the wall at the far end of the house. I had just enough of light where we were lying to see a person walking or standing near us: and there was no more noise than if it was a churchyard, except the cows chewing the fodder in the stalls.

'Just as I was thinking of getting up, as I told you – I won't belie my father, sir, he was a good father to me – I saw him standing at the bedside, holding out his right hand to me, and leaning his other on the stick he used to carry when he was alive, and looking pleasant and smiling at me, all as if he was telling me not to be afeard, for I would not lose the child. "Is that you, father?" says I. He said nothing. "If that's you," says I again, "for the love of them that's gone, let me catch your hand." And so he did, sir; and his hand was as soft as a child's. He stayed about as long as you'd be going from this to the gate below at the end of the avenue, and then went away. In less than a week the child was as well as if nothing ever ailed him; and there isn't to-night a healthier boy of nineteen, from this blessed house to the town of Ballyporeen, across the Kilworth mountains.'

'But I think, Tom,' said Mr Martin, 'it appears as if you are more indebted to your father than to the man recommended to you by Shamous; or do you suppose it was he who made favour with your enemies among the good people, and that then your father – '

'I beg your pardon, sir,' said Bourke, interrupting him; 'but don't call them my enemies. 'T would not be wishing to me for a good deal to sit by when they are called so. No offence to you, sir. Here's wishing you a good health and long life.'

'I assure you,' returned Mr Martin, 'I meant no offence, Tom; but was it not as I say?'

'I can't tell you that, sir,' said Bourke; 'I'm bound down, sir. Howsoever, you may be sure the man I spoke of and my father, and those they know, settled it between them.'

There was a pause, of which Mrs Martin took advantage to inquire of Tom whether something remarkable had not happened about a goat and a pair of pigeons, at the time of his son's illness – circumstances often mysteriously hinted at by Tom.

'See that, now,' said he, turning to Mr Martin, 'how well she remembers it! True for you, ma'am. The goat I gave the mistress, your mother, when the doctors ordered her goats' whey?'

Mrs Martin nodded assent, and Tom Bourke continued, 'Why, then, I'll tell you how that was. The goat was as well as e'er goat ever was, for a month after she was sent to Killaan to your father's. The morning after the night I just told you of, before the child woke, his mother was standing at the gap leading out of the barnyard into the road, and she saw two pigeons flying from the town of Kilworth off the church down towards her. Well, they never stopped, you see, till they came to the house on the hill at the other side of the river, facing our farm. They pitched upon the chimney of that house, and after looking about them for a minute or two, they flew straight across the river, and stopped on the ridge of the cow-house where the child and I were lying. Do you think they came there for nothing, sir?'

'Certainly not, Tom,' returned Mr Martin.

'Well, the woman came in to me, frightened, and told me. She began to cry. "Whist, you fool?" says I; " 'tis all for the better." 'Twas true for me. What do you think, ma'am; the goat that I gave your mother, that was seen feeding at sunrise that morning by Jack Cronin, as merry as a bee, dropped down dead without anybody knowing why, before Jack's face; and at that very moment he saw two pigeons fly from the top of the house out of the town, towards the Lismore road. 'Twas at the same time my woman saw them, as I just told you.'

''Twas very strange, indeed, Tom,' said Mr Martin; 'I wish you could give us some explanation of it.'

'I wish I could, sir,' was Tom Bourke's answer; 'but I'm bound down. I can tell but what I'm allowed to tell, any more than a sentry is let walk more than his rounds.'

'I think you said something of having had some former knowledge of the man that assisted in the cure of your son,' said Mr Martin.

'So I had, sir,' returned Bourke. 'I had a trial of that man. But that's neither here nor there. I can't tell you anything about that, sir. But would you like to know how he got his skill?'

'Oh! very much indeed,' said Mr Martin.

'But you can tell us his Christian name, that we may know him better through the story,' added Mrs Martin.

Tom Bourke paused for a minute to consider this proposition.

'Well, I believe that I may tell you that, anyhow; his name is Patrick. He was always a smart, 'cute[3] boy, and would be a great clerk if he stuck to it. The first time I knew him, sir, was at my mother's wake. I was in great trouble, for I did not know where to bury her. Her people and my father's people – I mean their friends, sir, among the good people, had the greatest battle that was known for many a year, at Dunmanwaycross, to see to whose churchyard she'd be taken. They fought for three nights, one after another, without being able to settle it. The neighbours wondered how long I was before I buried my mother; but I had my reasons, though I could not tell them at that time. Well, sir, to make my story short, Patrick came on the fourth morning and told me he settled the business, and that day we buried her in Kilcrumper churchyard, with my father's people.'

'He was a valuable friend, Tom,' said Mrs Martin, with difficulty suppressing a smile. 'But you were about to tell how he became so skilful.'

'So I will and welcome,' replied Bourke. 'Your health, ma'am. I'm drinking too much of this punch, sir; but, to tell the truth, I never tasted the like of it; it goes down one's throat like sweet oil. But what was I going to say? Yes – well – yes – Patrick, many a long year ago, was coming home from a *berrin* late in the evening, and walking by the side of a river, opposite the big inch,[4] near Ballyhefaan ford. He had taken a drop, to be sure; but he was only a little merry, as you may say, and knew very well what he was doing. The moon was shining, for it was in the month of August, and the river was as smooth and as bright as a looking-glass. He heard nothing for a long time but the fall of the water at the mill weir about a mile down the river, and now and then the crying of the lambs on the other side of the river. All at once there was a noise of a great number of people laughing as if they'd break their hearts, and of a piper playing among them. It came from the inch at the other side of the ford saw, through the mist that hung over the river, a whole crowd of people dancing on the inch. Patrick was as fond of a dance as he was of a glass, and that's saying enough for him; so he whipped off his shoes and stockings, and away with him across the ford. After putting on his shoes and stockings at the other side of the river he walked over to the crowd, and mixed with them for some time without being minded. He thought, sir, that he'd show them better dancing than any of themselves, for he was proud of his feet, sir, and a good right he had, for there was not a boy in the same parish could foot a double or treble with him. But pwah! his dancing was no more to theirs than mine would be to the mistress' there. They did not seem as if they had a bone in their bodies, and they kept it up as if nothing could tire them. Patrick was 'shamed within himself, for he thought he had not his fellow in all the country round; and was going away, when a little old man, that was looking at the company bitterly, as if he did not like what was going on, came up to him. "Patrick," says he. Patrick started, for he did not think anybody there knew him. "Patrick," says he, "you're discouraged, and no wonder for you. But you have a friend near you. I'm your friend, and your father's friend, and I think worse[5] of your little finger than I do of all that are here, though they think no one is as good as themselves. Go into the ring and call for a lilt. Don't be afeared. I tell you the best of them did not do it as well as you shall, if you will do as I bid you." Patrick felt something within him as if he ought not to gainsay the old man. He went into the ring, and called the piper to play up the best double he had. And sure enough, all that the others were able for was nothing to him! He bounded like an eel, now here and now there, as light as a feather, although the people could hear the music answered by his steps, that beat time to every turn of it, like the left foot of the piper. He first danced a hornpipe on the ground. Then they got a table, and he danced a treble on it that drew down shouts from the whole company. At last he called for a trencher; and when they saw him, all as if he was spinning on it like a top, they did not know what to make of him. Some praised him for the best dancer that ever entered a ring; others hated him because he was better than themselves; although they had good right to think themselves better than him or any other man that ever went the long journey.'

'And what was the cause of his great success?' inquired Mr Martin.

'He could not help it, sir,' replied Tom Bourke. 'They that could make him do more than that made him do it. Howsomever, when he had done, they wanted him to dance again, but he was tired, and they could not persuade him. At last he got angry, and swore a big oath, saving your presence, that he would not dance a step more, and the word was hardly out of his mouth when he found himself all alone, with nothing but a white cow grazing by his side.'

'Did he ever discover why he was gifted with these extraordinary powers in the dance, Tom?' said Mr Martin.

'I'll tell you that too, sir,' answered Bourke, 'when I come to it. When he went home, sir, he was taken with a shivering, and went to bed; and the next day they found he had got the fever, or something like it, for he raved like as if he was mad. But they couldn't make out what it was he was saying, though he talked constant. The doctors gave him over. But it's a little they knew what ailed him. When he was, as you may say, about ten days sick, and everybody thought he was going, one of the neighbours came in to him with a man, a friend of his, from Ballinlacken, that was keeping with him some time before. I can't tell you his name either, only it was Darby. The minute Darby saw Patrick he took a little bottle, with the juice of herbs in it, out of his pocket, and gave Patrick a drink of it. He did the same every day for three weeks, and then Patrick was able to walk about, as stout and as hearty as ever he was in his life. But he was a long time before he came to himself; and he used to walk the whole day sometimes by the ditch-side, talking to himself, like as there was some one along with him. And so there was, surely, or he wouldn't be the man he is today.'

'I suppose it was from some such companion he learned his skill,' said Mr Martin.

'You have it all now, sir,' replied Bourke. 'Darby told him his friends were satisfied with what he did the night of the dance; and though they couldn't hinder the fever, they'd bring him over it, an teach him more than many knew beside him. And so they did. For you see all the people he met on the inch that night were friends of a different faction; only the old man that spoke to him, he was a friend of Patrick's family, and it went again his heart, you see, that the others were so light and active, and he was bitter in himself to hear 'em boasting how they'd dance with any set in the whole country round. So he gave Patrick the gift that night, and afterwards gave him the skill that makes him the wonder of all that know him. And to be sure it was only learning he was at that time when he was wandering in his mind after the fever.'

'I have heard many strange stories about that inch near Ballyhefaan ford,' said Mr Martin. ' 'Tis a great place for the good people, isn't it, Tom?'

'You may say that, sir,' returned Bourke. 'I could tell you a great deal about it. Many a time I sat for as good as two hours by moonlight, at th' other side of the river, looking at 'em playing goal as if they'd break their hearts over it; with their coats and waistcoats off, and white handkerchiefs on the heads of one party, and red ones on th' other, just as you'd see on a Sunday in Mr Simming's big field. I saw 'em one night play till the moon set, without one party being able to take the ball from th' other. I'm sure they were going to fight, only 'twas near morning. I'm told your grandfather, ma'am, used to see 'em there too,' said Bourke, turning to Mrs Martin.

'So I have been told, Tom,' replied Mrs Martin. 'But don't they say that the churchyard of Kilcrumper is just as favourite a place with the good people as Ballyhefaan inch?'

'Why, then, may be you never heard, ma'am, what happened to Davy Roche in that same churchyard,' said Bourke; and turning to Mr Martin, added: ' 'Twas a long time before he went into your service, sir. He was walking home, of an evening, from the fair of Kilcumber, a little merry, to be sure, after the day, and he came up with a *berrin*. So he walked along with it, and thought it very queer that he did not know a mother's soul in the crowd but one man, and he was sure that man was dead many years before. Howsomever, he went on with the *berrin* till they came to Kilcrumper churchyard; and, faith, he went in and stayed with the rest, to see the corpse buried. As soon as the grave was covered, what should they do but gather about a piper that *come* along with 'em, and fall to dancing as if it was a wedding. Davy longed to be among 'em (for he hadn't a bad foot of his own, that time, whatever he may now); but he was loth to begin, because they all seemed strange to him, only the man I told you that he thought was dead. Well, at last this man saw what Davy wanted, and came up to him. "Davy," says he, "take out a partner, and show what you can do, but take care and don't offer to kiss her." "That I won't," says Davy, "although her lips were made of honey." And with that he made his bow to the *purtiest* girl in the ring, and he and she began to dance. 'Twas a jig they danced, and they did it to th' admiration, do you see, of all that were there. 'Twas all very well till the jig was over; but just as they had done, Davy, for he had a drop in, and was warm with the dancing, forgot himself, and kissed his partner, according to custom. The smack was no sooner off of his lips, you see, than he was left alone in the churchyard, without a creature near him, and all he could see was the tall tombstones. Davy said they seemed as if they were dancing too, but I suppose that was only the wonder that happened him, and he being a little in drink. Howsomever, he found it was a great many hours later than he thought it; 'twas near morning when he came home; but they couldn't get a word out of him till the next day, when he woke out of a dead sleep about twelve o'clock.'

When Tom had finished the account of Davy Roche and the *berrin*, it became quite evident that spirits, of some sort, were working too strong within him to admit of his telling many more tales of 'the good people.' Tom seemed conscious of this. He muttered for a few minutes broken sentences concerning churchyards, riversides, leprechans, and *dina magh*,[6] which were quite unintelligible, perhaps to himself, certainly to Mr Martin and his lady. At length he made a slight motion of the head upwards, as if he would say, 'I can talk no more'; stretched his arm on the table, upon which he placed the empty tumbler slowly, and with the most knowing and cautious air; and rising from his chair, walked, or rather rolled, to the parlour door. Here he turned around to face his host and hostess; but after various ineffectual attempts to bid them good-night, the words, as they rose, being always choked by a violent hiccup, while the door, which he held by the handle, swung to and fro, carrying his unyielding body along with it, he was obliged to depart in silence. The cowboy, sent by Tom's wife, who knew well what sort of allurement detained him, when he remained out after a certain hour, was in attendance to conduct his master home. I have no doubt that he returned without meeting any material injury, as I know that within the last month he was, to use his own words, 'as stout and hearty a man as any of his age in the county Cork'.

NOTE: – Croker has, perhaps, slandered our 'fairy doctors.' It was the custom of his day to take nothing 'supernatural' seriously. He could not drive out of his head the notion that every man who saw a spirit was commonly drunk as a piper. Things have changed since then. I quote the following from Lady Wilde's 'Ancient Legends,' as it describes a 'fairy doctor' of wholly other type.

'He never touched beer, spirits, or meat, in all his life, but has lived entirely on bread, fruit, and vegetables. A man who knew him thus describes him: "Winter and summer his dress is the same, merely a flannel shirt and coat. He will pay his share at a feast, but neither eats nor drinks of the food and drink set before him. He speaks no English, and never could be made to learn the English tongue, though he says it might be used with great effect to curse one's enemy. He holds a burial-ground sacred, and would not carry away so much as a leaf of ivy from a grave. And he maintains that the people are right to keep to their ancient usages, such as never to dig a grave on a Monday; and to carry the coffin three times round the grave, following the course of the sun, for then the dead rest in peace. Like the people, also, he holds suicides as accursed; for they believe that all its dead turn over on their faces if a suicide is laid amongst them.

' "Though well off, he never, even in his youth, thought of taking a wife; nor was he ever known to love a woman. He stands quite apart from life, and by this means holds his power over the mysteries. No money will tempt him to impart his knowledge to another, for if he did he would be struck dead – so he believes. He would not touch a hazel stick, but carries an ash wand, which he holds in his hand when he prays, laid across his knees; and the whole of his life is devoted to works of grace and charity, and though now an old man, he has never had a day's sickness. No one has ever seen him in a rage, nor heard an angry word from his lips but once, and then being under great irritation, he recited the Lord's Prayer backwards as an imprecation on his enemy. Before his death he will reveal the mystery of his power, but not till the hand of death is on him for certain." When he does reveal it, we may be sure it will be to one person only – his successor.'

1. Berrin, burying.
2. Shamous, James.
3. 'Cute, acute.
4. Inch, low meadow ground near a river.
5. Worse, more.
6. *Daine maithe – i.e.,* the good people.

GERALD GRIFFIN

1803–1840

Gerald Griffin was the son of a Limerick brewer. In his seventh year his family moved to Fairylawn, a place on the Shannon, twenty-eight miles from Limerick. Here as time went on he did a deal of shooting and fishing, and acquired that love of legend and historic scenery so visible in his writings. He went to school in the neighbourhood, but all that was most vital in his education came probably from his own reading. His favourite author, Virgil, may well have given him that sense of form that marks out his stories from those of other Irish writers. He soon began scribbling tales and poems, and worked on contentedly for some years, encouraged by mother and tutor.

In 1820, the family fortune having gradually dwindled away, his parents were compelled to emigrate to Pennsylvania. They left Gerald, a boy of seventeen, and his two sisters and his younger brother, in charge of their eldest son, a doctor at Adare. Gerald, instead of following his elder brother's example and studying medicine, as he was expected to, began writing for local papers. He now made the acquaintance of John Banim, at that time still obscure like himself.

In 1823, Gerald Griffin composed a tragedy called 'Aguire,' and started with it to London, where he remained until 1827, writing plays and stories, and half starving the while. The hard work and poverty of these four years completely wrecked his constitution. Banim, who had also moved over to London, befriended him so far as he would allow him to do so – and that was but little. To write for the stage was his ambition, but that failing he turned his hand to Irish stories, made hopeful by the success of the O'Hara tales, and published 'Holland Tide,' the volume from which I have taken 'The Knight of the Sheep.' In 1827 he returned home and wrote 'Tales of the Munster Festivals.' Next came incomparably his best work, 'The Collegians,' the source of Boucicault's 'Colleen Bawn,' and the most finished and artistic of all Irish stories. A little later came a historical novel full of research, named 'The Wonders'; but the stage remained always his ambition, and, Foster maintains, his true vocation. His now at last rising fame as a novelist brought him little comfort. His novels were constantly perhaps no more than so much wearisome toil to raise the wind. He had always been religious, and amidst his times of toil and care religion grew into a passion. In his later books one feels its presence perpetually, and by no means to the gain of the art. In 1837 he left the world altogether, where clearly he was of most use to his country, and having burnt a number of unpublished works, joined 'The Christian Brothers,' where he spent his time, according to the custom of the order, in teaching poor children. For three years he 'made his soul' in peace, and then caught fever and died at the 'North Monasery,' Cork, in 1840, in his thirty-sixth year. A twelvemonth later an early tragedy of his, called 'Gessipus,' was acted with great applause at Covent Garden Theatre, with Macready in the principal part. Miss Mitford has spoken of his life as telling more than all others of 'the broken heart of the man of genius.'

In appearance Gerald Griffin was tall and delicate-looking. It was possible to see in his face the gentle and elegiac temperament that made up, together with a feeble body, a man little capable of shouldering his way.

His novels, though far more polished and complete than those of any other Irishman, are in no way comparable in power and in knowledge of Irish life with those of Carleton and

Banim. For all that, their tender sentiment, chequered here and there with feelings of more tragic importance, have won them many friends. He is perhaps, more than all others, the novelist of middle-class Catholic Ireland. In verse, he wrote, beside his tragedies, of which 'Gessipus' alone has been preserved, many popular songs and ballads. They are musical and graceful rather than poetical in any deep sense. His care for finish and completeness, however, might have made him in time a writer of much importance.

THE KNIGHT OF THE SHEEP

By GERALD GRIFFIN

I

In the days of our ancestors it was the custom, when a 'strong farmer' had arrived at a certain degree of independence by his agricultural pursuits, to confer upon him a title in the Irish language, which is literally translated, 'The Knight of the Sheep.' Though not commonly of noble origin, these persons often exercised a kind of patriarchal sway, scarce less extensive than that of many a feudal descendant of the Butlers or the Geraldines.

In one of the most fertile townlands in one of our inland counties lived a person of this class, bearing the name of Bryan Taafe. No less than three spacious tenements acknowledged his sway, by the culture of which he had acquired, in the course of a long life, a quantity of wealth more than sufficient for any purpose to which he might wish to apply it.

Mr Taafe had three sons, on whose education he had lavished all the care and expense which could have been expected from the most affectionate father in his walk of life. He had a great opinion of learning, and had frequently in his mouth, for the instruction of his children, such snatches of old wisdom as: 'Learning is better than houses or land,' and

'A man without learning, and wearing fine clothes,
Is like a pig with a gold ring in his nose.'

Accordingly, the best teachers that Kerry and Limerick could afford were employed to teach them the classics, mathematics, and such other branches of science and letters as were current in those parts. The two elder sons showed a remarkable quickness in all their studies; but the youngest, though his favourite, disappointed both him and his instructors. So heavy was he at his book, that neither threats nor caresses could have any effect in making him arrive at any thing like proficiency. However, as it did not proceed from absolute indolence or obstinacy, his father was content to bear with his backwardness in this respect, although it in some degree diminished the especial affection with which he once regarded him.

One day as Mr Taafe was walking in his garden, taking the air before breakfast in the morning, he called Jerry Fogarty, his steward, and told him he wanted to speak with him.

'Jerry,' says Mr Taafe, after they had taken two or three turns on the walk together, 'I don't know in the world what I'll do with Garret.'

'Why so, masther?'

'Ah, I'm kilt from him. You know yourself what a great opinion I always had o' the learning. A man, in fact, isn't conshidered worth speakin' to in these times that hasn't it. 'Tis for the same raison I went to so much cost and trouble to get schoolin' for them three boys; and to be sure, as for Shamus and Guillaum, I haven't any cause to complain, but the world wouldn't get good o' Garret. It was only the other mornin' I asked him who was it discovered America, and the answer he made me was that he believed it was Nebuchodonezzar.'

'A' no?'

' 'Tis as thrue as you're standin' there. What's to be done with a man o' that kind? Sure, as I often represented to himself, it would be a disgrace to me if he was ever to go abroad in foreign parts, or any place o' the kind, and to make such an answer as that to any gentleman or lady, afther all I lost by him. 'Tisn't so with Shamus and Guillaum. There isn't many goin' that could thrace histhory with them boys. I'd give a dale, out o' regard for the poor woman that's gone, if Garret could come any way near 'em.'

'I'll tell you what it is, masther,' said Jerry; 'there's a dale that's not over bright at the book, an' that would be very 'cute for all in their own minds. Maybe Master Garret would be one o' them, an' we not to know it. I remember myself one Motry Hierlohee, that not one ha'p'orth o' good could be got out of him goin' to school, an' he turned out one of the greatest janiuses in the parish afther. There isn't his aiquals in Munsther now at a lamentation or the likes. Them raal janiuses does be always so full of their own thoughts, they can't bring themselves, as it were, to take notice of those of other people.'

'Maybe you're right, Jerry,' answered Mr Taafe; 'I'll take an opportunity of trying.'

He said no more, but in a few days after he gave a great entertainment to all his acquaintances, rich and poor, that were within a morning's ride of his own house, taking particular care to have every one present that had any name at all for 'the learning.' Mr Taafe was so rich and so popular amongst his neighbours, that his house was crowded on the day appointed with all the scholars in the country, and they had no reason to complain of the entertainment they received from Mr Taafe. Everything good and wholesome that his sheep-walk, his paddock, his orchard, his kitchen-garden, his pantry, and his cellar, could afford, was placed before them in abundance; and seldom did a merrier company assemble together to enjoy the hospitality of an Irish farmer.

When the dinner was over, and the guests busily occupied in conversation, the Knight of the Sheep, who sat at the head of the table, stood up with a grave air, as if he were about to address something of importance to the company. His venerable appearance, as he remained standing, a courteous smile shedding its light over his aged countenance, and his snowy hair descending almost to his shoulders, occasioned a respectful silence amongst the guests, while he addressed them in the following words:

'In the first place, gentlemen, I have to return you all thanks for giving me the pleasure of your company here today, which I do with all my heart. And I feel the more honoured and gratified because I take it for granted you have come here, not so much from any personal feeling towards myself, but because you know that I have always endeavoured, so far as my poor means would enable me, to show my respect for men of parts and learning. Well, then, here you are all met, grammarians, geometricians, arithmeticians, geographers, astronomers, philosophers, Latinists, Grecians, and men of more sciences than perhaps I ever heard the names of. Now there's no doubt learning is a fine thing, but what good is all the learning in the world, without what they call mother-wit to make use of it? An ounce o' mother-wit would buy an' sell a stone-weight of learning at any fair in Munsther. Now there are you all scholars, an' here am I a poor country farmer that hardly ever got more teaching than to read and write, and maybe a course of Voster, and yet I'll be bound I'll lay down a problem that maybe some of ye wouldn't find it easy to make out.'

At this preamble, the curiosity of the company was raised to the highest degree, and the Knight of the Sheep resumed, after a brief pause.

'At a farm of mine, about a dozen miles from this, I have four fields of precisely the same soil; one square, another oblong, another partly round, and another triangular. Now, what is the reason that, while I have an excellent crop of white eyes this year out of the square, the oblong, and the round field, not a single stalk would grow in the triangular one?'

This problem produced a dead silence amongst the guests, and all exerted their understandings to discover the solution, but without avail, although many of their conjectures showed the deepest ingenuity. Some traced out a mysterious connection between the triangular boundary and the lines of the celestial hemisphere; others said, probably from the shape of the field an equal portion of nutrition did not flow on all sides to the seed so as to favour its growth. Others attributed the failure to the effect of the angular hedges upon the atmosphere, which, collecting the wind, as it were, into corners, caused such an obstruction to the warmth necessary to vegetation, that the seed perished in the earth. But all their theories were beside the mark.

'Gentlemen,' said Mr Taafe, 'ye're all too clever – that's the only fault I have to find with yer answers. Shamus,' he continued, addressing his eldest son, 'can you tell the raison?'

'Why, then, father,' said Shamus, 'they didn't grow there, I suppose, because you didn't plant them there.'

'You have it, Shamus,' said the knight; 'I declare you took the ball from all the philosophers. Well, gentlemen, can any o' ye tell me, now, if you wished to travel all over the world, from whom would you ask a passport?'

This question seemed as puzzling as the former. Some said the Great Mogul, others the Grand Signior, others the Pope, others the Lord Lieutenant, and some the Emperor of Austria; but all were wrong.

'What do you say, Guillaum?' asked the knight, addressing his second son.

'From Civility, father,' answered Guillaum; 'for that's a gentleman that has acquaintances everywhere.'

'You're right, Guillaum,' replied the knight. 'Well, I have one more question for the company. Can anyone tell me in what country the women are the best housekeepers?'

Again the company exhausted all their efforts in conjecture, and the geographers showed their learning by naming all the countries in the world, one after another, but to no purpose. The knight now turned with a fond look towards his youngest son.

'Garret,' said he, 'can you tell where the women are good housekeepers?'

Garret rubbed his forehead for a while, and smiled, and shook his head, but could get nothing out of it.

'I declare to my heart, father,' said he, 'I can't tell from Adam. Where the women are good housekeepers? – Stay a minute. Maybe,' said he, with a knowing wink, 'maybe 'tis in America?'

'Shamus, do you answer,' said the knight in a disappointed tone.

'In the grave, father,' answered Shamus; 'for there they never gad abroad.'

Mr Taafe acknowledged that his eldest son had once more judged right; and the entertainments of the night proceeded without further interruption, until, wearied with feasting and music, such of the company as could not be accommodated with beds, took their departure, each in the direction of his own home.

II

On the following morning, in the presence of his household, Mr Taafe made a present to his two eldest sons of one hundred pounds each, and was induced to bestow the same sum on Garret, although he by no means thought he deserved it after disgracing him as he had done before his guests. He signified to the young men at the same time that he gave them the money as a free gift, to lay out in any way they pleased, and that he never should ask them to repay it.

After breakfast, the old knight, as usual, went to take a few turns in the garden.

'Well, Jerry,' said he, when the steward had joined him according to his orders; 'well, Jerry, Garret is no genius.'

A groan from Jerry seemed to announce his acquiescence in this decison. He did not, however, resign all hope.

'With submission to your honour,' said he, 'I wouldn't call that a fair thrial of a man's parts. A man mightn't be able to answer a little *cran* o' that kind, an' to have more sense for all than those that would. Wait a while until you'll see what use he'll make o' the hundred pounds, an' that'll show his sense betther than all the riddles in Europe.'

Mr Taafe acknowledged that Jerry's proposition was but reasonable: and, accordingly, at the end of a twelvemonth, he called his three sons before him, and examined them one after another.

'Well, Shamus,' said he, 'what did you do with your hundred pounds?'

'I bought stock with it, father.'

'Very good. And you, Guillaum?'

'I laid it out, father, in the intherest of a little farm westwards.'

'Very well managed again. Well, Garret, let us hear what you did with the hundred pounds.'

'I spent it, father,' said Garret.

'Spent it! Is it the whole hundred pounds?'

'Sure, I thought you told us we might lay it out as we liked, sir?'

'Is that the raison you should be such a prodigal as to waste the whole of it in a year? Well, hear to me, now, the three o' ye, and listen to the raison why I put ye to these trials. I'm an ould man, my children; my hair is white on my head, an' it's time for me to think of turning the few days that are left me to the best account. I wish to separate myself from the world before the world separates itself from me. For this cause I had resolved, these six months back, to give up all my property to ye three that are young an' hearty, an' to keep nothing for myself but a bed under my old roof, an' a sate at the table and by the fireplace, an' so to end my ould days in peace an' quiet. To you, Shamus, I mean to give the dairy-farm up in the mountains; the Corcasses and all the meadowing to you, Guillaum; and for

you, Garret, I had the best of the whole, – that is, the house
we're living in, and the farm belonging to it. But for what would
I give it to you, after what you just tould me? Is it to make
ducks and drakes of it, as you did o' the hundhred pounds?
Here Garret,' said he, going to a corner of the room and
bringing out a small bag and a long hazel stick; 'here's the legacy
I have to leave you – that an' the king's high road, an' my liberty
to go wherever it best plases you. Hard enough I airned that
hundhred pounds that you spent so aisily. And as for the farm I
mean to give you, I give it to these two boys, an' my blessing
along with it, since 'tis they that know how to take care of it.'

At this speech the two elder sons cast themselves at their
father's feet with tears of gratitude.

'Yes,' said he, 'my dear boys, I'm rewarded for all the pains I
ever took with ye, to make ye industrious, and thrifty, and
everything that way. I'm satisfied, under Heaven, that all will go
right with ye; but as for this boy, I have nothing to say to him.
Betther for me I never saw his face.'

Poor Garret turned aside his head, but he made no attempt
to excuse himself, nor to obtain any favour from his rigid father.
After wishing them all a timid farewell, which was but slightly
returned, he took the bag and staff and went about his business.

His departure seemed to give little pain to his relatives. They
lived merrily and prosperously, and even the old knight himself
showed no anxiety to know what had become of Garret. In the
meantime the two elder sons got married, and Mr Taafe, in
the course of a few years, had the satisfaction to see his
grandchildren seated on his knee.

We are often widely mistaken in our estimate of generosity.
It may appear a very noble thing to bestow largely, but, before
we give it the praise of generosity, we must be sure that the
motive is as good as the deed. Mr Taafe began, in the course of
time, to show that his views in bestowing his property on his
two sons were not wholly free from selfishness. They found it
harder to please him, now that they were masters of all, than

when they were wholly dependent on his will. His jealousies and murmurs were interminable. There was no providing against them beforehand, nor any allaying them when they did arise. The consequence was, the young men, who never really felt anything like the gratitude they had professed, began to consider the task of pleasing him altogether burdensome. In this feeling they were encouraged by their wives, who never ceased murmuring at the cost and trouble of entertaining him.

Accordingly, one night, while the aged knight was murmuring at some inattention which was shown him at table, Shamus and Guillaum Taafe walked into the room, determined to put an end forever to his complaints.

'I'd like to know what would plaise you!' exclaimed Shamus. 'I suppose you won't stop until you'll take house and all from us, an' turn us out, as you did Garret, to beg from doore to doore?'

'If I did itself, Shamus,' said the knight, looking at him for some moments with surprise, 'I'd get no more than I gave.'

'What good was your giving it,' cried Guillaum, 'when you won't let us enjoy it with a moment's comfort?'

'Do you talk that way to me, too, Guillaum? If it was poor Garret I had, he wouldn't use me so.'

'Great thanks he got from you for any good that was in him,' cried one of the women.

'Let him take his stick and pack out to look for Garret,' said the second woman, 'since he is so fond of him.'

The old knight turned and looked at the women.

'I don't wondher,' said he, 'at anything I'd hear ye say. You never yet heard of anything great or good, or for the public advantage, that a woman would have a hand in – only mischief always. If you ask who made such a road, or who built such a bridge, or wrote such a great histhory, or did any other good action o' the kind, I'll engage 'tis seldom you'll hear that it is a woman done it; but if you ask who it is that set such and such a pair fightin', or who it is that caused such a *jewel*, or who it is that let out such a sacret, or ran down such a man's character, or occasioned such a war, or brought such a man to the gallows, or caused diversion in such a family, or anything o' that kind, then, I'll engage, you'll hear that a woman had some call to it. We needn't have recoorse to histhory to know ye'r doin's. 'Tis undher our eyes. 'Twas the likes of ye two that burned Throy, an' made the King of Leinsther rebel again' Brian Boru.'

At this the two women pulled the caps off their heads, and set up such a screaming and shrieking as might be heard from thence to Cork.

'Oh, murther! murther!' says one of them, 'was it for this I married you, to be compared to people o' that kind?'

'What raison has he to me,' cried the other, 'that he'd compare me to them that would rebel again' Brian Boru? Would I rebel against Brian Boru, Shamus, a regal?'

'Don't heed him, a-vourneen; he's an ould man.'

'Oh, vo, vo! if ever I thought the likes o' that would be said to me, that I'd rebel again' Brian Boru!'

'There's no use in talking, Guillaum,' cried the second, who probably took the allusion to the fate of Troy as a slight on her own personal attractions; 'there's no use in talkin', but I never'll stay a day undher your roof with anybody that would say I'd burn Throy. Does he forget that ever he had a mother himself? Ah, 'tis a bad apple, that's what it is, that despises the three it sprung from.'

'Well, I'll tell you what it is, now,' said the eldest son, 'since 'tis come to that with you, that you won't let the women alone, I won't put up with any more from you. I believe, if I didn't show you the outside o' the doore, you'd show it to me before long. There, now, the world is free to you to look out for people that'll plaise you better, since you say we can't do it.'

'A', Shamus, agra,' said the old knight, looking at his son with astonishment; 'is that my thanks afther all?'

'Your thanks for what?' cried Guillaum; 'is it for plaisin' your own fancy or for making our lives miserable ever since, an' to give crossness to the women?'

'Let him go look for Garret, now,' cried one of the women, 'an' see whether they'll agree betther than they did before.'

'Ah – Shamus – Guillaum – a chree,' said the poor old man, trembling with terror at sight of the open door, 'let ye have it as ye will; I am sorry for what I said, a'ra gal! Don't turn me out on the high road in my ould days! I'll engage I never'll open my mouth again' one o' ye again the longest day I live. A', Shamus a-vich, it isn't long I have to stay wid ye. Your own hair will be as white as mine yet, plaise God, an' 't wouldn't be wishin' to you then for a dale that you showed any disrespect to mine.'

His entreaties, however, were all to no purpose. They turned him out, and made fast the door behind him.

Imagine an old man of sixty and upwards turned out on the high road on a cold and rainy night, the north wind beating on his feeble breast, and without the prospect of relief before him. For a time he could not believe that the occurrence was real, and it was only when he felt the rain already penetrating through his thin dress that he became convinced it was but too true.

'Well,' said the old man, lifting up his hands as he crept out on the high road, 'is this what all the teaching come to? Is this the cleverness an' the learning! Well, if it was to do again! No matther. They say there's two bad pays in the world – the man that pays beforehand an' the man that doesn't pay at all. In like manner, there's two kinds of people that wrong their lawful heirs – those that give them their inheritance before death, and those that will it away from them afther. What'll I do now at all, or where'll I turn to – a poor old man o' my kind that isn't able to do a sthroke o' work if I was ever so fain? An' the night gettin' worse an' worse! Easy! – isn't that a light I see westwards? There's no one, surely, except an unnatural son or daughter, that would refuse to give an old man shelter on such a night as this. I'll see if all men's hearts are as hard as my two sons'.'

He went to the house, which was situated at the distance of a quarter of a mile from that which he so lately looked on as his own. As he tottered along the dark and miry *borheen* which led to the cottage door, the barking of a dog inside aroused the attention of the inmates. Being already in bed, however, before he had arrived there, none of them were very willing to give admission to a stranger.

'Who's there?' cried the man of the house, as the old knight knocked timidly at the door. 'Do you think we have nothing else to do at this time o' night but to be gettin' up an' openin' the doore to every sthroller that goes the road?'

'Ah! if you knew who it was you had there,' said the knight, 'you wouldn't be so slow of openin' the doore.'

'Who is it I have there, then?'

'The Knight of the Sheep.'

'The Knight of the Sheep! Oh, you born villyan! 'Twas your son Shamus that chated me out o' thirty good pounds by a horse he sould me at the fair o' Killedy – an animal that wasn't worth five! Go along this minute with you; or if you make me get up, 'tis to give you something that you wouldn't bargain for.'

The poor old man hurried away from the door, fearing that the farmer would be but too ready to put his threat into execution. The night was growing worse and worse. He knocked at another door; but the proprietor of this in like manner had suffered to the extreme cleverness of Guillaum Taafe, and refused to give him shelter. The whole night was spent in going from door to door, and finding in every place where he applied that the great ability of his two sons had been beforehand with him in getting a bad name for the whole family. At last, as the morning began to dawn, he found himself unable to proceed farther, and was obliged to lie down in a little paddock close to a very handsome farmhouse. Here the coldness of the morning air and the keenness of his grief at the recollection of his children's ingratitude had such an effect upon him that he swooned away, and lay for a long time insensible upon the grass. In this condition he was found by the people of the house, who soon after came out to look after the bounds and do their usual farming work. They had the humanity to take him into the house, and to put him into a warm bed, where they used all proper means for his recovery.

When he had come to himself, they asked him who he was, and how he had fallen into so unhappy a condition. For a time the old knight was afraid to answer, lest these charitable people, like so many others, might have been at one time sufferers to the roguery of his two eldest sons, and thus be tempted to repent of their kindness the instant they had heard on whom it had been bestowed. However, fearing lest they should accuse him of duplicity in case they might afterwards learn the truth, he at length confessed his name.

'The Knight of the Sheep!' exclaimed the woman of the house, with a look of the utmost surprise and joy.

'Oh, Tom, Tom!' she continued, calling out to her husband, who was in another room. 'A', come here, asthore, until you see Misther Taafe, the father o' young Masther Garret, the darlin' that saved us all from ruin.'

The man of the house came in as fast as he could run.

'Are you Garret Taafe's father?' said he, looking surprised at the old knight.

'I had a son of that name,' said Mr Taafe, 'though all I know of him now is, that I used him worse than I would if it was to happen again.'

'Well, then,' said the farmer, 'my blessing on that day that ever you set foot within these doores. The rose in May was never half so welcome, an' I'm betther plaised than I'll tell you, that I have you undher my roof.'

'I'm obliged to you,' said the knight; 'but what's the raison o' that?'

'Your son Garret,' replied the man, 'of a day when every whole ha'p'orth we had in the world was going to be canted for the rent, put a hand in his pocket an' lent us thirty pounds till we'd be able to pay him again, an' we not knowin' who in the world he was, nor he us, I'm sure. It was only a long time afther that we found it out by others in various parts that he had served in like manner, and they told us who he was. We never seen him since; but I'm sure it would be the joyful day to us that we'd see him coming back to get his thirty pounds.'

When the old knight heard this, he felt as if somebody was running him through with a sword.

'And this,' said he, 'was the way poor Garret spent the hundhred pounds! Oh, murther! murther! my poor boy, what had I to do at all, to go turn you adhrift as I done, for no raison! I took the wrong for the right, an' the right for the wrong. No matther! That's the way the whole world is blinded. That's the way death will show us the differ of many a thing. Oh, murther! Garret! Garret! What'll I do at all with the thoughts of it! An' them two villyans that I gave it all to, an' that turned me out afther in my ould days, as I done by you! No matther.'

He turned into the wall for fear the people would hear him groaning; but the remorse, added to all his other sufferings, had almost killed him.

In a little time the old knight began to recover something of his former strength under the care of his new acquaintances, who continued to show him the most devoted attention. One morning the farmer came into his room with a large purse full of gold in his hand, and said:

'I told you, sir, I owed your son thirty pounds; an' since he's not comin' to ax for it, you're heartily welcome to the use of it until he does, an' I'm sure he wouldn't wish to see it better employed.'

'No, no,' replied Mr Taafe, 'I'll not take the money from you; but I'll borrow the whole purse for a week, an' at the end o' that time I'll return it safe to you.'

The farmer lent him the purse, and the knight waited for a fine day, when he set off again in the morning, and took the road leading to the dwelling from which he had been expelled. It was noon, and the sun was shining bright, when he arrived upon the little lawn before the door. Sitting down in the sunshine by the kitchen-garden wall, he began counting the gold, and arranging it in a number of little heaps, so that it had a most imposing effect. While he was thus occupied, one of his young daughters-in-law – the same whose beauty had drawn upon her the unhappy allusion to the mischief-making spouse of Menelaus – happened to make her appearance at the front door, and, looking around, saw the old knight in the act of counting his gold in the sunshine. Overwhelmed with astonishment, she ran to her husband, and told him what she had seen.

'Nonsense, woman!' said Shamus; 'you don't mean to persuade me to a thing o' that kind.'

'Very well,' replied the woman, 'I'm sure if you don't believe me, 'tis asy for ye all to go an' see for ye'rselves.'

So they all went, and peeping through the little window one after another, were dazzled by the sight of so much gold.

'You done very wrong, Shamus,' said Guillaum, 'ever to turn out the ould father as you done. See, now, what we all lost by it. That's a part o' the money he laid by from year to year, an' we never'll see a penny of it.'

At this they all felt the greatest remorse for the manner in which they had acted to the old man. However, they were not so much discouraged but that some of them ventured to approach and salute him. On seeing them draw nigh, he hastily concealed the gold and returned their greeting with an appearance of displeasure. It was by much persuasion, and after many assurances of their regret for what had passed, that he consented once more to come and take up his abode beneath their roof, desiring at the same time that an ass and cart might be sent to the farmer's for a strong box which he had left there.

At the mention of a *strong box*, it may easily be imagined what were the sensations of his hearers. The ass and cart were procured without delay, and, before evening, those grateful children had the satisfaction to behold a heavy box, of very promising dimensions, deposited in a corner of the small chamber which was to be reserved for the future use of their aged parent.

In the meanwhile, nothing could exceed the attention which he now received from the young people. They seemed only unhappy when not occupied in contributing in some way to his comfort, and perceiving his remorse for the manner in which Garret had been treated, used all the means in their power to discover whither he had gone. But it is not always in this life that one false step can be retraced. The old knight was not destined to see his son again, and his grief at this disappointment had no slight effect in aggravating the infirmities of his old age.

At length, perceiving that he was near his end, he called his sons and daughters to his bedside, and addressed them in the following words:

'Whatever cause I had once to complain of ye, Shamus and Guillaum, that's all past and gone now, and it's right that I should leave you some little remembrance for all the trouble I gave you since my comin' home. Do you see that chest over there?'

'Ah, father! what chest?' cried the sons. 'Don't be talking of it for a chest.'

'Well, my good boys,' said the knight, 'my will is in that chest, so I need tell ye no more.'

'Don't speak of it, father,' said Shamus, 'for, as the Latin poet says:

"Non possidentem
Recte beatum."

Only as you're talkin' of it at all for a chest, where's the key, father?'

'Ah, Shamus,' said the knight, 'you were always great at the Latin. The key is in my waistcoat pocket.'

Soon after he expired. The two sons, impatient to inspect their treasure, could hardly wait until the old man had ceased to breathe. While Shamus unlocked the box, Guillaum remained to keep the door fast.

'Well, Shamus,' said his brother, 'what do you find there?'

'A parcel of stones, Guillaum!'

'Nonsense, man! try what's undher 'em.'

Shamus complied, and found at the bottom of the box a rope with a running noose at the end, and a scroll of paper, from which Shamus read the following sentence aloud, for the information of his brother:

'THE LAST WILL AND TESTAMENT OF BRYAN TAAFE, COMMONLY CALLED THE KNIGHT OF THE SHEEP.

'*Imprimis.* To my two sons, Shamus and Guillaum, I bequeath the whole of the limestones contained in this box, in return for their disinterested love and care of me ever since the day when they saw me counting the gold near the kitchen-garden.

'Item. *I bequeath the rope herein contained for any father to hang himself, who is so foolish as to give away his property to his heirs before his death.'*

'Well, Shamus,' said Guillaum, 'the poor father laid out a deal on our education, but I declare all the taichin' he ever gave us was nothing to that.'

THE DEATH OF THE HUNTSMAN [1]

By GERALD GRIFFIN

Mr Cregan, with two other gentlemen, were drinking in the dining-room, and, as he might gather from the tumultuous nature of their conversation, and the occasional shouts of ecstatic enjoyment, and bursts of laughter which rang through the house, already pretty far advanced in the bacchanalian ceremonies of the night.

Feeling no inclination to join the revellers, Hardress ordered candles in the drawing-room, and prepared to spend a quiet evening by himself. He had scarcely, however, taken his seat on the straight-backed sofa, when his retirement was invaded by old Nancy, the kitchen-maid, who came to tell him that poor Dalton, the huntsman, was 'a'most off,' in the little green room, and that when he heard Mr Hardress had arrived, he begged of all things to see him before he'd go. 'He never was himself rightly, a'ra gal,' said old Nancy, wiping a tear from the corner of her eye, 'since the masther sold the hounds and took to the cock-fighting.'

Hardress started up and followed her. 'Poor fellow!' he exclaimed as he went along, 'Poor Dalton! And is that breath, that wound so many merry blasts upon the mountain, so soon to be extinguished? I remember the time when I thought a monarch on his throne a less enviable being than our stout huntsman, seated on his keen-eyed steed, in his scarlet frock and cap, with his hounds, like painted courtiers, thronging and baying round his horse's hoofs, and his horn hanging silent at his waist. Poor fellow! Every beagle in the pack was his familiar acquaintance, and was as jealous of his chirp or his whistle, as my cousin Anne's admirers might be of a smile or secret whisper. How often has he carried me before him on his saddle-bow, and taught me the true fox-hunting cry! How often at evening has he held me between his knees, and excited my young ambition with tales of hunts hard run, and neck-or-nothing leaps; of double ditches, cleared by an almost miraculous dexterity; of drawing, yearning, challenging, hunting mute, hunting change, and hunting counter! And now the poor fellow must wind his last recheat, and carry his own old bones to earth at length! never again to awaken the echoes of the mountain lakes – never again beneath the shadows of those immemorial woods that clothe their lofty shores –

"Aere ciere viros, Martemque accendere cantu!"

The fox may come from kennel, and the red-deer slumber on his lair, for their mighty enemy is now himself at bay.'

While these reflections passed through the mind of Hardress, old Nancy conducted him as far as the door of the huntsman's room, where he paused for a moment on hearing the voice of one singing inside. It was that of the worn-out huntsman himself, who was humming over a few verses of a favourite ballad. The lines which caught the ear of Hardress were the following:

> 'Ah, huntsman dear, I'll be your friend,
>   If you let me go till morning;
> Don't call your hounds for one half hour,
>   Nor neither sound your horn;
> For indeed I'm tired from yesterday's hunt,
>   I can neither run nor walk well,
> Till I go to Rock-hill amongst my friends,
>   Where I was bred and born.

Tally ho the fox!
Tally ho the fox!
Tally ho the fox, a collauneen.
Tally ho the fox!
Over hills and rocks,
And chase him on till morning.'

'He cannot be so very ill,' said Hardress, looking at the old woman, 'when his spirits will permit him to sing so merrily.'

'Oyeh, Heaven help you, agra!' replied Nancy; 'I believe if he was at death's doore this moment, he'd have that song on his tongue still.'

'Hush! hush!' said Hardress, raising his hand, 'he is beginning again.'

The ballad was taken up, after a heavy fit of coughing, in the same strain.

'I lock'd him up an' I fed him well,
An' I gave him victuals of all kinds;
But I declare to you, sir, when he got loose,
He ate a fat goose in the morning.
So now kneel down an' say your prayers,
For you'll surely die this morning.
"Ah, sir," says the fox, "I never pray,
For my father he bred me a quaker"
Tally ho the fox!
Tally ho the – '

Hardress here opened the door and cut short the *refrain*.

The huntsman turned his face to the door as he heard the handle turn. It was that of a middle-aged man in the very last stage of pulmonary consumption. A red night-cap was pushed back from his wasted and sunken temples, and a flush, like the bloom of a withered pippin, played in the hollow of his fleshless cheek.

'Cead millia fealtha! My heart warms to see you, my own Masther Hardress,' exclaimed the huntsman, reaching him a skeleton hand from beneath the brown quilt; 'I can die in peace now, as I see you again in health. These ten days back they're telling me you're coming an' coming, until I began to think at last that you wouldn't come until I was gone.'

'I am sorry to see you in this condition, Dalton. How did you get the attack?'

'Out of a could I think I got it first, sir. When the masther sold the hounds – (Ah, Masther Hardress! to think of his parting them dogs, an' giving up that fine, manly exercise, for a paltry parcel o' cocks an' hens!) – but when he sold them an' took to the cock-fighting, my heart felt as low an' as lonesome as if I lost all belonging to me! To please the masther, I turned my hand to the cocks, an' used to go every morning to the hounds' kennel, where the birds were kept, to give 'em food an' water; but I could *never warm* to the birds. Ah, what is a cock-fight, Masther Hardress, in comparison of a well-rode hunt among the mountains, with your horse flying under you like a fairy, an' the cry o' the hounds like an organ out before you, an' the ground fleeting like a dream on all sides o' you, an' ah! what's the use o' talking!' Here he lay back on his pillow with a look of sudden pain and sorrow that cut Hardress to the heart.

After a few moments, he again turned a ghastly eye on Hardress, and said in a faint voice: 'I used to go down by the lake in the evening to hear the stags belling in the wood; an' in the morning I'd be up with the first light to blow a call on the top o' the hill, as I used to do to comfort the dogs; an' then I'd miss their cry, an' I'd stop listenin' to the aychoes o' the horn among the mountains, till my heart would sink as low as my ould boots. An' bad boots they wor, too; signs on, I got wet in 'em; an' themselves an' the could morning air, an' the want o' the horse exercise, I believe, an' every thing, brought on this fit.'

During this conversation both speakers had been frequently rendered inaudible by occasional bursts of laughter and shouts of bacchanalian mirth from the dining-room. At this moment, and before the young gentleman could select any mode of inquiry into the particulars of the singular communication above mentioned, the door was opened, and the face of old Nancy appeared, bearing on its smoke-dried features a mingled expression of perplexity and sorrow.

'Dalton, a'ra gal!' she exclaimed, 'don't blame me for what I'm going to say to you, for it is my tongue, an' not my wish nor my heart, that speaks it. The masther and the gentlemen sent me in to you, an' bid me tell you for the sake of old times, to give them one fox-huntin' screech before you go.'

The old huntsman fixed his brilliant but sickly eyes on the messenger, while a flush, that might have been the indication of anger or of grief, flickered like a decaying light upon his brow. At length he said: 'An' did the masther send that message by you, Nancy?'

'He did, Dalton, indeed. Ayeh, the gentlemen must be excused.'

'True for you, Nancy,' said the huntsman, after a long pause; then, raising his head, with a smile of seeming pleasure, he continued: 'Why, then, I'm glad to see the masther hasn't forgot the dogs entirely. Go to him, Nancy, an' tell him that I'm glad to hear that he has so much o' the sport left in him still. And that it is kind father for him to have a feeling for his huntsman, an' I thank him. Tell him, Nancy, to send me in one good glass o' parliament punch, an' I'll give him such a cry as he never heard in a cock-pit, anyway.'

The punch was brought, and, in spite of the remonstrances of Hardress, drained to the bottom. The old huntsman then sat erect in the bed, and letting his head back, indulged in one prolonged 'hoicks!' that made the phials jingle on the table, and frightened the sparrows from their roosts beneath the thatch. It was echoed by the jolly company in the dining-parlour, chorused by a howling from all the dogs in the yard, and answered by a general clamour from the fowl-house. 'Another! Another! Hoicks!' resounded through the house. But the poor consumptive was not in a condition to gratify the revellers. When Hardress looked down upon him next, the pillow appeared dark with blood, and the cheek of the sufferer had lost even the unhealthy bloom that had so long masked the miner Death in his work of snug destruction.

1. From 'The Collegians'.

CHARLES LEVER

1806–1872

Charles Lever was born on the 31st of August, 1806. His father was a well-known Dublin architect, around whose table were wont to gather many who had been ruined by the union with England and the consequent flight from Dublin of the fashionable and the wealthy. With the exception of stray visits to Galway and Kilkenny – his mother's town, – Lever grew up in this circle, among people whose minds ran ever on the gay and brilliant past, on the period of orators and duellists. At school he does not appear to have been in any way industrious, but busied himself with such matters as organizing his schoolfellows into a regular army, with generals, captains, sergeants, pickets, and the rest, and in helping to lead them to battle against a neighbouring school. On one occasion, his side having fired a mine charged with several pounds of gunpowder under the hostile troops, they were all had up before the magistrate and fined. Lever, though little more than entered on his teens, won much honour and glory by addressing the court in favour of his fellows and himself.

He worked hard also at theatricals, being playwright, player, scene-painter, vocalist, and fiddler by turns.

In 1822 he entered Trinity, and together with his 'chum' Boyle – the original of Webber in 'Charles O'Malley,' – lived there through five years of tumultuous high spirits. Like Goldsmith, he wrote street ballads, but, unlike Goldsmith, was not content to creep at night into some by-street to hear them sung, and enjoy in the applause of the crowd a prophecy of fame. Having written some political verses too 'strong' for the trade, Lever went out disguised, together with his friend Boyle, and sang them through the streets. He roused great enthusiasm, and collected no less than thirty-six shillings in halfpence. From this we may judge that the 'strong' verses were against the government.

In 1829 he visited America, and lived for a time among the Canadian Indians. He was formally received into the tribe, and for a little all went well. At last he tired of endless fishing and hunting, and began to long for civilization. He tried, however, to hide his changed feelings, but one day a squaw read his thoughts, and looking fixedly at him, said: 'Your heart, stranger, is not with us now. You wish for your own people, but you will not see them again. Our chief will kill you if you leave us. It is the law of our tribe that none joining us can go away. No, you will never see the pale faces again, nor go back to your own country.' Even if he fled, she told him, and escaped those who would pursue, he could never find the track through the forest. At length Lever grew so ill with longing to get away that the same squaw who had warned him took pity on him. She persuaded an Indian who came every now and then to the camp to barter tobacco and other produce of the settlements, to promise to guide him through the woods for money. By her advice, Lever pretended to be disabled by sickness, and so was left behind among the women when the men went hunting. When all was quiet he and the Indian plunged into the forest. They were pursued, but reached Quebec in safety.

On his return to Europe Lever studied medicine at Gottingen and became Bachelor of Medicine in 1831. Returning to Ireland he commenced practice in the North. In the cholera epidemic of 1832 he won much reputation for skill and devotion. In 1833 *The Dublin University Review* was started, and Lever was amongst its first contributors. In 1837 'Harry

Lorrequer' appeared in its pages, and began his fame as a novelist. From 1837 to 1840 one finds him again out of Ireland, doctoring at Brussels and writing 'Charles O'Malley.' Its publication made him at once one of the most important story-tellers of his time. He gave up his practice and returned to Ireland, and was appointed editor of *The Dublin University Magazine*. About him gathered a circle of writers, some of whom have made their mark in Irish literature. There were among them men like Isaac Butt, the orator and politician; Maxwell and LeFanu, the novelists; and Samuel Ferguson, the antiquarian and chief ballad-writer of his day. About him circled these men, the most brilliant of conservative Ireland, in the same period in which the more able spirits of the radical Nationalists drew thought and life from Thomas Davis. Between the two parties – the party of the wits and the party of the thinkers – all that was best in literary Ireland divided itself. Not that the circle who gathered round him had any leader in the sense in which the circle of Davis had. It is the very nature of wit to dissolve all leadership. But Lever was more constantly before the world than any other of his side. Book after book came from his tireless mind. In 1845 he left Ireland, having obtained a diplomatic post at Florence, and spent his remaining years abroad. He died in 1872 at Trieste.

He is the most popular in England of all Irish writers, but has never won a place beside Carleton and Banim, or even Griffin, in the hearts of the Irish people. His books, so full of gaiety and animal laughter, are true merely to the life of the party of ascendancy, and to that of their dependants. It will be a long time before the world tires altogether of his gay, witty, reckless personages, though it is gradually learning that they are not typical Irish men and women.

TRINITY COLLEGE

By CHARLES LEVER

My First Day in Trinity

No sooner had I arrived in Dublin than my first care was to present myself to Dr Mooney, by whom I was received in the most cordial manner. In fact, in my utter ignorance of such persons, I had imagined a college fellow to be a character necessarily severe and unbending; and, as the only two very great people I had ever seen in my life were the Archbishop of Tuam, and the Chief Baron, when on circuit, I pictured to myself that a university fellow was, in all probability, a cross between the two, and feared him accordingly.

The doctor read over my uncle's letter attentively, invited me to partake of his breakfast, and then entered upon something like an account of the life before me, for which Sir Harry Boyle had, however, in some degree prepared me.

'Your uncle, I find, wishes you to live in college; perhaps it is better too; so that I must look out for chambers for you. Let me see; it will be rather difficult, just now, to find them.' Here he fell for some moments into a musing fit, and merely muttered a few broken sentences, as, 'To be sure, if other chambers could be had, – but – then – and, after all, perhaps as he is young – besides, Frank will certainly be expelled before long, and then he will have them all to himself. I say, O'Malley, I believe I must quarter you for the present with a rather wild companion; but as your uncle says you're a prudent fellow' – here he smiled

325

very much, as if my uncle had not said any such thing – 'why, you must only take the better care of yourself, until we can make some better arrangement. My pupil, Frank Webber, is at this moment in want of a "chum," as the phrase is, his last three having only been domesticated with him for as many weeks; so that, until we find you a more quiet resting-place, you may take up your abode with him.'

During breakfast the doctor proceeded to inform me that my destined companion was a young man of excellent family and good fortune, who, with very considerable talents and acquirements, preferred a life of rackety and careless dissipation to prospects of great success in public life, which his connection and family might have secured for him; that he had been originally entered at Oxford, which he was obliged to leave; then tried Cambridge, from which he escaped expulsion by being rusticated – that is, having incurred a sentence of temporary banishment; and lastly, was endeavouring, with what he himself believed to be a total reformation, to stumble on to a degree in the 'Silent Sister.'

'This is his third year,' said the doctor, 'and he is only a freshman, having lost every examination, with abilities enough to sweep the university of its prizes. But come over now, and I'll present you to him.'

I followed down stairs, across the court, to an angle of the old square, where, up the first floor left, to use the college direction, stood the name of Mr Webber, a large No. 2 being conspicuously painted in the middle of the door, and not over it, as is usually the custom. As we reached the spot, the observations of my companion were lost to me in the tremendous noise and uproar that resounded from within. It seemed as if a number of people were fighting, pretty much as banditti in a melodrama do, with considerable more of confusion than requisite; a fiddle and a French horn also lent their assistance to shouts and cries, which, to say the best, were not exactly the aids to study I expected in such a place.

Three times was the bell pulled, with a vigour that threatened its downfall, when, at last, as the jingle of it rose above all other noises, suddenly all became hushed and still; a momentary pause succeeded, and the door was opened by a very respectable-looking servant, who, recognizing the doctor, at once introduced us into the apartment where Mr Webber was sitting.

In a large and very handsomely furnished room, where Brussels carpeting and softly-cushioned sofas contrasted strangely with the meagre and comfortless chambers of the doctor, sat a young man at a small breakfast-table, beside the fire. He was attired in a silk dressing-gown and black velvet slippers, and supported his forehead upon a hand of most lady-like whiteness, whose fingers were absolutely covered with rings of great beauty and price. His long silky brown hair fell in rich profusion upon the back of his neck and over his arm, and the whole air and attitude was one which a painter might have copied. So intent was he upon the volume before him, that he never raised his head at our approach, but continued to read aloud, totally unaware of our presence.

'Dr Mooney, sir,' said the servant.

'*Ton dapamey bominos, prosephe, crione Agamemnon,*' repeated the student, in an ecstasy, and not paying the slightest attention to the announcement.

'Dr Mooney, sir,' repeated the servant, in a louder tone, while the doctor looked round on every side for an explanation of the late uproar, with a face of the most puzzled astonishment.

'*Be dakiown para thina dolekoskion enkos,*' said Mr Webber, finishing a cup of coffee at a draught.

'Well, Webber, hard at work I see,' said the doctor.

'Ah, doctor, I beg pardon! Have you been long here?' said the most soft and insinuating voice, while the speaker passed his taper fingers across his brow, as if to dissipate the traces of deep thought of study.

While the doctor presented me to my future companion, I could perceive, in the restless and searching look he threw around, that the fracas he had so lately heard was still an unexplained and *vexata questio* in his mind.

'May I offer you a cup of coffee, Mr O'Malley?' said the youth, with the air of almost timid bashfulness. 'The doctor, I know, breakfasts at a very early hour.'

'I say, Webber,' said the doctor, who could no longer restrain his curiosity, 'what an awful row I heard here as I came up to the door. I thought Bedlam was broke loose. What could it have been?'

'Ah, you heard it, too, sir?' said Mr Webber, smiling most benignly.

'Hear it! – to be sure I did. O'Malley and I could not hear ourselves talking with the uproar.'

'Yes, indeed; it is very provoking; but, then, what's to be done? One can't complain, under the circumstances.'

'Why, what do you mean?' said Mooney, anxiously.

'Nothing, sir, nothing. I'd much rather you'd not ask me; for, after all, I'll change my chambers.'

'But why? Explain this at once. I insist upon it.'

'Can I depend upon the discretion of your young friend?' said Mr Webber, gravely.

'Perfectly,' said the doctor, now wound up to the greatest anxiety to learn a secret.

'And you'll promise not to mention the thing except among your friends?'

'I do,' said the doctor.

'Well, then,' said he, in a low and confident whisper, 'it's the dean!'

'The dean!' said Mooney, with a start. 'The dean! Why, how can it be the dean?'

'Too true,' said Mr Webber, making a sign of drinking; 'too true, doctor. And then, the moment he is so, he begins smashing the furniture. Never was anything heard like it. As for me, as I am now become a reading man, I must go elsewhere.'

Now, it so chanced that the worthy dean, who albeit a man of most abstemious habits, possessed a nose which, in colour and development, was a most unfortunate witness to call to character; and as Mooney heard Webber narrate circumstantially the frightful excesses of the great functionary, I saw that something like conviction was stealing over him.

'You'll, of course, never speak of this except to your most intimate friends?' said Webber.

'Of course not,' said the doctor, as he shook his hand warmly, and prepared to leave the room. 'O'Malley, I leave you here,' said he; 'Webber and you can talk over your arrangements.'

Webber followed the doctor to the door, whispered something in his ear, to which the other replied, 'Very well, I will write; but if your father sends the money, I must insist – ' The rest was lost in protestations and professions of the most fervent kind, amidst which the door was shut, and Mr Webber returned to the room.

Short as was the interspace from the door without to the room within, it was still ample enough to effect a very thorough and remarkable change in the whole external appearance of Mr Frank Webber; for scarcely had the oaken panel shut out the doctor, when he appeared no longer the shy, timid, and silvery-toned gentleman of five minutes before, but, dashing boldly forward, he seized a key-bugle that lay hid beneath a sofa-cushion and blew a tremendous blast.

'Come forth, ye demons of the lower world,' said he, drawing a cloth from a large table, and discovering the figures of three young men coiled up beneath. 'Come forth, and fear not, most timorous freshmen that ye are,' said he, unlocking a pantry, and liberating two others. 'Gentlemen, let me introduce to your acquaintance Mr O'Malley. My chum, gentlemen. Mr O'Malley, this is Harry Nesbitt, who has been in college since the days of old Perpendicular, and numbers more cautions than any man who ever had his name on the books. Here is my particular friend, Cecil Cavendish, the only man who could ever devil kidneys. Captain Power, Mr O'Malley; – a dashing dragoon, as you see; aide-de-camp to his Excellency the Lord Lieutenant, and love-maker-general to Merrion-square West. These,' said he, pointing to the late denizens of the pantry, 'are jibs, whose names are neither known to the proctor nor the police office; but, with due regard to their education and morals we don't despair.'

Frank Webber

Among the many peculiar tastes which distinguished Mr Francis Webber was an extraordinary fancy for street-begging; he had, over and over, won large sums upon his success in that difficult walk; and so perfect were his disguises, both of dress, voice, and manner, that he actually, at one time, succeeded in obtaining charity from his very opponent in the wager. He wrote ballads with the greatest facility, and sang them with infinite pathos and humour; and the old woman at the corner of College-green was certain of an audience when the severity of the night would leave all other minstrelsy deserted. As these feats of *jonglerie* usually terminated in a row, it was a most amusing part of the transaction to see the singer's part taken by the mob against the college men, who, growing impatient to carry him off to supper somewhere, would invariably be obliged to have a fight for the booty.

Now, it chanced that, a few evenings before, Mr Webber was returning with a pocket well lined with copper from a musical *réunion* he had held at the corner of York Street, when the idea struck him to stop at the end of Grafton Street, where a huge stone grating at that time exhibited – perhaps it exhibits still – the descent to one of the great main sewers of the city.

The light was shining brightly from a pastry-cook's shop, and showed the large bars of stone between which the muddy water was rushing rapidly down, and plashing in the torrent that ran boisterously several feet beneath.

To stop in the street in any crowded city is, under any circumstances, an invitation to others to do likewise, which is rarely unaccepted; but when, in addition to this, you stand fixedly in one spot, and regard with stern intensity any object near you, the chances are ten to one that you have several companions in your curiosity before a minute expires.

Now, Webber, who had at first stood still, without any peculiar thought in view, no sooner perceived that he was joined by others, than the idea of making something out of it immediately occurred to him.

'What is it, agra?' inquired an old woman, very much in his own style of dress, pulling at the hood of his cloak.

'And can't you see for yourself, darlin?' replied he, sharply, as he knelt down, and looked most intensely at the sewer.

'Are ye long there, avick?' inquired he of an imaginary individual below, and then, waiting as if for a reply, said, 'Two hours! Blessed Vargin! he's two hours in the drain!'

By this time the crowd had reached entirely across the street, and the crushing and squeezing to get near the important spot was awful.

'Where did he come from?' 'who is he?' 'how did he get there?' were questions on every side, and various surmises were afloat, till Webber, rising from his knees, said, in a mysterious whisper, to those nearest him, 'He's made his escape tonight out o' Newgate by the big drain, and lost his way; he was looking for the Liffey, and took the wrong turn.'

To an Irish mob, what appeal could equal this? A culprit, any time, has his claim upon their sympathy! but let him be caught in the very act of cheating the authorities and evading the law, and his popularity knows no bounds. Webber knew this well; and, as the mob thickened around him, sustained an imaginary conversation that Savage Landor might have envied, imparting now and then such hints concerning the runaway as raised their

331

interest to the highest pitch, and fifty different versions were related on all sides – of the crime he was guilty of – the sentence that was passed on him – and the day he was to suffer.

'Do you see the light, dear?' said Webber, as some ingeniously benevolent individual had lowered down a candle with a string – 'do ye see the light? Oh, he's fainted? the creature.' A cry of horror from the crowd burst forth at these words, followed by a universal shout of 'Break open the street!'

Pickaxes, shovels, spades, and crowbars seemed absolutely the walking accompaniments of the crowd, so suddenly did they appear upon the field of action, and the work of exhumation was begun with a vigour that speedily covered nearly half of the street with mud and paving-stones. Parties relieved each other at the task, and, ere half an hour, a hole capable of containing a mail-coach was yawning in one of the most frequented thoroughfares in Dublin. Meanwhile, as no appearance of the culprit could be had, dreadful conjectures as to his fate began to gain ground. By this time the authorities had received intimation of what was going forward, and attempted to disperse the crowd; but Webber, who still continued to conduct the prosecution, called on them to resist the police, and save the poor creature. And now began a most terrific fray; the stones, forming a ready weapon, were hurled at the unprepared constables, who, on their side, fought manfully, but against superior numbers; so that at last it was only by the aid of a military force the mob could be dispersed, and a riot, which had assumed a very serious character, got under. Meanwhile Webber had reached his chambers, changed his costume, and was relating over a supper-table the narrative of his philanthropy to a very admiring circle of his friends.

Such was my chum, Frank Webber; and as this was the first anecdote I had heard of him, I relate it here that my readers may be in possession of the grounds upon which my opinion of that celebrated character was founded, while yet our acquaintance was in its infancy.

Dr Barrett

Dr Barrett, the Vice-Provost, was, at the time I speak of, close upon seventy years of age, scarcely five feet in height, and even that diminutive stature lessened by a stoop. His face was thin, pointed, and russet-coloured; his nose so aquiline as nearly to meet his projecting chin, and his small, gray eyes, red and bleary, peered beneath his well-worn cap with a glance of mingled fear and suspicion. His dress was a suit of the rustiest black, threadbare, and patched in several places, while a pair of large brown slippers, far too big for his feet, imparted a sliding motion to his walk, that added an air of indescribable meanness to his appearance; a gown that had been worn for twenty years, browned and coated with the learned dust of the *Fagel*, covered his rusty habiliments, and completed the equipments of a figure that it was somewhat difficult for the young student to recognize as the Vice-Provost of the University. Such was he in externals. Within, a greater or more profound scholar never graced the walls of the college; a distinguished Grecian; learned in all the refinements of a hundred dialects, a deep Orientalist, cunning in all the varieties of Eastern languages, and able to reason with a Monshee, or chat with a Persian ambassador. With a mind that never ceased acquiring, he possessed a memory ridiculous for its retentiveness even of trifles; no character in history, no event in chronology was unknown to him, and he was referred to by his contemporaries for information in doubtful and disputed cases, as men consult a lexicon or dictionary. With an intellect thus stored with deep and far-sought knowledge, in the affairs of the world he was a child. Without the walls of the college, for above forty years, he had not ventured half as many times, and knew absolutely nothing of the busy, active world that fussed and fumed so near him; his farthest excursion was to the Bank of Ireland, to which he made occasional visits to fund the ample income of his office, and add to the wealth which already had acquired for him a well-merited repute of being the richest man in college.

His little intercourse with the world had left him, in all his habits and manners, in every respect exactly as when he entered college, nearly half a century before; and as he had literally risen from the ranks in the university, all the peculiarities of voice, accent, and pronunciation, which distinguished him as a youth adhered to him in old age. This was singular enough, and formed a very ludicrous contrast with the learned and deep-read tone of his conversation; but another peculiarity still more striking belonged to him. When he became a fellow, he was obliged, by the rules of the college, to take holy orders as a *sine quá non* to his holding his fellowship; this he did, as he would have assumed a red hood or a blue one, as bachelor of laws, or doctor of medicine, and thought no more of it; but frequently, in his moments of passionate excitement, the venerable character with which he was invested was quite forgotten, and he would utter some sudden and terrific oath, more productive of mirth to his auditors than was seemly, and of which, once spoken, the poor doctor felt the greatest shame and contrition. These oaths were no less singular than forcible, and many a trick was practised, and many a plan devised, that the learned Vice-Provost might be entrapped into his favourite exclamation of 'May the devil admire me!' which no place or presence could restrain.

My servant, Mike, who had not been long in making himself acquainted with all the originals about him, was the cause of my first meeting the doctor, before whom I received a summons to appear, on the very serious charge of treating with disrespect the heads of the college.

The circumstances were shortly these: Mike had, among the other gossip of the place, heard frequent tales of the immense wealth and great parsimony of the doctor; of his anxiety to amass money on all occasions, and the avidity with which even the smallest trifle was added to his gains. He accordingly resolved to amuse himself at the expense of this trait, and proceeded thus: Boring a hole in a halfpenny, he attached a long string to it, and having dropped it on the doctor's step, stationed himself on the opposite side of the court, concealed from view by the angle of the Commons' wall. He waited patiently for the chapel bell, at the first toll of which the door opened, and the doctor issued forth. Scarcely was his foot upon the step, when he saw the piece of money, and as quickly stooped to seize it; but just as his finger had nearly touched it, it evaded his grasp and slowly retreated. He tried again, but with the like success. At last, thinking he miscalculated the distance, he knelt leisurely down, and put forth his hand, but lo! it again escaped him; on which, slowly rising from his posture, he shambled on towards the chapel, where, meeting the senior lecturer at the door, he cried out, 'H – to my soul, Wall, but I saw the halfpenny walk away!'

For the sake of the grave character whom he addressed, I need not recount how such a speech was received; suffice it to say that Mike had been seen by a college porter, who reported him as my servant.

I was in the very act of relating the anecdote to a large party at breakfast in my rooms, when a summons arrived, requiring my immediate attendance at the Board, then sitting in solemn conclave at the examination-hall.

I accordingly assumed my academic costume as speedily as possible, and escorted by that most august functionary, Mr M'Alister, presented myself before the seniors.

The members of the Board, with the Provost at their head, were seated at a long oak table, covered with books, papers, etc., and from the silence they maintained, as I walked up the hall, I augured that a very solemn scene was before me.

'Mr O'Malley,' said the dean, reading my name from a paper he held in his hand, 'you have been summoned here at the desire of the Vice-Provost, whose questions you will reply to.'

I bowed. A silence of a few minutes followed, when at length the learned doctor, hitching up his nether garments with both hands, put his old and bleary eyes to my face, while he croaked out, with an accent that no hackney-coachman could have exceeded in vulgarity:

'Eh, O'Malley; you're *quartus*, I believe, ain't you?'

'I believe not. I think I am the only person of that name now on the books.'

'That's thrue; but there were three O'Malleys before you. Godfrey O'Malley, that construed *Calve Neroni* to Nero the Calvinist – ha! ha! ha! – was cautioned in 1788.'

'My uncle, I believe, sir.'

'More than likely, from what I hear of you – *Ex uno*, etc. I see your name every day on the punishment roll. Late hours, never at chapel, seldom at morning lecture. Here ye are, sixteen shillings, wearing a red coat.'

'Never knew any harm in that, doctor.'

'Why, but d'ye see me now? "Grave raiment," says the statute. And then, ye keep numerous beasts of prey, dangerous in their habits, and unseemly to behold.'

'A bull terrier, sir, and two game-cocks, are, I assure you, the only animals in my household.'

'Well, I'll fine you for it.'

'I believe, doctor,' said the dean, interrupting in an undertone, 'that you cannot impose a penalty in this matter.'

'Ay, but I can. "Singing birds," says the statute, "are forbidden within the walls."'

'And, then, ye dazzled my eyes at Commons with a bit of looking-glass, on Friday. I saw you. May the devil – ahem! – As I was saying, that's casting *reflections* on the heads of the college; and your servant it was, *Michaelis Liber*, Mickey Free – may the flames of – ahem? – an insolent varlet! called me a sweep.'

'You, doctor; impossible!' said I, with pretended horror.

'Ay; but d'ye see me now? it's thrue, for I looked about me at the time, and there wasn't another sweep in the place but myself. Hell to – I mean – God forgive me for swearing! but I'll fine you a pound for this.'

As I saw the doctor was getting on at such a pace, I resolved, notwithstanding the august presence of the Board, to try the efficacy of Sir Harry's letter of introduction, which I had taken in my pocket, in the event of its being wanted.

'I beg your pardon, sir, if the time be an unsuitable one; but may I take the opportunity of presenting this letter to you?'

'Ha! I know the hand – Boyle's. *Boyle secundus*. Hem, ha, ay! "My young friend; and assist him by your advice." To be sure! Oh! of course. Eh, tell me, young man, did Boyle say nothing to you about the copy of "Erasmus," bound in vellum, that I sold him in Trinity term, 1782?'

'I rather think not, sir,' said I, doubtfully.

'Well, then, he might. He owes me two-and-four-pence of the balance.'

'Oh, I beg pardon, sir! I now remember he desired me to repay you that sum; but he had just sealed the letter when he recollected it.'

'Better late than never,' said the doctor, smiling graciously. 'Where's the money? Ay, half-a-crown. I haven't twopence – never mind. Go away, young man; the case is dismissed. *Vehementer miror quare huc venisti.* You're more fit for anything than a college life. Keep good hours; mind the terms; and dismiss *Michaelis Liber*. Ha, ha, ha! May the devil! – hem! – that is, do – ' So saying, the little doctor's hand pushed me from the hall, his mind evidently relieved of all the griefs from which he had been suffering by the recovery of his long-lost two-and-fourpence.

Such was my first and last interview with the Vice-Provost, and it made an impression upon me that all the intervening years have neither dimmed nor erased.

My Last Night in Trinity

It was to be my last night in Old Trinity, and we resolved that the farewell should be a solemn one. Mansfield, one of the wildest young fellows in the regiment, had vowed that the leave-taking should be commemorated by some very decisive and open expression of our feelings, and had already made some progress in arrangements for blowing up the great bell, which had more than once obtruded upon our morning convivialities; but he was overruled by his more discreet associates, and we at length assumed our places at table, in the midst of which stood a *hecatomb* of all my college equipments – cap, gown, bands, etc. A funeral pile of classics was arrayed upon the hearth, surmounted by my 'Book on the Cellar,' and a punishment-roll waved its length, like a banner over the doomed heroes of Greece and Rome.

It is seldom that any very determined attempt to be gay *par excellence* has a perfect success, but certainly, upon this evening ours had. Songs, good stories, speeches, toasts, bright visions of the campaign before us, the wild excitement which such a meeting cannot be free from, gradually, as the wine passed from hand to hand, seized upon all, and about four in the morning, such was the uproar we caused, and so terrific the noise of our proceedings, that the accumulated force of porters, sent one by one to demand admission, was now a formidable body at the door; and Mike at last came in to assure us that the Bursar, the most dread official of all collegians, was without, and insisted, with a threat of his heaviest displeasure, in case of refusal, that the door should be opened.

A committee of the whole house immediately sat upon the question, and it was at length resolved, *nemine contradicente*, that the request should be complied with. A fresh bowl of punch, in honour of our expected guest, was immediately concocted, a new broil put on the gridiron, and, having seated ourselves with as great a semblance of decorum as four bottles a man admits of, Curtis, the junior captain, being most drunk, was deputed to receive the Bursar at the door, and introduce him to our august presence.

Mike's instructions were that, immediately on Dr Stone, the Bursar's, entering, the door was to be slammed to, and none of his followers admitted. This done, the doctor was to be ushered in, and left to our own polite attentions.

A fresh thundering from without scarcely left time for any further deliberation; and at last Curtis moved towards the door, in execution of his mission.

'Is there anyone there?' said Mike in a tone of most unsophisticated innocence, to a rapping that, having lasted three quarters of an hour, threatened now to break in the panel. 'Is there anyone there?'

'Open the door this instant – the Senior Bursar desires you – this instant.'

'Sure it's night, and we're all in bed,' said Mike.

'Mr Webber – Mr O'Malley,' said the Bursar, now boiling with indignation, 'I summon you in the name of the Board, to admit me.'

'Let the gemman in,' hiccupped Curtis; and, at the same instant, the heavy bars were withdrawn, and the door opened, but so sparingly as with difficulty to permit the passage of the burly figure of the Bursar.

Forcing his way through, and regardless of what became of the rest, he pushed on vigorously through the ante-chamber, and before Curtis could perform his functions of usher, stood in the midst of us. What were his feelings at the scene before him, heaven knows. The number of figures in uniform at once betrayed how little his jurisdiction extended to the great mass of the company, and he immediately turned towards me.

'Mr Webber – '

'O'Malley, if you please, Mr Bursar,' said I, bowing with most ceremonious politeness.

'No matter, sir; *avcades ambo*, I believe.'

'Both archdeacons,' said Melville, translating, with a look of withering contempt upon the speaker.

The doctor continued, addressing me: 'May I ask, sir, if you believe yourself possessed of any privilege for converting this university into a common tavern?'

'I wish to heaven he did,' said Curtis; 'capital tap your old Commons would make.'

'Really, Mr Bursar,' replied I, modestly, 'I had begun to flatter myself that our little innocent gaiety had inspired you with the idea of joining our party.'

'I humbly move that the old cove in the gown do take the chair,' sang out one. 'All who are of this opinion say "Aye." ' A perfect yell of ayes followed this. 'All who are of the contrary say "No." The ayes have it.'

Before the luckless doctor had a moment for thought, his legs were lifted from under him, and he was jerked, rather than placed, upon a chair, and put sitting upon the table.

'Mr O'Malley, your expulsion within twenty-four hours – '

'Hip, hip, hurra, hurra, hurra,' drowned the rest; while Power, taking off the doctor's cap, replaced it by a foraging cap, very much to the amusement of the party.

'There is no penalty the law permits of that I shall not – '

'Help the doctor,' said Melville, placing a glass of punch in his unconscious hand.

'Now for a "Viva la Compagnie!" ' said Telford, seating himself at the piano, and playing the first bars of that well-known air, to which, in our meetings, we were accustomed to improvise a doggerel in turn:

'I drink to the graces, Law, Physic, Divinity,
                    Viva la Compagnie!
And here's to the worthy old Bursar of Trinity,
                    Viva la Compagnie!'

'Viva, viva la va!' etc., were chorused with a shout that shook the old walls, while Power took up the strain:

> 'Though with lace caps and gowns they look so like asses,
> > Viva la Compagnie!
> They'd rather have punch than the springs of Parnassus,
> > Viva la Compagnie!
> What a nose the old gentleman has, by the way,
> > Viva la Compagnie!
> Since he smelt out the devil from Botany Bay,[1]
> > Viva la Compagnie!'

Words cannot give even the faintest idea of the poor Bursar's feelings while these demoniacal orgies were enacting around him. Held fast in his chair by Lechmere and another, he glowered on the riotous mob around like a maniac, and astonishment that such liberties could be taken with one in his situation seemed to have surpassed even his rage and resentment; and every now and then a stray thought would flash across his mind that we were mad – a sentiment which, unfortunately, our conduct was but too well calculated to inspire.

'So you're the morning lecturer, old gentleman, and have just dropped in here in the way of business; pleasant life you must have of it,' said Casey, now by far the most tipsy man present.

'If you think, Mr O'Malley, that the events of this evening are to end here – '

'Very far from it, doctor,' said Power; 'I'll draw up a little account of the affair for *Saunders*. They shall hear of it in every corner and nook of the kingdom.'

'The Bursar of Trinity shall be a proverb for a good fellow that loveth his lush,' hiccupped out Fegau.

'And if you believe that such conduct is academical – ' said the doctor, with a withering sneer.

'Perhaps not,' lisped Melville, tightening his belt; 'but it's devilish convivial – eh, doctor?'

'Is that like him?' said Moreton, producing a caricature, which he had just sketched.

'Capital – very good – perfect. McCleary shall have it in his window by noon today,' said Power.

At this instant some of the combustibles disposed among the rejected habiliments of my late vocation caught fire, and squibs, crackers, and detonating shots went off on all sides. The Bursar, who had not been deaf to several hints and friendly suggestions about setting fire to him, blowing him up, etc., with one vigorous spring burst from his antagonists, and, clearing the table at a bound, reached the floor. Before he could be seized, he had gained the door, opened it, and was away. We gave chase, yelling like so many devils; but wine and punch, songs and speeches, had done their work, and more than one among the pursuers measured his length upon the pavement; while the terrified Bursar, with the speed of terror, held on his way, and gained his chambers, by about twenty yards in advance of Power and Melville, whose pursuit only ended when the oaken panel of the door shut them out from their victim. One loud cheer beneath his window served for our farewell to our friend, and we returned to my rooms. By this time a regiment of those classic functionaries, yclept porters, had assembled around the door, and seemed bent upon giving battle in honour of their maltreated ruler; but Power explained to them, in a neat speech, replete with Latin quotations, that their cause was a weak one, and that we were more than their match, and finally proposed to them to finish the punch-bowl – to which we were really incompetent – a motion that met immediate acceptance; and old Duncan, with his helmet in one hand, and a goblet in the other, wished me many happy days, and every luck in this life, as I stepped from the massive archway, and took my last farewell of Old Trinity.

Should any kind reader feel interested as to the ulterior course assumed by the Bursar, I have only to say that the terrors of the 'Board' were never fulminated against me, harmless and innocent as I should have esteemed them. The threat of giving publicity to the entire proceedings by the papers, and the dread of figuring in a caricature, were too much for the worthy doctor, and he took the wiser course, under the circumstances, and held his peace about the matter.

1. Botany Bay was the slang name given by college men to one of the squares of the college.

CHARLES KICKHAM

1825–1882

Charles Kickham, novelist, poet, and Fenian, was the son of a draper in Mullinahone, a small town in Tipperary. When Sir Charles Gavan Duffy and Thomas Davis started the *Nation* newspaper, in 1845, he was just twenty – the age when most men begin to form their opinions. The impassioned prose and verse of 'Young Ireland' found him a ready listener, and prepared him to take, together with his kinsman, John O'Mahoney, a prominent part in the attempted insurrection of '48. He was the leading spirit in the Confederate Club at Mullinahone, and after the collapse at Ballingarry, a little way from where he lived, he lay in hiding for a time. Soon after, he worked earnestly in the Tenant-Right League, and when that failed gave up all faith in legal agitation, and became one of the leaders of the Fenian movement. John O'Leary, T C Luby, and Charles Kickham were the triumvirate appointed to control its action in Ireland. In 1865 he was arrested, and sentenced to fourteen years' penal servitude. He had always had wretched health, and partly on this account was released in four years. He returned to Ireland, and lived there until his death at Blackrock, in 1882.

He was the most lovable of men. Women and children seem especially to have been attached to him. Some one asked him what did he miss most in gaol. 'Children, women, and fires,' he answered. One of the touching things in Kickham's character was an ever-present love for his native town; its mountains and its rivers are often referred to in his writings. A few months before his death, a friend found him gazing intently at the picture of a cow in a Dublin gallery. 'It is so like an old cow at Mullinahone,' he said. I have seen an unpublished poem of his written in gaol, in which he recalled watching from a bridge at his native place 'the sunset fading' away as though 'quenched by the dew.'

He bore cheerfully from his fourteenth or fifteenth year a burden of partial deafness and blindness, caused by an explosion of a flask of powder. His sentence had to be announced to him through an ear-trumpet, and both deafness and blindness were greatly increased by imprisonment.

Kickham's three novels, 'Salley Kavanagh,' 'Knocnagow,' and 'For the Old Land,' are devoted to one subject – a conscientious, laborious study of Irish life and Irish wrongs. 'Salley Kavanagh,' the most impassioned and direct, was written before his imprisonment, the others after. One feels through all he wrote that in him were much humour and character-describing power of wholly Celtic kind, but marred by imperfect training. His books are put together in a haphazard kind of way – without beginning, middle, or end. His ballads are much more perfect than his stories. 'Blind Sheehan,' and 'She Dwelt beside the Anner,' will last for many a long day yet.

THE PIG-DRIVING PEELERS [1]

By CHARLES KICKHAM

He had just quickened his pace, lest the patient might go away
under the impression that he had gone some distance from
home, and the poor fellow's hand was in so bad a state, and the
walk from the mountain was so long, it wouldn't do to
disappoint him, Rody thought, when three long-legged, wild-
looking pigs rushed past him at full gallop. Turning round, he
saw two policemen running breathlessly after the pigs, greatly
encumbered by their rifles. There was a shallow pool of mud at
the turn of the road, a hundred yards or so farther on, into
which the three wild pigs plunged and commenced rooting
with all their might.

'For heaven's sake, as they have stopped at last, let us take a
little rest,' said Acting-Constable Finucan – who was a slender-
waisted and military-looking young man, with well-oiled hair
and whiskers, – just as they had come up with Rody Flynn.

'I wouldn't take a five-pound note to go through the same
hardships again,' returned Sub-Constable Joe Sproul, letting
himself fall on his back against the slanting fence of Rody
Flynn's field, crushing numberless primroses, and pushing his
head under the hawthorns on the top, feeling the coolness
pleasant to his heated face.

A tall figure, in whitish cord knee-breeches and long-tailed
blue body-coat, caught his eye near the next turn of the road.
It was Sammy Sloane's clever rival, Murty Magrath, who, no

doubt, had been out on business that morning, like Sammy himself, to soothe in some measure his irritation at the turn affairs had taken in regard to the election of a fit and proper person to represent the county in the Imperial Parliament of Great Britain and Ireland.

Murty Magrath, who had been loitering at the turn of the road, as soon as he saw that he was observed, moved on at an ordinary walking pace, and bade Rody Flynn and the policemen the time of day very civilly, passing the forefinger of his right hand, while he spoke, all round his unusually long neck, inside the high white cravat which covered the long neck up to the ears, and seemed to press uncomfortably upon his windpipe.

'What o'clock might it be?' Murty asked, in the most innocent and natural way imaginable, as if the question had been suggested by the watch-key which the military-looking acting-constable managed to display below his belt.

'A quarter to two,' the acting-constable replied, having, with much trouble, got his Geneva watch from the fob of his tight-fitting trousers.

'Good God!' exclaimed Joe Sproul, getting his head from under the hedge, and staring in amazement at his superior officer, 'you said it was only eleven when we had the misfortune to meet these three devils. How far is it from the cross beyond the second hill?' he asked, turning to Rody Flynn. 'It seems we took two hours and three quarters to come from that.'

' 'Tis about three miles,' was the reply; 'ye must walk mighty slow.'

'Walk!' said Joe Sproul, getting upon his legs with a groan, like a man very bad with the rheumatism; 'the devil a walk! 'Twas all running and tumbling. I never saw the like of it,' continued the sub-constable solemnly, as he buttoned up his jacket, 'That black pig must have an "open sesame," for d – n the gate along the whole way that didn't fly open the minute he pointed his nose at it.' Rody Flynn chuckled, but Murty Magrath passed his finger between his white cravat and his windpipe, and looked innocently unconscious as he asked Rody Flynn was he coming home.

'I am,' said Rody, stepping out to keep up with the policeman, with whom he seemed disposed to be companionable.

The three lean pigs, with an abrupt grunt, rushed out of the pool of mud and stood in line across the road, as if determined to defend the pass against all comers. Joe Sproul fell' back a step, and clutching his rifle, dropped upon one knee and 'prepared for cavalry,' without waiting for the word of command from his superior officer.

'Begob, it is dangerous,' muttered Murty Magrath, thrusting all his four fingers between his cravat and his windpipe. 'Let us non-combatants stand aside.'

'Hush-h-h!' said Joe Sproul, advancing cautiously for a yard or two.

But the three lean pigs stood firm, with their snouts pointed to the enemy.

'I'll show 'em the cold steel,' said Joe Sproul, drawing his sword, but never for a second removing his eye from the three pigs. The flash of the cold steel had the desired effect, for the three lean pigs wheeled round with another abrupt grunt, and scampered off in the way they should go.

'They're Glenmoynan pigs,' Murty Magrath remarked, as the party moved on again. 'They seem to breed for speed and endurance in Glenmoynan. Look at the limbs of that black fellow. Did you ever see such bone and muscle? Not an ounce of idle flesh. 'Tis quite different down here. The trouble you'd have here,' Murty Magrath observed feelingly, turning to the military-looking acting-constable, who was showing symptoms of feebleness about the knees, 'the trouble you'd have down here is to make them walk at all. There's a very gentlemanly herd of pigs about Shannaclough,' added Murty Magrath impressively, turning to Rody Flynn, as if for corroboration of the assertion.

'Well, there's a great change both in pigs and people in regard of walking,' said Rody Flynn. 'I remember when every man and every pig walked to the fair of Cloughbeg as a matter of course. Now both man an' pig must drive – even coming into our own little market.'

'Yes,' returned Murty Magrath, 'you won't find a more gentlemanly herd of pigs in Ireland. They take the world easy, and are always contented so long as their bellies are full. But if you put the Glenmoynan pigs in a coach they wouldn't be satisfied.'

'Did you see that!' exclaimed Sub-Constable Joseph Sproul, in amazement. 'Isn't it just as I said – "open sesame"?'

'Go, turn 'em back,' said Acting-Constable Finucan, faintly.

'That's an intelligent fellow,' Murty Magrath remarked, when Joe Sproul had started off to drive the three lean pigs out of a ploughed field, the gate of which had yielded to a push of the black one's nose. 'He read "Ali Baba and the Forty Thieves." The police are nearly all reading men now, and, as a consequence, are more wide-awake and up to everything, and capable of performing their duties. The police are a most useful and intelligent body of men.'

The acting-constable glanced at the speaker, noting his high white cravat, his long-tailed blue body-coat, whitish cord breeches, and light gray stockings, and said to himself that this well-spoken man must be a respectable school-master. Joe Sproul, unconscious of the eulogy of which he was the subject, pursued the three lean pigs through the ploughed field, sinking ankle-deep in the rich loam, and stumbling at every step, till, as he himself declared, he became quite dizzy, and thought the ploughed field was rolling and tumbling around him like the sea. Three times did he succeed in bringing his tormentors back to the gate, and as often did they – always led by the black one – double back upon him, one rushing to the right, one to the left, and the black one out between his legs – all three meeting again, with every sign of mutual satisfaction, in the very middle of the ploughed field.

When this manoeuvre had been successfully executed for the third time, in spite of a sharp thrust of the rifle muzzle into the snout of the ringleader, Joe Sproul sat down in despair upon the soft clay, muttering that it was too much for 'human nature.'

'You don't understand pigs,' said Murty Magrath, craning his long neck over the fence, and making as much room as possible for his windpipe in the white cravat.

'Don't I?' muttered Joe Sproul, sulkily.

'Can't you say hurrish! hurrish! bogh! bogh! to 'em – like a Christian,' said Murty Magrath reproachfully, but mildly.

'Well, I'll try,' returned Sproul, submissively, getting up from the ground, pressing his knuckles against his spine, and making up his mind for an inevitable attack of lumbago.

'Hurrish! hurrish! bogh! bogh!' cried the sub-constable, as earnestly and persuasively as he could to them, and after another long run he had these extraordinary animals near the gate once more.

To his great relief they condescended to pass out this time, and Joe Sproul resumed his place by the side of his superior officer, panting and gasping for breath.

'Ah!' sighed Sproul, 'when my mother's first cousin, the head-constable, came to my father to get leave for me to "join," and told the poor old man that I'd have a "gentleman's life" – how little he or I thought 'twould ever come to this.'

'The police have their hardships as well as the rest of us,' Murty Magrath remarked to Rody Flynn. 'I believe the Queen herself and the rest of the royal family have their troubles. There's no wan without 'em in this ugly world. To my own personal knowledge, Barrister Howley himself has his cares, and so has the Clerk of the Peace, and the Sub-Sheriff.'

'Nothin' to do but walk up and down,' continued Joe Sproul, recalling his early dreams. 'Your boots shinin' an' the heels soundin' on the curb-stone. Pintin' your baton to a dung-heap an' sayin' "Take that out o' that" an' findin' it gone when you'd come again. Comin' to a row when 'twould be over, an' runnin' the fellow in that you'd known 'ud go quiet. Keepin' your cap on in the court-house, and calling "Silence" whenever you'd like. Standin' at the corner with a little varnished cane in your hand, admired by the young women, gentle an' simple; goin' occasionally to a dance in coloured clothes, an' given' sixpence to the fiddler.'

'Sperited!' remarked Murty Magrath to Rody Flynn, and with an admiring glance at the speaker, who went on without heeding the interruption.

'Learnin' the key-bugle; brushin' your hair; sittin' on the seat outside the barrack door, with your legs stretched straight, your heels together, an' your toes turned out – readin' wan of Bulwer's.'

'What did I tell you?' exclaimed Murty Magrath in a suppressed 'aside' to Rody Flynn. 'I knew he was a readin' man. Ah! there's nothing like literature to smarten up a policeman. There's no blinkin' the readin' policeman; he's equal to anything. No use tryin' to come round him. When I see a Bo – ahem! – a member of the constabulary on the table, the first thing I ask myself is, "Is he a readin' man?" I won't have long to wait before I know whether he is or not; for if he be a readin' man he'll be sure to speak of the people sometimes as the "mob" and sometimes as the "civilians." The minute I hear the "civilians," I say to myself no danger of him on cross-examination. That,' continued Murty Magrath, turning to the sub-constable, 'that is a truthful and most beautiful description you have given us of the rural policeman's paradise. No man but a readin' man could do it.'

'But what's the reality?' rejoined Joe Sproul, suddenly halting and looking Murty Magrath straight in the face.

The whole party stood still. The genteel acting-constable dropped the butt of his rifle on the ground, glad of the chance of taking a rest. Rody Flynn, surprised into seriousness, thrust his hands into his coat pockets, looking up expectantly into the half-indignant, half-lugubrious countenance of the sub-constable, who also grounded arms, and leant upon his rifle. Murty Magrath made room for his windpipe, with a look of profound gravity and deep and respectful sympathy stamped upon every lineament of his thin, pale face.

'What's the reality?' repeated Joe Sproul, pressing his left hand upon his forehead for a moment, and then letting it drop again to the muzzle of his rifle. 'I know what still-huntin' in the mountains of Donegal is,' he resumed. 'I know what it is to be on the broad of my back in Sandy-row, with the Orangeman dancing on my stomach, whistling "Lillibulero," an' keeping time with his feet. That's a tinker's wife in Limerick,' said Joe Sproul, raising his upper lip with his forefinger and exhibiting two broken front teeth. 'A blow of a tin kettle,' he added, turning to Rody Flynn. 'I'll never forget the sound of that tin kettle. 'Twas like fifty thousand cannons. The sun was flashing on it, an' I thought the skull flew off my head in a blaze of lightnin'. An' just look at this,' said Joe Sproul, taking off his cap and tapping his poll. 'That's a *memento mori* of Cappawhite.'

'Blood-an'-ounk-adeers!' exclaimed Murty Magrath, making a step backwards and raising his hands in astonishment. 'He's a Latinist!'

'I know what hairbreadth escapes mean,' continued the sub-constable, gloomily, but proudly. 'Movin' accidents by flood an' field are not incomprehensible to me; I had to wade up to my belly through a bog, in the Donegal campaign. But,' added Joe Sproul, impressively, 'may I never get my V's – ' The awfulness of this asseveration seemed to startle the military-looking Acting-Constable Finucan from the state of lassitude and general collapse into which he was fast getting, as, with his cap pulled over his brows, he rested droopingly upon his rifle. Acting-Constable Finucan looked earnestly up at his comrade, who, with his clenched hand raised as if he were about to fling something with all his might against the ground, repeated the startling words a second time, looking defiance at his horrified superior officer. 'That I may never get my V's,' said Joe Sproul, 'if I have not gone through more hardships this blessed day since five minutes past eleven A.M. by Finucan's Geneva, to the present instant, between the Cross of Glenmoynan an' that wooden gate, than all the ordeals of my whole existence put together an' rolled into wan, owing to the perverse divilry of that black pig. 'Twas all his doin'. He was the planner and the leader – that was obvious. The other two were comparatively civilized an' incapable of such devices. The Orangeman was an archangel; the four-year-old a philanthropist; the tinker's wife a lamb, a dove, a goddess of chastity and meekness,' added Joe Sproul, at a loss for a moment for a suitable cap for his climax, 'contrasted with that black pig.' He was going to say 'compared,' but substituted 'contrasted' – strongly emphasized – as the more forcible expression. Having relieved his feelings by this outburst, Sub-Constable Sproul shouldered his rifle and resumed his march, looking neither to the right nor to the left till he came to a heap of bog-mould on the side of 'Casey's forge.' The three pigs were peacefully reposing upon the bog-mould close together, the black one in the middle.

'Look at 'em!' exclaimed Joe Sproul, in amazement. 'Snorin' like lambs! Ah,' he added, spitefully, presenting his rifle, and taking aim at the black pig's forehead. 'How I'd like to send a "conical" through him!'

'Drive them on,' said the acting-constable, faintly, ' 'tis very late.'

'Well, draw,' returned Joe Sproul. 'Let 'em see the steel, or they'll run back again. Hush!'

The three pigs got up quietly enough, and trotted on without showing the least sign of ill-humour.

'Well,' Murty Magrath observed, consolingly, 'so far as the job in hands is concerned, you're not like the young bears at any rate; your troubles are behind you. The priest's gate is the only gate between you and the Pound now; and 'tis fifty to one it will be shut and bolted. "Open sesame" may do for a gad or even a latch, but not for a bolt.'

'Ye're all right,' added Rody Flynn, 'if they don't rush into Bully's Acre, and get into the river.'

'Is the river deep?' Acting-Constable Finucan asked, with a shudder.

'No,' Rody Flynn replied, encouragingly. 'There's not six inches of water in it at present. But there's a good deal of sink.'

Acting-Constable Finucan looked down at his high-heeled stylish boots, plastered all over with clay and mud, and groaned.

'What did you mean by saying I didn't understand pigs?' Joe Sprout asked, darting an indignant glance at Murty Magrath, in the corner of whose eye he saw something he did not like at all.

'I thought,' returned Murty mildly, 'that you relied too much on compulsion. Compulsion is effective when judiciously applied, and at the proper moment. But there are times when nothing will tell upon a pig like persuasion. And, to be candid with you,' added Murty Magrath, lifting his chin out of his high cravat, 'I thought I noticed a deficiency of generalship in you that surprised me in a reading man.'

'Would you want me to take 'em in my arms?' Joe Sproul asked indignantly.

'By no means,' replied Murty Magrath. 'I wouldn't have you stoop to that. Nor even to twisting your hand in the tail and pulling it, pretending 'twas the other way you wanted 'em to go. That may do well enough for a spalpeen, but not for a reading man. But to keep quiet and let them have their own way during paroxysms; to leave them under the impression that their conduct is a matter of indifference to you; to adopt a decisive course at the critical moment – and to know when to say "hurrish! hurrish! bogh! bogh!" That's the way to manage pigs.'

'I've had thirteen years' official experience of pigs,' broke in Sub-Constable Sproul with dignity – drawing himself up to his full height and throwing back his shoulders – 'besides being intimately acquainted with them in my own father's house since before I was able to walk.'

'There's pigs an' pigs in it,' rejoined Murty Magrath blandly. 'But wait till you know the Glenmoynan pigs as well as I do, and the correctness of my views will be self-evident to you.'

'If that black pig be a typical pig,' interrupted Sub-Constable Sproul, 'if he is not a *rara avis* – *a lusus naturae* – then all I can say is, that I may be promoted before this day week to the most distant station in Kerry, where the only earthly motive for the exercise of either shoe-brush, clothes-brush, or hair-brush is a possible surprise from the sub-inspector; where promotion would be an anachronism, and where you are perpetually reminded, either by sight or sound, of that insulting lyric, "The Bansha Peelers Went Out One Day." That's all,' Joe Sproul added decisively.

'I knew the author of "The Peeler and the Goat" well,' Murty Magrath remarked gravely, 'one Darby Ryan of Bansha. A very decent man. Now I wonder some genius never tried his hand on "The Peeler and the Pig." I can't see why a pig is not as fit a subject for poetry as a goat.

    ' "Oh, mercy, sir!" replied the goat,
      "And let me tell my story Oh,
   I am no Rogue or Ribbonman,
     A Croppy, Whig, or a Tory Oh."

'That's neat, but why not –

    ' "Mercy, sir," replied the pig,
      "Just wait till I my tail unfold;
   I'm not an Orangeman at all,
     Nor a tinker's wife, nor a four-year-old."

If Darby Ryan was alive, or if his mantle had fallen on any of his posterity, I'd suggest to him to try what he could do with the peeler and the pig. Don't say it would be trying to make a silk purse of a pig's ear. Not at all. There's as much poetry in a pig any day as in a goat.

> "Meg-geg-geg-geg, let go my leg,
>   Or I'll puck you with my horn Oh." '

'Ah!' exclaimed Murty Magrath, tapping his forehead, and then holding up his finger, after the manner of the poet Moore's statue in College Street, Dublin, 'there is the difficulty! I realize now why Darby Ryan never tried his hand on "The Peeler and the Pig." I thought it might be the horns and the head that constituted the goat's superiority as a subject for poetry. But no, it is the language. The man was never born,' added Murty Magrath with a melancholy shake of the head, 'who could put the pig's vernacular in print, and more's the pity. But for that one disadvantage there's not an animal in creation that has more poetry in him than a pig. I don't expect you to coincide in my opinion,' said Murty Magrath, observing Joe Sprout's eyes fixed suspiciously upon him. 'You should be more or less than man to be unprejudiced in your present state of mind. But if you reflect upon what I say in cooler moments you'll find I'm right.'

'Do you belong to this part of the country?' Joe Sproul asked.

'Yes,' was the reply. 'I was bred, born, and reared in that little village whose smoke you can see peacefully curling, if you move to this side of the road.'

' 'Tis like a dream to me that I saw you before,' muttered the sub-constable, eyeing the tall figure beside him suspiciously, 'but I can't remember where. Do you smoke?'

'I take a blast now and then,' said Murty Magrath. 'There's no law against it that I ever heard of.'

They walked on in silence for another while, Rody Flynn, who had dropped a little behind presenting an admirable illustration of laughter, holding both his 'sides.' The silence was broken by the exclamation, 'Hulloo!' from Murty Magrath. 'Did you see that?' he continued, turning round to Rody Flynn, who had just wiped the tears from his eyes and become comparatively calm. 'Wasn't it beautifully done?'

'Ponsonby's white greyhound couldn't do it better,' said Rody Flynn.

'Like a steeplechase,' rejoined Murty Magrath. 'And see how beautifully they're keeping together across the field, the black leading and the other two well up. Ah,' continued he, turning to the two policemen, 'when you come to know the Glenmoynan pig ye'll admire his speed and his bottom. Aren't they as fresh now as they war the minute ye picked 'em up?' Murty asked with enthusiasm 'And ye'll see 'em thrust their snouts through the Pound gate – when ye have 'em in – without a hair turned and not the least blown.'

'What's to be done?' said Joe Sproul, gasping for breath.

'Go turn them back,' replied Acting-Constable Finucan, absently.

'Heavens and earth! What do you mean?' shouted Joe Sproul, breaking into open insubordination, and looking as if there and then he would dash his rifle against the ground, and trample upon the jacket in which he once fondly hoped he was to have a gentleman's life.

'You cannot say,' returned the genteel acting-constable reproachfully, 'that I did not do my full share of the day's duty.'

'If they take the next fence,' interrupted Murty Magrath, who seemed to be getting uneasy at the turn things were taking, 'they'll be into a magistrate's turnips.'

'Well,' said the sub-constable, calmed by the fear of a 'report,' 'will you hold my rifle and my belt an' I'll see what I can do?'

The acting-constable hung the sub-constable's belt on his arm, and, with a rifle in each hand, watched his comrade pursuing the three pigs through the large field, the fence of which they had cleared in a manner that the winner of the 'Rock Stakes' might have envied. Unencumbered as he was, and having the firm greensward under his feet, Joe Sproul found his chase almost exhilarating, compared with that through the ploughed field; and the three pigs, seeming conscious of the altered state of things, cantered back to the road and again cleared the fence in a manner that called forth the plaudits of Murty Magrath, and made Rody Flynn's round black eyes sparkle like diamonds.

'Hulloo!' exclaimed Murty Magrath, 'the black fellow is facin' this way.'

The military-looking acting-constable stood paralyzed in the middle of the road, with a rifle in each hand. He opened his mouth till the chin-strap of his cap got into it like a bit – giving him the look of an over-ridden and used-up steed – as the black pig came on at a fearful pace, ignoring obstruction. The acting-constable stood spell-bound, and never moved a muscle – except those connected with the under jaw – till the black pig had rushed past him. Then the acting-constable turned 'right about face,' and tore frantically down the road in pursuit of the black pig, a rifle in each hand, and Joe Sproul's sword swinging from his arm and striking him behind and before about the legs.

'I thought it wasn't in him,' said Murty Magrath. 'He can put on a quiet spurt. He's gainin' on him. If he can keep it up he'll get before him in less than no time.' The black pig seemed to think so too, or he may have suddenly remembered that his two companions were gone the other way. Not sharing Sub-Constable Joe Sproul's prejudices, we don't care to suggest diabolism pure and simple on the part of the black pig. We content ourselves with simply recording the fact – without stopping to inquire into motives – that just as Acting-Constable Finucan was straining every nerve for a final and successful spurt, the black pig wheeled round without a moment's warning, and, rushing right against Acting-Constable Finucan's shins, 'whipped the legs from under him,' as Rody Flynn afterwards expressed it, when describing the catastrophe to his friend Davy Lacy, and brought that promising officer flat upon his face, with a terrible crash.

'If the rifles were loaded I'd feel uneasy,' Murty Magrath remarked.

'I was afraid he was hurt,' said Rody Flynn, looking relieved on seeing the acting-constable rise to his feet, and gaze all around the horizon as if he were making astronomical observations.

'Let the pig pass,' said Murty Magrath, as the black pig trotted leisurely back to join his companions, looking quite innocent and showing no sign of excitement whatever. 'They'll get on all right now,' he continued. 'I was getting a little uneasy for fear they'd give it up when the pigs got into the field. But 'tis all right now. They're d—d decent fellows.' Unfortunately Joe Cooney left the gate open when returning with Mr O'Keeffe's horse from the forge, and didn't mind closing it, when riding out again an hour or two later.

'I suppose that is the priest's gate,' said Joe Sproul.

'Yes,' Rody Flynn replied.

The black pig seemed to have overheard the question. He held up his nose as if to inhale the odour of the lilac blossoms, and then moved sideways to the gate, pushing it open, and, waiting politely till his two companions had passed, walked leisurely up the avenue, and looked into the parlour window with rustic curiosity. It was plain he had never seen so fine a house as that in his life.

The priest and his nephew went outside the hall door, and stood on the steps, looking with some surprise at the three lean pigs, who, with their snouts in the air, seemed to be trying to count the windows in the front of the house.

'Let us leave 'em there and be d—d,' cried Joe Sproul.

'That's Sub-Inspector O'Keeffe's brother,' Murty Magrath remarked. 'And the parish priest is his uncle.'

The two policemen immediately marched up the avenue, keeping the step.

Rody Flynn and Murty Magrath walked on through the village street, the one stopping at his own house and the other continuing his way over the bridge.

The three pigs behaved very decently this time, and allowed themselves to be driven back to the gate and down the village street without demur. Joe Sproul wondered whether respect for the priest might have had anything to do with this gratifying and unexpected change of behaviour. If it had, and if it was to be his fate to remain long at the Gurthnabohill station, the sub-constable devoutly hoped that the parish priest of Shannaclough might soon pay a visit to that neighbourhood, and particularly to the townland of Glenmoynan.

'The little man is a cooper,' Joe Sproul remarked. 'That's a very nice little house he has. And I suppose that nice girl is his daughter. But I wonder what is that tall fellow? He's a tradesman I think.'

'I thought he might be a country school-master,' Acting-Constable Finucan replied. 'He reminded me of a picture I saw of a school-master in some magazine.'

'He's a bright fellow, whatever he is,' said Joe Sproul. 'But you couldn't be sure sometimes but he was humbuggin' you. Maybe 'twas in a picture I saw him before, with a pipe in his mouth an' his hat back on his poll. 'Twas runnin' in my mind, too, where did I see the little man. But now I remember – 'twas a picture I saw called "Mine Host of the Cherrytree," that was the dead image of him; when he was laughin' – which was mostly always – the other fellow was always serious,' mused Joe Sproul. 'But you'd see somethin' about the left cheek an' the corner of the eye that looked suspicious. Did you ever see anything like the change for the better in the pigs? There they're turnin' the right way of their own accord. Just as if they knew where they were goin', and hadn't the laste objection. I wish there was some change in the law with regard to the pigs,' Sub-Constable Sproul continued, as he and his comrade passed over the bridge. 'To let them have their own way altogether, or to reduce their number by taxation instead of the dogs. I see no use in taxin' dogs, except that, as a rule, now only wan at a time barks at you instead of two or three. Where's the advantage of that? I was never put to any trouble by a dog but once; an' there was a licence for that fellow. Very quare notions get into the head of Parliament. But if they'd tax the pigs 'twould be something creditable. That black fellow, in all probability, wouldn't be in existence today if he were taxed,' added Sub-Constable Sproul. 'There's reason in what the long fellow said about the peeler and the pig. The pig is our natural enemy, and not the goat. The goat is fiction. Why should a sensible man take offence at fiction? But the pig is reality. The pig is a stubborn fact. 'Tis the pig we ought to abominate, an' not the goat. 'Tis a mercy, as the long fellow remarked, that the pigs' vernacular is not spellable. If it was we'd never know an hour's peace. We wouldn't be let pass through a village in this peaceable manner if the pigs' vernacular could be put into a ballad. That chap with the ankles there,' said the sub-constable, scowling at Jacky, the cobbler, who was waiting all alone in Bully's Acre for school to break up, 'that fellow wouldn't be silent at the present moment if the pigs' vernacular could be put into print, like "meg-geg-a-geg." There's that much to be thankful for,' continued Joe Sproul with a grateful sign. 'But if agitation an' the force were not antagonistic an' incompatible – natural enemies in fact – I'd go in with all my heart an' soul for an agitation to abolish pigs; or at least to reduce the number by taxation, an' make dogs compulsory – if not muzzles.'

The tall man with the long neck enveloped in the white cravat was standing at the Pound gate. The three pigs passed mutely and reverentially with their noses close to the ground.

' 'Tis amazin',' Joe Sproul remarked, looking somewhat awestruck. 'I thought we'd have the divil to pay up and down the lane. But now you'd think 'twas into a cathedral, while the bishop was preachin', they were goin'. The Glenmoynan pigs must be a very peculiar race, for in all my experience I never met the like of 'em.'

'Thank ye,' said Murty Magrath, with a polite bow to the two policemen, as he handed a paper to the Pound-keeper, when the three pigs had passed in through the gate.

The two policemen stared at him.

'I always said,' continued Murty Magrath, complaisantly, 'that we never could get on without the Bo – ahem! – constabulary. A most useful body of men is the constabulary, especially now when, as a rule, they are readin' men.'

Joe Sproul opened his eyes wider while the military-looking acting-constable began to show signs of being frightened.

' "Open sesame," ' continued Murty Magrath, surveying Joe Sproul with bland admiration, 'satisfied me that you were a readin' man. And when you spoke of "wan of Bulwer's," I was sure of it. But I confess,' added Murty Magrath, fixing his eyes upon the ground and with a solemn movement of the head; 'I confess I was unprepared for the Latin. An uncle of my mother's,' Murty Magrath went on confidently, looking from one to the other of the dumbfounded constabulary officers, 'was a classical teacher. He took great pains to get some Latin into me. But I resisted. Like yourself,' he remarked, addressing himself specially to Joe Sproul, 'he relied too much upon compulsion. And I believe I always had a spice of the Glenmoynan pig in me; the devil wouldn't fatten me, or make me do anything I didn't like myself. But my mother's' uncle was a tough wan. Lord, what a kithouge he had!' exclaimed Murty Magrath, twisting his shoulders and wincing at the bare recollection of that classical left hand. 'And as for the rod, as he called it – but it was a compressed shillelagh – the essence of everything stinging was infused into that instrument. No matter how low down he'd hit you with that rod, you'd instantaneously feel it comin' into your throat; you'd be tryin' to swally something the minute that rod touched your person. Ah, wasn't there venom in it!'

The Pound-keeper grinned; but Joe Sproul and the acting-constable only stared.

'Well, he did whale a trifle of Lilly's Grammar into me,' Murty Magrath continued. ' 'Tis no very useful so far as I can see; but 'tis pleasing to the mind sometimes. When I saw them pigs trotting so elegant over the bridge, Lilly's Grammar came to my mind, and I said *Numquam sera est ad bonos mores via,* which means good manners on the road – to the Pound or elsewhere – is better late than never. And in like manner, when ye so kindly took charge of 'em at the Cross of Glenmoynan, I just got over the ditch for fear ye'd be anyway shy – I at once said *Nemo mortalium omnibus horis sapit,* which, as near as I can make out, is no mortal policeman is wise at all hours.'

'What are you?' Acting-Constable Finucan asked falteringly.

'A sheriff's officer,' was the reply, 'or, if you prefer the more commonly used term – a bailiff. The decree was only for one pound fifteen and fourpence halfpenny. But I thought it would be cruel to separate the creathers. So I seized the three.'

' 'Tis an awful sell,' said Acting-Constable Finucan, looking piteously into Joe Sproul's face.

'You're a man of few words,' said Murty Magrath, pleasantly. 'But don't tell me you're not a readin' man. I see "The Stories of Waterloo" in your eye. Tell the truth now, don't people call you captain, just as if they couldn't help it? Now if you volunteered the time of the Indian war, I'm lookin' at you,' continued Murty Magrath, shutting one eye, and fixing the other on the black pig, reposing in the far corner of the Pound, 'on the broad of your back on a sofy in the mess-room, smokin' a cigar. Or' – here Murty Magrath moved his feet genteelly, and turned half round, with an air and look which we think the word coquettish will best convey an idea of – 'all round the room you know; waltzin'. I'm sorry you didn't volunteer for India, though your loss to the constabulary would be felt. I hope,' Murty asked with concern, 'that fall on the heap of stones in the quarry didn't hurt you much?' Acting-Constable Finucan stooped down and rubbed his left shin. 'As for the fall on the road,' added Murty Magrath, 'I wouldn't mind that. A fall on the flat is nothing; you just feel upset; that's all. But that tumble in the quarry looked ugly.'

The tall bailiff had lit his pipe while delivering these last remarks, and now stood leaning against the Pound gate, puffing contemplatively with his hat back on his poll. He thrust his hands into his breeches pockets, and raised one shoulder up nearly to his ear. A light seemed to break upon Joe Sproul as he gazed upon the tall bailiff, who had undergone quite a metamorphosis in a moment.

'I remember now,' Joe Sproul muttered. ''Twasn't a picture. 'Twas you was sittin' on the lime-kiln while we were chasin' 'em round the quarry?'

''Twas,' was the reply. 'And d—n smart fellows ye are. 'Twas a pleasure to be looking at ye. Sure I might have known even then that ye were readin' men. That wary expression, "try 'em diagonally, as they won't go straight," taken in conjunction with the way ye got over the large heap, might have satisfied me that I had cultivated minds to reply upon.'

'You didn't give us much assistance,' said Joe Sproul.

'No,' replied Murty Magrath. 'I said I'd act magnanimously and leave ye all the credit. And I'm not sorry for it. It would be unworthy of a sheriff's officer, of thirty years' standing, to step in and rob ye of an iota of the glory. I leave such meanness to Sammy Sloane and the likes of him. He's a little Saxon without an idea in his head; knows nothing about pigs but to put a fat slice between two pieces of bread and chaw it. If it was him instead of me, ye couldn't talk of this day's work, as ye can now, of a winter's night, sittin' round the fire like the farmer's rosy children, when some gentle hand will tap at the bolted door, maybe to tell you that your friend the tinker's wife was sending some poor fellow's front teeth inside his shirt. But you didn't say whether yours went down,' said Murty Magrath, thrusting his finger inside his cravat. 'But don't suppose,' the bailiff added, 'that I want to deny that I am under an obligation to you. I am; and I acknowledge it. Good evenin' and safe home. I'll drop in to see ye the next day I am passing. You'll know by that time whether that black pig is very like a black swan, or only a common character in Glenmoynan.'

'Where did you pick up your Latin?' he asked, turning round after having walked half a dozen yards from the Pound gate.

'In the "Spellin' Book Superceded,"' replied Joe Sproul, evidently doubtful as to whether the tall bailiff was not after all a civil and sociable person.

''Twasn't whaled into you?' the tall bailiff inquired.

'No,' replied the sub-constable, 'Finucan and me studied the Latin and French phrases, of our own accord.'

'Ha! ye haven't the Glenmoynan pig in yer insides,' said the bailiff. 'There's nothing gives a young man confidence like a few Latin phrases, besides the comfort to the mind when a fellow feels cast down. Try it, and you'll find I'm right. The next time you make an ass of yourself just say *Nemo mortalium omnibus horis sapit*, and you'll find how comforting it is. But mind say sapit like a Christian,' added the bailiff, benevolently, 'and not say-pit, like Parson Latouch. And above all,' he continued imploringly, raising his hand and waving it there several times towards Joe Sproul, 'don't make a saw-pit of it. That's worse even than say-pit, for 'tis barbarous and would be uncommonly out of place in the mouth of an intelligent policeman whose teeth have met with accidents.'

Having delivered himself of this impressive lecture, Murty Magrath put his hands under his coat-tails and walked leisurely away, softly whistling 'The Peeler and the Goat.'

1. From 'For the Old Land'.

MISS ROSA MULHOLLAND

Miss Mulholland is the novelist of contemporary Catholic Ireland. She has not the square-built power of our older writers, Banim, Carleton, and their tribe, but has, instead, much fancy and style of a sort commoner in our day than theirs, and a distinction of feeling and thought peculiar to herself.

THE HUNGRY DEATH

By ROSA MULHOLLAND

I

It had been a wild night in Innisbofin, an Irish island perched far out among Atlantic breakers, as the bird flies to Newfoundland. Whoever has weathered an ocean hurricane will have some idea of the fury with which the tempest assaults and afflicts such lonely rocks. The creatures who live upon them, at the mercy of the winds and waves, build their cabins low, and put stones on the roof to keep the thatch from flying off on the trail of Mother Carey's chickens; and having made the sign of the cross over their threshold at night, they sleep soundly, undisturbed by the weird and appalling voices which have sung alike the lullaby and death-keen of all their race. In winter, rain or storm is welcome to rage round them, even though fish be frightened away, and food be scarce, but when wild weather encroaches too far upon the spring, then threats of the 'hungry death' are heard with fear in its mutterings.

Is any one to blame for this state of things? The people have a good landlord; but the greater part of the island is barren bog and rock. No shrub will grow upon it, and so fiercely is it swept by storm that the land by the northern and eastern coasts is only a picturesque wilderness, all life sheltering itself in three little thatched villages to the south. The sea is the treasury of the inhabitants, and no more daring hearts exist than those that fight these waves, often finding death in their jaws; but a want

369

of even the rudest piers as defence against the Atlantic makes the seeking of bread upon the waters a perilous, and often an entirely impossible, exploit.

Bofin is of no mean size, and has a large population. Light-hearted and frugal, the people feel themselves a little nation, and will point out to you with pride the storied interest of their island. In early ages it was a seat of learning, witness the ruins of St Coleman's school and church; in Elizabeth's day the handsome masculine queen, Grace O'Malley, built herself a fort on a knoll facing the glories of the western sky; and on the straggling rocks which form the harbour Cromwell raised those blackened walls, still welded into the rock and fronting the foam. The island has a church, a school, a store where meal, oil, soap, ropes, etc., can be had, except when contrary winds detain the hooker which plies to and from Galway with such necessaries.

Foreign sailors, weather-bound in Bofin, are welcomed, and invited to make merry. Pipers and fiddlers come and go, and when times are good are kept busy making music for dancing feet. Even when the wolf is within a pace of the door laughter and song will ring about his ears, so long as the monster can be beaten back by one neighbour from another neighbour's threshold. But there comes a day when he enters where he will, and the bones of the people are his prey.

Last night's was a spring storm, and many a 'Lord have mercy on us!' went up in the silent hours, as the flooding rain that unearths the seedlings was heard seething on the wind; yet Bofin wakened out of its nightmare of terror green and gay, birds carolling in a blue sky, and the ring of the boat-maker's hammer suggesting peace and prosperity.

Through the dazzling sunshine a girl came rowing herself in a small boat that darted rapidly along the water. The oars made a quick, pleasant thud on the air, the larks sang in the clouds, and the girl poured out snatches of a song of her own in a plaintive and mellow voice. The tune was wild and mournful;

the Irish words of the ever-recurring refrain might be freely translated thus:

> Fearful was her wooing,
>> Ululu!
> All her life undoing.
>> Ululu!
> When his face she sighted,
> Back she fell affrighted,
> Death and she were plighted,
>> Ululu!

A strange song for such a gay, glittering morning! Thud, thud, went the oars, and the girl's kerchief fell back from her head as the firm elastic figure swayed with the wholesome exercise. Never was a fairer picture of health, strength, and beauty. Her thick, dark-red hair filled with the sunshine as a sponge fills with water; her red-brown eyes seemed to emit sparks of fire as the shadows deepened round them in the strong light. Two little round dimples fixed at the corners of the proud curved mouth whispered a tale of unusual determination lying at the bottom of a passionate nature. There was nothing to account for her curious choice of a song this brilliant morning, except the love of dramatic contrasts that exists in some eager souls. Suddenly she shipped her oars, and sat listening to the waves lapping the edges of the seaweed-fringed cliffs. 'I thought I heard some one calling me,' she muttered, looking up and down with a slight shudder but a bold gaze – 'Brigid, Brigid, Brigid!' then, with a little laugh, she dipped her oars again, burst into a lively song, so reeling with merriment that it was wonderful how she found breath for it, and her boat flew along the glittering waves like a gull.

Above the broad, shelving, shingly beach within the harbour stood the school, the store, and some of the best dwellings on the island, and high and dry on the dreaming shingle the boat-maker was at work with a knot of gossips around him. The sky over their heads was a soft vivid blue; the brown-fringed rocks loomed against a sea almost too dazzling to look upon; the dewy green fields lay like scattered emeralds among the rocks and hollows.

'Lord look to us!' said a man in a sou'-wester hat, 'if the spring doesn't mend. Half my pratees was washed clane out o' the ground last night.'

'Whist, man, whist,' said the boat-maker cheerfully. 'Pick them up an' put them in again.'

'Bedad,' said an old fisherman, 'the fish has got down to the bottom of all etarnity. Ye might as well go fishin' for mermaids.'

'Aren't yez ashamed to grumble,' cried a hearty voice joining the group, 'an' sich a mornin' as this? I tell ye last night was the last o' the rain.'

'Ye have the hopes o' youth about ye, Coll Prendergast,' said the old fisherman, looking at the strong frame and smiling bronzed face of the young man before him. 'If yer words is not truth, it's the seaweed we'll be atin' afore next winther's out.'

'Faix, some of it doesn't taste so bad,' said Coll, laughing, 'an' a little of it dried makes capital tabaccy. But whist! if here isn't Brigid Lavelle, come all the way from West Quarter in her pretty canoe.'

The sound of oars had been heard coming steadily nearer, and suddenly Brigid's boat shot out from behind a mass of rock, making, with its occupant, such a picture on the glittering sea that the men involuntarily smiled as they shaded their eyes with their hands to look. Resting on her oars she smiled at them in return, while the sunshine gilded her perfect oval face, as brown as a berry, burnished the copper-hued hair rippling above her black, curved brows, and deepened the determined expression of her full red mouth. Her dress, the costume of the island, was only remarkable for the freshness and newness of its material – a deep crimson skirt of wool, with a light print bodice and short tunic, and a white kerchief thrown over the back of her head.

As she neared the shore Coll sprang into the water, drew her canoe close to the rocks, and, making it fast, helped her to land.

'That's a han'some pair,' said the old fisherman to the boat-maker. 'I hear their match is as good as made.'

'Coll's in luck,' said the other. 'A rich beauty is not for ivery man.'

'She's too proud, I'm thinking. Look at the airs of her now, an' him wet up to the knees in her sarvice.'

'Yer ould, man, an' ye forgot yer coortin'. Let the crature toss her head while she can.'

Brigid had proceeded to the store, where her purchases were soon made – a sack of meal, a can of oil, a little tea and sugar, and some white flour. The girl had a frown on her handsome brows as she did her business, and took but little notice of Coll, who busied himself gallantly with her packages. When all were stored in the boat, he handed her in, and stood looking at her, wondering if she would give him a smile in return for his attentions.

'Let me take the oars, Brigid. Ye'll be home in half the time.'

'No, thank ye,' she answered shortly. 'I'll row my own boat as long as I can.'

Coll smiled broadly, half amused and half admiring, and again sought for a friendly glance at parting, but in vain. The face that vanished out of his sight behind the cliff was cold and proud as though he had been her enemy. After he had turned and was striding up the beach the look that he had wanted to see followed him, shot through a rift in the rocks, where Brigid paused and peered with a tenderness in her eyes that altered her whole face. If Coll had seen that look this story might never have been written.

As the girl's boat sped past the cliffs towards home she frowned, thinking how awkward it was that she should have met Coll Prendergast on the beach. He must have known the errand that brought her to the store, and how dare he smile at her like that before he knew what answer she would give him?

Coll's uncle and Brigid's father had planned a match between the young people, and the match-making was to be held that night at Brigid's father's house. Therefore had she come early in the morning in her boat to the store, to buy provisions for the evening's entertainment. Obedience to her father had obliged her to do this, but her own strong will revolted from the proceeding. She was proud, handsome, and an heiress, and did not like to be so easily won.

Brigid's father was sitting at the fire – a consumptive-looking man, with a wistful and restless eye.

'Father, I have brought very little flour. The hooker hasn't got in.'

'Sorra wondher, an' sich storms. 'Tis late in the year for things to be this ways.'

Brigid arranged her little purchases on the dresser and sat down at the table, but her breakfast – a few roasted potatoes and mug of buttermilk – remained untasted before her.

'Father, isn't you an' me happy as we are? Why need I marry in sich a hurry?'

'Because a lone woman's better with a husband, my girl.'

'I'm not a lone woman. Haven't I got you?'

'Not for long, avourneen machree. I'm readyin' to go this good while.'

'But I will hold you back,' cried Brigid, passionately, throwing her strong arms around his neck.

'You can't, asthoreen. I'm wanted yonder, and it's time I was gettin' on with my purgatory. An' there's bad times comin', an' I will not let you face them alone.'

'I could pack up my bundles and be off to America,' said Brigid, stoutly, dashing away tears.

'I will not have you wanderin' over the world like a stray bird,' said the father, emphatically; and Brigid knew there was nothing more to be said.

Lavelle's prosperity appeared before the world in a great deal of clean whitewash outside the house, and an interior more comfortable than is usual on the island. The cabin consisted of two rooms – the kitchen, with earthen floor and heather-lined roof, roosting-place for cocks and hens, and with its dresser, old and worm-eaten, showing a fair display of crockery; and the best room, containing a bed, a few pictures on sacred subjects, some sea-shells on the chimney-piece, an ornamental tray, an old gun, and an ancient, time-blackened crucifix against the wall, this last having been washed ashore one morning after the wreck of a Spanish ship. This was the finest house in Bofin, and Tim Lavelle, having returned from seeing the world and married late in life, had settled down in it, and on the most fertile bit of land on the island. It was thought he had a stockingful of money in the thatch, which would of course be the property of his daughter; so no wonder if the handsome Brigid has grown up a little spoiled with the knowledge of her own happy importance.

As she went about her affairs this morning she owned to herself that she would not be sorry to be forced to be Coll's wife in spite of her pride. True, he had paid her less court hitherto than any other young man on the island, and she longed to punish him for that; but what would become of her if she saw him married to another? Oh, if they had only left the matter to herself she could have managed it so much better – could have plagued him to her heart's content, and made him anxious to win her by means of the difficulties she would have thrown in his way. Had Coll been as poor as he seemed to be, with nothing but his boat and fishing-tackle, she would have been easier to woo, for then eagerness to bestow on him the contents of that stocking in the thatch would have swept away the stumbling-block of her pride. But his uncle had saved some money, which was to be given to Prendergast on the day of his marriage with her. It was a made-up match like Judy O'Flaherty's, while Brigid's proud head was crazed on the subject of being loved for her love's sake alone.

'I'll have to give him my hand tonight,' she said, folding her brown arms, and standing straight in the middle of the room she had been dusting and decorating. 'I be to obey father, an' I'll shame nobody afore the neighbours. But match-makin' isn't marryin'; and if it was to break my heart an' do my death I'll find means to plague him into lovin' me yet.'

Having made this resolve, she let down her long hair, that looked dark bronze while she sat in the corner putting on her shoes, and turned to gold as she walked through a sunbeam crossing the floor, and having brushed it out and twisted it up again in a coil round her head, she finished her simple toilet and went out to the kitchen to receive her visitors.

The first that arrived was Judy O'Flaherty, an old woman with a smoke-dried face, who sat down in the chimney corner and lit her pipe. Judy was arrayed in a large patchwork quilt folded like a shawl, being too poor to indulge in the luxury of a cloak. But the quilt, made of red and white calico patches, was clean, and the cap on her head was fresh and neat.

'I give ye joy of Coll Prendergast,' said Judy heartily. 'Ye ought to be the glad girl to get sich a match.'

'Why ought I be glad?' asked Brigid, angrily. 'It's all as one may think.'

'Holy Mother, girl! don't be sendin' them red sparks out o' yer eyes at me. Where d' ye see the likes o' Coll, I'm askin', with his six feet if he's an inch, an' his eyes like the blue on the Reek afore nightfall!'

Brigid's heart leaped to hear him praised, and she turned away her face to hide the smile that curled her lips.

'An' yer match so aisy made for ye, without trouble to either o' ye. Not like some poor cratures, that have to round the world afore they can get one to put a roof over their heads or a bit in their mouths. It's me that knows. Sure wasn't I a wanderin' bein' doin' day's works in the mountains, and as purty a girl as you, Miss Brigid, on'y I hadn't the stockin' in the thatch, nor the good father to be settlin' for me. An' sore and tired an' spent I was when one night I heard a knock at the door o' the house I was workin' in, an' a voice called out: "Get up, Judy; here's a man come to marry you!" Maybe I didn't dress quick; an' who was there but a woman that knew my mother long ago, an' she had met a widow-man that wanted somebody to look after his childer. An' she brought him to me, an' wakened me out o' my sleep for fear he'd take the rue. An' we all sat o'r the fire for the rest o' the night to make the match, and in the first morning light we went down to Father Daly and got married. There's my marriage for ye, an' the rounds I had to get it, an' many a wan is like me. An' yet yer tossin' yer head at Coll, you that hasn't as much as the trouble o' bein' axed.'

The smile had gone off Brigid's face. This freedom from trouble was the very thing that troubled her. She would rather have had the excitement of being 'axed' a hundred questions. As they talked the sunshine vanished and the rain again fell in torrents. Brigid looked out of the door with a mischievous hope that the guests might be kept at home and the match-making postponed. Judy rocked herself and groaned: 'Oh, musha, the piatees, the piatees! Oh, Lord, look down with mercy on the poor!' then suddenly became silent and began telling her beads.

A slight lull in the storm brought the company in a rush to the door, with bursts of laughter, groans for the rain and the potatoes, shaking and drying of cloaks and coats, and squealing and tuning up of pipes. Among the rest came Coll, smiling and confident as ever, with an arch look in his eyes when they met Brigid's, and not the least symptom of fear or anxiety in his face. Soon the door was barred against the storm, the fish-oil lamp lighted, laughter, song, and dancing filled the little house, and the rotting potatoes and the ruinous rains were forgotten as completely as though the Bofin population had been goddesses and gods, with whose nectar and ambrosia no such thing as weather could dare to interfere.

'Faith, ye must dance with me, Brigid,' said Coll, after she had refused him half-a-dozen times.

'Why must I dance with you?'

'Oh, now, don't you know what's goin' on in there?' said Coll, roguishly, signing towards the room where father and uncle were arguing over money and land.

'I do,' said Brigid, with all the red fire of her eyes blazing out upon him. 'But, mind ye, this match-makin' is none o' my doin'.'

'Why then, avourneen?'

'I'm not goin' to marry a man that on'y wants a wife, an' doesn't care a pin whether it's me or another.'

'Bedad, I do care,' said Coll, awkwardly. 'I'm a bad hand at the speakin', but I care entirely.'

But Brigid went off and danced with another man.

Coll was puzzled. He did not understand her the least. He was a simple straightforward fellow, and had truly been in love with Brigid – a fact which his confident manner had never allowed her to believe. Latterly he had begun to feel afraid of her; whenever he tried to say a tender word, that red light in her eyes would flash and strike him dumb. He had hoped that when their 'match was made' she would have grown a little kinder; but it seemed she was only getting harsher instead. Well, he would try and hit on some way to please her; and, as he walked home that night, he pondered on all sorts of plans for softening her proud temper and satisfying her exacting mind.

On her side, Brigid saw that she had startled him out of his ordinary easy humour, and, congratulating herself on the spirit she had shown, resolved to continue her present style of proceeding. Not one smile would she give him, till she had, as she told herself, nearly tormented him to death. How close she was to keep to the letter of her resolution could not at this time be foreseen.

Every evening after this Coll travelled half the island to read some old treasured newspaper to the sickly Lavelle, and bringing various little offerings to his betrothed. Everything that Bofin could supply in the way of a love-gift was sought by him, and presented to her. Now it was a few handsome shells purchased from a foreign sailor in the harbour, or it was the model of a boat he had carved for her himself; and all this attention was not without its lasting effect. Unfortunately, however, while Brigid's heart grew more soft, her tongue only waxed more sharp, and her eyes more scornful. The more clearly she perceived that she would soon have to yield, the more haughty and capricious did she become. Had the young man been able to see behind outward appearances he would have been thoroughly satisfied, and a good deal startled at the vehemence of the devotion that had grown up and strengthened for him in that proud and wayward heart. As it was he felt more and more chilled by her continued coldness, and began to weary of a pursuit which seemed unlikely to be either for his dignity or his happiness.

Meanwhile the rain went on falling. The spring was bad, the summer was bad, potatoes were few and unwholesome, the turf lay undried and rotting on the bog. Distress began to pinch the cheerful faces of the islanders, and laughter and song were half-drowned in murmurs of fear. At the sight of so much sorrow and anxiety around her, Brigid's heart began to ache and to smite and reproach her for her selfish and unruly humours. One night, softened by the sufferings of others, she astonished herself by falling on her knees and giving humble thanks to heaven for the undeserved happiness that was awaiting her. She vowed that the next time Coll appeared she would put her hand in his, and let the love of her heart shine out in the smiles of her eyes. Had she kept this vow it might have been well with her, but her habit of vexing had grown all too strong to be cured in an hour. At the first sight of her lover's anxious face in the doorway all her passion for tormenting him returned.

It was an evening in the month of May; the day had been cold and wet, and as dark as January, but the rain had ceased, the clouds had parted, and one of those fiery sunsets burst upon the world that sometimes appear unexpectedly in the midst of stormy weather. In Bofin, where the sun drops down the heavens from burning cloud to cloud, and sinks in the ocean, the whole island was wrapped in a crimson flame. Brigid stood at her door, gazing at the wonderful spectacle of the heavens and sea, looking herself strangely handsome, with her bronze hair glittering in the ruddy sun light, and that dark shadow about her eyes and brows which, except when she smiled, always gave such a look of tragedy to her face. She was waiting for Coll, with softened lips and downcast eyes, and was so lost in her thoughts that she did not see him when he stood beside her.

He remained silently watching her for a few moments, thinking that if she would begin to look like that he would be ready to love her as well as he had ever loved her, and to forget that he had ever wearied of her harassing scorn. At this very moment Brigid was rehearsing within her mind a kind of little speech which was to establish a good understanding between them.

'I'm sorry I vexed you so often, for I love you true,' were the words she had meant to speak; but suddenly seeing Coll by her side, the habitual taunt flew involuntarily to her lips.

'You here again!' she said disdainfully. 'Then no one can say but you're the perseverinest man in the island!'

'Maybe I'm too perseverin,' said Coll, quietly, and, as Brigid looked at him with covert remorse, she saw something in his face that frightened her. His expression was a mixture of weariness and contempt. He was not hurt, or angry, or amused, as she had been accustomed to see him, but tired of her insolence, which was ceasing to give him pain. A sudden consciousness of this made Brigid turn sick at heart, and she felt that she had at last gone a little too far, that she had been losing him all this time while triumphantly thinking to win him. Oh, why could she not speak and say the word that she wanted to say? While this anguish came into her thoughts her brows grew darker than ever, and the warmth ebbed gradually out of her cheek. They went silently into the house, where Brigid took up her knitting, and Coll dropped into his seat beside Lavelle. The bad times, the rotting crops, the scant expectations of a harvest, were discussed by the two men while Brigid sat fighting with her pride, and trying to decide on what she ought to say or do. Before she had made up her mind, Coll had said good-evening abruptly, and gone out of the house.

The young fisherman's home was in Middle Quarter Village, a cluster of gray stone cabins close to the sea, and to reach it Coll had to cross almost the whole breadth of the island. He set out on his homeward walk with a weary and angry heart. Brigid's dark unyielding face followed him, and he was overwhelmed by a fit of unusual depression. He whistled as he went, trying to shake it off. Why should he fret about a woman who disliked him, and who probably loved another whom her father disapproved? Let her do what she liked with herself and her purse. Coll would persecute her no more.

The red light had slowly vanished off the island, and the dark cliffs on the oceanward coast loomed large and black against the still lurid sky. Deep drifts of brown and purple flecked with amber swept across the bogs, and filled up the dreary horrors of the barren and irreclaimable land which Coll had to traverse on his way to the foam-drenched village where the fishermen lived. The heavens cooled to paler tints, a ring of yellow light encircled the island with its creeping shadows and ghost-like rocks. Twilight was descending when Coll heard a faint cry from the distance, like the call of a belated bird or the wail of a child in distress.

At first he thought it was the wind or a plover, but straining his eyes in the direction whence it came he saw a small form standing solitary in the middle of a distant hollow, a piece of treacherous bog, dangerous in the crossing except to knowing feet. Hurrying to the spot he found himself just in time to succour a fellow-creature in distress.

Approaching as near as he could with ease to the person who had summoned him, he saw a very young girl standing gazing towards him with piteous looks. She was small, slight, poorly and scantily clad, and carried a creelful of sea-rack on her slight and bending shoulders. A pale after-gleam from the sky fell where she stood, young and forlorn, in the shadowy solitude, and lit up a face round and delicately pale, reminding one of a daisy; a wreath of wind-tossed yellow hair, and eyes as blue as forget-me-nots. Terror had taken possession of her, and she stretched out her hands appealingly to the strong man, who stood looking at her from the opposite side of the bog. Coll observed her in silence for a few moments. It seemed as if he had known her long ago, and that she belonged to him; yet if so, it was in another state of existence, for he assured himself that she was no one with whom he had any acquaintance. However that might be, he was determined to know more of her now, for, with her childlike, appealing eyes and outstetched hands, she went straight into Coll's heart, to nestle there like a dove of peace for evermore.

'Aisy, asthoreen,' cried Coll across the bog, 'I'm goin' to look after ye. Niver ye fear.'

He crossed the morass with a few rapid springs, and stood by her side.

'Give me the creel, avourneen, till I land it for ye safe.'

A few minutes and the burthen was deposited on the safe side of the bog, and then Coll came back and took the young girl in his arms.

'Keep a good hoult round my neck, machree.'

It was a nice feat for a man to pick his way through this bog, with even so small a woman as this in his arms. The girl clung to him in fear, as he swayed and balanced himself on one sure stone after another, slipping here and stumbling there, but always recovering himself before mischief could be done. At last the deed was accomplished – the goal was won.

'Ye were frightened, acushla,' said Coll, tenderly.

'I was feared of dhrownin' ye,' said the girl, looking wistfully in his face with her great, blue eyes.

'Sorra matther if ye had,' said Coll, laughingly, 'except that maybe ye 'd ha' been dhrowned too. Now, which ways are ye goin'? and maybe ye 'd be afther tellin' me who ye are?'

'I'm Moya Maillie,' said the girl; 'an' I live in Middle Quarter Village.'

'Why, yer niver little Moya that I used to see playing round poor Maillie's door that's dead an' gone! And how did ye grow up that ways in a night?'

'Mother says I'll niver grow up,' laughed Moya; 'but I'm sixteen on May mornin', and I'll be contint to be as I am.'

'Many a fine lady would give her fortune to be contint with that same,' said Coll, striding along with the creel on his shoulders, and glancing down every minute at the sweet white-flower-like face that flitted through the twilight at his side. Thus Brigid's repentance would now come all too late, for Coll had fallen in love with little Moya.

How he brought her home that night to a bare and poverty-stricken cabin in the sea-washed fishing village, and restored her like a stray lamb to her mother, need not be told. Her mother was a widow and the mother of seven, and Moya's willing labour was a great part of the family support. She mended nets for the fishermen, and carried rack for the neighbour's land, knitted stockings to be sent out to the great world and sold, and did any other task which her slender and eager hands could find to do. Coll asked himself in amazement how it was that having known her as a baby he had never observed her existence since then. Now an angel, he believed, had led her out into the dreary bog to stand waiting for his sore heart on that blessed day of days. And he would never marry any one but little Moya.

It was impossible they could marry while times were so bad, but, every evening after this, Moya might be seen perched on an old boat upon the shingle, busy with her knitting – her tiny feet, bare and so brown, crossed under the folds of her old worn red petticoat, with a faint rose-pink in her pale cheeks, and a light of extraordinary happiness in her childlike blue eyes. Coll lay on the shingle at her feet, and these two found an elysium in each other's company. There was much idleness perforce for the men of Bofin at this time, and Coll filled up his hours looking after the concerns of the Widow Maillie, carrying Moya's burdens, and making the hard times as easy for her as he could. When people would look surprised at him and ask: 'Arrah, thin, what about Brigid Lavelle?' Coll would answer: 'Oh, she turned me off long ago. Everybody knows that she could not bear the sight of me.'

In the meantime Brigid, at the other end of the island, was watching daily and hourly for Coll's reappearance. As evening after evening passed without bringing him, her heart misgave her more and more, and she mourned bitterly over her own harshness and pride. Oh, if he would only come again with that wistful, questioning look in his brave face, how kindly she would greet him, how eagerly put her hand in his grasp! As the rain rained on through the early summer evenings there would often come before sunset a lightening and a brightening all over the sky, and this was the hour at which Brigid used to look for her now ever-absent lover. Climbing to the top of the hill, she would peer over the sea-bounded landscape, with its dark stretches of bog, and strips and flecks of green, towards the gray irregular line of the fishing village, the smoke of which she could see hanging against the horizon. Her face grew paler and her eyes dull, but to no one, not even to her father, would she admit that she was pining for Coll's return. She had always lived much by herself, and had few gossiping friends to bring her news. At last, unable to bear the suspense any longer, she made an excuse of business at the store on the beach; and before she had gone far among the houses of that metropolis of the island, she was enlightened as to the cause of her lover's defection.

'So ye cast him off. So ye giv' him to little Moya Maillie,' were the words that greeted her wherever she turned. She smiled and nodded her head, as if heartily assenting to what was said, and content with the existing state of things; but as she walked away out of the reach of observing eyes, her face grew dark and her heart throbbed like to burst in her bosom. Almost mechanically she took her way home through the Middle Quarter Village, with a vague desire to see what was to be seen, and to hear whatever was to be heard. She passed among the houses without observing anything that interested her, but, as she left the village, by the sea-shore she came upon Coll and Moya sitting on a rock in the yellow light of a watery sunset, with a mist of sea-foam around them, and a net over their knees which they were mending between them. Their heads were close together, and Coll was looking in her face with the very look which, all these tedious days and nights, Brigid had been wearying to meet. She walked up beside them, and stood looking at them silently with a light in her eyes that was not good to behold.

'Brigid,' said Coll, when he could bear it no longer, 'for heaven's sake, are ye not satisfied yet?'

She turned from him, and fixed her strange glance on Moya. 'It was me before, an' it's you now,' she said shortly. 'He's a constant lover, isn't he?'

'I loved ye true, and ye scoffed and scorned me,' said Coll, gently, as the gleam of anguish and despair in her eyes startled him. 'I wasn't good enough for Brigid, but I'm good enough for Moya. We're neither of us as rich nor as clever as you, but we'll do for one another well enough.'

Brigid laughed a sharp, sudden laugh, and still looked at Moya. 'For heaven's sake, take that wicked look off yer face,' cried Coll, hastily. 'What somdever way it is betune us three is yer own doin'; an', whether ye like it or not, it cannot now be helped.'

'I will never forgive either of you,' said Brigid, in a low, hard voice; and then, turning abruptly away, she set out on her homeward walk through the gathering shadows.

II

All through that summer the rain fell, and, when autumn came in Bofin, there was no harvest either of fuel or of food. The potato-seed had been for the most part washed out of the earth without putting forth a shoot, while those that remained in the ground were nearly all rotted by a loathsome disease. The smiling little fields that grew the food were turned into blackened pits, giving forth a horrid stench. Winter was beginning again, the year having been but one long winter, with seas too wild to be often braved by even the sturdiest of the fishermen, and the fish seeming to have deserted the island. Accustomed to exist on what would satisfy no other race, and to trust cheerfully to Providence to send them that little out of the earth and out of the sea, the people bore up cheerfully for a long time, living on a mess of Indian-meal once a day, mingled with such edible seaweed as they could gather off the rocks. So long as shopkeepers in Galway and other towns could afford to give credit to the island, the hooker kept bringing such scanty supplies as were now the sole sustenance of the impoverished population. But credit began to fail, and universal distress on the mainland gave back an answering wail to the hunger-cry of the Bofiners. It is hard for anyone who has never witnessed such a state of things to imagine the condition of ten or twelve hundred living creatures on a barren island girded round with angry breakers; the strong arms around them paralyzed, first by the storms that dash their boats to pieces, and rend and destroy their fishing gear, and the devastation of the earth that makes labour useless, and later by the faintness and sickness which comes from hunger long endured, and the cold from which they have no longer a defence. Accustomed as they are to the hardships of recurring years of trial, the Bofiners became gradually aware that a visitation was at hand for which there had seldom been a parallel. Earth and sea alike barren and pitiless to their needs, whence could deliverance come unless the heavens rained down manna into their mouths? Alas! no miracle was wrought, and after a term of brave struggle, hope in Providence, cheerful pushing off of the terrible fears for the worst – after this, laughter, music, song faded out of the island; feet that had danced as long as it was possible now might hardly walk, and the weakest among the people began to die. Troops of children that a few months ago were rosy and sturdy, sporting on the sea-shore, now stretched their emaciated limbs by the fireless hearths, and wasted to death before their maddened mothers' eyes. The old and ailing vanished like flax before a flame. Digging of graves was soon the chief labour of the island, and a day seemed near at hand when the survivors would no longer have strength to perform even this last service for the dead.

Lavelle and his daughter were among the last to suffer from the hard times, and they shared what they had with their poor neighbours; but in course of time the father caught the fever which famine had brought in its train, and was quickly swept into his grave, while the girl was left alone in possession of their little property, with her stocking in the thatch and her small flock of 'beasts' in the field. Her first independent act was to despatch all the money she had left by a trusty hand to Galway to buy meal, in one of those pauses in the bad weather which sometimes allowed a boat to put off from the island. The meal arrived after a long, unavoidable delay, and Brigid became a benefactor to numbers of her fellow-creatures. Late and early she trudged from village to village and from house to house, doling out her meal to make it go as far as possible, till her own face grew pale and her step slow, for she stinted her own food to have the more to give away. Her 'beasts' grew lean and dejected. Why should she feed them at the expense of human life? They were killed, and the meat given to her famishing friends. The little property of the few other well-to-do families in like manner melted away, and it seemed likely that 'rich' and poor would soon all be buried in one grave.

In the Widow Maillie's house the famine had been early at work. Five of Moya's little sisters and brothers had one by one sickened and dropped upon the cabin floor. The two elder boys still walked about looking like galvanized skeletons, and the mother crept from wall to wall of her house trying to pretend that she did not suffer, and to cook the mess of rank-looking sea-weed, which was all they could procure in the shape of food. Coll risked his life day after day trying to catch fish to relieve their hunger, but scant and few were the meals that all his efforts could procure from the sea. White and gaunt he followed little Moya's steps, as with the spirit of a giant she kept on toiling among the rocks for such weeds or shell-fish as could be supposed to be edible. When she fell Coll bore her up, but the once powerful man was not able to carry her now. Her lovely little face was hollow and pinched, the cheek-bones cutting through the skin. Her sweet blue eyes were sunken and dim, her pretty mouth purple and strained. Her beauty and his strength were alike gone.

Three of the boys died in one night, and it took Coll, wasted as he was, two days to dig a grave deep enough to bury them. Before that week was over all the children were dead of starvation, and the mother scarcely alive. One evening Coll made his way slowly across the island from the beach, carrying a small bag of meal which he had unexpectedly obtained. Now and again his limbs failed, and he had to lie down and rest upon the ground; but with long perseverance and unconquerable energy he reached the little fishing village at last. As he passed the first house, Brigid Lavelle, pallid and worn, the spectre of herself, came out of the door with an empty basket. Coll and she stared at each other in melancholy amazement. It was the first time they had met since the memorable scene on the rocks many months ago, for Coll's entire time had been devoted to the Maillies, and Brigid had persistently kept out of his way, striving, by charity to others, to quench the fire of angry despair in her heart. Coll would scarcely have recognized her in her present death-like guise, had it not been for the still living glory of her hair.

The sight of Coll's great frame, once so stalwart and erect, now stooping and attenuated, his lustreless eyes, and blue, cold lips, struck horror into Brigid's heart. She utttered a faint, sharp cry and disappeared. Coll scarcely noticed her, his thoughts were so filled with another; and a little further on he met Moya coming to meet him, walking with a slow, uneven step that told of the whirling of the exhausted brain. Half blind with weakness she stretched her hands before her as she walked.

'The hungry death is on my mother at last. Oh, Coll, come in and see the last o' her!'

'Whist, machree! Look at the beautiful taste o' male I am bringin' her. Hard work I had to carry it from the beach, for the eyes o' the cretures is like wolves' eyes, an' I thought the longin' o' them would have dragged it out o' my hands. An', Moya, there's help comin' from God to us. There's kind people out in the world that's thinkin' o' our needs. The man that has just landed with a sack, an' giv' me this, says there's a hooker full o' male on its road to us this day. May the great Lord send us weather to bring it here.'

'I'm 'feared – I'm 'feared it's too late for her,' sobbed Moya, clinging to him.

They entered the cabin where the woman lay, a mere skeleton covered with skin, with the life still flickering in her glassy eyes. Coll put a little of the meal, as it was, between her lips, while Moya hastened to cook the rest on a fire made of the dried roots of heather. The mother turned loving looks from one to the other, tried to swallow a little of the food to please them, gasped, shuddered a little, and was dead.

It was a long, hard task for Coll and Moya to bury her, and when this was done they sat on the heather clasping each other's wasted hands. The sky was dark; the storm was coming on again. As night approached a tempest was let loose upon the island, and many famishing hearts that had throbbed with a little hope at the news of the relief that was on its way to them, now groaned, sickened, and broke in despair. Louder howled the wind, and the sea raged around the dangerous rocks towards which no vessel could dare to approach. It was the doing of the Most High, said the perishing creatures. His scourge was in His hand. Might His ever blessed will be done!

That evening Moya became delirious, and Coll watched all night by her side. At morning light he fled out and went round the village, crying out desperately to God and man to send him a morsel of food to save the life of his young love. The suffering neighbours turned pitying eyes upon him.

'I'm 'feared it's all over with her when she can't taste the sayweed any more,' said one.

'Why don't ye go to Brigid Lavelle?' said another. 'She hasn't much left, poor girl; but maybe she'd have a mouthful for you.'

Till this moment Coll had felt that he could not go begging of Brigid; but, now that Moya's precious life was slipping rapidly out of his hands, he would suffer the deepest humiliation she could heap upon him, if only she would give him so much food as would keep breath in Moya's body till such time as, by Heaven's mercy, the storm might abate, and the hooker with the relief-meal arrive.

Brigid was alone in her house. A little porridge for some poor creature simmered on a scanty fire, and the girl stood in the middle of the floor, her hands wrung together above her head, and her brain distracted with the remembrance of Coll as she had seen him stricken by the scourge. All these months she had told her jealous heart that the Maillies were safe enough since they had Coll to take care of them. So long as there was a fish in the sea he would not let them starve, neither need he be in any danger himself. And so she had never asked a question about him or them. Now the horror of his altered face haunted her. She had walked through the direst scenes with courageous calm, but this one unexpected sight of woe had nearly maddened her.

A knock came to the door which at first she could not hear for the howling of the wind; but when she heard and opened there was Coll standing before her.

'Meal,' he said faintly – 'a little meal, for the love of Christ! Moya is dying.'

A spasm of anguish and tenderness had crossed Brigid's face at the first words; but at the mention of Moya her face darkened.

'Why should I give to you or Moya?' she said coldly. 'There's them that needs that help as much as ye.'

'But not more,' pleaded Coll. 'Oh, Brigid, I'm not askin' for myself. I fear I vexed ye, though I did not mean it. But Moya niver did any one any harm. Will you give me a morsel to save her from the hungry death?'

'I said I niver would forgive either o' ye, an' I niver will,' said Brigid, slowly. 'Ye broke my heart, an' why wouldn't I break yours?'

'Brigid, perhaps neither you nor me has much longer to live. Will ye go before yer Judge with sich black words on yer lips?'

'That's my affair,' she answered in the same hard voice, and then suddenly turning from him, shut the door in his face.

She stood listening within, expecting to hear him returning to implore her, but no further sound was heard; and, when she found he was gone, she dropped upon the floor with a shriek, and rocked herself in a frenzy of remorse for her wickedness.

'But I cannot help everyone,' she moaned; 'I'm starving myself, an' there's nothin' but a han'ful o' male at the bottom o' the bag.'

After a while she got up, and carried the mess of porridge to the house for which she had intended it, and all that day she went about, doing what charity she could, and not tasting any thing herself. Returning, she lay down on the heather, overcome with weakness, fell asleep, and had a terrible dream. She saw herself dead and judged; a black-winged angel put the mark of Cain on her forehead, and at the same moment Coll and Moya went, glorified and happy, hand in hand into heaven before her eyes. 'Depart from me, you accursed,' thundered in her ears; and she started wide awake to hear the winds and waves roaring unabated round her head.

Wet and shivering she struggled to regain her feet, and stood irresolute where to go. Dreading to return to her desolate home, she mechanically set her face towards the little church on the cliff above the beach. On her way to it she passed prostrate forms, dying or dead, on the heather, on the roadside, and against the cabin walls. A few weakly creatures, digging graves, begged from her as she went past, but she took no notice of anything, living or dead, making straight for the church. No one was there, and the storm howled dismally through the empty, barn-like building. Four bare, whitewashed walls, and a rude wooden altar, with a painted tabernacle and cross – this was the church. On one long wall was hung a large crucifix, a white, thorn-crowned figure upon stakes of black-painted wood, which had been placed there in memory of a 'mission' lately preached on the island; and on this Brigid's burning eyes fixed themselves with an agony of meaning. Slowly approaching it she knelt and stretched out her arms, uttering no prayer, but swaying herself monotonously to and fro. After a while the frenzied pain of remorse was dulled by physical exhaustion, and a stupor was stealing over her senses when a step entering the church startled her back into consciousness. Looking round she saw that the priest of the island had come in, and was wearily dragging himself towards the altar.

Father John was suffering and dying with his people. He had just now returned from a round of visits among the sick, during which he had sped some departing souls on their journey, and given the last consolation of religion to the dying. His own gaunt face and form bore witness to the unselfishness which had made all his little worldly goods the common property of the famishing. Before he had reached the rails of the altar Brigid had thrown herself on her face at his feet.

'Save me, father, save me!' she wailed. 'The sin of murther is on my soul!'

'Nonsense, child! No such thing. It is too much that you have been doing, my poor Brigid! I fear the fever has crazed your brain.'

'Listen to me, father. Moya is dying, an' there is still a couple o' han'fuls o' male in the bag. Coll came an' asked me for her, an' I hated her because he left me, and I would not give it to him, an' maybe she is dead.'

'You refused her because you hated her?' said the priest. 'God help you, my poor Brigid. 'Tis true you can't save every life; but you must try and save this one.'

Brigid gazed up at him, brightly at first, as if an angel had spoken, and then the dark shadow fell again into her eyes.

The priest saw it.

'Look there, my poor soul,' he said, extending a thin hand towards the figure on the cross. 'Did He forgive His enemies, or did He not?'

Brigid turned her fascinated gaze to the crucifix, fixed them on the thorn-crowned face, and, uttering a wild cry, got up and tottered out of the church.

Spurred by terror lest her amend should come too late, and Moya be dead before she could reach her, she toiled across the heather once more, over the dreary bogs, and through the howling storm. Dews of suffering and exhaustion were on her brow as she carefully emptied all the meal that was left of her store into a vessel, and stood for a moment looking at it in her hand.

'There isn't enough for all of us,' she said, 'an' some of us be to die. It was always her or me, her or me; an' now it'll be me.

May Christ receive me, Moya, as I forgive you.' And then she kissed the vessel and put it under her cloak.

Leaving the house, she was careless to close the door behind her, feeling certain that she should never cross the threshold again, and straining all her remaining strength to the task, she urged her lagging feet by the shortest way to the Middle Quarter Village. Dire were the sights she had to pass upon her way. Many a skeleton hand was outstretched for the food she carried; but Brigid was now deaf and blind to all appeals. She saw only Coll's accusing face, and Moya's glazing eyes staring terribly at her out of the rain-clouds. Reaching the Maillies' cabin, she found the door fastened against the storm.

Coll was kneeling in despair by Moya, when a knocking at the door aroused him. The poor fellow had prayed so passionately, and was in so exalted a state, that he almost expected to see an angel of light upon the threshold bring the food he had so urgently asked for. The priest had been there and was gone, the neighbours were sunk in their own misery; why should anyone come knocking like that, unless it were an angel bringing help? Trembling, he opened the door; and there was Brigid, or her ghost.

'Am I in time?' gasped she, as she put the vessel of food in his hand.

'Aye,' said Coll, seizing it. In his transport of delight he would have gone on his knees and kissed her feet; but before he could speak, she was gone.

Whither should she go now? was Brigid's thought. No use returning to the desolate and lonesome home where neither food nor fire was any longer to be found. She dreaded dying on her own hearthstone alone, and faint as she was she knew what was now before her. Gaining the path to the beach, she made a last pull on her energies to reach the whitewashed walls, above which her fading eyes just dimly discerned the cross. The only face she now wanted to look upon again was that thorn-crowned face which was waiting for her in the loneliness of the empty and wind-swept church. Falling, fainting, dragging herself on again, she crept within the shelter of the walls. A little more effort, and she would be at His feet. The struggle was made, blindly, slowly, desperately, with a last rally of all the passion of a most impassioned nature; and at last she lay her length on the earthen floor under the cross. Darkness, silence, peace, settled down upon her. The storm raved around, the night came on, and when the morning broke, Brigid was dead.

Mildly and serenely that day had dawned, a pitiful sky looked down on the calamities of Bofin, and the vessel with the relief-meal sailed into the harbour. For many even then alive, the food came all too late, but to numbers it brought assuagement and salvation. The charity of the world was at work, and though much had yet to be suffered, yet the hungry death had been mercifully stayed. Thanks to the timely help, Moya lived for better times, and when her health was somewhat restored, she emigrated with Coll to America. Every night in their distant backwoods hut they pray together for the soul of Brigid Lavelle, who, when in this world, had loved one of them too well, and died to save the life of the other.

*The following is from an old chapbook called 'The Hibernian Tales.'
I quote it not so much for its own sake, though it is not altogether
unamusing, as for its value as a representative of the chapbook
literature, once the main reading of the people.*

THE JACKDAW

Tom Moor was a linen-draper in Sackville Street. His father,
when he died, left him an affluent fortune, and a shop of
excellent trade.

As he was standing at his door one day, a countryman came
up to him with a nest of jackdaws, and accosting him, said:
'Master, will you buy a nest of daws?' 'No, I don't want any.'
'Master,' replied the man, 'I will sell them all cheap; you shall
have the whole nest for ninepence.' 'I don't want them,'
answered Tom Moor, 'so go about your business.'

As the man was walking away one of the daws popped out
his head, and cried, 'Mawk, mawk.' 'Damn it,' says Tom Moor,
'that bird knows my name; halloo, countryman, what will you
take for the bird?' 'Why, you shall have him for threepence.'
Tom Moor bought him, had a cage made, and hung him up in
the shop.

The journeymen took much notice of the bird, and would
frequently tap at the bottom of the cage, and say: 'Who are
you? Who are you? Tom Moor of Sackville Street.'

In a short time the jackdaw learned these words, and if he wanted victuals or water, would strike his bill against the cage, turn up the white of his eyes, cock his head, and cry: 'Who are you? who are you? Tom Moor of Sackville Street.'

Tom Moor was fond of gaming, and often lost large sums of money; finding his business neglected in his absence, he had a small hazard table set up in one corner of his dining-room, and invited a party of his friends to play at it.

The jackdaw had by this time become familiar; his cage was left open, and he hopped into every part of the house; sometimes he got into the dining-room, where the gentlemen were at play, and one of them being a constant winner, the others would say: 'Damn it, how he nicks them.' The bird learned these words also, and adding them to the former, would call: 'Who are you? who are you? Tom Moor of Sackville Street. Damn it, how he nicks them.'

Tom Moor, from repeated losses and neglect of business, failed in trade, and became a prisoner in the Fleet; he took his bird with him, and lived on the master's side, supported by friends, in a decent manner. They would sometimes ask, What brought you here? when he used to lift up his hands and answer: 'Bad company, by G—.' The bird learned this likewise, and at the end of the former words, would say: 'What brought you here? Bad company, by G—.'

Some of Tom Moor's friends died, others went abroad, and by degrees he was totally deserted, and removed to the common side of the prison, where the jail distemper soon attacked him; and in the last stage of life, lying on a straw bed, the poor bird who had been for two days without food or water, came to his feet, and striking his bill on the floor, calls out: 'Who are you? Tom Moor of Sackville Street; damn it, how he nicks them, damn it, how he nicks them. What brought you here? Bad company, by G—, bad company, by G—.'

Tom Moor, who had attended to the bird, was struck with his words, and reflecting on himself, cried out: 'Good God, to what a situation am I reduced! My father, when he died, left me a good fortune and an established trade. I have spent my fortune, ruined my business, and am now dying in a loathsome jail; and to complete all, keeping that poor thing confined without support. I will endeavour to do one piece of justice before I die, by setting him at liberty.'

He made a struggle to crawl from his straw bed, opened the casement, and out flew the bird. A flight of jackdaws from the Temple were going over the jail, and Tom Moor's bird mixed among them. The gardener was then laying the plants of the Temple gardens, and as often as he placed them in the day the jackdaws pulled them up by night. They got a gun and attempted to shoot some of them; but, being cunning birds, they always placed one as a watch in the stump of a hollow tree; who, as soon as the gun was levelled cried 'Mawk,' and away they flew.

The gardeners were advised to get a net, and the first night it was spread they caught fifteen; Tom Moor's bird was amongst them. One of the men took the net into a garret of an uninhabited house, fastened the doors and windows, and turned the birds loose. 'Now,' says he, 'you black rascals, I will be revenged of you.' Taking hold of the first at hand, he twists his neck, and throwing him down, cries. 'There goes one.' Tom Moor's bird, who had hopped up to a beam at one corner of the room unobserved, as the man lays hold of the second, calls out, 'Damn it, how he nicks them.' The man, alarmed, cries: 'Sure I heard a voice, but the house is uninhabited, and the door is fast; it could only be imagination.' On laying hold of the third, and twisting his neck, Tom's bird again says: 'Damn it, how he nicks them.' The man dropped the bird in his hand, and turning to where the voice came from, seeing the other with his mouth open, cries out, 'Who are you?' to which the bird answered: 'Tom Moor of Sackville Street, Tom Moor of Sackville Street.' 'The devil you are; and what brought you here?' Tom Moor's bird, lifting up his pinions, answered: 'Bad company, by G—,

399

bad company, by G—.' The fellow, frightened almost out of his wits, opened the door, ran down stairs, and out of the house, followed by all the birds, who by this means regained their liberty.

DARBY DOYLE'S VOYAGE TO QUEBEC

ANONYMOUS[1]

I *tuck* the road, one fine morning in May, from Inchegelagh, an' got up to the Cove safe an' sound. There I saw many ships with big broad boords fastened to ropes, everyone ov them saying, 'The first vessel for Quebec.' Siz I to myself, 'Those are about to run for a wager; this one siz she'll be first, and that one siz she'll be first.' At any rate, I pitched on one that was finely painted, and looked long and slender like a corragh on the Shannon. When I wint on boord to ax the fare, who shou'd come up out ov a hole but Ned Flinn, an ould townsman ov my own. 'Och, is it yoor-self that's there, Ned?' siz I; 'are ye goin' to Amerrykey?' 'Why, an' to be sure,' siz he; 'I'm *mate* ov the ship.' 'Meat! that's yer sort, Ned,' siz I; 'then we'll only want bread. Hadn't I betther go and pay my way?' 'You're time enough,' siz Ned; 'I'll tell you when we're ready for sea – leave the rest to me, Darby.' 'Och, tip us your fist,' siz I; 'you were always the broath ov a boy; for the sake ov ould times, Ned, we must have a dhrop.' So, my jewel, Ned brought me to where there was right good stuff. When it got up to three o'clock I found myself mighty weak with hunger. I got the smell ov corn beef an' cabbage that knock'd me up entirely. I then wint to the landleddy, and siz I to her, 'Maybee your leddyship id not think me rood by axin' iv Ned an myself cou'd get our dinner ov that fine hot mate that I got a taste ov in my nose?' 'In troath you can,' siz she (an' she look'd mighty pleasant), 'an' welkim.' So,

401

my darlin' dish and all came up. 'That's what I call a *flaugholoch* mess,' siz I. So we eat and drank away. Many's the squeeze Ned gave my fist, telling me to leave it all to him, and how comfortable he'd make me on the voyage. Day afther day we spint together, waitin' for the wind, till I found my pockets begin to grow very light. At last, siz he to me, one day afther dinner, 'Darby, the ship will be ready for sea on the morrow – you'd betther go on boord, an' pay your way.' 'Is it jokin' you are, Ned?' siz I; 'shure you tould me to leave it all to you.' 'Ah! Darby,' siz he, 'you're for takin' a rise out o' me; shure enough, ye were the lad that was never without a joke – the very priest himself couldn't get over ye. But, Darby, there's no joke like the thrue one. I'll stick to my promise; but, Darby, you must pay your way.' 'O Ned,' siz I, 'is this the way you're goin' to threat me afther all? I'm a rooin'd man; all I cou'd scrape together I spint on you. If you don't do something for me, I'm lost. Is there no place where you cou'd hide me from the captin?' 'Not a place,' siz Ned. 'An' where, Ned, is the place I saw you comin' out ov?' 'Oh, Darby, that was the hould where the cargo's stow'd.' 'An' is there no other place?' siz I. 'Oh, yes,' siz he, 'where we keep the wather casks.' 'An', Ned,' siz I, 'does any one live down there?' 'Not a mother's soul,' siz he. 'An', Ned,' siz I, 'can't you cram me down there, and give me a lock ov straw an' a bit?' 'Why, Darby,' siz he (an' he look'd mighty pittyfull). 'I must thry. But mind, Darby, you'll have to hide all day in an empty barrel, an' when it comes to my watch, I'll bring you down some grog; but if you're diskiver'd, it's all over with me, an' you'll be put on a dissilute island to starve.' 'O Ned,' siz I, 'leave it all to me.' 'Never fear, Darby, I'll mind my eye.' When night cum on I got down into the dark cellar, among the barrels; poor Ned fixt a place in a corner for me to sleep, an' every night he brought me down hard black cakes an' salt meat. There I lay snug for a whole month. At last, one night, siz he to me, 'Now, Darby, what's to be done? we're within three days' sail of Quebec; the ship will be overhauled, and all the passengers' names call'd over; if you are found, you'll be sould as a slave for your passage money.' 'An' is that all that frets you, my jewel,' siz I; 'can't you leave it all to me? In throath, Ned, I'll never forget your hospitality at any rate. But, what place is outside of the ship?' 'Why, the sea, to be sure,' siz he. 'Och! botheration,' siz I, 'I mean what's the outside the ship?' 'Why, Darby,' siz he, 'part of it's called the bulwark.' 'An' fire an' faggots,' siz I, 'is it bulls work the vessel along?' 'No, nor horses,' siz he, 'neither; this is no time for jokin'; what do you mean to do?' 'Why, I'll tell you, Ned; get me an empty meal-bag, a bottle, an' a bare ham-bone, and that's all I'll ax.' So, begad, Ned look'd very queer at me; so he got them for me, anyhow. 'Well, Ned,' siz I, 'you know I'm a great shwimmer; your watch will be early in the mornin'; I'll jist slip down into the sea; do you cry out, there's a man in the wather, as loud as you can, and leave all the rest to me.'

Well, to be sure, down into the sea I dropt without so much as a splash. Ned roared out with the hoarseness of a brayin' ass – 'a man in the sea! a man in the sea!' Every man, woman, and child came running up out of the holes, the captin among the rest, who put a long red barrel like a gun to his eye – gibbet me, but I thought he was for shootin' me! down I dived. When I got my head over the wather agen, what shou'd I see but a boat rowin' to me, as fast as a throut afther a pinkeen. When it came up close enough to be heard, I roared out: 'Bad end to yees, for a set ov spalpeen rascals, did ye hear me at last?' The boat now run 'pon the top ov me; down I dived agen like a duck afther a frog, but the minnit my skull came over the wather, I was gript by the scruff ov the neck, and dhragged into the boat. To be shure, I didn't kick up a row – 'Let go my hair, ye blue devils,' I roared, 'it's well ye have me in your marcy in this dissilute place, or by the powthers I'd make ye feel the strinth ov my bones. What hard look I had to follow yees, at all at all – which ov ye is the masther?' As I sed this every mother's son began to stare at me, with my bag round my neck, an' my bottle by my side, an' the bare bone in my fist. 'There he is,' siz they, pointin' to a little yellow man in a corner of the boat. 'May the – rise blisthers on your rapin'-hook shins,' siz I, 'you yellow-lookin' monkey, but it's a'most time for you to think ov lettin' me into your ship – I'm here plowin' and plungin' this month afther ye; shure I didn't care a *thrawneen* was it not that you have my best Sunday clothes in your ship, and my name in your books. For three sthraws, if I don't know how to write, I'd leave my mark, an' that on your skull'; so saying I made a lick at him with the ham-bone, but I was near tumblin' into the sea agen. 'An', pray, what is your name, my lad?' siz the captin. 'What's my name! What id you give to know?' siz I, 'ye unmannerly spalpeen, it might be what's your name, Darby Doyle, out ov your mouth – ay, Darby Doyle, that was never afraid or ashamed to own it at home or abroad!' 'An', Mr Darby Doyle,' siz he, 'do you mean to persuade us that you swum from Cork to this afther us?' 'This is more ov your ignorance,' siz I – 'ay, an' if you sted three days longer and not take me up, I'd be in Quebec before ye, only my purvisions were out, and the few rags ov bank notes I had all melted into paste in my pocket, for I hadn't time to get them changed. But stay, wait till I get my foot on shore; there's ne'er a cottoner in Cork iv you don't pay for leavin' me to the marcy ov the waves.'

All this time the blue chaps were pushin' the boat with sticks through the wather, till at last we came close to the ship. Everyone on board saw me at the Cove, but didn't see me on the voyage; to be sure, everyone's mouth was wide open, crying out Darby Doyle. 'The – stop your throats,' siz I, 'it's now you call me loud enough; ye wouldn't shout that way when ye saw me rowlin' like a tub in a millrace the other day fornenst your faces.' When they heard me say that, some of them grew pale as a sheet – every thumb was at work till they a'most brought the blood from their forreds. But, my jewel, the captin does no more than runs to the book, an' calls out the names that paid, and them that *wasn't* paid – to be shure, I was one ov them that didn't pay. If the captin looked at me before with *wondherment*, he now looked with astonishment! Nothin' was tawk'd ov for the other three days but Darby Doyle's great shwim from the Cove to Quebec. One sed, 'I always knew Darby to be a great schwimmer.' 'Do ye remimber,' siz another, 'when Darby's dog was nigh been drownded in the great duck hunt, when Darby peeled off and brought in the dog, and made afther the duck himself, and swum for two hours endways; and do ye remimber when all the dogs gother round the duck at one time; whin it wint down how Darby dived afther it, and sted down for a'most an hour – and sted below while the creathur was eatin' a few frogs, for she was weak an' hungry; and when everybody thought he was lost, up he came with the duck by the leg in his kithogue (left hand).'

Begar, I agreed to all they sed, till at last we got to Amerrykey. I was now in a quare way; the captain wouldn't let me go till a friend of his would see me. By this time, my jewel, not only his friends came, but swarms upon swarms, starin' at poor Darby. At last I called Ned. 'Ned, avic,' siz I, 'I want to go about my *bisness*.' 'Be easy, Darby,' siz he; 'haven't ye your fill ov good aitin', an' the Captain's got mighty fond ov ye entirely.' 'Is he, Ned?' siz I; 'but tell us, Ned, are all them crowds ov people goin' to sea?' 'Augh, ye omadham,' siz Ned, 'sure they are come to look at you.' Just as he said this, a tall yellow man, with a black curly head, comes and stares me full in the face. 'You'll know me agen,' says I, 'bad luck to yer manners and the schoolmasther that taught ye.' But I thought he was goin' to shake hands with me, when he tuck hould ov my fist and opened every finger, one by one, then opened my shirt and look't at my breast. 'Pull away, mabouchal,' siz I, 'I'm no desarthur, at any rate.' But never an answer he made, but walk'd down into the hole where the captin lived. 'This is more ov it,' siz I; 'Ned, what cou'd that tallah-faced man mean?' 'Why,' siz Ned, 'he was lookin' to see iv your fingers were webb'd, or had ye scales on your breast.' 'His impidence is great,' siz I; 'did he take me for a duck or a bream? But, Ned, what's the meanin' ov the boords acrass the stick the people walk on, and the big white boord up there?' 'Why, come over and read,' siz Ned. But, my jewel, I didn't know whether I was stannin' on my head or on my heels when I saw in great big black letters –

THE GREATEST WONDHER OF THE WORLD!!!
TO BE SEEN HERE,
A Man that beats out Nicholas the Diver!
He has swum from Cork to Amerrykey!!
Proved on oath by ten of the Crew and twenty Passengers.
Admittance Half a Dollar.

'Bloody wars! Ned,' siz I, 'does this mean your humble sarvint?' 'Divil another,' siz he, – so I makes no more ado, than with a hop, skip, and jump, gets over to the captin, who was now talkin' to the yellow fellow that was afther starin' me out ov countenance. 'Pardon my rudeness, your honour,' siz I, mighty polite, and makin' a bow – at the same time Ned was at my heels – so rising my foot to give the genteel scrape, sure I scraped all the skin off Ned's shins. 'May bad luck to your brogues,' siz he. 'You'd betther not curse the wearer,' siz I, 'or – ' 'Oh, Darby!' siz the captin, 'don't be unginteel, an' so many ladies and gintlemin lookin' at ye.' 'The never an other mother's soul shall lay their peepers on me till I see sweet Inchegeiagh agen,' says I. 'Begar ye are doin' it well. How much money have ye gother for my shwimmin'?' 'Be quiet, Darby,' siz the captin, and he looked very much friekened. 'I have plenty, an' I'll have more for ye iv ye do what I want ye to do.' 'An' what is it, avic?' siz I. 'Why, Darby,' siz he, 'I'm afther houldin' a wager last night with this gintleman for all the worth ov my ship, that you'll shwim against any shwimmer in the world; an', Darby, if ye don't do that, I'm a gone man.' 'Augh, give us your fist,' siz I; 'did ye ever hear ov Paddys dishaving any man in the European world yet – barrin' themselves?' 'Well, Darby,' siz he, 'I'll give you a hundred dollars; but, Darby, you must be to your word, and you shall have another hundred.' So sayin', he brought me down into the cellar; but, my jewel, I didn't think for the life ov me to see such a wondherful place – nothin' but goold every way I turned, and Darby's own sweet face in twenty places. Begar I was a'most ashamed to ax the gintleman for the dollars. 'But,' siz I to myself agen, 'the gintleman has too much money, I suppose he does be throwin' it into the sea, for I often heard the sea was richer than the land, so I may as well take it anyhow.' 'Now, Darby,' siz he, 'here's the dollars for ye.' But, begar, it was only a bit of paper he was handin' me. 'Arrah, none ov yer tricks upon thravellers,' siz I; 'I had betther nor that, and many more ov them, melted in the sea; give me what won't wash out ov my pocket.' 'Why, Darby,' siz he, 'this is an ordher on a marchant for the amount.' 'Pho, pho!' siz I, 'I'd sooner take your word nor his oath' – lookin' round mighty respectful at the goold walls. 'Well, Darby,' siz he, 'ye must have the real thing.' So, by the powthers, he reckon'd me out a hundred dollars in goold. I never saw the like since the stockin' fell out of the chimly on my aunt and cut her forred. 'Now, Darby,' siz he, 'ye are a rich man, an' ye are worthy of it all – sit down, Darby, an' take a bottle ov wine.' So to please the gintleman, I sat down. Afther a bit, who comes down but Ned. 'Captin,' siz he, 'the deck is crowded; I had to block up the gangway to prevint any more from comin' in to see Darby. Bring him up, or, blow me, iv the ship won't be sunk.' 'Come up, Darby,' siz the captin' lookin' roguish pleasant at myself. So, my jewel, he handed me up through the hall as tendher as iv I was a lady, or a pound ov fresh butther in the dog days. When I got up, shure enough, I couldn't help starin'; such crowds of fine ladies and yellow gintlemen never was seen before in any ship. One ov them, a little rosy-cheek'd beauty, whispered the captin somethin', but he shuk his head, and then came over to me. 'Darby,' siz he, 'I know an Irishman would do anything to please a lady.' 'In throth you may say that with yer own ugly mouth,' siz I. 'Well, then, Darby,' siz he, 'the ladies would wish to see you give a few strokes in the sea.' 'Och, an' they shall have them in welcome,' siz I. 'That's a good fellow,' siz he; 'now strip off.' 'Decency, Katty,' siz I; 'is it in my mother-naked pelt before the ladies? Bad luck to the undacent brazen-faced – but no matther! Irish girls for ever, afther all!' But all to no use. I was made to peel off behind a big sheet, and then I made one race and jumpt ten yards into the wather to get out ov their sight. Shure enough, everyone's eyes danced in their head, while they look'd on the spot where I went down. A thought came into my head while I was below, how I'd show them a little divarsion, as I could use a great many thricks on the wather. So I didn't rise at all till I got to the tother side, and everyone run to that side; then I took a hoult ov my big two toes, and makin' a ring ov myself, rowled like a hoop on the top ov the wather all round the ship. I b'leeve I opened their eyes! Then I yarded, back-swum, an' dived, till at last the captin made signs for me to come out, so I got into the boat an' threw on my duds. The very ladies were breakin' their necks runnin' to shake hands with me. 'Shure,' siz they, 'you're the greatest man in the world! !' So for three days I showed off to crowds ov people, though I was *fryin'* in the wather for shame.

At last the day came that I was to stand the tug. I saw the captin lookin' very often at me. At last, 'Darby,' siz he, 'are you any way cow'd? The fellow you have to shwim agenst can shwim down waterfalls an' catharacts.' 'Can, he, avic?' siz I; 'but can he shwim up agenst them? Wow, wow, Darby, for that! But, captin, come here; is all my purvisions ready? – don't let me fall short ov a dhrop ov the rale stuff above all things.' An' who shou'd come up while I was tawkin' to the captin but the chap I was to shwim with, an' heard all I sed. Begar! his eyes grew as big as two oysther shells. Then the captin call'd me aside. 'Darby,' siz he, 'do ye put on this green jacket an' white throwsers, that the people may betther extinguish you from the other chap.' 'With all hearts, avic,' siz I, 'green for ever – Darby's own favourite colour the world over; but where am I goin' to, captain?' 'To the shwimmin' place, to be shure,' siz he. 'Divil shoot the failers an' take the hindmost,' siz I; 'here's at ye.' I was then inthrojuiced to the shwimmer. I look'd at him from head to foot. He was so tall that he could eat bread an' butther over my head – with a face as yellow as a kite's foot. 'Tip us the mitten,' siz I, 'mabouchal,' siz I. (But, begad, I was puzzled. 'Begar,' siz I to myself, 'I'm done. Cheer up, Darby! If I'm not able to kill him, I'll frighten the life out ov him.') 'Where are we goin' to shwim to?' But never a word he answered. 'Are ye bothered, neighbour?' 'I reckon I'm not,' siz he, mighty chuff. 'Well, then,' siz I, 'why didn't ye answer your betthers? What id ye think iv we shwum to Keep Cleer or the Keep ov Good Hope?' 'I reckon neither,' siz he agen, eyein' me as iv I was goin' to pick his pockets. 'Well, then, have ye any favourite place?' siz I. 'Now, I've heard a great deal about the place where poor Boney died; I'd like to see it, iv I'd anyone to show me the place; suppose we wint there?' Not a taste of a word cou'd I get out ov him, good or bad. Off we set through the crowds ov ladies an' gintlemen. Such cheerin' and wavin' ov hats was never seen even at *Dan's* enthry; an' then the row ov purty girls laughin' an' rubbin' up against me, that I cou'd har'ly get on. To be shure, no one cou'd be lookin' to the ground, an' not be lookin' at them, till at last I was thript up by a big loomp ov iron stuck fast in the ground with a big ring to it. 'Whoo, Darby!' siz I, makin' a hop an' a crack ov my fingers, 'you're not down yet.' I turn'd roun' to look at what thript me. 'What d'ye call that?' siz I to the captin, who was at my elbow. 'Why, Darby?' siz he; 'that's half an anchor.' 'Have ye any use for it?' siz I. 'Not in the least,' siz he; 'it's only to fasten boats to.' 'Maybee, you'd give it to a body,' siz I. 'An' welkim, Darby,' siz he; 'it's yours.' 'God bless your honour, sir,' siz I, 'it's my poor father that will pray for you. When I left home the creather hadn't as much as an anvil but what was sthreeled away by the agint – bad end to them. This will be jist the thing that'll match him; he can tie the horse to the ring, while he forges on the other part. Now, will ye obleege me by gettin' a couple ov chaps to lay it on my shoulder when I get into the wather, and I won't have to be comin back for it afther I shake hans with this fellow.' Begar, the chap turned from yallow to white when he heard me say this. An' siz he to the gintleman that was walkin' by *his* side, 'I reckon I'm not fit for the shwimmin' today – I don't feel *myself.*' 'An', murdher an Irish, if you're yer brother, can't you send him for yerself, an' I'll wait here till he comes. Here, man, take a dhrop ov this before ye go. Here's to yer betther health, and your brother's into the bargain.' So I took off my glass, and handed him another; but the never a dhrop ov it he'd take. 'No force,' siz I, 'avic; maybe you think there's poison in it – well, here's another good luck to us. An' when will ye be able for the shwim, avic?' siz I, mighty complisant. 'I reckon in another week,' siz he. So we shook hands and parted. The poor fellow went home – took the fever – then began to rave. 'Shwim up the catharacts! – shwim to the Keep ov Good Hope! – shwim to St Helena! – shwim to Keep Cleer! – shwim with an anchor on his back! – Oh! oh! oh!'

I now thought it best to be on the move; so I gother up my winners; and here I sit undher my own hickory threes, as independent as any Yankee.

1. From the once noted *Dublin Penny Jornal.*

APPENDIX

W B Yeats' Introduction to 'Stories from Carleton' (1889)

WILLIAM CARLETON

At the end of the last century there lived in the townland of Prillisk, in the parish of Clogher, in the county of Tyrone, a farmer named Carleton. Among his neighbours he was noted for his great memory. A pious Catholic, he could repeat almost the whole of the Old and New Testament, and no man ever heard tell of Gaelic charm, rann, poem, prophecy, miracle, tale of blessed priest or friar, revelation of ghost or fairy, that did not already lie on this man's tongue.

His wife, Mary, was even better known. Hers was the sweetest voice within the range of many baronies. When she went to sing at wake or wedding the neighbours for miles round would flock in to hear, as city folk do for some famous *prima donna*. She had a great store of old Gaelic songs and tunes. Many an air, sung once under all Irish roof-trees, has gone into the grave with her. The words she sang were Gaelic. Once they asked her to sing the air, 'The Red-haired Man's Wife,' to English words. 'I will sing for you,' she answered, 'but the English words and the air are like a quarrelling man and wife. The Irish melts into the tune: the English does not.' She could repeat many poems, some handed down for numberless years, others written by her own grandfather and uncle, who were noted peasant poets in their day. She was a famous keener likewise. No one could load the wild funeral song with so deep sorrow. Often and often when she caught up the cry the other keeners would become silent in admiration.

413

On Shrove-Tuesday, in the year 1798, when pitch-caps were well in fashion, was born to these two a son, whom they called William Carleton. He was the youngest of fourteen children.

Before long his mind was brimful of his father's stories and his mother's songs. In after days he recorded how many times, when his mother sat by her spinning-wheel, singing 'Shule agra' or the 'Trougha,' or some other 'song of sorrow,' he would go over with tears in his eyes, and whisper, 'Mother dear, don't sing that song; it makes me sorrowful.' Fifty years later his mind was still full of old songs that had died on all other lips than his.

At this time Ireland was plentifully stored with hedge school-masters. Government had done its best to crush out education, and only succeeded in doing what like policy had done for the priestcraft – surrounding it with a halo. Ditchers and plough-boys developed the strangest enthusiasm for Greek and Latin. The worst of it was, the men who set up schools behind the hedges were often sheer imposters. Among them, however, were a few worthy of fame, like Andrew Magrath, the Munster poet, who sang his allegiance to the fairy, 'Don of the Ocean Vats.'

The boy Carleton sat under three hedge school-masters in succession – Pat Fryne, called Mat Kavanagh in the stories; O'Beirne of Findramore; and another, the master in 'The Poor Scholar,' whose name Carleton never recorded, as he had nothing but evil to say of him. They were great tyrants. Pat Fryne caused the death of a niece of Carleton's by plucking her ear with such violence that some of the internal tendons were broken, and inflammation set in.

When Carleton was about fourteen, the unnamed schoolmaster was groaned out of the barony; and his pupil, after six months' dutiful attendance at all wakes, weddings, and dances, resolved to make his first foray into the world. He set out as 'a poor scholar,' meaning to travel away into Munster in search of education. He did not go beyond Granard, however, for there he dreamed that he was chased by a mad bull, and, taking it as an evil omen, returned home. His mother was delighted to have her youngest once more. She had often repeated, while he was away, 'Why did I let my boy go? Maybe I will never see him again.'

He now returned to his dances, fairs, and merry-making with a light heart. None came near him at jig or horn-pipe. He was great, too, with his big peasant's body, at all kinds of athletic contests, could swing a shillelah with any man, and leap twenty-one feet on a level. But in his own family he was most admired for his supposed learning, and showed a great taste, as he tells, for long words. Hence it was decided that he should become a priest.

When about nineteen he made his second foray into the world. His father often told him of St Patrick's Purgatory on an island in Lough Derg – how St Patrick killed the great serpent and left his bones changed into stone, visible to all men for ever, and of the blessing that falls upon all pilgrims thither. To the mind of the would-be priest, and tale-weaver that was to be, the place seemed full of endless romance. He set out, one of the long line of pilgrims who have gone thither these twelve hundred years to murmur their rosaries. In a short time a description of this pilgrimage was to start him in literature.

On his return he gave up all idea of the priesthood, and changed his religious opinions a good deal. He began drifting slowly into Protestantism. This Lough Derg pilgrimage seems to have set him thinking on many matters – not thinking deeply, perhaps. It was not an age of deep thinking. The air was full of mere debater's notions. In course of time, however, he grew into one of the most deeply religious minds of his day – a profound mystical nature, with melancholy at its root. And his heart, anyway, soon returned to the religion of his fathers; and in him the Established Church proselytisers found their most fierce satirist.

One day Carleton came on a translation of *Gil Blas*, and was filled at once with a great longing to see the world. Accordingly, he left his native village and went on his third foray, this time not to return. He found his way to the parish of Killanny, in Louth, and stayed for a while with the priest, who was a relation of the one in his native parish. At the end of a fortnight, however, he moved to a farmer's house, where he became tutor to the farmer's children. A quarter of a mile from the priest's house was Wildgoose Lodge, where, six months before, a family of eight persons had been burnt to ashes by a Ribbon Society. The ringleader still swung on a gibbet opposite his mother's door, and as she came in and out it was her custom to look up and say, 'God have mercy on the sowl of my poor martyr.' The peasants when they passed by would often look up too, and murmur, 'Poor Paddy.' The whole matter made a deep impression on the mind of Carleton, and again and again in his books he returns to the subject of the secret societies and their corruption of the popular conscience. He discusses their origin in book after book, and warns the people against them.

Presently he found that he was not seeing the world in this parish of Killanny, and finding, beside, that life in the farmer's household was very dull, he started for Dublin, and arrived with two shillings and ninepence in his pocket. For some time he had a hard struggle, trying even to get work as a bird-stuffer, though he knew absolutely nothing of the trade. He wrote a letter in Latin to the colonel of a regiment, asking his advice about enlisting. The colonel seems to have made out the Latin, and dissuaded him.

In those days there lived in Dublin a lean controversialist, Caesar Otway. A favourite joke about him was, 'Where was Otway in the shower yesterday?' 'Up a gun-barrel at Rigby's.' He also had been to Lough Derg. When he had looked down upon it from the mountains he had felt no reverence for the grey island consecrated by the verse of Calderon and the feet of twelve centuries of pilgrims. His stout Protestant heart had merely filled with wrath at so much 'superstition.'

Carleton and Otway came across each other somehow. The lean controversialist was infinitely delighted with this peasant convert, and seems to have befriended him to good purpose. By his recommendation, 'The Lough Derg Pilgrim' was written. A few years later, Carleton cleared away many passages. Caesar Otway would hardly approve its present form. As we have it now, the tale is a most wonderful piece of work. The dim chapel at night, the praying peasants, the fear of a supernatural madness if they sleep, the fall of the young man from the gallery – no one who has read it forgets these things.

From this on, there is little to be recorded but the dates of his books. He married, and for a time eked out his income by teaching. When about thirty he published the 'Traits and Stories,' and with them began modern Irish literature. Before long there were several magazines in Dublin, and many pens busy. Then came 'Fardarougha, the Miser,' the miser himself being perhaps the greatest of all his creations. In 1846 was published 'Valentine M'Clutchy': his pronouncement on the Irish Land Question, and on the Protestant-Catholic Controversy. The novel is full of wonderful dialogues, but continually the intensity of the purpose lowers the art into caricature. Most of the prophecies he made about the land question have been fulfilled. He foretold that the people would wake up some day and appeal to first principles. They are doing so with a vengeance. Many of the improvements also that he recommended have been carried out.

Young Ireland and its literature were now in full swing. The 'National Library,' founded by Davis, was elbowing the chapbooks out of the pedlars' packs. As 'Traits and Stories' had started the prose literature of Ireland, Ferguson's articles on Hardiman's minstrelsy, with their translations from the Gaelic, had sown a harvest of song and ballad. Young Ireland was crusading in verse and prose against the sins of Old Ireland. Carleton felt bound to do his part and wrote a series of short stories for the 'National Library' – 'Art Maguire,' a temperance tale; 'Paddy Go-easy,' finished in nine days to fill a gap left by the death of Davis, and attacking the bad farming and slovenly housekeeping of so many peasants; and 'Rody the Rover,' on his old theme – the secret societies. Rody is an *agent provocateur* – a creature common enough in Ireland, God knows. At the tale's end, with mingling of political despair and Celtic fatalism, evil is left triumphant and good crushed out.

A few years later, on the death of John Banim, an attempt was made to have his pension transferred to Carleton. It might have saved him from the break-up of his genius through hack-work. But some official discovered that this author of a notable temperance tale drank more than was desirable. 'The Red Well,' 'The Dream of a Broken Heart,' and all his beautiful and noble creations counted for nothing. Government, that did not mind a drunken magistrate, more or less, was shocked, and the pension refused.

The rest of his life was an Iliad of decadence, his genius gradually flickering out. Many a bright, heaven-ward spark on the way, though! At last, nothing left but the smoking wick, he died at Woodville, Sandford, near Dublin, on the 30th of January 1869, aged seventy, and was buried at Mount Jerome. A short time before his death he received the pension refused years before, but seems to have known much poverty.

William Carleton was a great Irish historian. The history of a nation is not in parliaments and battle-fields, but in what the people say to each other on fair-days and high days, and in how they farm, and quarrel, and go on pilgrimage. These things has Carleton recorded.

He is the great novelist of Ireland, by right of the most Celtic eyes that ever gazed from under the brows of story-teller. His equals in gloomy and tragic power, Michael and John Banim, had nothing of his Celtic humour. One man alone stands near him there – Charles Kickham, of Tipperary. The scene of the pig-driving peelers in 'For the Old Land,' is almost equal to the best of the 'Traits and Stories.' But, then, he had not Carleton's intensity. Between him and the life he told of lay years in prison, a long Fenian agitation, and partial blindness. On all things flowed a faint idealising haze. His very humour was full of wistfulness.

There is no wistfulness in the works of Carleton. I find there, especially in his longer novels, a kind of clay-cold melancholy. One is not surprised to hear, great humourist though he was, that his conversation was more mournful than humorous. He seems, like the animals in Milton, half emerged only from the earth and its brooding. When I read any portion of the 'Black Prophet,' or the scenes with Raymond the Madman in 'Valentine M'Clutchy,' I seem to be looking out at the wild, torn storm-clouds that lie in heaps at sundown along the western seas of Ireland; all nature, and not merely man's nature, seems to pour out for me its inbred fatalism.

W B Yeats

W B YEATS

IRISH FAIRY TALES
EDITED BY W B YEATS

'…giving gifts to the kindly, and plaguing the surly'

In this selection of Irish fairy and folk tales, W B Yeats allows us in to a world of stories, legends and magic that have been handed down through generations. In his introduction he shares his precious knowledge of this tradition and its significance in the history of a people. Full of simplicity and music, this is the literature of a class for whom everything has gathered meaning and symbol, and Yeats' anthology represents every kind of folk-faith.

OTHER TITLES BY W B YEATS AVAILABLE DIRECT
FROM HOUSE OF STRATUS

Quantity		£	$(US)	$(CAN)	€
☐ IRISH FAIRY TALES		8.99	14.99	19.49	15.00

ALL HOUSE OF STRATUS BOOKS ARE AVAILABLE FROM GOOD BOOKSHOPS
OR DIRECT FROM THE PUBLISHER:

Internet: www.houseofstratus.com including synopses and features.

Email: sales@houseofstratus.com
info@houseofstratus.com
(please quote author, title and credit card details.)

Tel: Order Line
0800 169 1780 (UK)
 800 724 1100 (USA)
International
+44 (0) 1845 527700 (UK)
+01   845 463 1100 (USA)

Fax: +44 (0) 1845 527711 (UK)
+01   845 463 0018 (USA)
(please quote author, title and credit card details.)

Send to: House of Stratus Sales Department   House of Stratus Inc.
Thirsk Industrial Park   2 Neptune Road
York Road, Thirsk   Poughkeepsie
North Yorkshire, YO7 3BX   NY 12601
UK   USA

PAYMENT

Please tick currency you wish to use:

☐ £ (Sterling)　☐ $ (US)　☐ $ (CAN)　☐ € (Euros)

Allow for shipping costs charged per order plus an amount per book as set out in the tables below:

CURRENCY/DESTINATION

	£(Sterling)	$(US)	$(CAN)	€(Euros)
Cost per order				
UK	1.50	2.25	3.50	2.50
Europe	3.00	4.50	6.75	5.00
North America	3.00	3.50	5.25	5.00
Rest of World	3.00	4.50	6.75	5.00
Additional cost per book				
UK	0.50	0.75	1.15	0.85
Europe	1.00	1.50	2.25	1.70
North America	1.00	1.00	1.50	1.70
Rest of World	1.50	2.25	3.50	3.00

PLEASE SEND CHEQUE OR INTERNATIONAL MONEY ORDER
payable to: HOUSE OF STRATUS LTD or HOUSE OF STRATUS INC. or card payment as indicated

STERLING EXAMPLE

Cost of book(s):..................... Example: 3 x books at £6.99 each: £20.97
Cost of order: .... Example: £1.50 (Delivery to UK address)
Additional cost per book:............. Example: 3 x £0.50: £1.50
Order total including shipping:.......... Example: £23.97

VISA, MASTERCARD, SWITCH, AMEX:

☐ ☐ ☐ ☐ ☐ ☐ ☐ ☐ ☐ ☐ ☐ ☐ ☐ ☐ ☐ ☐ ☐ ☐ ☐

Issue number (Switch only):

☐☐☐

Start Date:　　　　　　　Expiry Date:

☐☐/☐☐　　　　　　　☐☐/☐☐

Signature: _____

NAME: _____

ADDRESS: _____

COUNTRY: _____

ZIP/POSTCODE: _____

Please allow 28 days for delivery. Despatch normally within 48 hours.

Prices subject to change without notice.
Please tick box if you do not wish to receive any additional information. ☐

House of Stratus publishes many other titles in this genre; please check our website (**www.houseofstratus.com**) for more details.